CHAPLINIANA

VOLUME I

The Keystone Films

Harry M. Geduld

CHAPLIN

A COMMENTARY
ON CHARLIE CHAPLIN'S
81 MOVIES

Indiana University Press

IANA

VOLUME I

The Keystone Films

BLOOMINGTON & INDIANAPOLIS

Manufactured in the United States of America

Library of Congress Cataloging-in-Publication Data

Geduld, Harry M.
    Chapliniana: a commentary on Charlie Chaplin's
81 movies.

    Includes index.
    Bibliography: p.
    Contents: v. 1. The Keystone films.
    1. Chaplin, Charlie, 1889–1977—Criticism and
interpretation. I. Title.
PN2287.C5G36 1987   791.43'028'0924   86-45479
ISBN 0-253-31336-8 (v. 1)

1 2 3 4 5 91 90 89 88 87

FOR DANIEL JOEL GEDULD,

*through whom I rediscovered my delight in seeing
Charlie Chaplin's films for the first time,*

with love.

How well we know the image of Charlie in flight—turning a corner somewhat like a sailboat, frantically holding onto his hat and pivoting on the immobile axis of one foot, while the other leg lifted high and bent, poises for the next stride, with the hand holding the cane at arm's length to maintain balance. The eyes start out with terror beneath the already terrified brows; the mouth seems insignificant, lips pressed diminishingly together under the black, symmetrical patch of the moustache. . . .

—Parker Tyler

All I need to make a comedy is a park, a policeman and a pretty girl.

—Chaplin

CONTENTS

INTRODUCTION

This is the first volume of a three-volume commentary on Chaplin's eighty-one films, prepared in commemoration of the centenary of the comedian's birth (1989). The second volume will be devoted to the twenty-seven movies Chaplin made for the Essanay and Mutual companies (1915–16), and the final volume to his nineteen First National and feature films (1918–67).

Chaplin learned his craft as a film actor and director in 1914, his first year in the movies. In that year he made no less than thirty-five of his eighty-one films. These were his Keystone comedies, named for the studio at 1712 Allessandro Street in Edendale, California, where he worked for Mack Sennett, the so-called King of Comedy. Chaplin's Keystone comedies were the films that established his movie career. When he joined Keystone at the end of 1913 he was already a successful music hall comedian but was totally unknown to movie audiences. A year later his Keystone movies had set him well on the way to becoming the world's most popular film comedian.

Paradoxically, Chaplin's critics and commentators have paid least attention to this period of his work. Some idea of the superficial treatment his thirty-five Keystone films have received can be gained from noting the amount of space that several of the most widely known books by and about Chaplin have devoted to them: 9 out of 320 pages in Theodore Huff's *Charlie Chaplin* (1952), 10 out of 240 pages (half a chapter) in Roger Manvell's *Chaplin* (1974), 15 out of 297 pages in John McCabe's *Charlie Chaplin* (1978), 21 out of 512 pages in Chaplin's *My Autobiography* (1964), and 32 out of 792 pages in David Robinson's *Chaplin: His Life and Art* (1985).

The scope of the present volume may be seen by comparing it with such surveys as *The Films of Charlie Chaplin* (1965) by Gerald McDonald, Michael Conway, and Mark Ricci and *Chaplin's Films* (1976) by Uno Asplund. These books provide—for each of the films in question—production credits (with varying degrees of completeness and accuracy), brief and often inaccurate plot summaries, and little if any analysis.

In their haste to discuss Chaplin's later films, scholars and commentators who devote any time at all to the Chaplin Keystones tend to describe them impressionistically rather than accurately or to lump them all together as "mere slapstick" intermittently enlivened by flashes of Chaplin's comic business.

The present study is intended to rectify this inadequate treatment of nearly one-third of the output of the cinema's foremost creative artist. For each film it provides significantly more factual information than is available elsewhere, a detailed description, and a commentary. The first substantial discussions of many of Chaplin's Keystones will be found in these commentaries.

The credits and preliminary facts provided for each film have been drawn from a wide variety of sources. But I am particularly indebted to *Charles Chaplin: A Guide to References and Resources* by Timothy J. Lyons. My use of other works has been fully documented in the text.

Unfortunately, there are no original scenarios for Chaplin's Keystone films, and one can never be certain of having seen the most complete print of any of them. In this respect, comparing the length of a given print with the maximum known footage is not always very helpful. Length by itself reveals nothing about content. As I have discovered all too often, two equally long prints of the same film can actually contain different footage.

Moreover, thirty-five millimeter footage measurements for individual Keystone films differ considerably from one work on Chaplin to another. The major discrepancies are those between the footages provided by Asplund 1976, 205–206, and those given in Lyons 1979, 38–52. The footages in Lyons are those of the original release prints; the footages in Asplund are taken from the Danish sources and from the records of the Swedish Board of Censors which, from 1915 onward, maintained a register of the lengths (prior to censorship) of all films imported into Sweden.* I have provided *both* 35mm footage counts for each film. (Note that the footage ratio between 8mm, 16mm, and 35mm is 1:2:5. Thirty feet of 35mm film contains approximately as many frames as ten feet of 16mm or three feet of standard 8mm film.) The variations between the footage counts given by Asplund and Lyons are curious and often inexplicable: e.g. the Swedish Censors apparently received a print of *Kid's Auto Race* (Keystone no. 2) that was nearly fifty feet longer than the original release print! In this respect it is worth noting that the Swedish footage count is often more precise than the original release figure.

My descriptions of each film are usually based on viewings of many different prints. Hereafter, anyone studying one of the Chaplin Keystones will be able to estimate the completeness of a print in two ways: first by checking its length against the maximum footage specified in the credits, and second by comparing what has been seen with the account provided in this volume.

Most shots in Chaplin's Keystones are medium shots or long shots;

---

*Asplund's longest footage count is given in each instance. For detailed information on the problem of footages see Asplund (1976, 203–205).

most transitions are straight cuts. Accordingly, my descriptions usually make no mention of shots and transitions. Exceptions to this include indications of occasional, creative uses of close-ups. Camera movement is mentioned whenever it seems of special significance.

All of Chaplin's later films are readily available to film scholars in videotape format. The same is not true of the Keystones, some of which are the rarest, least accessible, and therefore least known of his films. Hence the length and detail of my descriptions. I believe these descriptions will also enable a reader who *has* previously seen a particular Keystone—but no longer has access to a print—to recall the film in most important respects.

In virtually every instance I have provided notes on the structure of individual films. These notes should facilitate the reader's own analyses of the films. They should also dispel once and for all the widespread notion that Chaplin's Keystone films consist of nothing but formless slapstick episodes.

Originally I contemplated writing this particular volume of my commentary without much enthusiasm. The first time I screened all of Chaplin's films in chronological order, as they are presented here, I saw the Keystones as little more than forty-five reels of unfunny crudity. But when I embarked on this study I reran each film many times, and my enjoyment of the Keystones, my admiration for their inventiveness and vitality, and above all my fascination with all that they reveal of the development of Chaplin's artistry increased with every viewing.

If this volume persuades other film scholars to go back and look at Chaplin's Keystones with as much attention as they usually pay to his later films, my efforts here will have been handsomely rewarded.

FIRST FILMS

Although *Making a Living* is usually listed as Chaplin's first movie, there is evidence—albeit very questionable—of his previous appearance in at least three films:

1. An article in the *New York Times* (September 2, 1921, p. 9) notes that as a child, while playing hookey from school, Chaplin was inadvertently filmed by a news photographer who was shooting a movie of a parade in St. James's Park, London.

2. Another article, "How Pictures Found Charlie," in *Photoplay* (April 1919), records that in the summer of 1912 Chaplin was filmed—this time quite deliberately—by a news photographer who was shooting the annual Battle of the Flowers festivities at St. Helier, Jersey, in the Channel Islands. Chaplin (who had been engaged with the Karno Company to perform at the St. Helier Opera House) became curious about the photographer's activities and stepped in front of the camera—an anticipation of his performance in his second Keystone movie, *Kid's Auto Race*. Then, realizing that he was being filmed, he began an impromptu mime. A prescient French child tugged at his mother's sleeve and said, "Maman, je veux voir encore ce comique!" If the story is true, the child was the earliest of Chaplin's innumerable film fans.

3. *Charlie Chaplin's Own Story* (1916), mentions yet another film prior to *Making a Living*. This would have been his first Keystone picture. It was a 2,000-foot comedy (untitled) that was never publicly shown. According to this account the film was scrapped by Mack Sennett immediately after its completion because it turned out to be unequivocally bad. Chaplin's reactions to this film—the first time he had ever seen himself on the screen—are quoted thus: "Funny? A blind man couldn't have laughed at it. I had ironed out entirely any trace of humor in the scenario. It was stiff, wooden, stupid. . . . Halfway through the picture Mr. Sennett took pity on me and stopped the operator. . . . 'Yes, it's plain we can't release this,' the director put in moodily" (See further *Charlie Chaplin's Own Story*, reprint, 1985, 169).

Not one of these films is known to exist.

Note that Chaplin's *My Autobiography* indicates that he had considered working in movies even before signing up with Keystone. As he recalls it: "I . . . offered to go into partnership with [Alf] Reeves, our manager, to buy the rights of all Karno's sketches and make movies of them. But Reeves had been skeptical, and sensibly so, because we knew nothing about making them" (1964, 138).

Chaplin's Keystone Films

1.

Making a Living

(1914)

Original working title: *The Reporters*
Other titles: *Doing His Best, Take My Picture, Troubles, A Busted Johnny;* French: *Charlot journaliste, Charlot reporter, Pour gagner sa vie;* German: *Man schlägt sich durch;* Spanish: *Charlot periodista, Charlot reportero;* Italian: *Charlot giornalista, Per guadagnarsi la vita*

Length: 1 reel; 951 feet (Asplund), 1030 feet (Lyons)
Playing time: 16 minutes at 16 frames per second
Producer: Keystone
Director: Henry Lehrman
Screenplay: Reed Heustis (?)
Photography: E. J. Vallejo or Frank D. Williams
Cast:

A sharper	Chaplin*
His rival	Henry Lehrman
A mother	Alice Davenport
Her daughter	Virginia Kirtley
A wife	Minta Durfee
Cop and laborer	Chester Conklin

Finished or shipped: January 14, 1914
Released: February 2, 1914

SYNOPSIS

A street. Charlie—not a tramp but an unscrupulous, quick-witted rogue or sharper—accosts Lehrman, his rival-to-be. Indicating by mime that he is hungry and broke, he flatters Lehrman and tries to

---

*For this, his first-released film, Chaplin had not yet assumed his famous outfit. Instead he sports a drooping mustache and wears a monocle, a top hat, and a frock coat. The idea for this costume apparently derived from one he had worn in vaudeville for the role of the Hon. Archibald Binks in Fred Karno's *The Wow-Wows*. He used a variation on the same costume for his portrayal of the flea-circus proprietor, Professor Bosco, in *The Professor* (a discarded film of his First National period, included in the compilation series *The Unknown Chaplin*).

panhandle him. Virtually broke himself, the latter is about to give the sharper a hand-out when he changes his mind. Muttering "Bum!" he exits. Alone, Charlie suddenly abandons his servility. He jauntily tosses his cane into the air and catches it. Then, with top hat askew, he swaggers away from the camera with his cane under his arm in the manner of a British army drill sergeant.

Driveway of mansion. The mother (looking smug) and her daughter are awaiting a visitor.

Street lined with palm trees. Charlie comes into view, walking briskly toward the camera. He observes the mother and daughter but they don't see him. He hesitates, points toward them, and tidies his trouser cuff. Now the ladies notice him. He raises his hat and approaches. They are obviously flattered by his attention. He kisses the daughter's hand, then pokes out his tongue in mock nausea—to the amusement of both ladies. The mother moves discreetly away and watches fondly as the sharper slips a ring on her daughter's finger. A manservant also watches—with contempt—and she rebukes him. Chastened, he turns and disappears into the house. Meanwhile, Charlie is displaying his amorous technique. He kisses the daughter's hand and continues the kiss up the full length of her arm. But enough is enough. Anxious to wrap things up, she directs her "fiancé" to talk to mother, and Charlie courteously obliges. Mother is delighted with her future son-in-law, and Charlie considerately removes his hat so that she can kiss the crown of his head.

At this point, Charlie's rival (Lehrman) appears. He offers the daughter a nosegay and a ring, but she spurns them, proudly showing him the ring she has just received from her "fiancé." Now the sharper approaches, arm-in-arm with his prospective mother-in-law. The daughter tries to introduce the two men, but Lehrman denounces his rival and makes a grab at him. Charlie pulls away, flanked by the protective shield of mother and daughter. At an apparently safe distance, he clenches his fists and glares at Lehrman. But the latter dashes over, seizes him by the scruff of the neck, and hurls him to the ground. Staggering to his feet, Charlie endeavors to fight back. The two men trade a few ineffective blows, then Charlie swings wildly, loses his balance, and hits the ground again. Lehrman promptly picks up a broom and beats him over the head. The ladies watch, aghast. Charlie gets up again and taunts his rival who responds with threatening gestures with the broom. The mother faints, and the daughter bends down to render assistance. Now Charlie moves to the offensive. He leaps onto Lehrman, clasping him around the neck. He is whirled around. The manservant reenters and is instantly felled by Charlie's flailing legs. Desperately, the latter drags Lehrman down on top of him. Now the manservant gets to his feet and starts to throttle Lehrman, who is trying to throttle Charlie. Intertwined, the three men manage to stand upright—but the manservant seizes the initiative, grabs Lehrman, and gives him the bum's rush. Charlie, looking very disheveled, tries to strike a dignified pose as his enemy is flung off the driveway and out of sight. Belatedly, mother and daughter come to Charlie's aid. The former straightens his cravat while the latter dusts his jacket and hands him his cane. Replacing his top hat on his head, he offers his arms to the two ladies.

Street. Lehrman glares back at the house and stalks away—right into an overhanging branch.

Driveway of mansion. The mother orders the manservant back into the house and resumes her chat with Charlie.

Office of a newspaper editor. Lehrman enters, diffidently, in search of a job. The editor appears dubious about him and indicates that he has nothing available.

Driveway of mansion. Charlie takes his leave and marches off with an exaggerated swagger.

Street. He looks back at the house and snickers.

Driveway. Mother and daughter enter mansion.

Office. Lehrman pleads with the editor, then exits to printing shop next door.

Printing shop. Lehrman converses with a linotype operator.

Street outside newspaper building. Charlie notices a placard: "Reporter Wanted: See Editor." He quickly spruces himself up—to the derision of an ill-dressed laborer (Chester Conklin) who is holding up a lamp post. Glancing contemptuously at the laborer, he strides into the building, shoving aside a newsboy who is standing by the door.

Office. Charlie enters, walks over to the editor, and slaps him on the back. After introducing himself, he looks up and notices Lehrman who has just reentered from the printing shop. The rivals glower at each other. Lehrman whispers to the editor and points disparagingly at Charlie. Not to be outdone, Charlie twirls the editor's head to face *him* and proceeds to denounce Lehrman. Unexpectedly, the editor gestures to Lehrman to leave him alone with the sharper.

Printing shop. Lehrman, beside the linotype operator, angrily looks back at Charlie. (There is, presumably, an open door between the office and the printing shop.)

Office. Charlie sits on his own hat, then jumps up and retrieves it.

Printing shop. Lehrman laughs at Charlie.

Office. Charlie, now seated, begins to describe his qualifications. Excitedly, he taps the editor on the knee. When the latter withdraws it, Charlie pulls the knee back so that he can continue to tap on it.

Printing shop. Lehrman anxiously watches his rival who seems to be making progress with the editor. He dashes back to the office.

The editor's office. Lehrman approaches and whispers in the editor's ear. Charlie rises to his feet to confront his rival. This time the editor orders Charlie to leave at once. Angrily, Charlie strikes the floor with his cane—at which one of his starched cuffs falls off his wrist and slides down the cane. He bends down and retrieves the cuff. Lehrman orders Charlie to clear out. The latter reacts by peeling off his jacket for a fight, but having second thoughts, he puts his jacket back on and beats a hasty exit.

Office annex. Charlie, in a threatening pose, glares back at the editor's office.

Office. Lehrman resumes his talk with the editor.

Road near a cliff. Rear view of a convertible careening wildly.

Footpath near the cliff. Lehrman appears carrying a still camera.

Top of cliff. The car moves out of control, narrowly missing the cliff edge.

Footpath. Lehrman quickly poses his camera.

Cliff face. Tilt shot of car plunging over the cliff.

Footpath. Lehrman, having taken a photograph, races toward the accident.

Foot of cliff. The wrecked car lies on its side. Lehrman rushes onto the scene. He frantically looks for the driver and then notices him moving feebly beside the wreck. Putting down his camera, he turns to the injured victim.

Footpath. A Keystone Kop (Chester Conklin) observes the accident. He gesticulates, screams for help, and runs away from the wreck.

At the wrecked car. Close shot of Lehrman beside the victim.

Footpath. The cop returns, accompanied by several people. He waves in the direction of the wreck.

At the wrecked car. Close shot of Lehrman, the would-be reporter, *interviewing* the supine victim.

Footpath. Cop and people walk toward the wreck.

At the wrecked car. Cop and people crowd around the smashed vehicle. With much gesticulation, the cop assumes command of the situation.

Footpath. Charlie appears, notices the accident, advances towards it, then hesitates.

At the wrecked car. A crowd mills around the accident.

Footpath. Charlie still hesitates. Then, after a little soul-searching, he heads toward the wrecked car.

At the wrecked car. Charlie appears in the background. Unable to see what's going on, he crouches down and peers under the legs of the crowd. Then he leaps up and tries to climb over their heads. At last he discovers Lehrman's camera and makes off with it, triumphantly waving his hat in the air.

Footpath. He hesitates and looks back at the accident.

At the wrecked car. Lehrman suddenly realizes that his camera has vanished. He waves his hands in despair.

Footpath. Charlie stumbles—then hastens away out of sight.

At the wrecked car. Lehrman sets off in pursuit of Charlie.

Footpath. Lehrman stumbles too—then he continues his pursuit.

Ground level of frame house with exterior staircase. Charlie bumps into a cop, who cautions him and then lets him go. He flees up the staircase, falls, and slides halfway down.

First-floor balcony of frame house. He inadvertently runs into a young girl and knocks a basin of water out of her hand. She pursues him back to the top of the staircase.

Ground level. He cautiously descends the staircase and has nearly reached the bottom when Lehrman arrives and chases him back up.

Almost at the top, Lehrman grabs hold of him, but Charlie pushes his rival back and regains the balcony once more.

Balcony. The young girl, terrified, watches Lehrman seize Charlie and throw him to the floor. He drags him to his feet and shakes him. Charlie struggles to extricate himself, falling into the young girl's washtub in the process. To get them off the balcony, the young girl opens the nearest door. They tumble through.

Bedroom. Charlie throws his hat onto the bed—where a woman (the wife) is sleeping—and leaps onto Lehrman's neck.

Ground level. The husband arrives at the foot of the staircase.

Bedroom. Charlie shoves his rival onto the bed and dashes out of the room.

Balcony. He turns the key in the lock and checks that the door is securely fastened.

Ground level. The husband is about to ascend the staircase.

Balcony. Charlie picks up the stolen camera, waves his hat, and starts down the steps.

Staircase. Charlie collides with the husband and pushes him down to ground level. They fight.

Bedroom. The wife pushes Lehrman out of her bed. He tries in vain to open the locked door. She gesticulates helplessly.

Ground level. Close shot of Charlie struggling with the husband. The cop (whom Charlie had bumped into earlier) reappears and tries to break up the fight. Charlie punches him in the stomach, shoves the husband over his prostrate body, and flees with the camera in hand.

A crowded city street with trolley car in background. Charlie comes into view and runs along the trolley tracks toward the movie camera.

Bedroom. Lehrman grapples with the wife.

City street. Pull back tracking shot of Charlie as he runs madly toward the movie camera.

Bedroom. The husband enters and finds his wife in bed, embracing Lehrman. The guilty couple look up and see him pointing an accusing finger at them. The wife nods a denial of guilt, but the husband is unconvinced. He threatens Lehrman who seeks refuge under the sheet. Now the husband leaps onto the bed, pushes his wife aside, and grapples with Lehrman.

City street. Pull back tracking shot of Charlie running madly toward the movie camera.

Bedroom. The two men roll off the bed. While they are locked in conflict, the wife goes to the window and clasps her hands in prayer. The two men fall back onto the bed again.

Exterior of newspaper building. Charlie runs past the placard which falls to the ground. He stumbles, then gets up and gives the lounging laborer a shove before dashing into the building.

Bedroom. The wife calls through the window for help. Lehrman leaps up from the bed and hurls pillows at his attacker.

Balcony. Cops arrive. The young woman directs them toward the bedroom.

Bedroom. Lehrman wrestles with the door handle.

Balcony. Lehrman exits from the bedroom and collides with the cops. They hit the floor in a heap.

Bedroom. The husband wrestles with the door handle.

Balcony. The husband also collides with the cops. We see a tangled mass of arms and legs.

Office of editor. Charlie dashes in and confronts the editor.

Ground level of frame house. The husband pursues Lehrman down the staircase and catches him.

Balcony. The wife hurls a bowl of water down at the two men.

Ground level. The husband is drenched. Lehrman escapes his clutches. The husband dashes back upstairs to deal with his wife.

Office of editor. The editor congratulates Charlie on his "scoop." Charlie reacts by kissing him on his bald pate.

Printing shop. Charlie gives instructions to the linotype operator.

City street. Lehrman racing in hot pursuit.

Printing shop. The operator processes the photos of the accident.

Office of editor. The editor and his assistant scrutinize a freshly printed newspaper.

Alley. Bundles of newspapers are tossed out of the newspaper building where Charlie is waiting to load them, single-handed, onto the wagons of the newsvendors. Some of the bundles knock him down, but he jumps up and continues loading.

Office of editor. Lehrman arrives. The editor indicates that Charlie has already left.

Alley. Charlie supplies bundles of papers to newsboys on bicycles.

Office of editor. The editor shows Lehrman a copy of the newspaper displaying the purloined photograph. He is appalled.

Printing shop. Miming Charlie's appearance, Lehrman asks the operator the whereabouts of his rival.

Street. Charlie passes out bundles of papers to newsboys.

Printing shop. Operators tell Lehrman where he can find Charlie. He dashes out after him.

Alley. Lehrman rushes over to a man reading a newspaper and asks if he has seen Charlie.

Street. Lehrman pursues Charlie—toward the movie camera. Charlie suddenly stops. The rivals confront each other and start to peel off their jackets, but Charlie changes his mind and turns to flee. Lehrman seizes his jacket. Charlie promptly slips out of it and Lehrman sprawls backwards.

City street with trolley car tracks. Charlie is pursued by Lehrman away from the movie camera. Then, as a trolley car approaches, Charlie turns and leaps onto Lehrman's neck. The trolley car scoops the rivals up on its cowcatcher. Still struggling, they pass out of view on the front end of the trolley car.

COMMENTS

1. David Robinson notes that there were four main kinds of Keystone productions:

> The simplest . . . were the "park" films, always shot in Westlake Park. . . . Another variety of production used locations: Sennett would take advantage of some public occasion . . . and send a unit to film the comedians fooling and playing out some impromptu farce with the crowd and the spectacle of the event as free background. More formal films were shot in sets which seem to have stood more or less permanently on the stage. . . . The fourth category of films . . . combined location and studio sets. (Robinson 1985, 110–11)

Making a Living made use of studio sets, external locations, and the linotype room (or printing shop) of the *Los Angeles Times*. *Between Showers*, Chaplin's fourth Keystone film, is the first of his movies in which Westlake Park makes a prominent appearance. See my comment 3 to *Between Showers*.

Robinson also notes (1985, 111): "The usual number of shots for a one-reel [Keystone] film was between fifty and sixty." In fact, he has considerably underestimated this average, as many of my descriptions indicate.

2. *Making a Living* has often been dismissed as formless slapstick. However, it has a definable structure consisting of a prologue, five

episodes, and an epilogue, as follows: Prologue: Charlie panhandles Lehrman. (i) Charlie steals Lehrman's girl. (ii) Lehrman gets the job—his only victory. (iii) Charlie steals Lehrman's camera. (iv) Bedroom struggle—Charlie escapes Lehrman. (v) Charlie scoops Lehrman. Epilogue: Cowcatcher—the rivalry remains unresolved.

3. Although this is an unimpressive first film for the man who was soon to become the world's greatest comedian, *Making a Living* does contain—in a few bits of comic business—some hints of things to come. Note particularly Chaplin's tricks with his cane and cuff, his mock-amorous "great lover" performance in kissing the heroine, his mock-belligerent technique of swinging around Lehrman's neck, his twirling of the editor's head, and his game with the editor's knee. In Chaplin's attempt to define the sharper's character through a distinctive walk, we may also discern an anticipation of the more famous walk he was soon to create for the Tramp character.

4. During his first weeks at Keystone, Chaplin had serious problems in adjusting to the world of moviemaking and in his relationships with Mabel Normand (who sneeringly referred to him as the "Little Englander") and with his director, Henry "Pathe" Lehrman. Lehrman's overbearing, egotistical manner grated on him, and they were soon quarreling as furiously as the rivals in *Making a Living*.

He was also bewildered by the apparent chaos of the studio: the incessant movement of hordes of extras wandering around in a multiplicity of costumes, the hammering and ripping of new sets being built and old ones being demolished, the glare of the California sunlight intensified by numerous reflectors, the screaming of commands, and the irritating whirring and clicking of the cameras while he was trying to play a scene. The discovery that the scenes of a movie were not shot in chronological order mystified him.

All in all, his frame of mind was totally unprepared for the kind of performance that Sennett expected and Lehrman tried to bully him into providing.

Thus, almost inevitably, *Making a Living* is a disappointment. Sadly miscast and insensitively directed, Chaplin was, for the most part, singularly unfunny and he knew it. "I was stiff," he recalled only two years later. "I took all the surprise out of scenes by anticipating the next motion. When I walked against a tree, I showed that I knew I would hit it, long before I did. I was so determined to be funny that every muscle in my body was stiff and serious with the strain." Assuming that he had been hired to perform in the Karno tradition, Chaplin developed some elaborate comic business for the film—only to discover that it had all been cut out in the editing. My synopsis of the movie indicates that there were far too many brief scenes to have allowed for any development of either comic business or character. Lehrman's notion of comedy was a succession of rapid-fire slapstick gags used to create fast-paced action. Indeed, he is said to have been more instrumental than Sennett in establishing breakneck movement as a basic ingredient of Keystone comedy. The very idea of extending a scene to develop characterization or to enrich a situation was quite alien to him, and so he ignored Chaplin's special talents and rejected his suggestions for improving the picture.

However, no doubts about the film or Chaplin were reflected in the advertising for *Making a Living* which proudly announced the "First appearance in Keystone Comedies of . . . the famous English pantomimist," and declared that "Chaplin proves himself a film player of the first rank by his performance in this film, which is full of farcical and unexpected incident, and which will cause roars of laughter from beginning to end."

Subsequently, the gossip column of the *New York Dramatic Mirror* for February 4, 1914, noted that "Charles Chapmann [sic], formerly with Fred Karno's Company in the vaudeville hit *A Night in an English Music Hall* and one of the great English pantomime actors, has signed a long contract with the Keystone Company and is seen to advantage in his first lead in a farce-comedy, *To Make a Living* [sic]." With far less restraint, the reviewer for *Moving Picture World* singled out the Chaplin of *Making a Living* as "a comedian of the first water." Both comments read suspiciously like studio publicity "plants."

5. Chester Conklin (1888–1971), who had two minor roles in *Making a Living*, was cast in various roles in thirteen other Chaplin Keystones. Kalton Lahue (1971, 87–92) notes Conklin's three typical characterizations: "Fishface" (portraying innocent stupidity), "Droppington" (a bumbling know-it-all), and "Walrus" (a spiteful nuisance). He reappeared in two of Chaplin's features. In *Modern Times* (1936) he played a mechanic (Charlie crushed his "family heirloom" in the steam press). In *The Great Dictator* (1940) he played a customer (the Jewish barber shaved him to the strains of Brahms).

OTHER VIEWS

"*Making a Living* was one of Keystone's more elaborate productions. It had a comparatively well developed story line. . . . Chaplin's costume, make-up and character . . . [showed] nothing as yet of the Charlie figure to come. . . . The first characteristically Chaplin gag is where he disdainfully rejects the proffered coin as too mean, but then hastily grabs it back before the friend can change his mind" (Robinson 1985, 109).

"Certainly it makes no particular impression today: the bouncing 'toff' character has only the slightly weird historical interest of being played by the (barely recognizable) creator of Charlie" (Quigly 1968, 20).

"Making a Living in its fifteen-minute span lacks everything but a sense of urgency. It is a typical Keystone gallop. . . . Yet a distinctive Chaplin hallmark is established in his very first film—his serene belligerence in times of self-need. Chaplin is at the newspaper office trying to browbeat an editor. He keeps slapping the man on the knee, and when the man moves his knee away, Chaplin simply pulls it back automatically in order to continue the intimidation, not even looking at the knee. Chaplin, Walter Kerr points out, has 'established what would become a permanent, immensely productive pattern: he is adjusting the rest of the universe to his merely reflexive needs.' Charlie [is] making the world his" (McCabe 1978, 51–52).

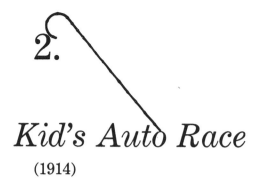

2.

Kid's Auto Race

(1914)

Other titles*:*Kid Auto Races at Venice, The Kid Auto Race, The Pest, The Children's Automobile Race*; French: *Charlot est content de lui, Course d'autos pour gosses*; German: *Seifenkistenrennen in Venedig*; Spanish: *Carreras de autos para ninos*; Italian: *Charlot si distingue*

Length: Split reel; 669 feet (Asplund), 572 feet (Lyons)**
Playing time: 11 minutes at 16 frames per second
Producer: Keystone
Director: Henry Lehrman
Screenplay: Henry Lehrman
Photography: Hans Koenekamp***
Cast:

A tramp	Chaplin
A film director	Henry Lehrman
A cinematographer	Frank D. Williams?
Keystone Kids in minor roles	Gordon Griffith
	Billy Jacobs
	Thelma Salter
	Charlotte Fitzpatrick

Location: Venice, California
Finished or shipped: January 17, 1914****
Released: February 7, 1914

SYNOPSIS

The entire film is located on or beside the track of a Soap Box Derby.

Charlie is dressed in his Tramp's costume for the first time. Swing-

---

Kid's Auto Race is the title of this film as it appears under the original Keystone logo. Commentators frequently refer to it as *Kid Auto Races at Venice*, but this is actually a slight abbreviation of the movie's first insert title: "Kid Auto Races at Venice, California."
**Originally released with a purchased educational short, *Olives and Their Oil*.
***According to Robinson (1985, 700).
**** According to Kalton C. Lahue (1971b, 294).

ing his cane and puffing a cigarette, he watches the leading cars in the
Soap Box Derby. He politely doffs his hat to the director (off-camera),
who orders him off the track, then wanders toward the camera and
stands with his back to it until he is once again ordered out of range.
After pausing to preen himself, he momentarily obliges, then casually
saunters back into view, swinging his cane and pretending he doesn't
know which way to go to avoid the camera, but meanwhile taking the
opportunity to remain in full view for a while longer. This sets the
pattern of his repeated efforts to hog the attention of the camera.

Moving over to the grandstand, he again "steals the picture" while
the cinematographer is trying to get some shots of the judges. He
persistently remains in view as the camera pans along the grandstand
and over the bystanders.

When ordered away yet again, he approaches to medium close shot
position, gesticulating his apparent bewilderment as to which way to
turn. The director angrily pushes him off camera, but he darts back
with a mock-serious expression on his face. Shoved out of view once
more, he returns almost immediately, strikes a match on his rump,
lights a cigarette, and elbows a bystander out of his path.

Next, from long shot position he runs and stumbles wildly along
the track toward the camera, comes to a halt and assumes a few osten-
tatious poses. The director dashes over and flings him violently out of
camera range.

Observing that the camera has been set up for filming the race at
"Death Curve," Charlie nonchalantly comes up from behind the filmmakers, then turns, inviting the cinematographer to film him in profile.
He has just back-kicked his discarded cigarette butt when the director
marches over and tells him to clear off. As he shows no inclination to
leave, the director smacks his face and pushes him aside. Undaunted, he
returns—this time with his back to the camera—and is almost run down
by a speeding soapbox car. Despite the director's increasingly violent
reactions, he repeatedly meanders in front of the camera. Now the director tries politeness once more. Charlie responds by doffing his hat and
obligingly withdrawing—but only momentarily. He wanders into the
center of the track—to the annoyance of a bystander who hurls him out of
the path of the racing cars. Eventually, having forced Charlie away from
the camera yet again, the frantic director tries flinging his hat onto the
track. Bending down to pick it up, Charlie is almost run down a second
time by one of the speeding cars.

COMMENTS

1. In chapter 10 of *My Autobiography* Chaplin informs us that the
next film he made after *Making a Living* was *Mabel's Strange Predicament* and that *this* was the movie in which he made his first appearance

as the Tramp character. But on this matter most scholars agree with John McCabe: Chaplin's "memory fails him here. Minta Durfee and Chester Conklin both recall the tramp's genesis in *Kid Auto Races* and the film's date also verifies this" (McCabe 1978, 53). The film was released on February 7, 1914, two days earlier than *Mabel's Strange Predicament*. Examination of the latter film shows that Chaplin's role is that of a drunken masher—not the Tramp. (See my comment 2 to *Mabel's Strange Predicament*.) Nevertheless, David Robinson argues that *Mabel's Strange Predicament* may well have been the earlier film.

> For many years it has been accepted that the second film, and the first appearance of Chaplin's tramp character, was *Kid Auto Races at Venice, California*. It now seems much more likely that the film was *Mabel's Strange Predicament*. In order of release, *Kid Auto Races* was certainly the first of the two. . . . Yet Chaplin clearly remembered that it was in *Mabel's Strange Predicament* that he first wore the costume, and his memory on such details rarely failed him. Hans Koenekamp who was cameraman on *Mabel's Strange Predicament*, also remembers this as being the first appearance of the costume. The answer most likely is that *Mabel's Strange Predicament* was *shot* first. *Kid Auto Races* was one of Sennett's location films, said to have been filmed in forty-five minutes . . . and consisting of no more than twenty shots. It could have been shot, cut, printed and slipped into the release schedule while the more elaborate film, *Mabel's Strange Predicament*, was being assembled. (Robinson 1985, 113–14)

2. The action of *Kid's Auto Race* was improvised, and, as David Robinson noted, tradition has it that the film was shot in a mere forty-five minutes. Mack Sennett had learned that the resort town of Venice, near Los Angeles, was to have a Soap Box Derby. Deciding that such an event would be an interesting setting for a slapstick comedy, he told Lehrman to go there with Chaplin and a cinematographer and return as soon as possible with a comedy shot. Chaplin was instructed to dress in a funny outfit of his own choice.

In *My Autobiography* Chaplin tells us:

> I had no idea what make-up to put on. I did not like my getup as the press reporter in *Making a Living*. However, on the way to the wardrobe I thought I would dress in baggy pants, big shoes, a cane and a derby hat. I wanted everything a contradiction: the pants baggy, the coat tight, the hat small and the shoes large. I was undecided whether to look old or young, but remembering Sennett had expected me to be a much older man, I added a small moustache, which, I reasoned, would add age without hiding my expression. (Chaplin 1964, 144)

In *The Parade's Gone By* Kevin Brownlow quotes Chester Conklin's more detailed account of the origin of that immortal costume:

"I remember one rainy morning, Roscoe Arbuckle, Ford Sterling and myself were sitting in the dressing room playing pinochle. Charlie wandered in and went up to the make-up bench. In those days we used crepe hair a lot. Charlie held up various pieces of this crepe hair under his nose, then looked at himself in the mirror. Finally, he found a piece that he liked, and he stuck it on there with spirit gum, went over and got Roscoe Arbuckle's hat and his pants, my coat (a cutaway, we called it in those days; now it's called a morning coat) and he took his own cane and went out on the set." (Brownlow 1968, 498)

Maurice Bessy quotes the following recollection of Henry Lehrman:

"[Chaplin] borrowed Fatty's trousers, Chester Conklin's old shoes, and got the rest of his clothes from the dressing-room he shared with the other comics and from the studio wardrobe. A few days later we were getting ready to go out to Venice, where there is an amusement park, like Coney Island but on a smaller scale of course, and I saw Chaplin arrive wearing the costume that was to make him famous. His moustache consisted of a rectangle of black crêpe glued under his nose. He seemed delighted with his appearance and twirled his walking-stick with his fingers, a big safety pin took the place of the button missing from his jacket. . . . And that's how we got to see Charlie Chaplin for the first time in his 'trampy' disguise, in the film *Kid Auto Races*, which wasn't supposed to be anything more than a light-hearted documentary about kids, but which became his second film." (Bessy 1985, 54)

An entirely different account appears in Charles Chaplin, Jr.'s book, *My Father, Charlie Chaplin:*

My father told me once that the costume had originated years before [he went to work for Keystone]. One night while he was janitoring in a London music hall, the frantic manager came to him with the dismal news that the star comedian was sick and he needed a fill-in. Would Dad help out? The comedian was a big man and his clothes were oversize for Dad—the pants baggy, the shoes too large. But the derby was too small, because Dad's head was larger than the comedian's. "I just put them on and there was my tramp outfit," my father told me. . . . (Chaplin, Jr. 1961, 22)

Two details of this anecdote cast doubts about its reliability. First, there is no evidence that Chaplin ever worked as a janitor in a music hall; second, it seems highly unlikely that the manager of a music hall would ask the janitor to stand-in for the star comedian. However, the story does lend some support to the idea that the Tramp costume and character originated much earlier than *Kid's Auto Race*.

Indeed, Chaplin himself mentions that at the age of eight he dreamed of appearing in a music hall act consisting of "two boys dressed as comedy tramps . . . but, alas, it never materialized" (Chaplin 1964, 45). It should be noted that tramp acts were not uncommon on the English variety circuits when Chaplin was a member of the Eight Lancashire Lads clog-dancing troupe, and he informs us that one such act he tried, unsuccessfully, to imitate was Zarmo "the comedy tramp juggler" (Chaplin 1964, 47).

Presumably, like so many British comedians at the beginning of the century, Chaplin was also influenced by the great Dan Leno, who frequently appeared on stage wearing absurdly elongated boots and oversized pants that flapped loosely about his frail body. (See further *Charlie Chaplin's Own Story*, reprint, 1985, xiii–xiv.)

Another possible anticipation of the Tramp costume can be traced to 1906, when Chaplin joined the company of *Casey's Circus*, appearing with a cast of juveniles who wore clothes many sizes too big for them.

Incidentally, it is possible that the famous Charlie Chaplin walk antedated the Tramp costume and character. If we are to believe "Charlie Chaplin's Million Dollar Walk," *McClure's* 47 (July 1916), p. 26, the walk was derived from Chaplin's childhood parody of the splay-footed gait of a local eccentric, Rummy Binks, who earned his liquor by holding cabmen's horses outside the Queen's Head, Lambeth Walk. (See further G. J. Mellor, "The Making of Charlie Chaplin," *Cinema Studies* [London], 2, no. 2 [June 1966], p. 19.)

Whatever the Tramp's origins may have been, he seems to have sprung to life for the first time during the making of *Kid's Auto Race*. In *My Autobiography* Chaplin recalls how

> the moment I was dressed, the clothes and the make-up made me feel the person he was. I began to know him, and by the time I walked onto the stage [at Keystone] he was fully born. . . . Gags and comedy ideas went racing through my mind. (Chaplin 1964, 144)

In 1923, fifty or so films later than *Kid's Auto Race*, Chaplin enlarged on the symbolic significance of the Tramp's appearance:

> "That costume helps me to express my conception of the average man, of myself. The derby, too small, is a striving for dignity. The moustache is vanity. The tightly-buttoned coat and the stick and his whole manner are a gesture toward gallantry and dash and 'front.' He is trying to meet the world bravely, to put up a bluff, and he knows that too. He knows it so well that he can laugh at himself and pity himself a little." (Huff 1952, 17)

3. A virtually plotless movie, *Kid's Auto Race* consists of numerous repetitions and variations on the same simple situation. Its significance, however, is far from simple.

It is, of course, one of the first self-reflexive films in the history of the motion picture. The movie forces its audiences into an awareness of two contrasting uses of cinema: the movie camera as a mere recording device (Lehrman's approach) and the movies as a medium that the artist can manipulate creatively (Chaplin's approach). Whether Lehrman was aware that the picture embodied this highly significant dichotomy must remain doubtful, but *Chaplin* must have realized it. The film was turned by him into a clever retaliation for Lehrman's butchery of his performance in *Making a Living*. In *Kid's Auto Race* the director is trying to film an *event;* he wants to keep his own and everyone else's personality out of the picture. Charlie, on the other hand, refuses to accept such cinematic objectivity. He repeatedly tricks the camera into capturing a *persona* and in so doing relegates the event to the inferior status of "background." Subjectivity triumphs time and again. "Look at me, Me, ME!" is the recurrent theme of Charlie's insatiable scene-stealing. Approaching the camera, he suddenly makes us realize that we are seeing him through the eye of the cameraman. Then, taunting the director to shove him out of camera range, he compels Lehrman to make repeated appearances in his own movie. Just as he turns the public event into his personal background, so he transforms the supposedly objective camera and the would-be offscreen and anonymous director into functional elements of his own personal comedy.

At the same time, anticipating a major theme of *The Circus* (1928), the film contrasts contrived performance (the race) with improvised artistry (Charlie's scene-stealing). We are left in no doubt as to the superiority of the latter. The race is orderly; it imposes rules and restraints on participants and bystanders alike. In so doing it comes across as an impersonal event observed by a sheepish mass of people. But Charlie refuses to become part of any organized activity. He's an individualist, and he's there to be seen and not just to see. (Chaplin's fascination with the theme of *seeing*, as in *City Lights*, may be traced to this little film.) In *Kid's Auto Race* the Tramp distracts our attention (and the bystanders) from the race by spontaneously cooking up a series of mini "turns" that suggest effective moments from various vaudeville acts. Simultaneously unpredictable and innovative, he contributes all the vitality that the film possesses.

Yet the Tramp in *Kid's Auto Race* is merely a preliminary sketch for a character who was to become more complex with every film in which he would appear. Robert Payne's (1952) ecstatic description of the film as an "epiphany of Charlie on the streets of Venice" is a considerable exaggeration of the truth. Chaplin wears the famous costume, of course, and there are a few gestures and traits—back-kicking a cigarette, the clumsy, lolloping jog trot, the mock-dignified poses—which were to become Charlie's hallmarks, but there is not much else to support the fully rounded character. However, *Kid's Auto Race* does introduce Charlie the *pest or intruder*—one of the most characteristic of his Keystone roles.

OTHER VIEWS

An important commentary on the film appears in James Naremore, "Film and the Performance Frame," *Film Quarterly*, Winter 1984–85, pp. 8–15.

"From the very beginning . . . Charlie announces that his enemies are the cops and the cameramen and that he is on the side of natural man. He has no patience with law and order. . . . He is the exhibitionist in all of us" (Payne 1952, 17–18).

"Chaplin must have realized the importance of the occasion. The idea was simple and he would develop it. . . . It was obvious that even with Lehrman directing him, he was going to be able to impose his own style and pace on the picture. It was a golden opportunity to find out whether what he considered right for himself was also right for the screen. In the event, the discovery was a happy one. . . . There is something of the 'Little Fellow' there. . . . It is in the silhouette, slightly less exaggerated than it was to become, but altogether as visually clear cut as a cartoon" (Sobel and Francis 1977, 123–24).

3.

Mabel's Strange Predicament

(1914)

Original working title: *Pajamas*
Other titles: [*The*] *Hotel Mixup;* French: *Charlot à l'hôtel, L'étrange aventure de Mabel;* German: *Mabels Missliche Lage;* Spanish: *Charlot en el hotel, Primavera;* Italian: *La strana avventura di Mabel*

Length: 1 reel; 1030 feet (Asplund), 1016 feet (Lyons)
Playing time: 17 minutes at 16 frames per second
Producer: Keystone
Directors: Henry Lehrman and Mack Sennett
Screenplay: Reed Heustis or Henry Lehrman
Photography: Frank D. Williams (?)
Cast:

A drunken masher	Chaplin
Mabel	Mabel Normand
Mabel's admirer	Harry McCoy
A jealous wife	Alice Davenport
Her husband	Chester Conklin
Hotel manager	Al St. John
Bellboy	Hank Mann

Finished or shipped: January 20, 1914*
Released: February 9, 1914

SYNOPSIS

Hotel lobby. Charlie, a drunken masher, tries to get acquainted with an elegantly dressed lady (Mabel Normand) who has a collie in tow. She snubs him and walks off, leaving him gazing forlornly after her. Shrugging his shoulders, he turns his attention to another young woman, in a tuxedo-like outfit, who is seated in a rocking chair. She

---

* Some authorities consider this Chaplin's *second* film for Keystone. See *Kid's Auto Race*, comment 1.

also spurns his attentions and exits hastily. Charlie flops heavily onto the edge of a vacant chair which tips back and almost flings him to the floor. Regaining his balance, he takes a swig from a bottle of liquor.

Hotel garden. A smiling Mabel shakes hands with an admirer. As he departs, she waves farewell and trots back into the hotel, followed by her dog.

Hotel lobby. Charlie seizes the dog's tail and is dragged off his chair. Mabel tugs at the dog's head. Charlie, losing his grip on the tail, sprawls backward onto the carpet. Mabel marches off in a huff while Charlie sits up and takes another swig from the bottle. The hotel manager dashes onto the scene, picks Charlie up, and orders him out of the hotel. Charlie responds by pressing a wad of bank notes into the manager's hand. That does the trick. The manager walks away, leaving Charlie to his own devices. He trots around the lobby and spruces himself up for the next encounter.

Hotel corridor. Mabel is snubbed by a middle-aged lady (the jealous wife).

Jealous wife's room. The wife enters and closes the door, looking angrily in the direction of Mabel's room (opposite). Removing her hat, she hands it to her obedient husband.

Mabel's room. Mabel enters and begins playing with her dog.

Hotel lobby. Charlie has sat down in the rocking chair. The lady in the tuxedo passes him. He tries to get acquainted but she walks on, nose high in the air. Turning to follow her movements, he falls backward off the chair and plunges his hand into a spittoon. The manager rushes over and helps him back onto the chair.

Mabel's room. Mabel, now in pajamas, is playing ball with the dog. Excitedly, it bounds towards her and knocks her over.

Jealous wife's room. The wife is seated on the bed, reading a book. Her husband is standing before a mirror, adjusting his collar. Infuriated by the noise from Mabel's room, the wife rises from the bed and flings her arms into the air.

Title: *"I'm going to complain."*

Hotel corridor. Shaking her fists, the wife heads along the corridor in search of the manager.

Hotel lobby. Charlie, still seated, ogles a young woman sitting nearby. The wife rushes over to the reception desk. Charlie gets up and accosts her. She shakes him off and exits. He aims a back-kick in her direction.

Mabel's room. The game continues. She bounces the ball but has forgotten to close the door. The ball bounces out of the room and lands at the far end of the corridor. She gazes down at her pajamas, looks around to see if anyone else is around, then runs out to get the ball. The dog tries to follow her but pushes the door shut instead.

Corridor. Mabel runs back to her room and finds the door locked against her. She tugs at door handle. Meanwhile, Charlie appears at the far end of the corridor, having lost sight of a young woman he had been following. At first Mabel doesn't notice him. Eventually he toddles up to her and becomes aware of her "strange predicament." Now she notices him and screams. He responds by doffing his hat while stifling a laugh. She begs him to leave, but he starts to make advances and winds up chasing her down the corridor.

Rounding a corner of the corridor, she observes ahead of her a male guest clad in pajamas similar to her own. The man is placing a jug outside his room. Recoiling, she crouches behind a sofa. Charles charges round the corner, flings his arms around the male guest and kisses him. As a "reward" he is flung to the floor. Mabel, meanwhile, runs back toward her room.

Corridor outside Mabel's room. She hesitates momentarily in front of her locked door; then, observing that the opposite door is open, she enters.

Jealous wife's room. Unseen by the husband, she throws herself under the bed.

Corridor. Charlie races back after Mabel. He observes her entering the other room but arrives there just as she closes the door. A bellboy wanders along the corridor and discovers Charlie peeking through the keyhole. He orders him to clear off, but Charlie makes faces at him and remains outside the room.

Jealous wife's room. Mabel, terrified, hides under the bed. The husband sits on the bed and removes his boots.

Corridor. Charlie straightens his hat, braces himself, tries the door handle, and enters the room.

Jealous wife's room. The husband watches, bewildered, as Charlie wanders around the room, opens a dressing-table drawer and peers into it. A distraught Mabel watches from under the bed. Charlie does a side-kick, swings his cane (which he has been holding by the wrong end), eyes the husband suspiciously, shrugs his shoulders, and exits—momentarily catching his foot in the door. The husband, standing beside the door, gestures angrily and then scratches his head.

Hotel lobby. Charlie plucks a flower from a bouquet held by Mabel's admirer. The admirer rebukes him and then bends down to pick up a fallen blossom—whereupon Charlie whacks him smartly across the rear end. Ignoring his victim's anger, Charlie gallantly offers his freshly plucked flower to a girl seated in the rocking chair.

Mabel's room. A bellboy ushers in the admirer. As he does so, the dog trots out and wanders down the corridor. Finding the room empty, the admirer decides to leave.

Corridor. He speaks to the bellboy.

Title: *"I'll wait with my friend."*

Jealous wife's room. The admirer enters and shakes hands with the husband. The dog enters at the same time and crawls under the bed. Frantic, Mabel tries to keep the animal quiet, but the admirer has noticed it. Peering under the bed he discovers none other than his girlfriend, Mabel! In a jealous rage, he drags her out. Mabel and the husband plead innocence, but to no avail. The furious admirer starts to throttle his "rival." Manslaughter is only prevented when Mabel alerts the two men to the sound of voices outside the room. Released from the admirer's grip, the terrified husband peeks out the door.

Corridor. The manager opens Mabel's door and shows the wife that there is no one inside to make any noise.

Jealous wife's room. Aware that his wife is about to enter, the husband insists that Mabel get back under the bed.

Corridor. The wife thanks the manager for his assistance.

Jealous wife's room. The wife enters, looking smug and self-satisfied. Then she notices the admirer and orders him to clear out. He leaves under protest as the husband makes signals to him to say nothing. The wife gives her husband a withering look.

Corridor. Charlie reappears and begins mocking the admirer. He gets shoved aside and flops back onto a conveniently placed chair.

Jealous wife's room. The wife discovers Mabel under the bed. Assuming the worst, she pounces on her. Mabel fights back. The husband intervenes, pushing Mabel out of the room.

Corridor. The melee continues outside the room. The admirer attacks the husband. Charlie resumes his pursuit of Mabel who flees back to her room. The husband gets in Charlie's way and gets kicked by him.

Mabel's room. The husband staggers back onto Mabel, then flops against the door, closing it.

Corridor. Charlie swings a heavy punch at the admirer and misses. A return blow sends him sprawling. The wife tries, unsuccessfully, to break into Mabel's room.

Mabel's room. Mabel assaults the husband who slaps her back in self-defense.

Corridor. The wife and admirer beat at the door of Mabel's room. Charlie removes his jacket.

Mabel's room. Mabel grabs the husband by his shirt front and flings him out into the corridor.

Corridor. The wife drags her husband back into their room. As they pass, Charlie aims a swift kick at the latter. He misses and falls on his rump. The admirer continues beating on Mabel's door.

Jealous wife's room. The wife starts throttling her husband.

Corridor. Charlie elbows the admirer aside and knocks on Mabel's door. The admirer does the same to Charlie. Mabel timorously opens her door. Charlie goes on one knee to proclaim his love, but she orders him to leave. The admirer follows this up by hurling Charlie the full length of the corridor and throwing his jacket after him. Taking the hint at last, Charlie lurches to his feet and disappears round the bend of the corridor. Mabel and her admirer laugh.

Jealous wife's room. The wife beats her husband ferociously.

Mabel's room. The admirer kisses Mabel. They laugh again. She looks at him coyly, and he holds her hand and gazes after her happily as she moves away from him. . . .

COMMENTS

1. Keystone slapstick farce was already a well-established form when Chaplin joined the studio. He was to chafe at the style and pacing of Keystone comedy but could respond enthusiastically to many of the plots—for they dealt, typically, with the kind of environment he had known in his childhood and that he was to describe many years later in the first chapter of *My Autobiography*—an environment characterized by human behavior at its most unpleasant: male lechery and drunkenness, female vindictiveness, sexual jealousy, marital discord, infidelity, and violence. Like the classic farces of Feydeau, this environment was shaped by misunderstanding and coincidence, both of which were to become fundamental to Chaplin's vision of life in such films as *A Woman of Paris* and *The Gold Rush*.

2. In chapter 10 of *My Autobiography* Chaplin overlooks *Kid's Auto Race* and refers to *Mabel's Strange Predicament* as the first film in which he wore the Tramp outfit. (See note 2 to *Kid's Auto Race*.) Actually his role was that of a drunken masher, not a tramp. The film was his first with Mabel Normand, who directed or codirected him in four and costarred with him in ten Keystones. It was also his first screen depiction of a drunkard, a role he had played many times in the music hall.

Chaplin tells us that Mack Sennett asked him at short notice to improvise a walk-on part for a hotel lobby scene and that all that he knew about the plot was that it concerned Mabel, a lover, and a husband. "In all comedy business," he continues, "an attitude is most important, but it is not always easy to find an attitude. However, in the hotel lobby I felt I was an impostor posing as one of the guests, but in reality I was a tramp just wanting a little shelter. . . . " (Chaplin 1964, 146) Here Chaplin's memory has failed him. A character who passes out bank notes and chases girls around a hotel cannot possibly be a tramp seeking shelter. Chaplin's recollection of the opening lobby scene is also faulty in most of its details: "I entered and stumbled over the foot of a lady," he writes. "I turned and raised my hat apologetically, then turned and stumbled over a cuspidor." Amusing, perhaps, but these actions are somewhat different from what occurs in the film. Regrettably, many commentators seem to have borrowed from Chaplin's description (or Theodore Huff's) rather than looked at the movie itself.

Close examination of the film's plot dispels the notion that Chaplin's role was inserted into the picture "at short notice"—as he himself maintained. His drunken masher character is clearly integral to the complicated chain of events. Not only does Charlie provide most of the film's comedy, he also aggravates Mabel's predicament by forcing her to hide in a married man's bedroom, and he is inextricably involved in all the madcap activity that follows. The most reliable assumption, therefore, is that for this Keystone film at least, Charlie *interpreted* a role rather than created it. This is not to belittle his achievement. The *intended* star was Mabel Normand, but, as Chester Conklin remarked, Chaplin "stole the picture" (Brownlow 1968, 498). His eloquent body language, his idiosyncratic gait, his suggestive shuffling little dance in the foyer (reprised years later for one of *Limelight's* music hall numbers), his impish grins and chuckles, his inventive byplay with hat and cane—all contributed to his transformation of a conventional comedy type into a hilariously eccentric character.

Chaplin's accomplishment was evident to everyone who saw the film being made. As he recalls it:

> . . . by the time we had finished rehearsing we had quite a large audience laughing. Very soon I saw Ford Sterling peering over the shoulders of others. When it was over I knew I had made good. . . . That evening I went home on the street car with one of the small bit players. Said he, "Boy, you've started something; nobody ever got those kinds of laughs on the set before, not even Ford Sterling—and you should have seen his face watching you, it was a study!" (Chaplin 1964, 146)

Despite the obvious success of Chaplin's comic business, his director, Henry Lehrman, wanted to cut most of the opening sequence. He was reluctant to let any scene exceed ten feet, but this one ran to seventy-five. Sennett could not make up his mind about it until Chaplin intervened. "If it's funny," he said, "does length really matter?" This time he prevailed over Lehrman. It was a first, tentative step toward creating his own kind of comedy.

For Mabel Normand, on the other hand, the film was merely a run-of-the-mill effort. There is nothing memorable about *her* performance, and the film would soon have been forgotten if it had not also been a vehicle for Chaplin.

However, a few comments are worth making about Mabel that have nothing to do with her performance. First, her embarrassment at being caught in her pajamas prefigures a similar scene in *Mabel's Married Life* (Keystone no. 19). It was obviously considered a sexy touch to show her in pajamas; Capra latched onto the same idea years later when he showed Claudette Colbert wearing (Clark Gable's) pajamas in *It Happened One Night* (1934). Second, the precise nature of Mabel's role in *Mabel's Strange Predicament* is open to question. It is not clear that she is *merely* a young lady with an admirer. Why, exactly, does the wife snub her at their very first encounter? Does she make an assumption about her that the film's original audiences may also have made as they pondered why she was staying, unchaperoned, at the hotel? And a rather special hotel, it seems. Its lobby has a curious attraction for unescorted young women. Charlie may be drunk, but he knows that it's just the right place to pick up a pretty girl (compare with his escapades in *Caught in the Rain* [Keystone no. 13]), and the manager is rather easily bribed to turn a blind eye to his lechery. Perhaps "admirer" is a polite description for Mabel's gentleman friend who is shown into her bedroom as a matter of course. Their relationship ends the film on a curious note of ambiguity. Is Mabel about to get undressed for him?

3. Mabel Normand (1892–1930) was Keystone's leading comedienne. She appeared with Chaplin in ten other Keystones, including *Tillie's Punctured Romance* (Keystone no. 33) and directed or codirected four of his films. She made many features in the teens and twenties, perhaps the most popular one being *Mickey* (1917). Her later career was disrupted by her association with Hollywood director William Desmond Taylor who was murdered under mysterious circumstances. (See Fussell 1982, 151–69.)

Al St. John (1893–1963), the hotel manager in *Mabel's Strange Predicament*, was Roscoe Arbuckle's nephew and a skilled stunt man. A minor player at Keystone, he appeared with Chaplin in nine Keystones. His career peaked in the 1920s when he became a popular character actor ("Fuzzy") in numerous comedies. In the thirties and forties he often played a sidekick in Westerns.

Alice Davenport (1864–?), the mother in *Making a Living* and the jealous wife of *Mabel's Strange Predicament*, appeared with Chaplin in seven other Keystones. An original member of the Keystone company, she became a leading character comedienne in the teens (e.g., *Fickle Fatty's Fall, Wife and Auto Trouble, Maggie's First False Step*), working for Fox and other companies.

Hank Mann (1888–1971), who played the bellboy in *Mabel's Strange Predicament*, was also one of the Keystone Kops. He appeared with Chaplin in five other Keystones. Chaplin later cast him in three features: as the boxer Charlie fights in *City Lights* (1931), as Charlie's hefty cell mate in *Modern Times* (1936), and as a storm trooper in *The Great Dictator* (1940).

OTHER VIEWS

"There was nothing in the action of *Mabel's Strange Predicament* except chases in and out of hotel rooms, with a husband, a lover, and Charlie as the hotel gate-crasher. Here the mannerisms that were to become so characteristic—the outsize dignity preserved at all costs, the gesture of absurd delicacy in unsuitable situations—began to appear" (Quigly 1968, 23).

"The lobby scene became Chaplin's scene. . . . Lehrman wanted to cut it but found he couldn't: Chaplin had quickly learned how to outwit the 'butchers.' He introduced gags at his entrance and exit which virtually sealed him into the sequence" (Gifford 1974, 34).

"Brutalising. Chaplin, a hotel guest, gets mixed up in a series of amorous complications, some of which are of the most tasteless sort . . ." (Swedish Film Censors, quoted in Asplund 1976, 30).

"Mabel Normand . . . [the] silent screen's finest comedienne, with a natural fluency of timing and a bubbling imagination . . . was the first to recognize Chaplin's talent and to nurture its development. After *Mabel's Strange Predicament*, the first film in which he played opposite her, Chaplin showed a steady improvement in his style. After an exhaustive study of the films she made before Chaplin arrived on the scene, Sam Peeples, a film historian, was forced to conclude that they contained 'entire routines, gestures, reactions, expressions, that were later a part of Chaplin's characterizations' " (Sobel and Francis 1977, 207–209).

4.

Between Showers

(1914)

Original working title: *A Rainy Day*
Other titles: *Charlie and the Umbrella, The Flirts, In Wrong, Thunder
and Lightning;* French: *Charlot et le parapluie, Charlot sous l'averse,
Charlot flirt;* German: *Regenschauer;* Spanish: *Entre Chubascos, Char-
lot y el paraguas, Todo por un paraguas;* Italian: *Charlot e l'ombrello,
Charlot e il parapioggia*

Length: 1 reel; 886 feet (Asplund), 1020 feet (Lyons)
Playing time: 15 minutes at 16 frames per second
Producer: Keystone
Director(s): Henry Lehrman (and Mack Sennett?)
Screenplay: Reed Heustis (?)
Photography: Frank D. Williams (?)
Cast:

A masher	Ford Sterling
A rival masher	Chaplin
A cop	Chester Conklin
His girlfriend	Sadie Lampe
A young lady in distress	Emma Clifton

Finished or shipped: February 7, 1914
Released: February 28, 1914

SYNOPSIS

Exterior of house. A masher (grimacing Ford Sterling) is in a bad
mood: his umbrella is broken, and he has hurt his finger trying to open
it. He suddenly notices another umbrella in perfect condition.

A barn door alongside the masher's house. A cop (Chester Conklin)
is quarreling with his girlfriend about who should hold their umbrella.
He kisses her to make up. While they are thus occupied, the masher's
arm steals into the picture from the right and exchanges the bad umbrella for the good one.

Exterior of house. Unnoticed, the masher runs back into his house with the purloined umbrella.

Barn door. The cop's girlfriend discovers that their good umbrella is missing. Bewildered, she and the cop look in every direction.

Exterior of house. She walks back to the barn after spurning the cop for his incompetence. He stamps off in a rage after tossing away the broken umbrella.

Curbside of a street just after the shower. The masher dips "his" umbrella into a puddle to test its depth. A young lady (Emma Clifton) appears and finds her path blocked by the same puddle. The masher sizes her up and decides that it might be to his advantage to be courteous. He offers to assist her across the street. Then, estimating the width of the puddle, he changes his mind and asks her to hold his umbrella while he dashes off to get assistance. Now Charlie (a rival masher) appears on the scene, dressed in his tramp's outfit. At first he tries to flirt with the young lady; then, realizing her predicament, he too offers to assist her.

A fence nearby. The masher tries to pull up a post to use as a bridge across the puddle.

Curbside. Charlie peeks down at the puddle, loses his balance, and plunges one foot into it. Holding the lady's shoulder, he pulls off his sopping wet boot and sock. Angrily, she shakes his hand loose. Undeterred, he exits after indicating that he will soon be back to help her.

A building site nearby. Charlie has his eye on a large wooden strut beside a workman's feet.

Curbside. A cop (not Conklin!) appears. Without further ado, he picks up the young lady and starts carrying her over the puddle.

Fence. The masher observes what is happening. He rushes away.

Other side of street. The cop deposits the young lady on dry land.

Curbside. The masher returns, still holding the fence post. Enraged, he slams it down on his foot.

Building site. Charlie slips the strut from under the workman's feet and runs off with it.

Other side of street. The young lady smiles at the cop and waves farewell to him. She glares across the street at the masher.

Curbside. The masher snarls at the cop, then dashes across the street.

Other side of the street. The masher demands the return of "his" umbrella.

Curbside. Charlie appears and has an altercation with the cop. As the latter walks away, Charlie thumbs his nose after him and starts swaggering across the street. He stops to snigger at the sight of the young lady making short work of the masher.

Other side of the street. The young lady hurls the masher to the sidewalk and beats him over the head with the umbrella. As he gets to his feet, she shoves him backwards.

Curbside. He staggers back onto the surprised Charlie. As the latter gets up, the masher flings him to the ground again.

Other side of the street. The masher dashes over and grabs the young lady by the hair.

Curbside. Charlie rises dazedly, picks up his hat, makes a few practice feints, and rushes to the rescue.

Other side of the street. At first the masher gets the better of the struggle—although Charlie does manage to get in one good kick. However, his antagonist grabs him by the neck and trots him into a nearby park.

A nearby park [actually Westlake Park, Los Angeles]. The masher flings him down beside a lake, disrupting the siesta of a local hobo. Down but not out, Charlie returns to the fray, lobbing the hobo's boots into his adversary's face. The masher promptly flings them back—but they miss Charlie and hit the hobo, knocking him into the lake. The battle of the boots continues until Charlie is beaten to the ground. Then the masher sets off in pursuit of the young lady.

Another part of the park. He catches up with her. They struggle. He seizes the umbrella. But Charlie reappears, beats him over the head, grabs the umbrella, and pokes it up the masher's rear end. He then returns the umbrella to the young lady. She smiles and thanks him, but he indicates that what he did was a mere nothing.

Street. Infuriated, the masher dashes away in search of a cop. He falls over the curb, kicks it in a fury, and hops around nursing an injured foot.

A tree-lined street nearby. A melancholy cop (Conklin) is on his beat.

The park. His back to the camera, Charlie tries to flirt with the young lady. She spurns him, and he retaliates by seizing the umbrella and poking his tongue out at her.

Tree-lined street. The masher locates the cop and reports that he has been robbed. Together, they rush off to apprehend the thief.

The park. The young lady exits, haughtily. Unabashed, Charlie grins after her. He parades up and down, swinging the umbrella and generally showing off.

Curbside. The masher falls; the cop stumbles over him. They get up and rush into the park.

The park. The masher grabs "his" umbrella from Charlie. Charlie tries to retrieve it. The cop intercedes—and to his astonishment discovers that it's *his own*. Charlie freely admits that he had taken the umbrella from the masher, who has no plausible explanation of how *he* had acquired it. The film ends with a self-satisfied Charlie, whistling and with hands in pocket, watching the arrest of his rival.

COMMENTS

1. *Between Showers* was intended mainly as a vehicle for the rather limited talents of Ford Sterling, Keystone's leading male comic at this period. But even for Sterling it seems a pretty routine effort. Under Lehrman's uninspired direction he merely repeated rather mechanically a role he had played in dozens of previous pictures, while Chaplin, obligated to conform to Sterling's style, was reduced to creating an unsubtle caricature, a simplistic version of the masher he had played in *Mabel's Strange Predicament*. A viewing of the film certainly does not bear out the assertion of McDonald, Conway, and Ricci that "Chaplin's screen characterization, as it was to be seen in the later Keystone comedies, was almost fully developed in this film" (1974, 32).

2. *Between Showers* was to be the last Chaplin film directed by Henry "Pathe" Lehrman. It was also the first of two films in which Chaplin appeared with Ford Sterling: the second was *Tango Tangles* (Keystone no. 6). Denis Gifford observes that Sterling was Chaplin's rival in more ways than one.

> Sterling, Sennett's star since their Biograph days, was working out his Keystone contract. Sennett had made Sterling . . . world famous, and naturally Sterling wanted a rise. This was the reason Sennett played a hunch and hired Chaplin. (1974, 37)

Uno Asplund emphasizes:

> Sterling left Keystone in February 1914, not—as many have averred— because he felt outclassed by Chaplin, but because he felt that he was getting too little money. . . . He had already left when the first Chaplin films began to come out. (1976, 30–31)

Sennett himself comments:

> One of the legends about Chaplin is that he tangled with Ford Sterling when he arrived at the studio and that the two comedians fought it out to the death. Sterling lost the battle and departed, leaving Chaplin in command as top comic. . . . The truth is that we brought Charlie in because we already knew that Ford Sterling was quitting. As a matter of fact, Sterling was thirty-two years old and a major star when twenty-four-year-old Charlie entered the scene. Ford did not consider Chaplin a competitor. (Sennett and Shipp 1954, 159)

It is evident—just from *Between Showers*—that Sterling would have posed no serious challenge to Chaplin even if he had remained at Keystone during Chaplin's tenure with that company. Sterling's unsubtle comic persona never developed significantly after he entered movies in 1911. A onetime circus clown, he graduated to the screen via repertory theater and quickly established himself as the movies' number one comic villain. In *Mack Sennett's Keystone* Kalton Lahue and Sam Gill vividly describe Sterling's comic style:

> A malicious mugging at the camera; his tip-toe strutting while gleefully engaged in the deepest of comic villainy; the broad asides to the audience which telegraphed his next move—these formed an unusual pantomimic style, not native to the screen and more exaggerated than the stage required. . . . Sterling was not really a screen comic in the true sense of the word, but more of a cardboard caricature of the stereotyped Victorian villain—a limitation above which he was seldom able to rise. (1971, 62)

In *Making a Living*, his first film, Chaplin was almost inevitably modeling his screen character on that of Keystone's star, whom he had been hired to replace. But as early as his second film he had nothing to learn from Sterling.

Sterling was lured away from Keystone by Fred J. Balshofer who established a new production unit, the Sterling Film Company (incorporated February 1914), that released its films through Carl Laemmle's Universal Pictures Corporation. Balshofer had promised Laemmle a comedy series starring Mabel Normand and Ford Sterling or Chaplin. To create his company he raided Keystone. Aside from enticing Sterling to join him, he signed up Lehrman as director and netted at least twenty of Sennett's other actors, including several of the Keystone Kops. Up to this time Mabel Normand had no contract with Keystone, but Sennett got wind of Balshofer's designs on her and signed her up before she too could be lured away. As a substitute for Mabel, Balshofer took Emma Clifton (the young lady in distress from *Between Showers*), whom Lahue and Gill (1971b, 22) regarded as a Mabel Normand look-alike. (Isabel Quigly [1968, 37–38] less generously referred to Emma Clifton as "a stout girl," while Theodore Huff [1952, 283] settled for describing her as "buxom.") The new company was soon running a handsome profit, and Sterling and Lehrman were sharing in the dividends. But they squandered their money as quickly as they received it. Then they started quarreling. Eventually their disagreements totally disrupted their work. Balshofer fired Lehrman but found Sterling just as unreliable on his own. The comedian made a habit of reporting sick, but he was actually sleeping off his nightly binges. After removing him for breach of contract, Balshofer completed his comedy series with a Sterling look-alike, then, early in 1915, he wound up the company. Sterling returned to work for Sennett (a procedure he would repeat several more times before his career finally hit the skids). By this time Chaplin had moved over to Essanay and was well on his way to becoming the world's best-known comedian. (See further: Fred J. Balshofer and Arthur C. Miller, *One Reel a Week*, 1967.)

3. Uno Asplund maintains that *Twenty Minutes of Love* (Keystone no. 11) was "the first in a long row of 'park' films shot in Westlake Park outside Los Angeles" (1976, 37). In fact, about half the action of the earlier *Between Showers* is located in Westlake Park. Other films in Chaplin's "park" series are *The Star Boarder, Caught in the Rain, The Fatal Mallet, Mabel's Married Life, Recreation, His New Profession, The Rounders, Those Love Pangs, His Trysting Places, Getting Acquainted* (all Keystones), and the two Essanay pictures *In the Park* and *A Woman*. The lake that appears in many of these films was Echo Lake in Westlake Park.

When Chaplin began to direct his own films he told Sennett: "All I need to make a comedy is a park, a policeman and a pretty girl" (1964, 159). Those ingredients are already present in *Between Showers*, but the film's park setting has no special significance. However, in the later park films—those written or directed by Chaplin—the setting would, more obviously, function as a location for the free play of sexual possibilities and temptations. (See further *Twenty Minutes of Love* note 6.)

Chaplin's commentators have been too quick to assume that his park films simply evolved out of one of his British music hall acts for Karno. But he seems also to have been continuing a comedy subject established in American vaudeville and American silent cinema several years before he joined the Karno company.

Kemp Niver's description of a 1903 Biograph film, *On the Benches in the Park*, points to a striking anticipation of several of Chaplin's park films (e.g., *Twenty Minutes of Love* and *Recreation*):

This film was photographed as if from the audience at a vaudeville show. It opens on a stage set with a painted backdrop of sky and trees, etc. In the foreground to the right of the camera is a park bench where a young woman is seated. She is reading from a book and declaiming. A man wearing tattered garments peers through the foliage at her. The tramp approaches the bench, sits down, and places his arm about the young woman. She jumps up from the bench and yells for a policeman who arrives. The policeman takes the tramp by his tattered garments, shakes him, and hits him on the head with a club. Just then, a little pug dog enters the scene. He grabs the tramp by the seat of his trousers.

The picture ends as the tramp, with the dog firmly affixed to his coat tail, is seen running off through the bushes. The final scene is of the policeman comforting the young woman by putting his arm round her and fanning her with his hat. (1967, 74)

The direction of Biograph's *The Masher*, another movie with a setting and situations anticipating Chaplin's park films, has been attributed to Mack Sennett. It was released on October 14, 1910. See further Kemp Niver, *Motion Pictures from the Library of Congress Paper Print Collection 1894–1912* (1967), pp. 63, 74; also comment 8 to *His Favorite Pastime*.

4. The film has five main sequences. (i) Sterling steals the umbrella from the first cop. (ii) The "rescue" of the young lady in distress. (iii) The young lady rejects Sterling and hangs on to the umbrella. (iv) Charlie gets the umbrella—but not the young lady. (v) The cop regains his umbrella and Sterling is arrested.

5. The motivating action of *Between Showers* is, of course, Sterling's theft of the umbrella. Unused for its intended purpose, the umbrella becomes a symbol of dominance. Whoever possesses it is in temporary control of the situation. Conversely, its loss represents (sexual) weakness or incapacity. Thus for the cop (Conklin) who initially loses the umbrella to Sterling, its theft is tantamount to a loss of virility: first his flirtation is disrupted, then he receives the scorn of the girl he was flirting with. Having filched the umbrella, Sterling makes the mistake of handing it over to the young lady in distress for safe keeping. But she refuses to give it back. Thereafter, reflecting his loss of control, Sterling becomes increasingly frantic. Meanwhile, the young lady is "rescued" by a second, more virile cop who conspicuously flourishes his nightstick— an obviously phallic alternative to the umbrella. When Sterling tries to flirt with the lady and simultaneously reclaim "his" umbrella, she ignominiously beats him over the head with it. He retaliates by abandoning the chivalry he had displayed at their first encounter and grabbing her by the hair in the manner of a caveman. At this point Charlie dashes to the rescue.

The rest of the film focuses on the rivalry of the two main characters (in which respect it parallels *Making a Living*). Each man wants the young lady *and* the umbrella, but if he can't get both he'll settle for one. Having been repudiated by the young lady, Sterling seizes the umbrella. But Charlie grabs it from him, and, as a sexual coup de grace, pokes it up his behind. So far so good, but the young lady is not interested in Charlie either—she just wants the umbrella. That means "no deal" as far as Charlie is concerned.

Denis Gifford singles out this film as the one that establishes "a curious characteristic of the Tramp: despite his shabbiness he is utterly irresistible to the opposite sex" (1974, 37). But this is quite untrue of *Between Showers*. The young lady unmistakably gives Charlie the brush-off; whereupon he seizes the umbrella and pokes his tongue out at her as she exits.

Now Sterling reappears with the first cop. By overreaching to claim the stolen umbrella as his own he is effectively hoisted with his own petard. The cop promptly arrests him and retrieves his umbrella, thereby regaining the control he had lost at the outset.

6. Aside from its slapstick elements, *Between Showers* is a comedy of contrasts—of character, action, and motive. Charlie and Ford Sterling clearly belong to different classes. Sterling's costume marks him as a middle-class "gentleman." Apparently respectable, he quickly reveals himself as a thief. He loses his manners, but Charlie seems to have none to lose. If anything, he finds some soon after meeting the young lady. Gifford describes him as "Charlie the Tramp acting Raleigh to Emma Clifton's stranded Elizabeth." Well, not exactly: the second cop comes nearest to that. But in parallel circumstances Charlie the Tramp certainly behaves no worse than Sterling the bourgeois. Possibly better, depending on your view of the relative importance of courtesy vs. morality: Sterling pulls out an old fence post to help the lady, but Charlie goes to the extent of *stealing* for her. (Sterling doesn't have any qualms about stealing—but he does it only for himself.) Above all, Sterling's mean-spirited, irascible attitude contrasts at every turn with Charlie's good-humored, mischievous playfulness.

To reinforce this, almost everything in the film happens *at least* twice. Thus Sterling surreptitiously steals the umbrella, while Charlie surreptitiously filches a wooden strut. Each man makes his own approach to the young lady. Each treats her chivalrously at first but soon changes his attitude for the worst. Each has his own encounter with (and makes his own insulting gestures at) the second cop, and so on and so forth. (See further *Caught in the Rain* note 5.)

As far as motive is concerned, in rushing to help the young lady in distress, both Charlie and Sterling obviously expect "sexual favors" for services rendered. Charlie is perhaps more flirtatious than lecherous while Sterling comes across, more or less, as a dirty old man. Neither comes off looking very well in relation to the young lady. By contrast, the second cop helps the young lady out of courtesy and nothing more. *Between Showers* clearly defines some of the characteristics of a true gentleman—as opposed to a fake one like Sterling or a would-be one like Charlie.

OTHER VIEWS

"A screamingly funny comedy, featuring Charles Chaplin and a charming girl. All the trouble is caused by an umbrella, and the two men's rivalry for the favour of the lady. Their efforts to out-do each other in gallantry create many humorous situations" (*The Cinema*, quoted in McDonald, Conway, and Ricci 1974, 32).

"The flirtation [of Charlie and the young lady] is striking: for the first time in films it is carried out with the protagonist's back to the camera, a trick of the 'legit' absorbed into the Chaplin repertoire in the days of [H. A.] Saintsbury [who gave Chaplin his first engagement in legitimate theater]" (Gifford 1974, 37).

"Already Chaplin is beginning to find his form as Charlie. In this film it is interesting to study his playing against the Keystone star, Ford Sterling, who here develops his characteristic pattern of movements, including an original way of running with convulsive hops and flexed knees" (Asplund 1976, 30).

5.

A Film Johnnie

(1914)

Original working title: *A Movie Bug*
Other titles: *Charlie at the Studio, His Million Dollar Job, [The] Movie Nut;* French: *Charlot fait du cinéma;* German: *Ein Film-Fan;* Spanish: *Charlot en los estudios, Charlot y el fuego;* Italian: *Charlot fa del cinema*

Length: 1 reel; 915 feet (Asplund), 1020 feet (Lyons)
Playing time: 15 minutes at 16 frames per second
Producer: Keystone
Director: George Nichols
Screenplay: Craig Hutchinson
Photography: Frank D. Williams?
Cast:

The Film Johnnie*	Chaplin
The Keystone Girl	Virginia Kirtley**
Heroine (a movie actress)	Minta Durfee
Roscoe "Fatty" Arbuckle	as himself
Ford Sterling	as himself
The director	Mack Sennett
Firemen	The Keystone Kops

Finished or shipped: February 11, 1914
Released: March 2, 1914

SYNOPSIS

Exterior of a nickelodeon. Charlie in his Tramp's outfit scrutinizes a poster advertising a Keystone film, *The Champion Driver*, and depicting the film's heroine. Smitten with her, he blows her a kiss and

---

* *Johnnie* is old British slang for *a young fellow.* It was also, more specifically, a name given to playboys who hung around stage doors in order to pick up actresses.
**Virginia Kirtley, "The Keystone Girl," was the female lead in Chaplin's first film, *Making a Living.*

then reaches into his pants pocket and pulls out an old sock from which he extracts the price of admission.

Interior of darkened nickelodeon. Sauntering down the aisle, he proceeds to make a nuisance of himself. He treads on a man's foot and sits in the lap of a pretty girl who jumps up and protests. Apologizing, he waves his arm, inadvertently hitting another man in the face. Seated at last, he stares fixedly at the screen.

On the movie screen. A war scene is in progress. Two armies are firing at each other. It *looks* like an extreme long shot from a battle sequence of *The Birth of a Nation* (see comment 3 below), but Griffith's great epic of the Civil War was not even previewed until January 1915.

Interior of nickelodeon. Engrossed, Charlie casually puts his leg onto his neighbor's knee. The man throws it off and admonishes him.

On the movie screen. A scene of hand-to-hand combat.

Interior of nickelodeon. Charlie begins to weep at what he is watching. He pulls out his sock and uses it to dab his streaming eyes; then he wrings it out all over his pants. Uncomfortably wet, he gets up and starts back up the aisle. En route, he mischievously pokes his knee into his neighbor. The latter responds by grabbing at Charlie's jacket—at which Charlie turns and flings the wet sock in the man's face. An attendant runs down the aisle, collars both men, and shoves them back in their seats. Charlie now becomes preoccupied (momentarily) with shaking out his pants.

On the movie screen. A close-up of the smiling Keystone Girl, holding a nosegay.

Interior of nickelodeon. Charlie applauds noisily, to the annoyance of everyone seated near him. Flinging his arms wide, he smashes his derby hat into his neighbor's face.

On the movie screen. The Keystone Girl blows kisses at the audience.

Interior of nickelodeon. Charlie sighs and simpers with passion. His neighbor eyes him curiously. Charlie blows him a kiss. He puts his derby back on his head and makes it spring into the air; then he thumbs his nose at his neighbor.

On the movie screen. A portly man pulls the protesting Keystone Girl out of some bushes and kisses her.

Interior of nickelodeon. Aroused and angry, Charlie claps his hat on his head, rises to his feet, and shadowboxes the screen. Unable to see the screen, the man immediately behind him forces him back into his seat. Charlie gets up again, treads on his neighbor's foot, and swings his fist to hit the man behind him—he hits his neighbor instead. The latter retaliates by smacking his head. Charlie turns round to strike back, but his fist catches the man behind and sends him sprawling among the right aisle seats. Successfully landing a blow on his neighbor's jaw, he now sends *him* sprawling among the left aisle seats. At this point the attendant intervenes, giving the protesting Charlie the bum's rush out of the auditorium.

Exterior of nickelodeon. Charlie picks himself up and notices the poster again. Smiling and pointing at the name "Keystone," he suddenly has an idea. He marches off in the direction of Keystone Studios.

Street outside Keystone Studios. Several Keystone players arrive in automobiles. One falls out of his car and is helped to his feet by a passerby (Henry Lehrman?). The heroine (Minta Durfee) arrives in the company of Roscoe "Fatty" Arbuckle (out of make-up and wearing ordinary clothes).

Studio driveway. Charlie watches excitedly. He mimes Fatty's bulk. Then he accosts Fatty, touches his paunch, and compares it with his own. Fatty slips him a hand-out and walks on into the studio. Charlie dubiously scrutinizes the hand-out.

Studio door. The director (Mack Sennett) emerges with a cast list. He checks it over, then reenters the studio.

Studio driveway. Feigning high spirits, Charlie next accosts Ford Sterling (also out of make-up). He flatters and applauds him, and earns himself another hand-out.

Studio door. The director reappears, looking harassed.

Studio driveway. Relaxing, Charlie puffs on a cigarette as a number of extras pass by. Then he decides to follow them.

Studio door. He arrives in time to have the door slammed in his face. He treads on the foot of the director who tells him:

Title: *"I don't want any bums around here."*

Undaunted, Charlie follows him into the studio, mischievously slapping the bearded old doorkeeper on the head as he enters.

Interior of studio. Charlie watches a scene being filmed; then he wanders over to the director and interrupts him. For this he gets flung across the studio floor. As he gets up, two sceneshifters knock him down again with a rolled carpet. He rises to his feet in a daze. Behind him, a set is being rapidly dressed. The heroine comes into view. Charlie eyes her with interest—especially her bosom. When she walks past without noticing him, he tries to follow—right across the set—but one of the sceneshifters blocks his path and shoves him aside.

Prop room. Among the miscellaneous props, Charlie finds a revolver. Absentmindedly, he tries to pick his teeth with the gun barrel. A workman passes, carrying a large scenery panel. Charlie clings to it and gets himself a free ride.

Interior of studio. Charlie sits in an armchair and watches a fight scene being filmed—until a property man suddenly pushes him aside and takes the armchair. Aiming a kick at the property man, he misses and stubs his foot instead. He turns his attention back to the filming and is soon caught up in the action. He clutches at his heart while watching a love scene. When the villain appears and attacks the heroine, Charlie leaps to the rescue. He tosses the villain aside and embraces the heroine. The irate director protests, but Charlie kicks him in the stomach. He falls back and smashes into a large scenery panel. The heroine reacts by flinging Charlie to the floor. Outraged at his treatment, he staggers to his feet and starts firing in the direction of the hero and villain. The director makes a grab at him, but Charlie is too quick. He starts blazing away with the revolver, forcing everyone in sight to take cover. Then he stalks up and down the set, brandishing the weapon. Near the studio door he picks up a cigar butt and lights it by firing at the tip. Then he exits, shooting as he goes.

Studio door. He lunges a well-placed kick into the doorkeeper's paunch.

Interior of studio. Work now resumes on the disrupted film.

A residential street. A Keystone representative passes a burning house. Knowing that a fire scene is just what is needed to complete the movie, he calls up the studio from a nearby telephone box.

Interior of studio. Another representative answers the telephone. He informs the director.

Street outside the studio. Actors and crew pile into automobiles and speed toward the fire.

Road. Tracking shot of rear view of Charlie rushing to the fire.

Residential street. The filming proceeds against the background of the fire. All is going well until Charlie bursts onto the set. He warms his hands at the blaze. Then he once more disengages the heroine from the villain's clutches. The director politely orders him to clear off. This time he obeys with protest. Now the fire brigade arrives. Charlie helpfully returns with a bucket of water, which he pours onto a small (unburning) piece of wood that is lying on the ground near the camera tripod. For this "heroic" act he approaches the camera and tries to get himself filmed—in close up. Infuriated, the director picks up the piece of wood and goes after him. He hurls it, but Charlie ducks and the missile hits the camera, knocking it off the tripod. In a frenzy, the director attacks the hero as he is trying to replace the camera on its mount. The latter loses his grip on the tripod and the camera smashes to the ground. Charlie laughs hysterically. While the director slugs out with his crew, Charlie seizes the heroine and starts kissing her. Now the firemen turn their hoses on the camera crew. The heroine reacts to Charlie's embraces by giving him a thorough shake-up, after which she dumps him next to a fence—where he becomes the firemen's new target.

Close-up of Charlie. Thoroughly waterlogged, he twists one ear and squirts a jet of water from his mouth.

The heroine laughs.

Charlie responds by clasping his heart and gesturing that he has had enough of the movies and "love"—not to mention cold water.

COMMENTS

1. Chaplin did not consider George "Pop" Nichols an improvement over Lehrman. Nichols was an actor turned director, described by Chaplin as "an oldish man in his late fifties who had been in motion pictures since their inception." He was a friend of Lehrman and evidently shared many of his notions about film comedy: hence, in October 1914 when Lehrman was fired from Sterling Comedies and started up his own company, Lehrman-Knockout Comedies, he brought in Nichols as one of his four unit directors. Chaplin tells us:

> [Nichols] had but one gag, which was to take the comedian by the neck and bounce him from one scene to another. I tried to suggest subtler business, but he too would not listen. "We have no time, no time!" he would cry. All he wanted was an imitation of Ford Sterling. Although I mildly rebelled, it appears that he went to Sennett saying that I was a son of a bitch to work with. . . . I tried to reason with members of the cast, but they also were against me. "Oh, he knows, he knows, he's been in the business much longer than you have," said an old actor. (1964, 147–48)

But Chaplin underrated Nichols. Certainly in specific details *A Film Johnnie* is occasionally reminiscent of Chaplin's four films for Lehrman. Charlie's cadging from Fatty Arbuckle recalls his sharper character panhandling Lehrman in *Making a Living*, while his repeated frustrations of the Keystone director (Sennett) are bound to remind us of the Tramp's incessant disruptions of Lehrman in *Kid's Auto Race*. But there is no equivalent of Ford Sterling in *A Film Johnnie*, and Chaplin's put-down of Nichols totally ignores the important new developments that accompanied his change of director.

A Film Johnnie was the first film in which some evolution of the Tramp is discernible; it was also the first film in which Chaplin played the lead in a *preplanned* story film. *Kid's Auto Race* had been entirely improvised, and in the three other Lehrman films he had had to share the spotlight with Lehrman, Mabel Normand, and Ford Sterling, respectively. But *A Film Johnnie* was obviously conceived from the outset with some of Chaplin's special talents in mind. Chaplin claims sole credit for whatever creativity there was in his films directed by Nichols (and later by Mabel Normand and Sennett). "I had managed," he tells us, "to put over one or two bits of comedy business of my own, in spite of the butchers in the cutting room. Familiar with their method of cutting films, I would contrive business and gags just for entering and exiting from a scene, knowing that they would have difficulty in cutting them out" (1964, 148). However, this contrivance was less effective than Nichols's use of the camera—over which Chaplin could have had little or no control. (Whoever shot *A Film Johnnie*, it was under Nichols's direction that he gave us some of the earliest striking close-ups of Charlie.) Unlike Lehrman, Nichols realized that Chaplin's face was a major comic asset, and so he focused on it in several key scenes.

Many commentators have referred to that memorable final close-up in which Charlie turns his face into a faucet by tweaking his ear and spurting water out of his mouth. But there are other notable close-ups in the film—less funny perhaps, but certainly more expressive of the character Chaplin is playing. For example, the focus on Charlie's sigh as he is ignored by a movie actress (whose bosom he has just surreptitiously scrutinized). There are hints of wonderful things to come in this fleeting moment of *A Film Johnnie*. The discerning may see in it an anticipation of the Tramp's longing gaze as he first glimpses the apparently unattainable Georgia at the Monte Carlo nightclub in *The Gold Rush* (1925), and perhaps, too, of Charlie the "art fancier" peeking coyly at a nude statue in *City Lights*.

Nichols also allowed Chaplin to introduce some of the Tramp's most characteristic screen business: the swaggering walk, the now-perfected derby-hat flip, the polite raising of the hat as a cunning prelude to delivering a swift kick, the first elaborate play with the cane, etc. At the same time, despite his later insistence that Nichols restrained him as much as Lehrman, under his direction he demonstrated some of his earliest creative use of objects: turning a revolver into a toothpick and transforming an old sock successively into a purse and a handkerchief.

We also get to know quite a lot more about the Tramp. In *Kid's Auto Race* he is a self-advertising intruder, an irrepressible pest, and not much else. *A Film Johnnie* adds considerably to the portrait by showing us a tramp who can be tenderhearted (he weeps at the sight of onscreen carnage), passionate (he adores the Keystone Girl), mock-passionate (he clutches his heart while watching the filming of a love scene), protective (he tries to rescue the Keystone Girl and rushes to the defense of the Heroine), absentminded (he picks his teeth with a revolver), frenetic (he goes berserk with the gun), cunning (he is about to boot a sceneshifter, but when the man turns round Charlie pretends to be tying his shoelace), malicious (he slaps and kicks the old doorkeeper), mock-heroic (he wants to be filmed for his "courage" in dousing an unburning piece of wood), and so on. Clearly Chaplin himself was responsible for developing these new aspects of the Tramp, but he was able to do so because of—rather than in spite of—the context that Nichols (and screenwriter Craig Hutchinson) provided.

2. *A Film Johnnie* has three main "movements," in each of which Charlie creates his own performance by disrupting the performances of others: (i) mayhem at the film show, (ii) mayhem in the film studio, and (iii) mayhem at the fire.

3. Like *Kid's Auto Race*, and *The Masquerader* (Keystone no. 24), *A Film Johnnie* is an essay in self-reflexive cinema. Unlike *Kid's Auto Race*, the reflexivity of *A Film Johnnie* is elaborate and extensive rather than single-minded and intensive.

Certain Chaplin films form natural groups in terms of similarity of plot or theme or location, and hindsight enables us to see *A Film Johnnie* as the first of several Chaplin movies located partly or wholly in a film studio. The others were *The Masquerader, His New Job* (Essanay 1915), and *Behind the Screen* (Mutual 1916). Comparative study of these films could be rewarding not only to the student of Chaplin but to anyone interested in authentic glimpses of a silent film studio.

The reflexivity of *A Film Johnnie* begins with the film's title—which may well have been suggested by Chaplin since it made use of a slang term then popular in Britain rather than the U.S.A. "Film johnnie" has several interrelated meanings in terms of the movie: Chaplin, a disgruntled film actor for Keystone plays a film fan who "becomes" an inadvertent film actor for Keystone. Where *Kid's Auto Race* reflected Chaplin's conflict with Lehrman, *A Film Johnnie* can be seen as a parody of Chaplin's beginning discomfort with film in general and his general disagreements with the Keystone environment in particular.

Following the title we see a range of self-reflexive elements. The Tramp twice draws our attention to a poster advertising a Keystone film, *The Champion Driver*, which may have been an "in" joke reference to Lehrman's one-reeler *Racing* (originally titled *The Champion*). Behind that poster we can glimpse another ad—for a Bison picture. Bison, like Keystone, was one of Kessel and Bauman's companies, and both posters are prominently placed at the outset of the picture as unashamedly promotional gimmicks. (There was nothing particularly original about this sort of thing. Edison and other Patents Company studios had been doing it for years as much for the free advertising as a device intended to deter movie pirates.)

As the Tramp enters the nickelodeon, the film's self-reflexivity is heightened. The nickelodeon audience (including Charlie) is viewed repeatedly from the standpoint of the nickelodeon screen—so that we get, in a primitive way, something akin to the shots of the audience in Woody Allen's *Purple Rose of Cairo* (1985). Then, of course, there are the films within the film. The battle scenes at which Charlie weeps *look*, in retrospect, as if they were taken from *The Birth of a Nation*, but chronology makes that out of the question. It *is* possible that they were pirated from Griffith's Biograph film *The Battle* (1911). At any rate, what we see, momentarily, is a movie comic weeping at a movie epic. Then comes more studio self-advertising: the Keystone Girl takes the place of the epic. Charlie believes her kisses are for him and the cutting *almost* suggests that they are. Certainly he imagines that he is interacting with her: his shadowboxing is intended as a protective gesture when a portly man kisses her against her will, but he draws the line at trying to climb into the screen as Keaton would do in *Sherlock Jr.* (1924). This scene may actually have been a conscious recreation of an early Edison comedy, *Uncle Josh at the Moving Picture Show* (1902) in which a country bumpkin, watching his first movie, gets so involved with it that he tears down the screen in order to help the heroine.

After getting kicked out of the nickelodeon, Charlie, inspired by the poster of the Keystone Girl, heads for the actual studio. From this, presumably, many 1914 audiences would have realized for the first time that Keystone was not just a trademark but a studio where film comedies (such as the one they were watching) were made by people in front of and behind cameras. But before that, Chaplin in his onscreen persona encounters Keystone actors in their offscreen "reality." There are a couple of possible "in" jokes here. Minta Durfee arrives in the company of Fatty Arbuckle, her real-life husband (they were married in 1908); Charlie is totally oblivious or unaware of this later on when she has become the heroine and he rushes to "rescue" her from another man. Then there's the cadging business (his panhandling of Fatty), which seems like a deliberate parody of Chaplin's very first scene in *Making a Living*.

Once inside the studio, the Tramp interacts in various ways with the film-in-production. He uses the props and scenery for his own purposes. He interrupts the director and obstructs the sceneshifters. Unable to perceive that what is being filmed is dramatic illusion, he intrudes upon it as if it is reality, thereby becoming part of its action and reshaping it accordingly. In so doing, he totally disrupts the film-in-production just as he had disrupted the filmshow at the nickelodeon. Putting a stop to the film enables him to put on his own exclusive "performance," stalking up and down on the set with the property revolver.

In the movie's first movement, Charlie had interacted with the film image. In the second movement, his interaction is with the process of filmmaking. In the final movement, he interacts with the filmmakers' attempts to use "reality" (the burning house) as part of their dramatic illusion. In the course of his destructive intrusions, the camera gets smashed and the production unit gets totally "washed up" when the fire brigade appears. Just before the camera is ruined, Charlie plays the "hero" by dousing an unburning piece of wood. Then he tries unsuccessfully to achieve his objective of getting the cameraman to film him to the exclusion of everyone and everything else. But a thorough drenching and his final rejection by the heroine bring him to his senses at last. He gestures that he has had enough of the movies (at least the way they were being made at Keystone) but, significantly, the movie fades out with a focus on his performance.

4. Chaplin would reappear with Roscoe Arbuckle (1887–1933) in four other Keystones, including a notable cameo role in *The Knockout* (Keystone no. 17) which was essentially a "Fatty" picture. Minta Durfee (1897–1975), Arbuckle's wife, appeared with Chaplin in thirteen Keystones, including *Tillie's Punctured Romance* (Keystone no. 33). In 1921, at the height of his career, Arbuckle became the defendant in a notorious rape and murder case (the Virginia Rappe case) in which Henry Lehrman was a major witness for the prosecution. Arbuckle was acquitted but ruined. See further David Yallop, *The Day the Laughter Stopped* (1976).

OTHER VIEWS

"Mack Sennett, playing himself, hears of a nearby fire, and true to Keystone custom, despatches a company to the scene with orders to improvize a picture. Charlie tags along, mistakes the staged danger for the real thing, and ruins the take. They turn the firehose on him, a slapstick finale which Charlie tops by turning his ear and squirting water out of his mouth: a personal twist which refocuses the attention on the comedian instead of the comedy" (Gifford 1974, 37).

"At Keystone Charlie had any number of jobs and roles, while remaining himself; just occasionally Chaplin took over, in the cause of versatility, and played someone else. . . . But mostly he was Charlie in this or that situation, more or less tramp-like (sometimes more, sometimes less), raising uproar and confusion. In *A Film Johnnie* he invaded the Keystone studios and caused chaos among the filmmakers" (Quigly 1968, 29, 36).

6.

Tango Tangles ⟶⟶⟶⟶⟶⟶⟶⟶⟶⟶⟶⟶⟶)
(1914)

Original working title: *A Midnight Dance*
Other titles: *Music Hall, Charlie's Recreation*;* French: *Charlot au bal, Charlot danseur;* German: *Tango Tingeltangel;* Spanish: *Charlot en el baile;* Italian: *Charlot ballerino, I passi del tango*

Length: 1 reel; 702 feet (Asplund), 734 feet (Lyons)
Playing time: 12 minutes at 16 frames per second
Producer: Keystone
Director: Mack Sennett
Screenplay: Mack Sennett
Photography: Frank D. Williams (?)
Cast:

Drunken swell	Chaplin
Hatcheck girl	Minta Durfee
Band leader	Ford Sterling
Clarinettist	Roscoe "Fatty" Arbuckle
Male dancer	Chester Conklin

Finished or shipped: February 17, 1914
Released: March 9, 1914

SYNOPSIS

All the action of *Tango Tangles* is located in a dance hall and its adjoining cloak room.

Prologue. Title: *The professional dancers have their innings before the Masque Ball begins.*

A couple wearing dance costumes and ballet shoes dance a few tango steps and round off their brief appearance with a pirouette.

Charlie, clean-shaven and dressed in a tuxedo, toddles drunkenly onto the dance floor where two young girls are doing the cancan. He

---

*Under the alternative title *Charlie's Recreation*, this film has frequently been confused with *Recreation*, Chaplin's twenty-third Keystone film.

grasps the nearest girl's outstretched arm and joins in. When the girl suddenly withdraws her arm, he falls on his rump. The manager helps him to his feet and indicates where he can find a table. Politely taking his leave of the two girls, he bumps into a dancing couple and staggers off the dance floor.

Two ladies are chatting next to the hatcheck counter. Charlie proceeds to dust his clothes with one lady's foxtail and tries to hand his hat to the other lady. He is rebuffed. Spying the actual hatcheck girl, he places his hat on her head and hands her his cane; then he tries to flirt with her. She is unresponsive, so he flings his cloakroom ticket at her, gives a little back kick, and lurches off.

Title: *The Band leader has a sneaky feeling for the hat check girl.*

Ford Sterling's not unwelcome attentions to the hatcheck girl arouse the jealousy of Fatty, the clarinettist, who shoves Sterling aside and embraces the girl. Sterling recoils.

Title: *"She's mine: I saw her first."*

He pushes Fatty backward onto the feet of a passing guest. The guest protests. Fatty picks him up and threatens to fling him at Sterling—who beats a hasty retreat. Fatty has to be temporarily satisfied with booting the guest.

Fleeing Fatty's wrath, Sterling runs into Charlie and knocks him sprawling across the dance floor. Fatty reappears, in hot pursuit of his rival. Charlie tries to follow but falls down a staircase instead. Fatty meets up with his rival at last. But Sterling manages to placate him and persuades him to rejoin the band.

The dance resumes. The floor is crowded with couples in fancy dress. Charlie continues his flirtation with the hatcheck girl and invites her to dance with him. As they pass the band, she goes to work on Sterling's sense of courtesy by deliberately dropping her handkerchief. But before he can pick it up, Charlie gets there first. Enraged, Sterling dashes over, separates Charlie from his partner, and tries to drag him off the dance floor. It proves too slippery. The two men slither and fall all over the polished surface.

Title: *"We'll fight for her!"*

The dancing couples pull back and watch. Charlie and Sterling square off. Sterling quickly gets the upperhand. First he knocks Charlie to the floor; then he grabs him by the head and shoves him backward into the throng of laughing bystanders. Charlie staggers to his feet, smacks the face of the nearest onlooker, and lurches away. Sterling waves his arms victoriously.

Title: *The fat musician has grown suspicious.*

Fatty arrives on the dance floor. He catches sight of the hatcheck girl in Sterling's company and angrily flings his arms asunder, felling a bevy of bystanders.

Title: *"I'll break that sneak in two!"*

Sterling announces to all and sundry:

Title: *"She's my girl and anyone that tries to steal her is going to get beaten."*

He kisses the girl's hand. Fatty stands behind him and observes the scene ominously.

Title: *"And I bar no one!"* Turning, he notices Fatty and promptly tries to melt into the crowd. Fatty goes after him but slithers and falls, bringing several dancers down with him.

Charlie reappears and peels off his jacket for another bout with Sterling.

Title: *"I'm going to change your map."*

Sterling peels off his jacket, too. They square off again, and each man tears off his starched collar. But Sterling changes his mind about fighting. He marches off to the cloakroom.

Cloakroom. Sterling starts to put on his overcoat. Charlie enters and simultaneously tries to get into the same coat. Sterling pulls him out of it and throws him across the floor. Charlie gets up and knocks him down. The fight continues—back onto the dance floor (to the amusement of the bystanders) until they succeed in knocking each other out.

COMMENTS

1. This is one of the slighter Keystones, but it nevertheless has some aspects worthy of note.

First a few words about the tango. The dance was introduced to the United States by Vernon and Irene Castle shortly before World War I. It was an immediate sensation and generated a tango craze that swept the United States c. 1913–14. The craze was to have a resurgence after the war when Rudolph Valentino performed the tango in *The Four Horsemen of the Apocalypse* (1921).

The dance had a bad reputation. It had originated in the brothels of Argentina and had vague associations with white slavery. Moralists objected not only to its origins but also to its very nature. In her autobiography, *Castles in the Air*, Mrs. Castle observes: "its opponents objected to the man bending the woman over backwards and peering into her eyes with a smoldering passionate look."

Thus *Tango Tangles* probably sounded like a risqué subject when it was originally released. But despite the enticing title and the dance prologue, the film's treatment of the tango is brief and titillating rather than elaborate and revelatory. The tango of the exhibition dancers in the prologue begins with a glimpse of the dance's suggestiveness, but the female partner quickly transforms this into ballet by pirouetting on her toes. Thereafter there is no focus on the tango. The film's first insert title indicates that (despite the film's main title) what will follow the prologue is a "Masque Ball"—not a comic treatment of tango dancing. In fact, we get to see no more than glimpses of this masque ball. The film concentrates not on dancing but on a double rivalry for the hatcheck girl: Fatty vs. Sterling and Sterling vs. Charlie.

2. Commentators have often stated that the whole of *Tango Tangles* was shot in a real dance hall in Los Angeles—which would make it an exercise in on-location improvisation like *Kid's Auto Race*. But careful examination of prints of *Tango Tangles* reveals that much of the film was studio-made. The scenes taking place on the checkerboard floor and in the cloakroom were undoubtedly made back at Keystone and not in the dance hall. Note that where it would be easy and obvious to pan from the checkerboard floor to the main dance hall, there are straight cuts—although, through skillful editing, the action seems to move fluently from one location to the other. The question that has to be asked is why the whole film wasn't shot either at the dance hall or in the studio. There can be no certain answer to this. But one possible explanation is that Sennett originally planned to shoot the entire picture at the dance hall but found that he could not control the situation adequately. So he decided to complete the film at the studio, making use of footage he had already taken on location.

3. The film's main sequences: (i) prologue, (ii) Charlie's entrance: he tries to pick up the hatcheck girl, (iii) Sterling's first flight from Fatty, (iv) Sterling vs. Charlie—round one, (v) Sterling's second flight from Fatty, (vi) Sterling vs. Charlie—round two.

4. A curious feature of *Tango Tangles* is that none of the principals appear in make-up or costume. (Chester Conklin sports his walrus mustache and is dressed as a cop, but he is just one of the extras.) The abandonment of make-up for one group points up the distinctions between the exhibition dancers, the dance hall regulars, the dancers in fancy dress (studio extras), and the principals. None of these groups significantly interacts with the others. The exhibition dancers are seen in isolation, the regulars and fancy-dress dancers mingle in a few shots and form backgrounds to the main action, but it is the fancy-dress dancers who are most interested in the two rivalries.

Without make-up, Fatty, Sterling, and Charlie appear already "unmasked" at the masque ball. (However, in his challenge game with Charlie, Sterling draws the line at taking all his clothes off.) All three characters are one-dimensional. Fatty doesn't know his own strength and is more interested in the hatcheck girl than in playing the clarinet.

Sterling is a braggart who can't control Fatty—let alone the rest of the band. Charlie reprises the drunken swell role that he had originally popularized with the Karno Company, a variation of which he had recently essayed in *Mabel's Strange Predicament*. As we shall see, he went on to repeat this role in many other films, most notably in *One A.M.* (Mutual 1916) Curiously, in *Tango Tangles* his drunken swell seems more interested in women and fighting than in liquor.

Obviously, in the rivalry of Fatty and Sterling there is no real contest. Fatty's slow burn is enough to terrify Sterling—he doesn't wait to be manhandled by him. So Fatty winds up with the girl (which was perfectly appropriate since she was, after all, Mrs. Roscoe Arbuckle). The opposition of Sterling and Charlie was a different matter. Here the onscreen conflict unquestionably mirrored what Sennett saw as a rivalry of comic talent. *Tango Tangles*, as we know, was the second and last film in which Sterling and Chaplin appeared together. Upon Sterling's departure to what he thought were greener pastures, Chaplin gravitated into his place. So, in *Tango Tangles* Sennett pointedly shows us Charlie trying to get into Sterling's coat. Evidently unable to decide which of the two comedians he preferred, Sennett concludes the film with a dual knockout.

5. Slight as it is, *Tango Tangles* gave Chaplin several ideas that were to surface years later. Sterling slithered wildly across the polished dance floor in 1914; Chaplin would have the same difficulty twenty-two years later in *Modern Times* (1936). Variations on Charlie's choreographed "duel" with Sterling were to recur in his even more elaborate challenge-game conflict with John Rand in *The Pawnshop* (Mutual 1916). His curious "flamenco-style" rump movements—one of the comedy's few concessions to its title—were to be repeated in the gymnasium sequence of *The Cure* (Mutual 1917). Charlie shared Sterling's overcoat in *Tango Tangles* and Henry Bergman's in *Pay Day* (First National 1922). His drunk role without make-up was repeated thirty-eight years later when he made his first entrance in *Limelight* (1952). Even the prologue to *Tango Tangles* was not forgotten. The Café Royal sequence of *Monsieur Verdoux* (1947) opens with two professional dancers performing the tango: a scene that (like the prologue of *Tango Tangles*) is not explicitly connected with what follows.

OTHER VIEWS

"An impromptu film taken in a real dance-hall at a tango contest" (Huff 1952, 47).

"*A Film Johnnie* . . . and *Tango Tangles* were location films—the former at the Keystone lot itself, the latter at an actual dance hall. The films almost directed themselves, with Chaplin and others improvising at need" (McCabe 1978, 57).

"For its glimpse of dapper Chaplin, so young, so handsome, so acrobatic, this little film is unique" (Gifford 1974, 38).

7.

His Favorite Pastime

(1914)

Original working title: *The Drunk*
Other titles: *The Bonehead, Charlie's Reckless Fling, The Reckless Fling*; French: *Charlot est trop galant, Charlot entre le bar et l'amour*; German: *Sein Lieblingsvergnügen*; Spanish: *Un marido contra Charlot; Charlot hace el amor*; Italian: *Il suo passatempo preferito; Traditore di un Charlot*

Length: 1 reel; 945 feet (Asplund), 1009 feet (Lyons)
Playing time: 16 minutes at 16 frames per second
Producer: Keystone
Director: George Nichols
Screenplay: Craig Hutchinson
Photography: Frank D. Williams (?)
Cast:

A drunken tramp	Chaplin
Another drunkard	Roscoe "Fatty" Arbuckle
A lady	Peggy Pearce

Finished or shipped: February 19, 1914
Released: March 16, 1914

SYNOPSIS

A barroom. Charlie, a drunken tramp, is being watched by Fatty, an inebriated barfly. Charlie takes a bunch of sausages from the free lunch counter, breaks one off, and shoves it in his mouth as if it were a cigar. Then he strikes a match on his rear end and attempts to light the sausage. Unsuccessful, he tosses his "cigar" away and consoles himself by buying a beer. Fatty now starts up a diversionary conversation with him while trying, surreptitiously, to steal his drink. Aware of what he is up to, Charlie at first circumvents his maneuvers. Then, with a display of unexpected generosity, he hands him the glass of beer. Fatty blows off the froth and is about to take a swig when

Charlie cunningly pulls back the glass, downs the beer himself, and places the almost empty glass on the bar. Undaunted, Fatty reaches over to drink the dregs, but Charlie is too quick for him again. Gulping down most of the dregs, he pours the few remaining drops over Fatty's feet.

Driveway. A lady, her husband and her black maid enter a taxi.

Barroom. Fatty tries to ingratiate himself with Charlie until, to Fatty's disgust, he demonstrates how well he can spit. Then, in an apparent gesture of cordiality, Charlie offers him his hand, but when Fatty shakes it, he finds it soaking wet. This is the last straw. He staggers out of the tavern while Charlie wipes his hand and then turns back to the bar.

A busy street. The taxi pulls up. The three passengers get out. The husband goes into a store while the lady and her maid wait for him beside the taxi.

Exterior of tavern. Charlie staggers into the street and notices the lady. He doffs his hat and approaches her, swinging his cane. When he speaks to her she smiles but doesn't answer. He takes off his derby and uses his cane to crease it into a more stylish trilby shape. Then he puts it back on and straightens his waistcoat. At this point the husband reappears and orders Charlie to clear off. Sizing him up, Charlie decides that it's prudent to obey. He heads back to the tavern, stroking his face pensively and poking out his tongue to indicate renewed thirst.

Barroom. He enters, totters over to the bar, and orders a drink. A tough guy in a striped shirt enters. In his haste to get to the bar, he shoves Charlie aside and knocks him down. Another barfly helps Charlie up. The tough guy raises his fists and Charlie tries to look conciliatory. They get on with their drinking. Then the tough guy slaps Charlie on the back, knocking the breath out of him. Recovering, he heads for the men's room. En route he bangs his nose on the swinging door.

Men's room. A black attendant is brushing down a customer. Assuming incorrectly that the customer had swung the door in his face, Charlie boots him into the barroom. Then he lights up a cigarette. The attendant smiles at him. Then, with his back to Charlie, he furtively holds out his hand for a tip. Charlie obliges by giving him a red hot match. As the attendant dashes out in pain, Charlie smirks.

A busy street. The lady and her husband have a heated argument beside the taxi. He stalks off angrily.

Men's room. Charlie stands at the washbasin, wets his face, then rubs his back with a towel as if he had just got out of a bath. Another customer enters and Charlie smiles at him.

Barroom. The husband enters. He greets the customer whom Charlie had booted out of the men's room.

Men's room. Charlie flops down on the shoe-shine stool.

A busy street. The lady and her maid are talking beside the taxi.

Men's room. Another customer enters followed by the black attendant. The latter discovers Charlie snoozing on his shoe-shine stool. He wakes him. Noticing the customer bent over the washbasin, lathering his face and hands, Charlie whacks him smartly across the behind with his cane; then he throws him to the floor and grabs the towel. The customer, soap in his eyes, reaches for the towel, but Charlie is already using it to polish his shoes. The customer staggers blindly around the men's room until Charlie considerately hands him the towel. Now he watches the customer unsuspectingly wipe shoe polish all over his face. Eventually, realizing what has happened, the man starts protesting. Charlie responds by shoving him through the swinging doors into the barroom—but the doors swing back and smack Charlie in the mouth.

Barroom. The black-faced customer elbows his way to the bar, knocking down four barflies.

Men's room. Having spruced himself up, Charlie tries to reenter the barroom, but he is knocked down by the swinging doors every time he attempts to push his way through. At last, in desperation, he crawls under them.

Barroom. He sees five drinkers at the bar: two of them are the customers he had polished off in the men's room. At first they are not aware that he has entered the barroom. Meanwhile he gets his foot caught in a spittoon. Two other customers try to help him. They pull at the spittoon. As it works loose they sprawl backward. Charlie falls onto the husband who turns and swings a punch at him. But he ducks and the blow lands on one of his unfortunate men's room victims. He retaliates anyway, socking the husband squarely in the face. Then, doffing his hat, he toddles casually out of the tavern.

A busy street. Charlie spies the lady standing beside the taxi. He smiles, smirks, and covers his mouth with his hand. She starts walking. He goes after her, staggers, and tries to steady himself by leaning on the taxi. But the taxi suddenly drives off, leaving Charlie sprawling in the road. In a daze he picks himself up.

Leaping onto a passing streetcar, he almost falls onto the cow-catcher. The streetcar stops and he tumbles off.

Exterior of lady's house. The taxi arrives with the maid. She enters the house. Charlie catches up with the taxi and asks the driver where his passenger went. Then he stumbles up the front steps and enters the house.

Hallway of lady's house. He tries, unsuccessfully, to go upstairs. Falling back over the banisters, he flops onto a sofa—all the while contriving to continue smoking a cigarette. He gets up and wanders into the living room.

The living room. The maid, her head covered with a shawl, is seated in a rocking chair. Charlie makes a pass at her, thinking she's the lady—whereupon she drops the shawl. Charlie collapses in shock. The maid promptly attacks him with a pillow.

Hallway. The lady arrives home with some packages. She discovers a battered-looking Charlie who smiles at her wanly and puts his hand to his heart. She reacts to this declaration of love by knocking him down. At this point her husband arrives. Charlie tries to escape by fleeing back into the living room.

The living room. He flees out of the frying pan into the fire, for the maid renews her attack, flinging him into the clutches of the husband. Charlie swings a punch—but this time it's the husband who dodges the blow and Charlie loses his balance. Picking him up, the husband tosses him into another room.

Another room. In falling Charlie fells a group of inquisitive servants. He jumps up and tries to tackle *them*, but he is quickly overpowered and thrown out of the house.

Exterior of lady's house. Medium close shot of Charlie. His hair and tie are askew. He holds his nose, puffs out his cheeks, and glances back at the house with disgust.

COMMENTS

1. This film, the second Chaplin film directed by George Nichols, contains one of the comedian's more intriguing virtuoso performances and compares favorably with some of his Essanay pictures. Again, like *A Film Johnnie*, it demonstrates Chaplin's misjudgment of Nichols. In *My Autobiography* he rates Nichols as no better than Lehrman. But a comparison of *His Favorite Pastime* with *Making a Living* quickly dispels this notion. Nichols may have admired Lehrman's frenetic approach to comedy, but he also knew when to restrain fast-paced slapstick and allow free rein to Chaplin's comic business.

2. *His Favorite Pastime* reflects Chaplin's offscreen interest in Peggy Pearce, the film's leading lady. As Peggy wanted marriage and Chaplin only wanted an affair, their romantic involvement was short-lived; also she was never to appear in another Chaplin film.

3. The film has two main plot "movements": (i) Charlie in the tavern, and (ii) Charlie in the lady's house. The first of these movements is the more substantially developed and contains several sequences: Charlie vs. Fatty, Charlie and the tough guy, Charlie in the men's room (two sequences), Charlie at the bar. His streetcar ride provides a brief interlude. The second movement focuses mainly on Charlie's ejection from

the house, but there are three scenes preliminary to that: Charlie's attempt to go upstairs, his discovery of the black maid, and his unrequited declaration of love.

4. Fatty makes little more than a cameo appearance in this film, and even then he is completely upstaged by the Tramp. He serves merely as the opening foil in a prolonged display of the Tramp's obnoxious behavior. Like Charlie he plays a drunken bum, but he's a more bedraggled and somewhat pathetic one. Unlike Charlie he's obviously a born loser without any of the aggressiveness he had displayed as the clarinettist in *Tango Tangles*. He does, of course, try to steal Charlie's beer, but for that Charlie pays him back far more than his due.

5. What exactly *is* Charlie's "favorite pastime?" Boozing? Lechery? He tries to seduce another man's wife. Dirty tricks? Creating chaos? He teases Fatty not once but four times. He boots one customer, whacks another with his cane and tricks him into blacking his face. He takes pleasure in scorching the hand of the washroom attendant and creates havoc in the barroom. He was drunk and lecherous in previous films, but his sadistic behavior in this picture reveals a new, distinctly obnoxious aspect of his character that will reappear in many subsequent films. "Gentle, lovable, pathetic Charlie" is a much later development. In *His Favorite Pastime* the Tramp generates no sympathy, and audiences take pleasure in watching *him* suffer as he, in turn, is repeatedly knocked down by the swinging doors, catches his foot in a spittoon, gets pushed around by a tough guy, and beaten up by the black maid, the lady, and her husband. Ultimately it seems appropriate that one of his vices frustrates another. Bent on seduction, he heads upstairs toward the lady's bedroom, but he never makes it: his drunkenness causes him to lose his balance and topple over the banisters.

Charlie's activities in the tavern and in the lady's house have distinctly different outcomes. After disrupting the barroom (and landing a hefty punch on the husband's face), he merely doffs his hat and toddles out. Patently, he triumphs in a place where ladies are not admitted and men feel free to exercise their aggressions. In the house, by contrast, it's the women who are in control. There the lady proves to be more aggressive than her husband in protecting her respectability. She had been amused by Charlie's flirtations in the street but draws the line at his intrusion into her home. After being beaten up by the lady and her maid, Charlie is unceremoniously tossed into the street (at the husband's command). He discovers thereby that what he could get away with in a man's world is quite intolerable in a woman's. The medium close shot of Charlie that ends the film recalls the finale of *A Film Johnnie*. This sort of ending looks like a Nichols trademark.

6. *His Favorite Pastime*, like so many Keystones, raises questions of audience response. Modern audiences raised on anything more sophisticated than the Three Stooges usually consider much of Chaplin's Keystone output too crude and sadistic to be funny. They also find it impossible to reconcile the Tramp of the Keystones with the gentler Charlie of the feature films. But the original audiences for the Keystones were undoubtedly entertained by them, and their responses were not necessarily naive. Within the context of Keystone slapstick Chaplin was, at the outset, reaching for something akin to the farcical character-comedy of Molière. In both Chaplin and Molière contemptible aspects of human nature are held up to ridicule. Like such Molière protagonists as Harpagon (*L'Avare*) and Alceste (*Le Misanthrope*), the Tramp begins his screen life as an egotist, totally preoccupied with gratifying his own appetites and thereby creating his own problems. To try and reconcile such a character with the Tramp of *The Circus* (1928) and *City Lights* is a fruitless task. Chaplin did not strive for consistency from film to film. His Tramp character developed, sometimes in unexpected ways, as he began to understand its implications. Instead of seeking for a consistency that doesn't exist, it is more useful to see each film in turn as a different exploration of the character's possibilities—among them Charlie the drunkard, Charlie the flirt, Charlie the lecher, Charlie the sadist, and, later on, Charlie the savior, Charlie the dreamer, and Charlie the lover. The Tramp in his various manifestations vividly exemplifies Whitman's dictum that each of us contains multitudes.

7. Chaplin's comic business enlivens almost every scene of this film. Particularly memorable are his transformation of a sausage into a cigar (a gag he would repeat in many other films), his cunning and dextrous interplay with Fatty, his battles with the swinging door (a gag he derived from Fred Karno), and his feat of retaining his cigarette as he tumbles over the banisters. In each instance the comic business is an expression of the Tramp's character that dovetails neatly into the main action.

8. Ethnic and racist gags were legion in the silent cinema. *His Favorite Pastime* has three at the expense of blacks, one of which (the hot match) is doubly offensive not only for its cruelty but also because it involves the depiction of the washroom attendant as a stereotypical servile "coon." The gag of the Tramp and the black maid was a recreation of the plot of *The Masher* (1907), which Peter Noble describes thus: "a lady-killer . . . is unsuccessful in his wooing with everyone with whom he tries to flirt. Finally he becomes successful with a lady wearing a veil, who quickly responds to his flirtation. However, when he makes further advances and lifts her veil, he discovers to his consterna-

tion that the lady of his choice is colored" (1948, 28). Donald Bogle comments on the Masher's discovery: "He may have been looking for a blue heaven, but he certainly did not want a black one" (1973, 8). Chaplin's *A Day's Pleasure* (First National 1919) provides a variation on the gag of the white man getting a black face: in the shipboard sequence, a black musician gets seasick and his face turns white.

OTHER VIEWS

"This is the prototype of the 'unpleasant' tough films of which so many are found in Chaplin's 1914 output. It is hardly surprising that the censor was horrified at this story of the ravages of a drunken bar-lounger. . . . The American critics of 1914 were, oddly enough, delighted" (Asplund 1976, 32).

"*His Favorite Pastime* contains one bit of business that is a bit different. His 'favorite pastime' is drinking, and he attempts to enter his favorite place—a saloon—to do some. He meets the swinging saloon door. He pushes it, and it returns to boff him in the face. He kicks it, and it boots him back. He puts up his dukes and starts to spar with it; it gets in all the good punches. Charlie gives up and crawls under it. The saloon door is the ancestor of every inanimate thing that Charlie later succeeded in bringing to life; he turns a piece of wood into a living opponent. He succeeds in treating one kind of object as if it were a different kind of being. Although historians usually refer to this technique as Chaplin's 'transposition of objects,' 'metamorphosis' would be a much more accurate term, for the object is not instantaneously transposed into something else but undergoes the complete transformation process before our eyes" (Mast 1979, 69).

8.

Cruel, Cruel Love

(1914)

Original working title: *Poison*
Other titles: *Lord Helpus;* French: *Charlot marquis, Charlot fou d'amour;* German: *Liebe ist Grausam;* Spanish: *Charlot galante, Un amor cruel;* Italian: *Charlot aristocratico, Amore crudele*

Length: 1 reel; 961 feet (Asplund), 1035 feet (Lyons)
Playing time: 16 minutes at 16 frames per second
Producer: Keystone
Director: George Nichols or Mack Sennett
Screenplay: Craig Hutchinson
Photography: Frank D. Williams (?)
Cast:

Mr. Dovey/Lord Helpus	Chaplin
The lady	Minta Durfee
The maid	Alice Davenport
The butler	Chester Conklin

Finished or shipped: March 5, 1914
Released: March 26, 1914

SYNOPSIS

A drawing room. Charlie, a well-groomed gentleman, is on his knees proposing to a coy young lady.

Hallway (annex to the drawing room). A maidservant spies on the young couple and laughs at them.

Drawing room. Charlie gets to his feet and addresses the lady passionately. Then he tries to sit down beside her—forgetting that there is no chair for him—and lands on the floor. From that vantage point he continues, good-humoredly, to press his suit, miming a babe-in-arms as one of the joyful prospects of their union.

Hallway. The maid continues her spying.

Drawing room. The lady chucks Charlie under the chin. He clasps her hand. She repeats her caress. He puts his arm around her. In a transport of passion, he bites his handkerchief to shreds. They kiss.

Hallway. The maid shrieks with laughter.

Drawing room. Interrupted in midkiss, Charlie stand up guiltily and puts his hands in his pockets. The embarrassed lady pushes aside a curtain to investigate the disturbance.

Hallway. The lady catches her eavesdropping maid. In a fury, she dismisses her.

Exterior of house. The maid leaves via the front entrance.

Title: *"The girl has upset me. Leave me alone."*

Hallway. The lady hands Charlie his hat and stick.

Driveway. The maid sees the gardener and tells him what occurred.

Exterior of house. Coldly, the lady offers Charlie her hand.

Driveway. The gardener steals a kiss from the maid. She pretends to be angry, then smiles at him.

Exterior of house. The lady watches Charlie's departure.

Driveway. The maid persuades the gardener to hide in the bushes while she deals with Charlie. She pretends to slip on the path. Charlie appears and rushes to her rescue. She flings her arms around him.

Bushes. The gardener observes what is happening.

Driveway. Charlie escorts the maid—who is still embracing him—to a nearby bench.

Exterior of house. In high dudgeon, the lady observes Charlie's tête-à-tête with the maid.

Driveway. The maid starts to get fresh with Charlie.

Exterior of house. Angrily, the lady heads toward the bench.

Driveway. She confronts Charlie and the maid. Then she orders the maid to clear off.

Exterior of house. The maid looks back resentfully.

Driveway. Charlie stands up, trying to look innocent.

Title: *"Take your ring. I don't ever want to see you again."*

The lady returns her engagement ring. Charlie bows to her, loses his balance and falls back onto the bench. She orders him to leave. He braces himself, puts on his top hat, and departs.

Street. He flaps his arms in a gesture of futility.

Driveway. Livid, the lady heads back toward her house.

Street. Charlie climbs into his limousine. He stands up, waving his arms in despair. The Chauffeur drives off suddenly and Charlie flops into the back seat.

Exterior of lady's house. The lady continues to berate her maid who is standing beside the front entrance looking helpless. She orders her to leave.

Driveway. The gardener sees what is happening and runs toward the house.

Exterior of house. The maid, having apologized (presumably), is now ordered to return into the house. But at this point, the gardener comes up to the entrance and explains that he had seen everything, that the maid and Charlie are both "innocent." He takes the maid by the hand, indicating that he—not Charlie—is her lover.

Charlie's living room. He drinks what he believes to be a glass of poison.

Behind a curtain. The butler laughs as he watches Charlie's suicide bid. (The butler has, in fact, swapped the poison for a glass of water.)

Living room. Charlie rises from his chair and fingers his stomach.

Behind curtain. The butler is convulsed with laughter.

Living room. Holding his stomach, Charlie heads for the bedroom.

Behind curtain. The butler continues to observe his master.

Title: *A vision of inevitable destiny.*

Bedroom. Medium close shot of Charlie clasping his stomach. With one hand he reaches out toward the camera. Then he runs his fingers through his hair. His face is contorted with terror. Dissolve to . . .

Hell. Two devils are stoking a fire in the midst of which Charlie is burning. He tries to escape the flames, but one devil prods him in the rump with a fork. He turns to face his attacker, whereupon the other devil prods him in the same spot. Both devils fasten their forks—like a yoke—around Charlie's neck and force him back into the fire. They jerk him up and down in the flames.

Bedroom. Charlie is seated; one hand is on his forehead. As he emerges from his nightmarish vision, he clutches at his throat and clasps his hands in prayer.

Living room. The butler, laughing hilariously, points at the glass of water.

Street. The gardener races toward Charlie's house.

Bedroom. Close up of Charlie looking fiendishly into the camera. He clutches his head and stomach and falls backward.

Living room. The butler watches Charlie.

Entrance of Charlie's house. The gardener arrives, checks the address on a paper he is carrying, then enters.

Bedroom. Charlie is having a conniption fit. He seizes the curtains and drags them down over himself.

Living room. The gardener approaches the butler with a note from the lady.

Bedroom. Charlie's head is caught in the curtains. He struggles to free himself, forces his head through them, and flops onto a chair, clutching at his throat.

Living room. The butler admits the gardener to the bedroom.

Bedroom. The gardener hands the note to Charlie. He tears open the envelope and discovers that the lady still loves him. Astounded, he falls backward onto the floor. Leaping to his feet, he flings off the curtains and seizes hold of the gardener.

Title: *"Too late. I have poisoned myself!"*

He leaps forward and pushes the gardener back into . . .

Living room. The gardener crashes onto the butler. They hit the floor.

Bedroom. Charlie goes berserk, kicks his fallen chair, and stubs his toe.

Living room. The gardener runs off, leaving the butler sprawling on a sofa.

Bedroom. Charlie has a sudden idea: he reaches for the telephone.

Doctor's surgery. The telephone rings. The doctor answers Charlie's call.

Bedroom. Charlie writhes in agony while explaining his "symptoms."

Doctor's surgery. The doctor puts down the telephone, grabs his bag, and exits, accompanied by an assistant.

Park. The gardener heads back toward the lady's house.

Bedroom. Charlie bursts out of the room.

Living room. He tears his hair, clutches his heart, appeals to heaven, and leaps onto the sofa—which the butler had just vacated.

Behind a curtain. The butler peeks at Charlie.

Street. The doctor enters a horse-drawn ambulance and drives off.

Living room. Charlie has another brain wave.

Park. The gardener runs toward the lady's house.

Living room. In the midst of some melodramatic flourishes, Charlie drinks a bottle of milk.

Street. The ambulance races to the rescue.

Bedroom. To his obvious distaste, Charlie continues to drink the milk.

Park. The gardener leaps and runs down a wooded path.

Street. The ambulance is still on its way.

Bedroom. Charlie finishes the milk and tosses the bottle aside.

Behind curtain. The butler continues to peek at Charlie.

Entrance of lady's house. The gardener runs up and informs the lady of Charlie's condition. She almost faints. Steadying herself, she sets off for Charlie's house, accompanied by the gardener.

Street. The ambulance is still on its way.

Street outside lady's house. The lady and the gardener enter a limousine which then drives off.

Interior of limousine. Close up of the lady's anguished face.

Bedroom. Charlie makes more melodramatic dying gestures.

Living room. The butler laughs.

Exterior of Charlie's house. The ambulance pulls up. The doctor climbs out.

Interior of limousine. The gardener tries to calm the frantic lady.

Bedroom. Charlie falls on his knees and prays.

Living room. The butler is sprawled in a chair, laughing. The doctor and his assistant enter. They rush over to the butler, assuming that he is the patient.

Bedroom. Charlie continues praying.

Living room. The butler directs the doctor toward the bedroom.

Bedroom. Charlie genuflects frantically.

Interior of limousine. Close up of the anguished lady.

Living room. The butler laughs. The doctor and his assistant head for the bedroom.

Bedroom. They find Charlie praying.

Living room. The butler, still laughing, gets off his chair and makes for the bedroom.

Bedroom. The assistant pushes Charlie into a chair and shakes him.

Interior of limousine. The lady clasps her hands over her ears.

Bedroom. Charlie kicks violently as the doctor tries to force the tube of a stomach pump into his mouth.

Living room. The butler peeks into the bedroom.

Street. The limousine pulls up. The lady and the gardener exit.

Entrance to Charlie's house. They enter.

Living room. The lady appears; she stares at the butler who is still peeking in at the bedroom. He turns and sees her, then motions her not to enter the bedroom.

Bedroom. Charlie resists violently. He falls to the floor, dragging the doctor and his assistant down with him.

Living room. The butler shows the lady that Charlie had drunk a glass of water instead of poison. She flings up her arms in rejoicing.

Bedroom. She enters, rescues Charlie from the doctor, and tells him that he is merely the victim of his butler's prank. He throws up his hands in prayerful thanks. The butler enters and Charlie berates him.

Living room. The gardener dashes in and makes for the bedroom.

Bedroom. Charlie takes a flying kick at the butler.

Living room. The butler falls backward onto the gardener. They hit the floor. As they stagger to their feet, the gardener takes a flying kick at the butler. They hit the floor again.

Bedroom. Charlie kicks the assistant onto the bed.

Living room. The gardener is having the worst of a struggle with the butler.

Street. Hearing the commotion, two orderlies leave the ambulance and head for Charlie's house.

Bedroom. Charlie tries to throttle the doctor.

Living room. The orderlies are felled by the doctor as Charlie flings him out of the bedroom. In the background, the gardener and the butler continue their scrap.

Bedroom. Charlie boots the assistant into the living room.

Living room. The assistant crashes into the orderlies, etc.

Bedroom. Charlie and the lady confront each other and fall into an embrace.

Living room. The fighting has stopped. The butler motions everyone to be silent and observe what is going on in the bedroom.

Bedroom. The lady embraces Charlie. Behind her back, he whets his hands menacingly.

Living room. The onlookers gaze at each other in bewilderment.

COMMENTS

1. Chaplin scholars disagree as to who directed *Cruel, Cruel Love.* John McCabe (1978), Denis Gifford (1974), and Timothy Lyons (1979) attribute the film to George Nichols; Uno Asplund (1976) to Mack Sennett; Theodore Huff (1952) cautiously referred to it as "supervised by Mack Sennett." Chaplin is no help on this matter. In *My Autobiography*, p. 148, he tells us he "made about five pictures" before Sennett assigned Mabel Normand to direct his films, but Chaplin's first film for Normand was *Mabel at the Wheel*, his *tenth* Keystone, and he never mentions by title any of the films Nichols directed.

This writer is inclined, on the basis of internal evidence, to attribute the film to Sennett. First, Sennett was a disciple of D. W. Griffith, and the film contains a parody of Griffith's last-minute rescue. Second, the build-up toward the fast-paced slapstick finale is more typical of Sennett than Nichols. Third, close-ups are not used where and how Nichols tended to use them. There are a couple of striking close-ups not of Chaplin but of the lady in her limousine; there's one curious moment when Chaplin in his bedroom falls back out of close-up after looking fiendishly into the camera; and unlike *A Film Johnnie* and *His Favorite Pastime* the film doesn't end with a close-up of Chaplin.

2. Some sources and analogues: (i) The theatrical origins of the mischievous butler and maid of *Cruel, Cruel Love* are directly traceable to the *zannis*, or comic servants, of the *commedia dell'arte*—such as the rascally Arlecchino whose female counterpart was Columbina. The history of farce from Molière (*Les Fourberies de Scapin*) onward abounds with plots about servants who trick or outwit their masters and mistresses. (ii) Mr. Dovey's (Chaplin's) vision of hell was probably based on the nightmare scene in Edwin S. Porter's Edison film *Dream of a Rarebit Fiend* (1906), which, in turn, was imitative of similar scenes in films by Georges Méliès. (iii) The opening sequence of *Cruel, Cruel Love* recalls *Love's Perfidy* (1905), a Biograph comedy: A young man kisses a maidservant in the hallway. The outraged maid watches, surrepti-

tiously, as the young man enters the living room and proclaims his love for her mistress. Then, to their embarrassment, the maid deliberately enters the room and catches them locked in an embrace. (iv) Mr. Dovey's would-be suicide is, of course, a parody of romantic suicides, such as Romeo's in Shakespeare's tragedy. C. J. S. Thompson in *Poison Mysteries in History, Romance and Crime* (n.d.), pp. 92–93, recounts several actual cases of people who behaved not unlike Mr. Dovey when they mistakenly believed they had taken poison. (v) When Hynkel in *The Great Dictator* (1940) swallowed mustard with his strawberries he had a similar conniption fit to Mr. Dovey's. But a more remarkable parallel to *Cruel, Cruel Love* occurs in *Monsieur Verdoux* (1947). Believing that he has just drunk poison, Verdoux becomes as frenzied as Mr. Dovey and downs a bottle of milk as an antidote. Another, slighter analogue occurs in the same film: a mistress (Martha Raye) fires her maid, then impulsively rehires her.

3. The film falls naturally into the following sequences. (i) The lady dismisses her eavesdropping maid. (ii) She rejects Mr. Dovey when she sees the maid "embracing" him. (iii) The gardener tells the lady what really happened. (iv) Mr. Dovey swallows what he believes to be poison. (v) He has his "vision of inevitable destiny." (vi) His frenzy. (vii) The gardener arrives with news that the lady still loves him. He calls his doctor. (viii) More frenzy. He drinks a bottle of milk. (ix) The doctor and the lady rush to the rescue. (x) The treatment—and Mr. Dovey's resistance. (xi) The butler tells the lady that Dovey had drunk water, not poison. She tells her beloved. (xii) His violent reaction to the news. (xiii) Final embrace.

4. A slapstick farce with several themes, *Cruel, Cruel Love* is a mock-melodrama, a comedy of voyeurism, a play on the themes of deception and delusion, and a farcical contrast between masters and servants.

Farce may be considered a *reductio ad absurdum* of melodrama. In *Cruel, Cruel Love*, the wrongfully rejected hero, his attempted suicide, his last-minute rescue and reconciliation with the heroine are melodramatic staples reduced to the ludicrous by exaggeration. Melodrama was one of the most popular "serious" dramatic forms of the Victorian era, and Mr. Dovey's "vision of inevitable destiny" inevitably calls to mind moralizing Victorian sermons on hellfire and brimstone.

The entire action of the film develops out of the consequences of snooping. The maid is caught spying on her mistress and Mr. Dovey. In revenge she contrives to have her mistress observe her embracing Dovey while the gardener looks on from the bushes. The butler spies on Dovey as the latter takes "poison." In the finale, at the butler's behest, the other characters peek in at Dovey and the lady embracing. Thus, the film begins and ends with characters spying on other characters. We, the audience, are also involved in the film's voyeurism. Not only do we join in the spying (and amusement) of the maid and butler, but we are also privy to Mr. Dovey's vision and observe the lady's anguish (needless, and therefore ludicrous) as she races to the rescue.

The film's plot turns on two deceptions, the second dependent upon the first. (i) The maid tricks the lady into believing that Mr. Dovey is unfaithful to her. (ii) The butler lets the lovelorn Dovey believe he has drunk poison. But these deceptions are only effective because Dovey and the lady take what they see at face value, because they act unquestioningly on what they perceive without determining its truth or reality. The lady doesn't give Mr. Dovey a chance to explain his conduct with the maid; she promptly breaks off their engagement. Mr. Dovey assumes that what he is drinking is poison; he promptly reacts as if he *is* poisoned. Deception and delusion here introduced in the context of farce eventually become serious themes in Chaplin's films—as in *The Gold Rush* and *City Lights*.

The contrast of master/mistress and servant shows up in several ways in *Cruel, Cruel Love*. The maid's flip reactions to the gardener stealing a kiss are in sharp distinction to the ritual and "passion" of the upper-class couple. The lady quickly loses her temper, and Mr. Dovey quickly loses self-control, but the maid and butler take virtually nothing seriously. They trick and laugh at their employers. It is obvious that they have no respect for them and that they enjoy exploiting their gullibility.

Chaplin went on to deal more elaborately with relations between masters and servants or employers and employees in many of the films he directed: e.g., *The New Janitor* (Keystone no. 27), *Work* (Essanay 1915), *The Pawnshop* (Mutual 1916), *Sunnyside* (First National 1919), *The Circus* (1928), *Modern Times* (1936), and *Monsieur Verdoux* (1947). In *Cruel, Cruel Love* and *The Idle Class* (First National 1921) he plays a *real* upper-class gentleman, and in his penultimate film he appears as an exiled king. But in other films he plays *pseudo*aristocrats: e.g., *Caught in a Cabaret* (Keystone no. 12), *Her Friend the Bandit* (Keystone no. 16), *The Jitney Elopement* (Essanay 1915), *The Count* (Mutual 1916).

5. *Cruel, Cruel Love* is far from the subtlest of Chaplin's early performances. During most of the film he deliberately over-acts for comic effect. But he does give us a few finer brush strokes, mainly in the "wooing" sequence that opens the picture. Note, for example an in-character variation on the editor's knee gag in *Making a Living*: the lady repeatedly caresses Mr. Dovey's chin; when she stops, he demonstrates his mounting boldness as a lover by pulling her hand back to repeat the action.

OTHER VIEWS

"Most of his [Chaplin's] individual comedy [during the Keystone period] was lost in the speed of each film, and in such pictures as *Cruel, Cruel Love* and *Caught in a Cabaret*, to name only two, he had little chance to prove his ability" (John Montgomery, in McCaffrey 1971, 14).

"The clowns and character actresses at Keystone are outnumbered by the more innocuous ornamental heroines, and it was this role that became most important in Chaplin's later work. Minta Durfee, Cecile Arnold, and other more or less interchangeable lovelies are the objects and victims of Charlie's affections in the Keystones, doing little else than standing demurely around to be flirted with, on occasion rejecting his affections, but as often as not, tolerating them. Chaplin found in such women a vein of romantic and comic themes for his character that he would explore thoroughly in the coming years. A poster for Chaplin's eighth Keystone film, *Cruel, Cruel Love*, shows Charlie gazing worshipfully up at Minta Durfee; a label prophetically describes him as 'Sentimental Charlie' " (Kamin 1984, 66).

9.

The Star Boarder

(1914)

Other titles: *The Landlady's Pet, The Fatal Lantern, The/A Hash House Hero, In Love with his Landlady;* French: *Charlot aime la patronne, Charlot pensionnaire;* German: *Der Lieblingsgast;* Spanish: *Charlot ama a su patrona, La patrona de Charlot;* Italian: *Il cliente prediletto, Charlot pensionante*

Length: 1 reel; 958 feet (Asplund), 1020 feet (Lyons)
Playing time: 16 minutes at 16 frames per second
Producer: Keystone
Director: George Nichols or Mack Sennett
Screenplay: Craig Hutchinson
Photography: Frank D. Williams (?)
Cast:

The star boarder	Chaplin
His landlady	Minta Durfee
Her husband	Edgar Kennedy
Their son	Gordon Griffith
The landlady's friend	Alice Davenport

Finished or shipped: March 19, 1914
Released: April 4, 1914

SYNOPSIS

Title: *The master of the house.*

Kitchen of a boarding house. The well-dressed, bossy landlady is shouting at her husband as a female servant prepares food. She deals brusquely with her small son, aged about seven or eight.

Dining room. She enters with a vase of flowers which she places on the dining table. The servant follows, carrying crockery. Having put finishing touches to the table arrangement, the landlady rings the dinner bell.

Title: *Charlie—the Landlady's Pet.*

Star boarder's bedroom. The view at first discloses Charlie's cane hooked onto the edge of the dressing-table mirror. To the extreme left the soles of his shoes are visible. The camera now pans slightly more to the left to show Charlie in bed, fully dressed and smoking. He sits up, puffs out smoke, yawns slightly, and scratches his nose.

Title: *The other boarders aren't worth mentioning.*

Dining room. Five of the seven boarders are seated at the dining table. The landlady is still ringing the bell. A thickset guest—*not* Arbuckle—enters and sits at the end of the table furthest from the camera. In the foreground is an empty chair intended (eventually) for the landlady.

Star boarder's bedroom. Charlie looks at himself in the mirror and brushes his hair. His hat is visible, perched on a bedknob.

Dining room. All the other boarders are waiting for Charlie.

Hallway. The landlady goes to the foot of the staircase and rings the bell. Charlie meanders down the stairs.

Title: *"Good morning, Mrs. Winterbottom. And how is the cold in your head?"*

As he descends he drops his handkerchief over the banisters onto a loveseat. The landlady tries to pick it up, but Charlie bends over and retrieves it, almost falling over the banisters in the process. She clutches her wrist and smiles coyly at him. He smiles back. They chat briefly.

Title: *"What about a little tennis after breakfast?"*

She directs him into the dining room.

Dining room. The landlady is seated at the table in the foreground (back to the camera), and Charlie is seated to her left.

Title: *The landlady's husband always kept his place—under his wife's thumb.*

The husband, wearing an apron, serves the food as if he is merely a waiter. He offers the platter to a boarder on the landlady's right, but she snatches it and offers Charlie first choice. The husband is visibly annoyed. Charlie helps himself to an enormous portion. Then the landlady takes the platter and adds even more food to Charlie's plate.

Title: *The Son had won medals for mischief making.*

Back porch of boarding house. The son is sitting on the stairs.

Dining room. The meal is over. The landlady chats with Charlie and snubs another boarder who tries to speak with her.

Kitchen. The husband peers through the open door.

Dining room. The landlady is making up to Charlie. She holds his hand and peers into his eyes. Unseen by them, the husband enters. He is fuming. Charlie smirks, hand on face, as the landlady tries to look coy. He pats her hand. The husband takes a step forward and rolls up his sleeves. In the nick of time she turns her attention to clearing the table. Now Charlie notices the angry husband. He fingers his tie nervously and posthaste informs the landlady that her husband is in the room. Hands on hips, she turns round and orders her spouse to clear the table. Charlie takes this as a cue to thumb his nose at the husband. The latter is about to respond by throwing a piece of crockery at his rival when his wife glares at him. Charlie exits. The landlady shouts at her husband and then sweeps out, leaving him to the task of clearing the table.

Title: *The morning constitutional.*

Front of boarding house. A sign on the porch to the right reads: "Board by the day, week or month." Charlie and the landlady emerge from the house arm-in-arm, smiling sweetly at each other. He nearly falls down the steps. Doffing his hat, he smiles bashfully as they exit.

Title: *A love game.*

Tennis court. Charlie bounces a ball. It hits him on the nose and he falls down. He picks up a racket, takes a swing at the ball, and falls down again.

Back porch of boarding house. The husband looks round anxiously for his wife.

Tennis court. Charlie is now trying to play tennis with the landlady. His hat rolls onto the court. He swings the racket with both hands. She knocks the ball in the wrong direction—out of sight. Each signals to the other to go and find it. Charlie now gestures to the camera the futility of either the game or the landlady's tennis playing. Both drop their rackets and march off arm-in-arm to find the lost ball.

Exterior of boarding house. The husband sets off to find his wife.

In front of a clump of bushes. Charlie boasts of his "prowess" as a sportsman. He tries to use his cane as a bat but catches its crook around the landlady's arm. They laugh at the mishap. The landlady mimes Charlie's two-handed racket grip. He watches this tolerantly. Then she notices that his tie is askew and starts to straighten it.

At a nearby tree. The son is taking a photograph of them engaged in what looks like the prelude to a kiss. He is hysterically amused at the situation.

Another part of the park. The husband asks two ladies if they have seen his wife. They indicate where he can find her.

Title: *"It's a difficult world for a fellow who's cursed with beauty."*

In front of bushes. The landlady tickles Charlie as she straightens his tie. Unnoticed by them, her husband comes upon their tête-à-tête. He finds the ball while they are poking around in the bushes looking for it. Then they turn and discover his presence. She reacts by shrugging her shoulders and marching away imperiously. Charlie gives an innocent smile and lights a cigarette. But the husband confronts him with clenched fists, pushes him into the bushes, and stamps off after his wife. Charlie climbs out of the bushes and shouts angrily after his attacker. He shouts too soon—for the husband comes back, and Charlie, smiling nervously and covering his face with his hands, tries to be conciliatory. But the husband has only returned momentarily to give Charlie the ball. He exits. Charlie has a bout of nervous coughing and mops his face with his handkerchief.

At a nearby bush. The son takes another photograph.

An apple tree. The landlady is on a step ladder picking apples and, incidentally, exposing her ankles. [This is the scene that her son is photographing.] Charlie comes upon her as she is about to fall. He tries to catch her. They roll on the ground.

At a nearby bush. The son gets another photograph of them—as follows:

An apple tree. Charlie's arm is around the landlady as he tries to calm her.

At a nearby bush. The son laughs uproariously.

An apple tree. Charlie retrieves his hat and marches off arm-in-arm with the landlady. They are unaware that their pictures have been taken.

Another part of the park. The husband meets a buxom lady—one of the boarders. She takes his arm.

Kitchen of the boarding house. Charlie's arm is around the landlady as they enter. She smoothes her hair.

Title: *"Au revoir until next meal time."*

She exits. Left alone, Charlie smiles into the camera, covers his mouth, points after the landlady and then at himself. He looks around the kitchen, pulls out his pants top and looks down at his (supposedly) empty stomach. His tongue hangs out. He swings his cane, kicks up his heels, goes over to the icebox, does a little dance in front of it, looks around furtively to see if anyone is watching him, then swings open the icebox door to reveal a cache of beer. He claps his hand to his brow at the sight of such "riches."

The park, below a water tower. The buxom lady appears to faint and the husband catches her before she falls.

Beside a hedge. The son takes their picture. He laughs.

Kitchen of boarding house. Charlie is drunk. He doffs his hat to the camera and staggers out of the kitchen with the last two bottles of beer and a pie.

The park, below a water tower. The buxom lady gives the husband the eye and exits.

Hallway. As someone is coming Charlie tries to hide the stolen pie inside his jacket. He can't conceal it there so he puts it on the love seat and tries to hide the beer behind his back. Then he sits down on the pie. The buxom lady enters. Charlie smiles at her and doffs his hat.

Title: *A smiling face hides many a hard seat.*

She passes him with a scornful gesture. He gets up from the love seat, looks sadly at the flattened pie, and heads upstairs with what remains of his spoils.

The park, below a water tower. The husband leaves to return home.

Living room. The son is preparing a magic lantern slide show. A boarder is tinkering at the piano. The son asks him for assistance in hanging up a sheet—to be used as a screen.

Title: *"Give us a hand. . . . I'm showing some real good 'uns tonight."*

Hallway. Charlie and the landlady are joking with each other.

Living room. The son sets up his magic lantern at the back of the room.

Hallway. Charlie sits invitingly on the love seat but the landlady doesn't join him. He takes her arm and kicks up his heels as they go in to see the show.

Living room. The son is laughing as his audience (the boarders, etc.) settle down to see the show. Charlie toddles in; he is obviously tipsy. Laughing, the son begins his show.

First slide: a silhouette of two fighting cats.

Second slide: the son being butted by a goat.

Third slide: the husband clasping the buxom lady.

Charlie laughs at this, but the landlady accuses her husband of infidelity. The buxom lady protests her innocence; the husband is thunderstruck. Then, infuriated, he rises from his seat and hovers menacingly over Charlie. The son screams with laughter.

Fourth slide: Charlie straightening the landlady's skirt while she gazes at him rapturously.

At the sight of this the husband attacks Charlie. General consternation. Charlie peels off his jacket, knocks the husband down, and dashes out of the room.

Dining room. He runs into the female servant and falls over. As he gets up she tries to swing a punch at him, but he is quicker: he shoves her in the face, and she tumbles back into the kitchen.

Living room. The husband has shaken off the boarders' restraining hands, and he goes after Charlie. Trying to escape his pursuer, Charlie dashes back into the living room and runs into the hanging sheet (screen). Wrapped up in it he looks like a ghost. He shakes it off after yet another pratfall. As his attacker advances on him with a bread-knife, he hurls a pillow which knocks over the husband and the boarders standing behind him. But with the force of the throw he loses his balance and falls over. Meanwhile, the landlady is busy spanking her son. Charlie tries to escape but is knocked down by a fellow boarder. His exit is now blocked by almost everyone in the room. The landlord tosses aside the knife, seizes Charlie, and hurls him onto a table which collapses. As a result he gets entangled in the tablecloth. His ruthless adversary picks up the table and throws it at him. Down but not out, Charlie staggers to his feet and wades into the husband. Momentarily, the latter seems to be getting the upper hand, but Charlie delivers the *coup de grace*, and the husband lands face down on the floor with Charlie, the star boarder, biting his rear end.

COMMENTS

1. Once again there is no agreement among Chaplin scholars as to this film's director. This disagreement arises out of different interpretations of the following remarks made by Chaplin

> After Lehrman, I was assigned to another director, Mr. Nichols. . . . I had the same trouble with him. . . . Although I only mildly rebelled, it appears that he went to Sennett saying that I was a son of a bitch to work with. . . . I made about five pictures and in some of them I had managed to put over one or two bits of comedy business of my own. . . . Now I was anxious to write and direct my own comedies, so I talked to Sennett about it. But he would not hear of it; instead he assigned me to Mabel Normand. . . . (Chaplin 1964, 147–48)

Denis Gifford paraphrases Chaplin's remarks as follows: "when George Nichols, who had made four in a row with Chaplin, went to Sennett and called the new star 'a son-of-a-bitch,' Sennett simply passed Chaplin on to the next director in line. This happened to be Mabel Normand" (1974, 40). Gifford somehow assumes from Chaplin's words that Nichols directed *A Film Johnnie, His Favorite Pastime, Cruel, Cruel Love*—and *The Star Boarder*. However, although the comedian says he "made about five pictures" after his films for Lehrman, he does not state which films or how many Nichols directed.

John McCabe interprets that passage from *My Autobiography* in a totally different way from Gifford: "When Chaplin tried to interpolate his own more restrained gags, Nichols complained to Sennett, who again took over, supervising the next two Chaplin films, *Cruel, Cruel Love* and *The Star Boarder*" (1978, 58). But McCabe's reading of Chaplin's comments seems no more justified than Gifford's. Actually, the frenetic pacing of *The Star Boarder*, (especially in its final moments), its lack of "creative" close-ups and its fairly routine use of Chaplin all point to Sennett rather than Nichols; but I have no *hard evidence* to support my view.

2. The film contains two interesting "firsts" for a Chaplin film. One was the use of a child in a significant role. As Lahue and Gill note: "Children were malicious monsters in the world of Keystone, forever molesting the adult world . . ." (1971b 221). These children—mainly small boys—appeared from time to time in regular Keystone comedies as well as in films of their own. The latter became known as "Kid Komedies," and reviewers inevitably dubbed the children "The Keystone Kids." The most popular of these kids was Paul Jacobs (a discovery of Henry Lehrman), who became the star of the "Little Billy" series. Gordon Griffith, the mischievous youngster of *The Star Boarder*, was never to achieve comparable success. But Chaplin adopted the Keystone conception of the rascally boy in some of the films *he* directed, in particular *The Pilgrim* (1923) and *A King in New York* (1957). Jackie Coogan in *The Kid* (1921) may also come to mind, but Jackie was different. The richest of all child portrayals in Chaplin's movies, he was anarchic rather than mischievous, in many ways a miniature version of the Tramp.

The Star Boarder also marks Edgar Kennedy's debut in a Chaplin film. He went on to appear in at least eight more Keystone Chaplins—often playing a cop. But none of his movie encounters with Charlie was to be as memorable as his confrontations with Harpo in *Duck Soup* (1933).

3. *The Star Boarder* falls into the following sequences: (i) prologue—before breakfast, (ii) breakfast, (iii) in the park, (iv) the slide show, (v) epilogue—chaos. Most of the intertitles occur in sequences (i) and (ii), where the focus is on character rather than action. In the epilogue, where the action is at its most frenetic, there are no intertitles.

4. In *The Star Boarder* the comedy emphasis is on situation rather than character. Accordingly, the film is one of Chaplin's lesser Keystones. The main characters seem little more than illustrations of the cynical intertitles that precede them: "The master of the house" (i.e., the landlady), "Charlie—the Landlady's Pet," "The landlady's husband always kept his place—under his wife's thumb," and "The Son had won medals for mischief-making."

However, the star boarder's introduction is of special interest. Before we actually get to see Charlie, we are shown his cane and the soles of his boots; and later, while he brushes his hair, his hat becomes prominently visible, perched on a bedknob. Although this was only Chaplin's ninth film, it looks as if his famous costume—which had so far appeared in no more than four Keystones—was already so widely known to the movie-going public that it could be calculated to raise an immediate laugh of recognition even if Chaplin wasn't in it. (See also Other Views below. Gifford's note on the Chaplin advertisement seems to support my impression of the public's strong interest in Chaplin as early as April 1914.) Actually, Charlie himself does nothing particularly funny in this scene, but from personal experience in having shown *The Star Boarder* to college audiences, I can vouch for the fact that seventy years after its original screenings, the scene still gets instantaneous laughs before Charlie actually becomes visible.

The film's few inspired comic moments occur quite early: Charlie's interrupted descent of the staircase and his business with the landlady and her husband (during and after breakfast). At one point, basking in the landlady's protection, he thumbs his nose at her husband. His behavior here anticipates a scene in *The Gold Rush* where the Tramp, relying on his "alliance" with Big Jim, gets up the courage to gesture his defiance of Black Larsen. So far so good. However, in view of the hilarious meal-time scenes in many of Chaplin's later films (e.g., *The Count* [Mutual 1916], *Modern Times* [1936]), his breakfast table episode in *The Star Boarder* is disappointing. In addition, he doesn't do very much with his drunk scene, when he raids the icebox later in the film. Chaplin received praise for the tennis sequence from some commentators who should know better: at Keystone that sort of slapstick was pretty routine by 1914. All in all, there's little in this film that could have enhanced Chaplin's reputation at this period.

5. Roger Manvell lists *The Star Boarder* among a group of Keystone pictures "dependent on jealousy, rivalry, infidelity in love and marriage" (1974, 82). These films did not invariably take a predictable moral stance toward such themes. In *The Star Boarder*, for example, Charlie, the rival, is triumphant, and it's the husband who is the butt of the movie. His wife wears the pants, his son's prank humiliates him in front of all the boarders, and he winds up with his rival on top of him, biting his rear. Note that at the outset, the husband meekly tolerates Charlie's flirtations with his wife as long as they seem private. It's only when the slide show makes them public (and as a counterblast to the revelation of his own apparent infidelity) that he belatedly asserts himself and attacks Charlie with a knife!

6. Charlie is also a boarder at a rooming house in a later Keystone, *Those Love Pangs* (Keystone no. 28). In the first sequence of that film he competes with Chester Conklin for the affections of a different landlady (Norma Nichols).

7. In some respects, *The Star Boarder* is the comic antithesis of *His Favorite Pastime*, and it is rewarding to show these films back to back. In the earlier film, Charlie, an intruder and would-be rival, is thrown

out of the house by both husband and wife. *The Star Boarder*, by contrast, shows the chaotic consequences that follow when a husband lets himself be henpecked and allows his rival to gain acceptance in his home.

8. Two similar gags link *Cruel, Cruel Love* and *The Star Boarder*. In the first film Charlie gets tangled up in some curtains. In the second he gets caught up in a movie screen.

9. *Flim Flam Felix*, a 1920's "Felix the Cat" cartoon, recreated the prank from *The Star Boarder*. As a joke, little Felix surreptitiously takes movies of Daddy (Felix himself) flirting with some bathing beauties. He then shows his movies to *both* his parents—then sits back to enjoy the sight of his outraged Mommy beating up Daddy.

OTHER VIEWS

"The film was released on 4 April 1914, a key date in the rise of the new star, for on that day *Moving Picture World* carried the first advertisement to exploit Chaplin as a commodity. His 8 × 10 portrait was offered for sale as part of a set featuring Mack Sennett, Mabel Normand and Roscoe Arbuckle. You got all four by sending 50 cents to the Keystone Publicity Department. Thus Chaplin was now a fully made up member of the Keystone constellation, ranking third in the hierarchy over Arbuckle, if the arrangement of this advertisement is interpreted correctly" (Gifford 1974, 40).

"Chaplin's overtures to women were nearly always ambiguous: shy and tentative on the one hand, lewd and aggressive on the other. The two were never comfortably integrated. . . . [An accompanying still from *The Star Boarder* depicts an example of his more restrained side. It] shows him gently disengaging Alice Davenport's dress from a bush" (Sobel and Francis 1977, 179).

10.

Mabel at the Wheel

(1914)

Original working title: *Racing Queen*
Other titles: *A Hot Finish, His Daredevil Queen;* French: *Charlot contre Mabel, Charlot et Mabel au volant, Charlot et Mabel aux courses;* German: *Mabel am Steuer;* Spanish: *Mabel automobilista, Mabel al volante;* Italian: *Mabel sulle ruote, Mabel al volante*

Length: 2 reels; 2004 feet (Asplund), 1900 feet (Lyons)
Playing time: 34 minutes at 16 frames per second
Producer: Keystone
Directors: Mabel Normand and/or Mack Sennett
Screenplay: Mabel Normand and/or Mack Sennett
Photography: ?
Cast:

Mabel	Mabel Normand
Her father	Chester Conklin
Her boyfriend	Harry McCoy
The villain	Chaplin
First henchman	Al St. John
Second henchman	William Seiter
A rube	Mack Sennett*

Finished or shipped: March 31, 1914
Released: April 18, 1914

SYNOPSIS

Exterior of Mabel's house. Nearby, Harry (her boyfriend), in his racing car, is waving at Mabel and her girlfriend who are standing outside the porch. Mabel's father is seated on the porch reading a newspaper. They all wave back. Harry invites Mabel to join him.

---

*According to Uno Asplund in his *Chaplin's Films*, Mack Sennett is supposed to be a "press representative." I see no evidence for this in the film.

Highway. Rear view of Charlie (the villain) riding his motorcycle. His costume is similar to that in *Making a Living:* top hat and grey frock coat. He also sports a mustache and a little goatee on each side of his chin.

Exterior of Mabel's house. Mabel and Harry quarrel. She refuses to climb into his car. Her father tries to reconcile them. Charlie drives up and props his motorcycle against the racing car. He leans against his bike and puffs out his cheeks. To make Harry jealous, Mabel waves at Charlie. He waves back. She rushes over to him. He is now smoking and has his cane dangling on his arm. He doffs his hat to Mabel and invites her for a ride on his motorcycle. She accepts. Charlie climbs into the driver's seat and Mabel rides pillion. Harry looks on angrily, his fists clenched.

Highway. Mabel is backseat-driving. Charlie argues with her.

Exterior of Mabel's house. Harry climbs into his car and starts to follow them.

Highway. Mabel is "goosed" as they ride over bumps in the road. Charlie shouts at her to stop complaining. She falls off the motorcycle into a puddle.

Further along the highway. He rides on without realizing that she's gone and points out the sights "they" are passing. He passes out of view.

Highway. Harry appears on the scene. A mud-covered Mabel waves to him. He comes to her aid and brandishes his fist in Charlie's direction.

Further along the highway. Charlie reaches behind him and discovers that Mabel isn't there. The shock almost topples him off the bike. Mabel and Harry—in the racing car—gain on him and come up just in time to see him fall. Close-up of Mabel and Harry laughing at him. Charlie can't raise his bike up. Harry stops his car. He and Mabel get out. She shows him her muddied dress and angrily points to Charlie as the cause. A bystander helps Charlie to get his bike upright and gives him a push to start off. Mabel and Harry are chatting.

Exterior of a nearby hut. Charlie has got off his bike. Observing Mabel tête-à-tête with his rival, he behaves like a melodramatic villain, making a wringing motion with his hands to suggest what he would like to do with Harry's neck.

Highway. He approaches and confronts Harry. Mabel shows him her muddied dress and indicates that he should clear off. But he puts his hand over his heart, protesting love for her. Outraged, she responds by slapping his face. He slaps her back. Harry takes a swing at him, but Charlie ducks and Mabel gets the blow full in the face. Charlie flees. Harry consoles Mabel.

Exterior of hut. At a safe distance Charlie glowers at them and vows vengeance.

Highway. Enraged, Mabel rushes away followed by a pleading Harry.

Exterior of hut. Charlie, still vowing vengeance, accidentally winds himself with a blow to the stomach.

Exterior of Mabel's house. Close-up of Harry pleading with Mabel. Unseen by them, Charlie creeps up and jabs a nail into one of Harry's tires. He laughs evilly and shakes his fist at his rival. Then he marches off.

From here until the start of the racetrack sequence the film cuts back and forth from Charlie (near the hut) to Mabel and Harry (near the house). Charlie looks into the camera and leeringly says, "I did it." Mabel accepts Harry's apologies and heads back to the car with him. Charlie observes them from behind a tree. Harry discovers that he has a flat tire. Charlie smirks and gleefully swings his cane. Mabel suddenly notices gloating Charlie. He mocks them brazenly. They stare at him angrily. Then Mabel hurls a rock at him and knocks him down. Charlie retaliates with a brick that makes Harry stagger back onto his car. Then he throws another which downs him. Mabel and Charlie hurl more missiles at each other, but she proves to be the better shot. Charlie is bowled over. Bruised but undefeated, he gets up and enlarges the conflict with a rock that knocks father off the porch. Now Mabel and Harry chase him over to the hut. There is more rock throwing. Charlie is downed, but not before one of his rocks strikes father yet again. The latter tries to retaliate but hits Harry instead. Mabel and Harry now combine their attack and pelt Charlie until he begs for mercy. But Mabel ignores his pleas, and he is forced to take to his heels to avoid more direct hits. Father gets up, shakes his fist, and comes over to Mabel and Harry (who is nursing a sore head). Mabel explains what has happened. Father invites them back to the house.

High-angle shot of auto racetrack. The Stars and Stripes are flying over a large crowd.

Pit stop. Charlie approaches Harry's car which is being serviced for the race. He tries to jab a nail into one of the tires but sticks it into the rear end of a mechanic instead. For this he gets kicked and shoved out of the way.

Bleachers. Father and Mabel have arrived.

Fence near the track. Charlie is puffing at a cigarette. He sticks his nail into a man who is blocking his view. When the man turns to protest, Charlie raises his hat and walks on.

Bleachers. Mabel exits in search of Harry. Charlie approaches father, hooks his cane around the old man's neck, and asks him about Mabel. Father tries to ignore him, but Charlie uses his nail once again. The old man escapes onto a seat in the bleachers. Mabel returns. Charlie notices that she is trying to attract Harry's attention. He confronts her, doffing his hat. Shocked at encountering him again, she slaps his face. He slaps her back. She strikes even harder, and he staggers and falls. She rushes over to her father. Charlie picks himself up and tries to regain his dignity. He marches over to Mabel and her father with cane under his arm—like a drill sergeant. Determined to make a thorough nuisance of himself, he moves into their row and sits on the feet of a man in the row behind. Then he jabs Mabel's leg and gets into a shoving match with her. Now the man behind pushes his knees into Charlie's chin. Charlie reacts by biting the man's leg.

Pit stop. Harry's car is ready. He waves to Mabel.

Bleachers. Harry comes over to greet her, but Charlie moves over and jabs him from behind. Before he can strike back, Charlie pokes out his tongue, thumbs his nose at his rival, and flees.

Racetrack. High-angle pan shot of cars lined up for the start of the race.

Exterior of shed. An angry Charlie vows revenge.

Bleachers. Harry and Mabel kiss.

Exterior of shed. Charlie whistles and two whiskered henchmen appear. As Harry passes on his way to his car, they seize him and bundle him into the shed.

Interior of shed. Harry struggles with the henchmen. Inadvertently, he slams the door in Charlie's face.

Track. The race starts.

Interior of shed. Harry is tied to a post and taunted by Charlie.

Bleachers. Mabel looks anxiously for her missing Harry.

Interior of shed. Charlie slaps his helpless prisoner.

Pit stop. Frantic at Harry's absence, his codriver tears his hair. He is informed by a track marshal that he has only one minute left to join the race.

Interior of shed. Charlie jabs his nail into Harry.

Exterior of shed. On her way to the pit stop Mabel is grabbed by Charlie. She escapes by biting his hand. Frustrated, he smacks the faces of his henchmen and vows more vengeance.

Bleachers. A rube (Mack Sennett) saunters onto the scene and takes the seat beside father. The latter objects when Mack uses him as a spittoon.

Pit stop. Mabel persuades the marshal to let her take Harry's place.

Bleachers. Mack studies father's reactions on observing that Mabel is about to join the race. He pesters the old man with foolish questions. Father tells him to shut up.

Pit stop. Mabel puts on some make up and joins her codriver. Mabel is now at the wheel.

Exterior of shed. Charlie shakes his fist in her direction.

Track. Long shot of cars speeding toward the camera.

Bleachers. Father leaps up excitedly.

Track. Charlie runs onto the track, gesticulating angrily at Mabel's car. He orders his henchmen to hurl bombs at it, but the car passes unharmed through the smoke of the explosion. Charlie is nearly run over by passing cars as he stands on the track.

Interior of shed. Harry struggles to free himself from his bonds.

Track. High-angle shots of cars rounding a curve.

Bleachers. Mack and father watch the race with mounting excitement.

Track. Charlie himself hurls more bombs but fails to hit Mabel's car.

Pit stop. Mabel stops to refuel.

Bleachers. Father demonstrates to Mack that his hat is filled with perspiration. Mack obliges by pouring it out.

Track. Charlie's henchmen throw more bombs—still to no effect. Charlie becomes furious with his henchmen. By now Mabel is leading by several laps.

Near the track. Charlie appears holding a hosepipe. He falls over its coils. Then he orders the henchmen to turn on the water.

Track. Charlie sprays water across the path of the oncoming cars. This softens the surface of the track and Mabel's car skids, but she maintains control. Charlie and his henchmen fall over on the slippery track. All the cars spin into a 180-degree skid and continue the race in the opposite direction. There are more skids. Mabel's car turns over on its side but it is quickly uprighted and continues the race.

Interior of shed. Harry escapes at last.

Near the track. Enraged at his failure to stop Mabel's car, Charlie vents his wrath on his henchmen by throwing bombs at them.

Bleachers. Harry rushes excitedly over to father.

Track. Mabel's car is the winner.

Bleachers. Mack pats Harry on the head. Harry and father dash away to greet Mabel.

Track. A movie camera films the winner. The joyful Harry lifts Mabel out of the car and carries her off triumphantly.

Bleachers. Mack applauds—then tries to follow Harry's example by seizing a girl for himself. She resists and another woman comes to her aid. Mack kicks her but is shoved aside.

Near the track. Charlie is beaten up by his henchmen. He suddenly discovers the last remaining bomb. He gloats. Then he throws it in the air. It lands among Charlie and his henchmen and explodes, leaving them unconscious or dead.

Track. Harry carries the victorious Mabel past a cheering crowd.

COMMENTS

1. By this time Chaplin was chafing to write and direct his own films, but, to his chagrin, Sennett would not give his approval, and he nettled Chaplin further by assigning him to work with Mabel Normand. The film was to be his first two-reeler, *Mabel at the Wheel*. In *My Autobiography* Chaplin maintains that Mabel "had just started directing her own pictures" (1964, 148). Actually, she had already directed four or five films; her first, *Mabel's Stormy Love Affair*, had been completed exactly a month before Chaplin appeared in *his* first. No matter how much Sennett may have cared for her, it is most unlikely that he would have let her continue directing if she had proved inadequate. Chaplin "doubted her competence as a director" and said so to Sennett. But, as Betty Fussell says, "Mabel had proved her competence in over 121 comic films made in the three years before Chaplin made his first. It was not Mabel's competence that nettled Chaplin. It was her sex" (1982, 73). It was also her youth (she was six years younger than Chaplin) and, above all, the differences in their notions of comedy.

Conflict flared up on the very first day of shooting. Mabel ordered Chaplin to do the scene in which the villain hoses down the road to make the leading car skid. (In *My Autobiography* he mistakenly recalls this as the villain's car.) He told Mabel he didn't think the scene was funny. He had a better idea. "I suggested standing on the hose so that the water can't come out, and when I look down the nozzle I unconsciously step off the hose and the water squirts in my face." Chaplin seems to have been unaware then (and when he wrote his autobiography) that this was the oldest gag in the movies: the Lumières had used it in their very first film program. Mabel promptly rejected it. "We have no time!" she told him. "Do what you're told." Chaplin refused. He would not carry on working unless Mabel listened to his suggestions. Now *she* refused. It was an impasse. Mabel was unable to continue the picture and Sennett was furious. He ordered Chaplin to obey Mabel or get out. But Chaplin wouldn't budge and expected to be fired. Surprisingly, next day Sennett was quite cordial. He urged him to swallow his pride and help out with the picture. But Chaplin stuck to his guns: "If you'll let me direct myself, you'll have no trouble," he replied, and he offered to provide his own story and even to deposit $1500 to pay for the film if it was a flop. This time Sennett didn't immediately reject the idea: "Finish the picture with Mabel, then I'll see," he said. Much later Chaplin discovered the reason for Sennett's unexpected cordiality. He had been about to fire Chaplin when he received a telegram from Kessel and Bauman requesting more Chaplin movies—they were doing better than all the other Keystones. In the meantime, Chaplin apologized to Mabel and went back to work on the picture. After their initial blowup, he tells us,

"Mabel could not have been sweeter. She even came to me for suggestions and ideas."

Whatever those suggestions and ideas may have been, a viewing of *Mabel at the Wheel* reveals Chaplin spraying the road with the hosepipe—just as Mabel originally wanted, and there is no sign of the gag *he* had suggested.

2. Films about motor races were immensely popular at this period. Sennett had tried his hand at a farce-comedy on this subject (*The Speed Demon*, Biograph 1912) even before Keystone, and one of his most successful early Keystones was *Barney Oldfield's Race for a Life* (1913), in which Oldfield, a real-life speedway champion, raced to the rescue of Mabel Normand who had been tied to the railroad tracks by dastardly Ford Sterling.

By 1914 there was a vogue of serial queens (Pearl White, Ruth Roland, Helen Holmes, etc.) whose courage and athleticism outstripped their male counterparts. Comedy quickly followed suit with its own heroines, among them Mabel Normand, who starred not only in *Mabel at the Wheel* but also in such other Keystone motor-racing comedies as *The Speed Queen* (1913), and *Love and Gasoline* (1914). David Robinson notices that "the week before *Mabel at the Wheel* was begun [Pearl White] had appeared on American screens in the first episode of the most famous of all serial thrillers, *The Perils of Pauline*. *Mabel at the Wheel* was a take-off of the Pearl White style . . ." (1985, 120). "The Deadly Turning," one episode of the Pearl White serial, typifies what Robinson is talking about. Pauline and a male codriver enter a cross-country motor race. Determined to sabotage their efforts, the villainous Kerner's accomplices (like Charlie's henchmen) scatter nails across the path of the car. But they are outwitted by skillful driving. The car that crashes is the one Kerner had backed, and Pauline's vehicle wins the race.

3. *Mabel at the Wheel* falls naturally into two main segments: before the race, and the race. The first segment may be further subdivided into three sequences: (i) Mabel quarrels with Harry, (ii) her motorcycle ride with Charlie, and (iii) the rock-throwing battle. The second segment has many more plot strands: (i) Charlie makes a nuisance of himself, (ii) he kidnaps Harry, (iii) Mack makes a lesser nuisance of himself, (iv) Mabel takes Harry's place, (v) the attempts of Charlie and his henchmen to sabotage her car, (vi) they fail—and are blown up, (vii) Mabel is victorious.

4. As the film's title indicates, *Mabel at the Wheel* was primarily intended as a Mabel Normand picture. Her job was to provide the thrills

and to demonstrate her spunkiness; Chaplin's was merely to provide the slapstick. Mabel's spunkiness is demonstrated by her own activities and by comparison with the male characters. She enthusiastically rides a motorcycle and a racing car which at that time were both considered to be exclusively male activities. Since she wins the race, it is obvious that as a driver she is as good as, if not better than, her boyfriend, Harry. In other respects she also proves her superiority to Harry (as well as to Charlie). In the rock-throwing scene Charlie puts Harry temporarily out of action, but Mabel makes Charlie beg for mercy and then drives him away. Harry never really stands up to Charlie and eventually gets kidnapped by him, but she proves stronger than Charlie at slapping faces, evades his attempt to kidnap *her,* and frustrates all his efforts to prevent her from winning the race.

5. Mabel's attitude to comedy was expressed in her words to Chaplin: "We have no time!" Like Sennett and Lehrman she was a devotee of the school of fast-paced slapstick. On the other hand, time was precisely what Chaplin needed to develop more elaborate characterization and comic business. It was obviously in short supply in *Mabel at the Wheel.* Moreover, he was asked to do little more than reprise his earliest film role. Another routine performance from Chaplin, but it looks like Academy Award stuff alongside Sennett's lamentable portrayal of a barbarian of the bleachers.

At first sight, from the rear, he seems amusingly incongruous: a man in a top hat and frock coat riding a motorcycle and precariously doffing his hat in an effort at politeness. We know he's not going to wind up with Mabel when he props up his mere motorcycle against Harry's splendid racing car. His cane is a tantalizing reminder of the Tramp—but he plays it down in favor of his more aggressive nail. That nail is one of many indications that he doesn't remain a merely incongruous figure. His character changes in midfilm as a result of Mabel's attitude. At the outset he is a ludicrous figure who turns up just in time to be exploited by her in a manner that somewhat anticipates Georgia's use of Charlie at the Monte Carlo dance hall in *The Gold Rush:* i.e., he becomes the heroine's foil to arouse the jealousy of the man she loves. After the motorcycle ride, when Mabel rejects his love and returns to Harry, he turns vicious. His threats are translated into action, and he becomes a comic villain, jabbing people and tires with his nail, kidnapping his rival and employing henchmen to commit sabotage. After his dastardly behavior, blowing himself up seems no less than he deserves, but it's hardly what we'd have expected at the start of the film.

6. Keaton borrowed the idea of the motorcycle ride and elaborated on it for one of the funniest sequences of *Sherlock Jr.* (1924).

OTHER VIEWS

"Since the first films were shown as 'chasers' in the music hall, the early film comedies reflected the kind of humor that music-hall audiences enjoyed. It was often vulgar and cruel, as in. . . *Mabel at the Wheel* [in which] Chaplin gives Harry McCoy a hefty slap across the face" (Sobel and Francis 1977, 141). [But note that it is *Mabel* who first starts the slapping, using Charlie's face as a target.]

"By the tenth film, *Mabel at the Wheel*, Chaplin's first two-reeler, Sennett may have contemplated forcing Chaplin into the mold of the now departed Ford Sterling because the Tramp costume is gone and Chaplin actually wears Sterling's old frock coat" (McCabe 1978, 58).

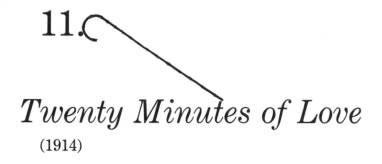

11.

Twenty Minutes of Love

(1914)

Original working title: *Passing of Time*
Other titles: *Cops and Watches, He Loved Her So, [The] Love-Fiend;*
French: *Charlot et le chronomètre, Vingt minutes d'amour;* German:
Zwanzig Minuten Liebe; Spanish: *Charlot y el reloj; Charlot y el
cronómetro;* Italian: *Charlot pazzo per amore, Venti minuti d'amore*

Length: 1 reel; 961 feet (Asplund), 1009 feet (Lyons)
Playing time: 16 minutes at 16 frames per second
Producer: Keystone
Director: Mack Sennett or Joseph Maddern or Chaplin (see note 1 below)
Screenplay: Chaplin (?)*
Photography: Frank D. Williams (?)
Cast:

A tramp	Chaplin
An ardent suitor	Edgar Kennedy
His beloved	Minta Durfee
Another beauty	Emma Clifton
A watch-stealer	Chester Conklin (?)
A sleeping watch-owner	Joseph Swickard
A boy	Gordon Griffith

Finished or shipped: March 28, 1914
Released: April 20, 1914

SYNOPSIS

The entire action of *Twenty Minutes of Love* takes place in a park.
Near the first park bench. Wandering through the park, Charlie, a
tramp, glances back angrily at some bushes. (He has, evidently, just
been given the brush-off by a girl.) Pausing in his stroll to puff at a

*Asplund says that *Twenty Minutes of Love* was "presumably" Chaplin's first scenario.
Lyons has no doubt about it. But Chaplin himself did not verify this in *My Autobiography*.
See comment 2 to this film.

cigarette, he suddenly notices a couple kissing on the bench. He peers
at them; then he smirks and parodies their passion, using a tree as a
partner and putting his hand over his heart. He laughs as the woman
plays with her suitor's mustache. Taking off his hat, he feigns that he
is swooning, throws his arms around a tree and kisses it. The couple
kiss more ardently. Charlie wanders over to them. He looks into the
camera, smirking again, removes his hat again, peers closely at the
passionate kiss, and sits down on the edge of the bench beside the
woman. The couple fail to notice him until he taps the woman on the
shoulder. Then they separate—shocked at realizing that someone else
is present. Charlie merely laughs. Then he digs the woman in the ribs
and taps her on the knee. Her suitor promptly switches places with
the woman. Charlie doesn't notice this; his hand gropes for the
woman's leg, and he utters what are probably endearments. Suddenly
the suitor speaks, and Charlie turns and realizes that the limb he is
caressing is a man's. The suitor is about to strike Charlie, but the
woman restrains him. The couple resume their embrace while the
suitor simultaneously tries to edge Charlie off the bench. Then Charlie
whispers something in his ear—and gets pushed off. Irrepressible, he
climbs back on the bench. The two men push at one another with their
rear ends until the suitor gives an extra strong push—whereupon
Charlie suddenly gets up and lets his rival fall off the bench. Charlie
now takes the suitor's place beside the woman, but the latter grabs
him and forces him onto his feet. They confront each other. The suitor
rolls up his sleeves and orders Charlie to clear off. He seems to take
the hint—but as he turns to leave, he gives the suitor a back kick in
the stomach. The suitor collapses onto the bench, and Charlie follows
up his surprise attack with a side kick to the head, after which he
shuffles off through the bushes.

A second park bench. A man wearing a cloth cap (the watch-
stealer) is declaring his love for a girl. She indicates that she wants a
token of his love. He feels in his pockets: they are empty, so he goes
off to find something for her.

Among the bushes. Charlie tramps along swinging his cane.

Pathway. The watch-stealer sees a man sleeping on a third bench,
his pocket watch exposed. He wanders over to the bench without disturbing the sleeper.

First bench. The couple are locked in an embrace. Charlie reappears, taps the suitor on the rump with his cane, and thumbs his nose
at him. He smirks at the suitor's annoyance.

Third bench. The watch-stealer filches the sleeper's pocket watch.

Second bench. The lady is tired of waiting for her boyfriend's return. She shrugs her shoulders and exits.

First bench. The lady comes face to face with Charlie standing in front of the couple. She starts to flirt with him. Charlie is obviously smitten, and he follows her into the bushes. The couple throw up their hands with relief at Charlie's departure. They return to their kissing.

Second bench. The watch-stealer appears and finds that the lady has gone.

Bushes. The lady leads Charlie on. He loses sight of her and tries to call her back by whistling.

First bench. The watch-stealer interrupts the couple in his search for his girlfriend.

Fourth bench. The lady sits down, waiting for Charlie.

Among the bushes. Charlie pulls aside the foliage and discovers a third couple making love. He retreats, raising his hat apologetically; then he changes his mind, goes back, stands over them and grins.

Among other bushes. The watch-stealer calls out for the lady.

Beside bushes. Charlie rolls out, scratching his head. He has, presumably, been knocked down by the man whose courtship he has just interrupted.

Among trees. The watch-stealer is still calling out for the lady.

Among bushes. Charlie stands up and straightens his clothes.

Among trees. The watch-stealer looks admiringly at the watch he has stolen. He listens to it. Charlie appears and observes him dangling the watch. The watch-stealer puts the watch in his pocket and calls out for the lady once more. Charlie filches the watch and tiptoes away without being noticed.

Pathway. Charlie examines the watch.

Fourth bench. The watch-stealer comes upon the lady at last. He indicates that he has a surprise for her. Reaching in his pocket for the watch, he finds that it has disappeared. The lady spurns him. Upset, he wanders off to search for the watch.

Among trees. The watch-stealer searches the area where he had been standing.

Pathway. A cop comes along and finds Charlie examining the watch. He asks to see it. Guiltily, Charlie hands it over and is about to flee when the cop hands it back: he had merely wanted to know the time. As the cop walks on Charlie gives a deep sigh, holds his heart, and wipes the sweat from his brow.

Among bushes. The watch-stealer searches frantically for the watch.

Pathway. Charlie swings the watch around by its chain and drops it neatly into his waistcoat pocket. He buttons up his coat and thumbs his nose at the cop. Then he heads off in search of the lady.

First bench. The watch-stealer searches for the watch under the bench. He interrupts the couple by crawling under the suitor's legs. The suitor picks him up and boots him out of sight. The couple resume their embrace.

Among trees. Charlie is still searching for the lady. He almost bumps into a tree. He raises his hat to it, then signals into the camera that he is nonplussed.

Third bench. The watch-stealer searches the sleeper's pockets without awakening him. He indicates his bewilderment directly into the camera.

Fourth bench. Charlie comes upon the lady. He raises his hat to her. She stands and pretends to be coy. Using his cane, Charlie dents his derby into a trilby—a repeat of a gag from *His Favorite Pastime*, Chaplin's seventh Keystone. He puts the hat on and offers her the watch. She is delighted. Charlie swings himself and his cane around in a mixed expression of swank and joy. Straightening his tie, he joins her on the park bench. Then he takes her hand and declares his love. She pecks his cheek; he swoons. Then he says something that offends her and she slaps him. He responds by kissing her on the lips.

Among trees. The watch-stealer suddenly notices Charlie kissing his girlfriend.

Fourth bench. The watch-stealer rushes over. The lady (with the watch pinned to her dress) jumps up, horrified. Charlie doesn't immediately notice the intruder until he is tapped on the shoulder. Then he turns, recognizes the "owner" of the watch, and realizes he's in trouble. Removing his hat, he tries to cover up the watch. The watch-stealer removes the hat and grabs the watch. He demands to know where the lady had got it. She points to Charlie. Charlie tries to make a hasty exit but he is stopped. Thinking quickly, he raps the watch-stealer's knuckles with his cane, pushes him onto the bench, grabs the watch, and runs off with it.

Pathway. Charlie, in flight, goes round the corner on one leg—the first time in any Keystone that we see this bit of business. He slows down and walks at a normal pace when he notices the cop. The latter gives him a friendly greeting. Smiling, Charlie returns the watch to his waistcoat pocket and walks on swinging his cane.

Third bench. Charlie sits down next to the sleeper.

Pathway. The lady and the watch-stealer pursue Charlie. They meet up with the cop. The watch-stealer tries to prevent her from talking to him, but she insists on telling the cop that Charlie has stolen her boyfriend's watch. They dash off in pursuit of Charlie.

Third bench. Charlie tries to filch the sleeper's watch—only to find he doesn't have one. The sleeper wakes up. Charlie offers him the stolen watch for two dollars, but the owner of the watch recognizes it. Charlie grabs it back. There is a brief struggle which ends when Charlie bites the owner's hand and boots him in the stomach.

Pathway. Charlie runs off, rounding the bend on one leg. The owner of the watch pursues him. Charlie meets up with the watch-stealer and the lady. They grab him. The watch-stealer bites Charlie's hand until he gives up the watch. Then he knocks him down. Charlie gets up, boots the watch-stealer in the rear end, kicks him in the face, and jumps on his stomach as he tries to get up. But the watch-stealer retaliates by hurling Charlie into the bushes. When Charlie gets up he punches him down again.

Nearby on the pathway. The owner of the watch reports the theft to the cop.

Pathway. Charlie, now back on his feet, aims a blow at the watch-stealer. The latter ducks, and the blow knocks the lady down. The watch-stealer kicks Charlie; Charlie trips him up.

Lakeside. Three picnickers watch the lady and the watch-stealer beat Charlie.

Pathway. Charlie is collapsing under their blows when the cop appears with the owner of the watch. He arrests Charlie. The watch-stealer contrives to slip the watch into Charlie's hand so that he is actually caught in possession of the stolen property. But Charlie has no intention of being carted off to jail. He suddenly punches the cop, who staggers backward and pushes the picknickers into the lake. Next he shoves the owner of the watch onto the cop, knocking the latter into the water. Now the watch-stealer intervenes. He boots Charlie in the stomach, sending him staggering back onto the owner of the watch who also lands in the lake. A second cop arrives on the scene. The watch-stealer removes his shoe and hurls it at Charlie—who ducks. It knocks the second cop into the lake.

Lakeside. Charlie and the watch-stealer struggle at the water's edge until Charlie boots his adversary into the water. The film ends as he marches off triumphantly with the watch, his arm around the lady.

COMMENTS

1. David Robinson provides questionable evidence that this was the first film that Chaplin directed. In *My Autobiography* Chaplin says that he made his directorial debut with *Caught in the Rain*. However, citing a manuscript from Chaplin's own files (reproduced by Robinson), Robinson notes: "On 9 August 1914 . . . he sent [his brother] Sydney a list of the films in which he had appeared during his seven months at Keystone. On it he very deliberately marked as 'My Own' six films which he had already directed." The first was *Twenty Minutes of Love* (released April 20); *Caught in the Rain* (released May 4) was second. Robinson continues: "It is notable that Chaplin does not include in the list of his own films three which existing filmographies record as collaborations with Mabel Normand: *Caught in a Cabaret, Her Friend the*

Bandit and *Mabel's Busy Day*. On the other hand he *does* include the fourth of these alleged collaborations: *Mabel's Married Life*" (1985, 121–22).

When writing about Chaplin's recollection of his first use of the Tramp costume, Robinson says that the comedian's memory rarely failed him when it came to such details (p. 113). Yet he also tells us: "Chaplin might understandably have forgotten fifty years later that he directed *Twenty Minutes of Love*, or have simply written it off as apprentice practice, since it is the first and one of the slightest of the 'park' films" (p. 122). Why "understandably"? The evidence is confusing. Is it likely that Chaplin—who quarreled with Lehrman and Nichols over *their* directing, who had a run-in with Mabel Normand over *her* direction of *Mabel at the Wheel*, and who had chafed almost from the outset, to direct *his own* films—could have forgotten, even fifty years later, which film was his directorial debut? *Twenty Minutes of Love* was apparently made three days before *Mabel at the Wheel*. If Chaplin actually did direct the former film, why did he have to persuade Mack Sennett to let him direct *Caught in the Rain* (Chaplin 1964, 148–51)? On the other hand, why, if he had considered *Twenty Minutes of Love* worth singling out as "my own" in 1914, should he have "written it off as an apprentice practice" in 1964? Robinson assumes that "my own" referred to directing. Chaplin could have meant that the films so indicated were his own *story ideas or scenarios* (see comment 2 below). Anyway, how much importance should we give to that list of films Chaplin sent to Sydney in 1914? As reproduced in Robinson's biography it looks like something that Chaplin hastily jotted down in the midst of a very busy schedule. Even Robinson indicates that there are some curious exclusions from it. On the other hand, Chaplin spends several carefully written pages of *My Autobiography* recounting how he had to reach a compromise with Mabel before Sennett allowed him, at last, to direct his first film— *Caught in the Rain*.

2. In *My Autobiography* (p. 210) Chaplin implies that the story idea for *Twenty Minutes of Love* was his. After remarking that "simple little tunes" gave him "the image" for some of his early comedies, he adds: in "*Twenty Minutes of Love* . . . I weaved in and out of situations to the tune of 'Too Much Mustard,' " a popular two-step in 1914. He also tells us (p. 157) that the film was made in a single afternoon. Like *Between Showers* it was shot on location in Westlake Park. Whether or not Chaplin did provide the story/script, the film unquestionably embodies many of his ideas for the Tramp character, and, as Theodore Huff (1952, 54) notes, he liked the film so much that he directed his own version of it for Essanay: *In the Park* (1915).

3. *Twenty Minutes of Love* was actually completed on March 28, 1914, three days before *Mabel at the Wheel*, but did not receive its first public screening until April 20th, two days after the premiere showing of *Mabel*.

Most commentators have attributed the direction of the film to Joseph Maddern or Madden. If so, this was probably his first film for Keystone; he may also have directed two other Keystones: *The Morning Paper* and *Down on the Farm*. I have no other information on this director.

Contrary to Asplund's statement, *Twenty Minutes of Love* was not Chaplin's first "park" film. See my comment 2 to *Between Showers* (Keystone no. 4).

4. *Twenty Minutes of Love* interweaves four plot strands: (i) Charlie's pestering of couples in the park, (ii) his flirtation with the lady, (iii) his conflict with her boyfriend, and (iv) the "adventures" of the stolen watch. Note that the introduction of strand (ii) resolves strand (i): i.e., Charlie's pestering ceases as soon as he begins his flirtation. The outcome of strands (iii) and (iv) determines the outcome of (ii): i.e., Charlie ends up with both the lady and the watch.

5. Careless descriptions of *Twenty Minutes of Love* have led to equally careless comments about the film. As an example of Chaplin's "lewdness," Sobel and Francis refer to his "sliding his hand up the thigh of a girl kissing her lover" (1977, 204). Actually he gropes for the *lover's* leg, thinking it's the girl's. As an example of a gesture that "anticipates Chaplin's introduction of the human element into his work," Kalton Lahue (1966, 79) cites the scene in which Charlie "tenderly" embraces a tree after watching a couple kissing on a park bench. Charlie is actually *parodying* the couple on the first bench. Enlarging on the same scene, Gerald Mast notes:

> Another important Chaplin motif—Charlie's ability to experience human happiness vicariously but not directly—also pops up in one of the Keystones. In *Twenty Minutes of Love*, Charlie observes two lovers kissing on a park bench while he sits on the branch of a tree. Carried away by this passion, Chaplin begins to hug and embrace the tree trunk. A tree is his only lover. . . . (1979, 70)

A sentimental and touching interpretation, but it ignores (a) the indication that Charlie is not acting out of passion and loneliness but is reacting out of disgust and mockery, probably at having just been given the brush-off by a girl, and (b) the fact that *he* winds up with a girl—who, incidentally, enjoys kissing him—while everyone else winds up in the lake.

6. In Chaplin's park films the location functions as an "island" (apart from the normal restraints of society) in which each character gives free rein to his impulses—sexual, violent, larcenous, etc.—usually in conflict with the impulses of one or more of the other characters. *Twenty Minutes of Love* is typical of this group of films. Its park is a haven for lovers (licit or illicit) and a "game reserve" where other characters freely and competitively indulge in pestering, infidelity, gold-digging, theft, and violence. In this environment Charlie first acts and then is transformed.

In the first half of the film the impressions he makes are distinctly negative. When we first see him he has either been driven away by a couple he has pestered or else he has just been rejected by a woman. My assumption is the latter, since when we actually see him driven away by other couples he never behaves as he did at the opening of the film. If I am right, his rejection by *one* woman has made him furious with *all* women. His behavior at the outset expresses two attitudes: (i) outrage at the insensitivity of women, (ii) contempt for the ingenuousness of men as far as women are concerned. Catching sight of the couple on the first bench, he is first aghast, then disgusted. After that he smirks, turns to a tree, and addresses it as if it were human. His gestures seem to be saying that women are as unfeeling as trees. Pointing at the couple, then at the tree, he mockingly puts his hand over his heart and laughs. Then he sneers some comment that I tentatively lip-read as "You tramp!" He is presumably referring to the woman. When she begins petting her complaisant lover (she plays with his mustache), Charlie reacts by imitating a man swooning in ecstasy, and it's at this point that he embraces and kisses the tree. After this he moves in on the couple. His "philosophy" here and later on, when he annoys a second couple, is evidently akin to that of the dog-in-the-manger: if *he* can't make it with a woman, he'll do his best to stop any other man in the park from doing so. Hence, until the flirtatious lady appears, he becomes the courting couples' pest.

I have spent so much time detailing this brief, preliminary section of the film for several reasons. (i) Close study of the opening reveals how (given the opportunity), even at this early phase of his film career, Chaplin's mime could be elaborate and complex in manner and meaning. This is in addition to a range of comic business that makes *Twenty Minutes of Love* the most inventive of all Chaplin's Keystones to date. Charlie introduces or reintroduces some of the Tramp's most enduring gags: doffing his hat to a tree (or other nonhuman object), a back-kick aimed at his rival's face, his running turn on one foot, and so on. (ii) As I noted earlier, the opening scene is frequently described and interpreted incorrectly. Yet a fairly precise account is necessary if we are to understand the full significance of what occurs later on. When the flirtatious lady appears and entices Charlie to pursue her through the bushes, he suddenly loses all interest in being a pest. Now that a female has demonstrated her interest in him, he forgets his former attitude to women and loses no time in stealing for her. Then, seated beside her on a bench, he becomes even more naively romantic than the lover of the first scene. When she kisses his cheek he swoons with ecstasy until she slaps him back to consciousness and demands to be kissed on the mouth. This is evidently a new sensation for Charlie: he promptly licks his lips to sample the taste of the kiss. With this scene, his transformation is complete. Having discarded his earlier misogyny and found a woman who likes him, we are not surprised when, in contrast to the opening scene, he exits, ultimately, with his arm around the lady.

Ironically, Charlie fails to notice that his initial, negative attitude to women is given ample justification by the behavior of the lady. She is a shameless gold digger who is impulsively unfaithful to her boyfriend. Her affections are available only to the man who will provide a suitable token of love. Consequently her impecunious boyfriend is driven to steal for her. But shortly after he exits, she gets tired of waiting for him and begins flirting with the first unattached man who comes into view, i.e., Charlie. When the boyfriend reappears and claims the watch, she promptly sides with him *against* Charlie. But she shifts her allegiance back to Charlie at the end of the film when it looks more advantageous. If Chaplin can be credited with the story idea for *Twenty Minutes of Love* the film must be regarded as the first in which we glimpse his views of women and of male-female relationships.

7. (i) As the watch-stealer, Chester Conklin (?) seems to have modeled his performance on Elmer Booth's gangster in D. W. Griffith's *The Musketeers of Pig Alley* (1912). (ii) An interesting contrast to the scene in which Charlie tries to sell the watch to its rightful owner occurs in the park-bench pickpocket scene of Chaplin's *The Idle Class* (First National 1921).

OTHER VIEWS

"Charlie, a romantic type, is strolling in the park and finds himself alone among a number of loving couples. He parodies one couple on a bench by embracing a tree only to join in the game himself" (Asplund 1976, 38).

"The director was Joseph Maddern and the story was 'written' by Chaplin. He improvised it after the earlier *Between Showers*, substituting a watch for the much-stolen umbrella. . . . Clearly Chaplin was breaking himself in as a movie-maker with standard Sennett stuff. For a first screenplay it presented nothing new. But it allowed a little more time for the star's spontaneities, as with the way he embraces a tree when he spots a spooning pair" (Gifford 1974, 41).

12.

Caught in a Cabaret

(1914)

Original working title: *The Waiter*
Other titles: *The Waiter, Charlie the Waiter, Jazz Waiter, Prime Minister Charlie, Faking with Society;* French: *Charlot garçon de café;* German: *Im Kabarett Ertrappt;* Spanish: *Charlot camarero, Charlot mozo;* Italian: *Charlot garzone di caffè, Nel caffè*

Length: 2 reels; 1968 feet (Asplund), 2053 feet (Lyons)
Playing time: 32 minutes at 16 frames per second
Producer: Keystone
Directors: Chaplin and Mabel Normand
Screenplay: Chaplin
Photography: Frank D. Williams (?)
Cast:

A waiter	Chaplin
Second waiter	Chester Conklin
Café proprietor	Edgar Kennedy
Café thug	Mack Swain
A society girl	Mabel Normand
Her mother	Alice Davenport
Her father	Hank Mann
Her admirer	Harry McCoy
A dancing waitress	Minta Durfee
A boy in the park	Gordon Griffith
Café staff and clientele	Alice Howell
	Phyllis Allen
	Leo White
	Joseph Swickard
	Wallace McDonald

Finished or shipped: April 11, 1914
Released: April 27, 1914

SYNOPSIS

A low-class "greasy spoon" café with an adjoining barroom. Charlie is a slovenly, booze-loving waiter. He is about to serve an order when he slips. The meal falls to the ground, but he serves it up anyway. Then he helps himself to the dregs of someone's unfinished drink.

Title: *A Society Bud.*

The garden of a country mansion.

Mabel, an expensively gowned society girl, flaunts herself before her wealthy parents. Her upper-class admirer calls on her. They enjoy a mild flirtation.

Barroom. Charlie steals some food and hides it underneath his hat. Then he collects his dog, a dachshund, from beneath the bar, and begins his exit via the café where a female dancer is doing the shimmy. As he is leaving, the proprietor confronts him.

Title: *"Remember, stupid, be back in an hour."*

Charlie politely touches his hat and exits.

Street outside the café. An attractive woman is entering the café. Charlie raises his hat to her and his concealed snack falls out. Continuing on his way, he encounters some pals. They shake hands, and he resumes his promenade.

A park. Charlie tries to get some water from a little waterfall, but he loses his balance and falls in. Some ladies observe his dog and start to pet it. Charlie tries to strike up an acquaintance with them, but they aren't interested in *him*. Meanwhile, his legs have become entangled in the dog's lead. He trips and the dog runs away. A small boy retrieves it. Dusting himself off, Charlie shoves the boy aside and takes his dog back.

Nearby in the same park. Mabel and her admirer are taking a stroll. Suddenly, a hoodlum leaps out of the trees and attacks them. The admirer flees. Charlie, observing that Mabel is in distress, rushes to the rescue, chasing the attacker out of sight with some well-aimed kicks. Then he returns to Mabel and introduces himself. He attempts a graceful bow, but unceremoniously falls back on his rump. Mabel is too impressed with his heroism to notice his *faux pas*. From a discreet distance, the admirer jealously observes Charlie replacing him in Mabel's affections. He comes forward hesitantly, but Mabel spurns him and walks off, escorted by Charlie, her new admirer.

Exterior of country mansion. Charlie is impressed with her wealthy home, and Mabel is even more impressed with Charlie when he offers her a card identifying himself as:

*BARON DOOBUGLE: Prime Minister of Greenland.**

---

*In some prints his card reads: *O. T. Axle, Ambassador for Grease.*

She loses no time in introducing him to her parents as her new suitor.

Title: *She invites him to her party.*

Realizing that his lunch hour is almost over, Charlie interrupts the flirtation and heads back to the café.

Street. The jealous admirer follows Charlie and gleefully discovers that he is merely a waiter.

Café. Glancing at his watch, the angry proprietor tells the second waiter:

Title: *"I'll knock that bum for a goal when he returns."*

He goes into the barroom. Charlie enters. The second waiter informs him that the proprietor is waiting to kick him for being late. But Charlie is unconcerned. He has begun to daydream.

Title: *Tender memories.*

Flashback of Mabel standing at her garden gate looking fondly after him.

Café. The proprietor enters and rudely awakens Charlie with a swift kick in the pants. Charlie reacts by kicking the second waiter.

Barroom. The two waiters tangle with each other.

Café. A burly thug enters, grabs the nearest girl, and perches her on his knee. The proprietor protests, but the thug brandishes a gun. The diners and waiters cower in fear.

Barroom. The proprietor enters and orders the second waiter to deal with the thug.

Café. The second waiter enters. The thug makes short work of him.

Barroom. The proprietor orders Charlie to deal with the thug.

Café. The thug knocks Charlie down. The proprietor orders him to retaliate, and Charlie obliges by cunningly serving the thug a drink—then beating him over the head with a huge mallet. A half-dozen men promptly eject the unconscious thug, while admiring ladies crowd around heroic Charlie. In a trice, everything in the café is back to normal.

Barroom. Charlie enters and clubs the second waiter with the mallet.

Title: *Off to the Party.*

Charlie, in tophat and frock coat, dashes out of the café to see his Mabel.

Garden party. Charlie is greeted by Mabel and her guests. He astonishes them by knocking back several drinks in quick succession and using his coat to wipe his mouth. The furious admirer watches him flirting with Mabel. When he tries to intervene, Charlie puffs cigarette smoke in his face and threatens to kick him out. Then Charlie snatches a bottle of liquor from a passing butler and swills it down his throat. He starts to get tipsy, burping, singing raucously, and blowing smoke in Mabel's face, but she is too entranced with him to be anything but amused. Eventually he staggers to his feet and departs for work at the café. The admirer tries to denounce him as an upstart, but Mabel refuses to hear anything against him.

Café. Charlie arrives late again. He finds the angry proprietor waiting for him as usual. Work resumes.

Title: *Slumming.*

Mabel's admirer has persuaded her to see how the other half lives.

Street. Mabel and her entourage take a limousine to the café.

Café. Mabel & co. are greeted by the proprietor as if they are visiting royalty. The female dancer gives another performance. Then—to Mabel's annoyance—she starts to flirt with Mabel's father. Ordered to serve the guests, Charlie arrives at Mabel's table balancing several plates of food in his arms. Catching sight of her, he drops everything. Then, thinking quickly, he assures her:

Title: *"I'm a slummer myself."*

She accepts his explanation, momentarily. But then the proprietor appears. Slapping Charlie, he orders him back to work. Mabel protests—but he tells her that Charlie is only a waiter. She recoils at the news. His dignity affronted, Charlie slaps the proprietor. Instantly, a free-for-all breaks out. The proprietor hurls a pie at Charlie—it hits Mabel instead. Going berserk, the proprietor pulls out a pair of six-guns and starts shooting up the place. Charlie cuts him short with a well-aimed brick. Now, triumphant amid the ruins of the café, Charlie turns to Mabel, expecting gratitude and love for having saved her once more. But this time his chivalry is of no avail. A chastened, weeping Mabel coldly rejects him.

COMMENTS

1. "Chaplin's aim was direction," says Denis Gifford (1974, 45), "and he achieved it by co-direction." *Caught in a Cabaret* was the first of four films he was to codirect with Mabel Normand. The remaining three were *Her Friend the Bandit* (Keystone no. 16), *Mabel's Busy Day* (Keystone no. 18), and *Mabel's Married Life* (Keystone no. 19). We shall probably never know the details of their collaboration on *Caught in a Cabaret*. Chaplin doesn't mention the film in the main text of *My Autobiography**, but the comparative subtleties of his performance convince me that he was solely responsible for the scenes in which he does *not* appear with Mabel. I would also hazard the guess that it was Mabel who directed the scenes in which they *did* appear together. The story and script were entirely his. So it seems fair to say that Mabel merely

*It *is* listed in his filmography (1964, 499).

contributed to a film that was *totally* Chaplin's in conception and *mainly* Chaplin's in execution.

2. Keystone did not provide screen credits, and for the first few months of 1914 press references to Chaplin had cited his name variously as Chapman[n] or Chatlin or Edgar English. However, as Theodore Huff notes: "His correct name was mentioned for the first time by the *Moving Picture World* in its notice of *Caught in a Cabaret* (April 27, 1914), which was announced as the first of a new series. Chaplin was catching on" (1952, 40).

3. The structure of *Caught in a Cabaret* anticipates that of many later Chaplin films (indeed, that of many silent feature films): a prologue, five "acts," and an epilogue. This film, specifically, breaks down as follows. Prologue: Charlie at the café—a mere waiter. (i) Charlie in the park, comprising (a) his problems with the dog and (b) his rescue of Mabel. (ii) Charlie's first visit to Mabel's house; he passes himself off as an aristocrat. (iii) Back at the café: (a) Mabel's admirer discovers he's a waiter and (b) Charlie gets rid of the thug. (iv) Charlie's second visit to Mabel's house: the garden party. (v) The café: Mabel and friends go "slumming"; Charlie tries to pretend he is slumming too, but he is 'unmasked.' Epilogue: Charlie overpowers the frenzied proprietor but is spurned by Mabel. He returns to being a mere waiter.

4. The plot of *Caught in a Cabaret* in some important respects prefigures that of Chaplin's Essanay picture *The Tramp* (1915), whose pathetic finale is, by critical consensus, regarded as a turning point in his creative development. Setting aside the fact that in the earlier film Charlie is a waiter and in the later a tramp, it is noteworthy that in both films (i) Charlie heroically rescues a girl from her attacker(s); (ii) the girl is grateful, but Charlie expects love as well as—or instead of—gratitude; (iii) she brings him home and he gets involved in her world; (iv) another man has prior claims on her; and (v) Charlie loses the girl.

The final moment of *Caught in a Cabaret*—when a tearful Mabel rejects her savior, Charlie—actually teeters on the edge of pathos. If only Chaplin had held onto it a little longer or at least abbreviated the frenetic pie-in-the-face, shoot-em-up slapstick that immediately precedes it. . . . But Sennett would never have bought that kind of ending.

5. *Caught in a Cabaret* also looks forward thematically to Chaplin's later pictures. (i) The theme of *masquerade and its consequences*. In order to win Mabel, Charlie the waiter pretends to be what he is not— only to be "unmasked" and disillusioned. The same theme (or variations on it) is evident in many later films, including *The Idle Class* and *City*

Lights. (ii) The theme of *acceptance of protection = love*. When Charlie rescues Mabel (twice) he expects love, not gratitude. In many later films, including *The Gold Rush* and *The Circus*, he has the same expectations although the outcome is not invariably his disillusionment.

Caught in a Cabaret also deals rather blatantly with irreconcilable class differences. We see each class incongruously encountering the other on its home turf. Vainly trying to win Mabel by adjusting to her upper-class world, Charlie attempts two different masquerades. At the garden party, in an effort to behave like a gentleman, he comes across like Eliza Doolittle's father. His clothes are almost right but his behavior isn't. Huff perceptively notices how he "nearly exposes himself when he crosses his legs, revealing a hole in the sole of his shoe. He retrieves the situation by hanging his hat on the toe" (1952, 46). (An analog to this occurs in *A Woman of Paris* [1923], when Jean Millet tries to conceal his threadbare poverty from Marie St. Clair.) Yet Mabel is too infatuated with him at this point to recognize what he really is or to believe what the jealous admirer says about him. Later, when Mabel & co. go "slumming" to the café, Charlie tries to explain away his presence there and his waiter outfit by blithely declaring, "I'm a slummer myself." Actually, there are quite a few indications that Charlie doesn't belong in that kind of café environment in any role. He's a lousy waiter and dreamy type (see title: *"Tender memories"*) who ignores the local women and doesn't relate to anyone else in the joint. The thug, of course, belongs there even less than Charlie—greasy spoon cafés have their standards too—and he is ejected to the obvious satisfaction of the clientele.

6. In *Caught in a Cabaret* far from being a pest Charlie is more sinned against than sinning. He is a wage slave, ill-treated by his boss, and a would-be lover betrayed by a vengeful, cowardly rival and spurned by the woman he loves. He displays meanness only briefly— towards Chester Conklin, his fellow waiter (who more or less deserves it) and towards a small boy in the park (whom he misjudges). He steals food from the café—but some of it is probably for the dog. He gets drunk but never makes a nuisance of himself. Otherwise he comes across as a courteous, gutsy, lower-class romantic who makes the mistake of losing his heart to a snobbish socialite.

Charlie's most negative traits are demonstrated in his manners (or rather, his lack of them) and not in mistreating others. The most slobbish of waiters (without the excuse of being a novice like the singing waiter in *Modern Times*), he serves up food that he has dropped, uses the same dishcloth to wipe his nose and to wipe the tables, and drinks up the dregs of his customer's drinks. At the garden party, as a would-be gentleman, he quickly lapses into his true nature by blowing smoke into Mabel's face, getting drunk, drinking out of the bottle, burping and spitting, and wiping his mouth on his morning-coat. He's also a klutz who gets caught in his dog's lead and falls into the water while trying to get a drink.

On the other hand, he is polite to almost everyone he encounters—even his ill-tempered boss. He has an eye for the ladies, of course, but he's not a masher. Unfortunately, he loses out in all of his contacts with them. The ladies in the park prove to be more interested in his dog than in him. The women in the café are briefly impressed with the heroism but quickly turn their attention elsewhere. And Mabel, whom he rescues twice, gives him the brush-off when she discovers he's only a waiter. By contrast with his unsuccessful encounter with those ladies in the park, his brief but amicable meeting with a few street cronies suggests that he relates to men better than women.

In the course of the film Charlie proves on no less than three occasions that he's the only man with guts: he deals with the hoodlum in the park (when the cowardly admirer flees), he deals with the thug in the café (when Chester fails), and he alone deals with his berserk boss (when virtually everyone else flees). None of this nets him any permanent advantage. The proprietor shows no appreciation of Charlie's work as a bouncer, and ultimately, neither Charlie's heroism nor his love make any difference to Mabel when she discovers that he doesn't have "class."

7. This is yet another film in which we can see an enrichment of Chaplin's repertoire of comic business. Notice particularly his byplay with the cane, using one end of it to clean his fingernails and hooking it into his breast pocket when he shakes hands. The scene with the mallet anticipates his use of the same weapon in *The Fatal Mallet* (Keystone no. 15) and *The Tramp* (1915), his choreographed conflict with Chester looks forward to the more elaborate duel of Charlie and John Rand in *The Pawnshop*, and his exaggerated bowing and swaggering after rescuing Mabel and ejecting the thug are unmistakable foretastes of his vain behavior as a violinist in *The Vagabond* (1916).

OTHER VIEWS

"The typical Chaplin contrast between rich and poor can be seen in *Caught in a Cabaret*" (Mast 1979, 70).

"Most of his individual comedy was lost in the speed of each film, and in such pictures as *Cruel, Cruel Love* and *Caught in a Cabaret*, to name only two, he had little chance to prove his ability" (John Montgomery in McCaffrey 1971, 14).

"Chaplin's first full-blown, two-reel screenplay was another compromise. He coupled a Keystone custard-pie climax to a class-conscious plot that allowed passages of personal impromptu. Whilst not presenting Charlie the Tramp, he maintained much of the Tramp's character. His lowly waiter aimed at the higher life, and was not above imposture to achieve it. There was something of the dundreary dude from his first film here, but with greater depth. Charlie was no longer the con man out for cash at any cost; he was looking for love" (Gifford 1974, 41).

13.

Caught in the Rain

(1914)

Original working title: *All Wrong*
Other titles: *In the Park,** At It Again, Who Got Stung?;* French: *Un béguin de Charlot, Charlot et la somnambule, Charlot est encombrant;* German: *Vom Regen Überrascht;* Spanish: *Charlot se emborracha, Charlot y la sonambula;* Italian: *Sotto la pioggia*

Length: 1 reel; 984 feet (Asplund), 1015 feet (Lyons)
Playing time: 16 minutes at 16 frames per second
Producer: Keystone
Director: Chaplin
Screenplay: Chaplin
Photography: Frank D. Williams (?)
Cast:

A philandering tramp	Chaplin
A husband	Mack Swain
His wife	Alice Davenport
Another woman	Alice Howell

Finished or shipped: April 18, 1914
Released: May 4, 1914

SYNOPSIS

[This is one of the few of Chaplin's Keystones for which a description has previously been published: David Robinson provides a summary in *Chaplin: His Life and Art*, pp. 689–93. He claims to be describing the film in its most complete form, but several prints that I have seen show scenes that he does not mention (e.g., the piquant moment when the maid enters the first hotel room). The following description conflates details of my account with Robinson's summary.]

*Under this title the film is frequently confused with the Essanay Chaplin film of the same name.

Title: *A Big Thirst and a Little Wife.*

Park. A husband and wife are seated on a park bench. When he goes for a drink at the park cafeteria, she remains behind, sniffing at a rose.

Title: *A wrecker of homes.*

Charlie, at a nearby fountain, catches sight of her and smiles hopefully. Inadvertently, he sprays himself with water, almost knocking his hat off. She is amused at his antics but recoils when he takes her laughter as an invitation to sit beside her. But he immediately leaps up from the bench—having sat down on her thorny rose.

Title: *"Something attacked me in the rear."*

Pulling it from the seat of his pants, he graciously hands it to her, but she tosses it to the ground and haughtily turns her back on him.

Title: *"We seem to be getting along well together."*

He turns away from her, masking a grin, and crossing his legs. He rubs her dress with his boot. When she protests, he tucks the offending boot under his knee and tries to strike up a conversation with her, but she ignores him again. Charlie is not to be put off that easily, however.

Park cafeteria. The husband, in the process of lighting a cigar, notices his wife apparently flirting with another man.

Title: *"My wife—with a lady-killer."*

He is outraged.

Actually, she is waggling her finger at Charlie to protest his unwelcome attentions. But Charlie seizes the opportunity to grasp her hand and kiss it. Then he puts both his legs on her lap. She is appalled, but Charlie finds the situation highly entertaining until the husband dashes up and starts slapping him. When he objects, the husband grabs him by the neck and shoves him over the bench into some bushes.

Title: *"Take a back seat—you rusty Romeo."*

He angrily grabs his wife by the arm and marches her away. Charlie picks himself up and exits.

Street. The husband and wife are heading home.

Exterior of tavern. Charlie has arrived.

Title: *Love is a thirsty business.*

Exterior of hotel. The husband pushes his wife through the entrance. View of hotel foyer as they enter.

Exterior of tavern. Charlie exits. He is drunk. He strikes a match on a cop. The cop brandishes his nightstick. Charlie flees.

Hotel foyer. Husband and wife pass through. Quarreling furiously, they head upstairs to their room.

Street. Charlie, obviously drunk, is narrowly missed by a car. He runs into difficulties negotiating his passage across the trolley-car tracks.

Exterior of hotel. Charlie flops down on a bench. He tries to flirt with a young woman, but she shoves him back onto the bench and enters the hotel. He tries to pursue her, but she slams the hotel door in his face.

Hotel foyer. Charlie is just in time to see the young woman heading upstairs. He makes his way over to the reception desk, tripping over the bandaged, gouty foot of a guest (who is promptly knocked off his chair).

Hotel room. The wife looks on with disgust as her husband takes a swig from a liquor bottle. Then she grabs the bottle and takes a swig for herself.

Hotel foyer. Charlie tries to flirt with two girls, but they are unresponsive.

Title: *"Who does the hat with the feathers belong to?"*

Charlie looks into the hotel register to see if he can locate the young woman's room number. The gouty guest protests Charlie's treatment of him, but Charlie merely laughs and tosses the register at him.

Hotel room. Husband and wife are quarreling.

Title: *"After twenty years of married life I find you flirting with a scavenger."*

Hotel room. Quarrel continues.

Hotel foyer. Charlie tries to get up the staircase. He almost reaches the top, but falls on his face and slides all the way down. Undaunted, he makes a second attempt—this time followed by the gouty guest. Unsuccessful again, he falls backward—onto the gouty guest—and the two men land in a heap at the foot of the staircase. The two girls help them up. Now the gouty guest goes up first, assisted by the girls. Faring no better than Charlie, he falls backward with the two girls and the threesome lands on top of Charlie. At last, the girls get the gouty guest all the way up. Charlie then makes his third assault on the staircase. Tottering from one step to another, he finally loses his balance and topples backward, doing a somersault right into the foyer.

Hotel room. As a maid brings a jug into the room, the husband and wife suspend their quarrel. The maid sniggers as she sees the wife, fully dressed, sitting coyly on the bed while her husband stares vacantly at her. As soon as the maid leaves, the quarrel starts up again.

Staircase. Charlie is wearing a hat belonging to one of the girls. She dashes down the stairs and grabs it from him. He tries to chase her up the staircase, and after two more failures, he finally succeeds.

Upstairs corridor. Smoking a cigarette, Charlie comes upon the gouty guest leaving his room. He kicks him back through the door; then he starts to lurch drunkenly along the corridor.

Hotel room. The wife is assaulting her husband and he endeavors to pacify her. They sit on the bed.

Corridor. Charlie tries to unlock the door of their room using a cigarette as a key.

Title: *"Ah, locked!"*

Corridor. Realizing that the door is unlocked, he enters the room.

Hotel room. The husband and wife, now locked in a passionate embrace, are horrified at his intrusion, but Charlie hasn't noticed them. Looking in a mirror, he tries to brush his hat as if it's his hair. He takes a swig of liquor, wipes his mouth on the wife's hairpiece, and inadvertently tosses it aside—into the husband's face. Seething with anger, the husband rises from the bed, accuses his wife of an intrigue with the intruder, and boots Charlie into the corridor.

Title: *"Out you go—you he-vamp."*

Hotel room. Husband and wife immediately resume their quarrel.

Corridor. He picks himself up and staggers into . . .

Opposite room. He starts undressing. He wipes his boots on his shirtfront and gets caught up in his own pants. He is wearing pajamas beneath his clothes. Then he flops into bed for a well-earned rest.

First hotel room. The husband gives up on the quarrel. Leaving his wife to sleep things off, he exits.

Opposite room. Charlie removes a hairbrush from his bed.

Corridor. The husband heads down the corridor—perhaps to solace himself at the nearest tavern.

Opposite room. Charlie places his boots under his pillow.

Title: *Midnight—the sleep walker.*

First hotel room. The wife rises from the bed and starts to walk in her sleep.

Street. The husband is caught in a rainstorm. He heads back to the hotel.

Opposite room. The wife enters, sleepwalking. She sits down on Charlie's bed. Charlie, also asleep, reaches out and touches her. Waking up, he is astonished to find her in his room.

Title: *"Whoever sent you must have owed me a grudge."*

Still in her sleep, she locates his pants—as if they are her husband's—and searches for money. Charlie gently removes them from her grasp.

First hotel room. The husband, soaking wet, has returned to discover that his wife is missing. Alarmed, he calls out for her.

Opposite room. Charlie hears the frantic husband. Anxious to allay his suspicions, he dashes into . . .

Corridor. He tells the husband:

Title: *"I'm itching to throttle someone."*

Corridor. The husband stamps away angrily.

Opposite room. Re-entering, Charlie is shocked to find the wife sleeping in his bed. He wakes her. She gets frantic. He tries to pacify her.

Corridor. He sees that the coast is clear.

Taking the wife by the hand, he leads her back to her own room.

Title: *"Keep calm—I'll be quite all right."*

Foyer. The husband questions the desk clerk and finds that his wife has not left the hotel. He heads upstairs again.

First hotel room. Charlie tries to calm the wife by offering her a drink. She refuses—so he takes a swig himself. He is about to leave when he spies the husband along the corridor. The wife hastily pushes him out onto the balcony.

Balcony. It's raining, and Charlie gets drenched.

Exterior of hotel. A passing cop notices him and thinks he's a burglar. Pulling out his gun, he blasts away.

Balcony. Charlie is hit in the rear end.

First hotel room. Howling with pain, Charlie leaps in, landing on top of the husband.

Charlie dashes back to his own room for safety.

Hotel foyer. Several Keystone Kops burst into the hotel.

Corridor. The Kops try to seize the husband. He manages to convince them that it is Charlie they are after. They rush to Charlie's room to arrest him.

Opposite room. Charlie regains his courage, flings open the door.

Corridor. He knocks down the Kops. They flee ignominiously while Charlie and the husband square off. Charlie kicks him into . . .

Opposite room. The husband flops onto Charlie's bed.

Corridor. The wife faints in Charlie's arms; the pair of them collapse onto the floor.

COMMENTS

1. This one-reeler was a landmark film for Chaplin: his first movie as solo director. It was also *his* story and script, and *he* was the star.

Surprisingly, in view of his struggles for a chance to direct, he tells us:

When I started directing my first picture, I was not as confident as I thought I would be; in fact, I had a slight attack of panic. But after Sennett saw the first day's work I was reassured. . . . *Caught in the Rain* . . . was not a world-beater, but it was funny and quite a success. When I finished it, I was anxious to know Sennett's reaction. I waited for him as he came out of the projection room. "Well, are you ready to start another?" he said. (Chaplin 1964, 151–52)

Chaplin provides two other impressions of what it was like to direct his first film. In *My Autobiography* he notes:

> The mechanics of directing were simple in those days. I had only to know my left from my right for entrances and exits. If one exited right from a scene, one came in left in the next scene; if one exited towards the camera, one entered with one's back to the camera in the next scene. These, of course, were primary rules. But with more experience I found that placing of a camera was not only psychological but articulated a scene; in fact, it was the basis of cinematic style. (1964, 151)

In *Charlie Chaplin's Own Story* Chaplin is quoted thus:

> Every morning when I reached the stage in make-up the actors who were to play with me stood waiting to learn what their parts were to be. I myself did not always know, but when I had limbered up a bit by a jig or clog dance and the camera began to click, ideas came fast enough. I told the other actors how to play their parts, played them myself to show how it should be done; played my own part enthusiastically, teased the camera man, laughed and whistled and turned handsprings. The clicking camera took it all in; later, in the negative room, we chose and cut and threw away film, picking out the best scenes, rearranging the reels, shaping up the final picture to be shown on the screens. I liked it all; I was never still a minute in the studio and never tired. (1916, 226–27; 1985, 135)

Sennett gives a different perspective on the film.

> When *Caught in the Rain* was shown in our screening room we had an unusual audience. Every director was present. I sat in my big rocking chair to see what would happen. I could hear Dell Henderson, Del Lord, Pathe Lehrman, and my other comedy makers suck in lungfuls of air, getting ready to let loose jeers and catcalls. Instead they applauded from the first scene. My rocking chair went into action and stayed at full gallop. (Sennett and Shipp 1954, 164)

2. Some critics have expressed disappointment that *Caught in the Rain* was not a more ambitious film, perhaps an embryonic version of a Mutual comedy or at least one of the better Essanays. Actually, D. W. Griffith's *The Adventures of Dollie* (1908) is, by any standards, a less promising directorial debut, but I can't recall anyone describing *Dollie* as "disappointing." Griffith, we know, had to be persuaded to switch from acting to directing, but Chaplin set his heart on directing almost from the outset. Once he had been given the opportunity, he wanted to go on directing. So he took no chances and created *Caught in the Rain* out of the motifs of three of his previous movies: (i) Charlie in a park trying to pick up another man's woman (*Twenty Minutes of Love*), (ii)

Charlie in a hotel foyer trying to pick up unattached women (*Mabel's Strange Predicament*), and (iii) Charlie in the house/flat of the woman he has been chasing, confronting her jealous husband (*His Favorite Pastime*). Chaplin reappears in his tipsy Tramp-as-pest role, and he even contrives to get the Keystone Kops into the picture. Brief and action-packed as it is, the film is one of the better-paced early Keystones, allowing adequately for Chaplin's comic business, for some clever details of characterization (especially in scenes involving the husband and wife), and for the inevitable slapstick finale. McCabe says: "Chaplin began to see that the Keystone rush-rush had a certain inherent virtue: swiftness allowed poor gags to be quickly left behind and, more importantly, the more gags in a film the better" (1978, 58). On the face of it there seems to be nothing in *Caught in the Rain* that hadn't previously been approved by Sennett and the movie-going public. Yet it caused something of a stir when it was originally released. Some American viewers considered it risqué. Uno Asplund (1976, 23) says that in Sweden it was banned no less than three times.

3. The structure of the film is as follows: Prologue—a park. Charlie tries to pick up the wife. (i) Hotel foyer. (a) Charlie tries to pick up girls; (b) his efforts to ascend the staircase. (ii) Charlie intrudes into the couple's room; the husband ejects him. (iii) The wife sleepwalks into Charlie's room. Charlie conceals her presence from her husband. (iv) Charlie returns the wife to *her* room. She conceals *his* presence from her husband. (v) The balcony. A cop shoots Charlie in the behind. Epilogue—hotel corridor. The cops flee; Charlie overcomes the husband; he collapses with the wife. The film has an obvious pattern of intrusion and concealment.

4. The hinge or crux of *Caught in the Rain* may not be immediately evident. It resides in the fact that Charlie, who tried to pick up the wife in the park, is no longer interested in her sexually when she sleepwalks into his bedroom. (If he *had* resumed making advances toward her, the film would, obviously, have taken a very different and quite nasty turn.) Nothing in the film directly accounts for Charlie's change of attitude. There are various possibilities, however. He's afraid of the lady's husband, and is possibly scared of creating a scandal that will get him thrown out of the hotel. It may also be that he is sobering up and takes a good look at her for the first time. (Gifford [1974] says, "You would have to be pretty tipsy to fancy Miss Davenport in or out of her tentlike nightie.") Perhaps extending a would-be flirtation as far as adultery is more than he had in mind. Or perhaps he doesn't want to get involved in sexual situations that he didn't initiate and can't control. Whatever the explanation, the film in effect shows us two rather different Charlies.

As we have noticed in comments on previous films, the park functions as a neutral zone where characters (the men, at least) feel free to abandon their inhibitions. In the park scene that opens *Caught in the Rain*, the husband casually wanders off for a drink on his own. (Later on, when he's back in the hotel, we see that his wife forces him to share the bottle with her.) In the park, Charlie's treatment of the wife begins with a display of graciousness (he hands her the rose he has just sat on) but quickly degenerates into downright impudence. He does not repeat any of this behavior toward her in the hotel.

Misperception, which evolves into a major theme of Chaplin's later films, initially motivates Charlie's behavior toward the wife. He takes her laughter at his antics as an invitation to join her on the park bench. Misperception also motivates the husband's reaction to the wife: he believes that she is flirting with Charlie—and this results in their quarrel. At the hotel, misperception (or concern for it) predominates. Only the viewer ever perceives correctly the fluctuating nature of the couple's relationship. (What's going on here is basic to Chaplin's comedy, indeed, to his overall vision of the human condition: *audience perception of the multiple misperceptions of characters*—an underscoring of the comic-pathetic notion that human beings seldom see or understand more than the surface impressions of their fellows.) Husband and wife put on a false front for the maid. Chaplin wittily capsulates the way in which married couples conceal the truth about their relationships from other people. Mast notes:

> As soon as the maid leaves, they [husband and wife] begin screaming at each other again. This bit brilliantly sums up the difference between real feelings and external appearances, the respectable class and the serving class, the fervor of rhetoric and the tepidness of a passion that can be quickly turned on and off. (1979, 71)

When Charlie wanders into their room (after misperceiving a cigarette as a door key), he doesn't even notice them. When the wife wanders into *his* room, the focus shifts to their fears for the husband's misperception of *their* connection. Then, thrust out of the couple's room, onto the balcony, Charlie is misperceived as a burglar and gets shot by a cop. Other cops rush in and try to seize the husband under the mistaken impression that *he's* the man they're after. The film's final moments—the husband alone in Charlie's bed while his wife, in Charlie's arms, collapses onto the floor, is a cunning invitation to *audience* misperception. When the wife faints into his arms, Charlie falls to the floor with her simply because she is too heavy to hold up. Yet this comic finale was misread by some of its original viewers as a scene of adultery triumphant. A plot summary by the Swedish censors—who banned the film until 1970—shows them trapped in their own misperceptions: "Undressed, he [Charlie] is lying in bed when the married woman, equally undressed, and walking in her sleep, comes in to him and joins him in bed. After various adventures thus lightly costumed, they sink down together" (Asplund 1976, 23).

5. Two scenes I have already mentioned draw attention to Chaplin's practice of duplicating actions in order to make significant comparisons and contrasts. I refer to (i) Charlie entering the couple's room without noticing them, and (ii) the wife sleepwalking into Charlie's room without noticing him. From one scene to the other the tables are turned on the masher. As a somnambulist, the wife's behavior toward Charlie in his bedroom is a variation on *his* behavior toward *her* in the park, and his reactions in the later scene are not unlike hers in the earlier one. *Caught in the Rain* has numerous other duplications like this. (i) Charlie tries to pick up a married woman in the park; later he tries to pick up unattached girls inside and outside the hotel. (ii) He repeats his efforts to ascend the staircase. (iii) In his hotel room the husband takes a swig of liquor; later Charlie wanders in and does the same. (iv) The maid, Charlie, and the wife all enter rooms unexpectedly. (v) In *his* room Charlie conceals the wife from her husband; in *her* room the wife conceals Charlie from her husband. (vi) Both Charlie and the husband get caught in the rain—with different consequences. (vii) A cop mistakenly shoots Charlie; other cops mistakenly try to arrest the husband. (viii) At different points in the film, first the wife and then the husband wind up in Charlie's bed. Such duplications become structurally integral to Chaplin's film *The Circus* (1928), in which virtually everything consequential is repeated—with significant variations. (See also *Between Showers* note 6.)

6. The film contains highly memorable comic business, much of it to be reprised in later movies by Chaplin—and other comedians. Huff (1952, 54) notes that *A Night Out* (Essanay 1915) is a Chaplin "expansion" of *Caught in the Rain* and *The Rounders* (Keystone no. 26). Flowers, repeatedly important symbols in Chaplin's movies, first show up in *Caught in the Rain*. In the context of that opening scene, Charlie's sitting on a rose and discovering it has thorns is quite piquant. When the lady brusquely tosses it away after he has graciously handed it to her, her action becomes the signal for him to woo her with a hilarious combination of charm and impudence that would eventually be borrowed in toto by Groucho Marx. He kisses her hand—then puts both his legs in her lap. (Compare with Groucho's treatment of the blonde vamp in *Horse Feathers*). Charlie's ill-treatment of the gouty guest looks forward to his even more aggressive mistreatment of gouty Eric Campbell in *The Cure* (1917), while his multiple assaults on the staircase prefigure

his similar efforts in another Mutual film, *One A.M.* (1916). Sobel and Francis (1977, 213) notice the "imaginative leap" of the alcoholic in the scenes where Charlie tries to open a door with a cigarette and when he pours whiskey on his hair instead of hair oil. (In the latter scene, he also brushes his hat as if it's his hair, calling to mind the similar behavior of the drunken spouse in Chaplin's *The Idle Class* [1921]). Many commentators have drawn attention one of the clever touches that characterizes the wife: in her sleep, as a reflex action, she searches Charlie's pockets as if they're her husband's. This is the sort of wifely behavior that Chaplin will enlarge on in *Pay Day* (1922), one of the few films in which Charlie himself appears as a married man. But *Caught in the Rain* and Chaplin's very next film, *A Busy Day*, are the earliest expressions of a jaundiced view of married life that probably reflects the comedian's memories of his parents' stormy relationship.

OTHER VIEWS

"Sennett began to realize that Chaplin would do better on his own . . . starting with his thirteenth film, *Caught in the Rain* (May, 1914), [Chaplin's films] . . . became a combination of the Keystone style and his own ideas" (Lahue 1966, 79).

"The lady came 'sleepwalking' into his room, arms outstretched. And here Chaplin extended himself. In a brief moment, his features and actions represented desire, fear of the husband, and contempt" (Hoyt 1977, 58–59).

14.

⌒

A Busy Day
(1914)

Original working title: *San Pedro*
Other titles: [A] *Militant Suffragette, Lady Charlie, Busy as Can Be;*
French: *La jalousie de Charlot, Madame Charlot;* German: *Ein aufre-
gender Tag;* Spanish: *Charlot señorita;* Italian: *Una giornata indaffarata*

Length: Split reel; 364 feet (Asplund), 441 feet (Lyons)*
Playing time: 6 minutes at 16 frames per second
Producer: Keystone
Director: Chaplin
Story: Chaplin
Photography: Frank D. Williams (?)
Cast:

Jealous wife	Chaplin
Her husband	Mack Swain
The other woman	Phyllis Allen

Location: San Pedro, California
Finished or shipped: April 18, 1914
Released: May 7, 1914

SYNOPSIS

Title: Gathered to see the parade and hear the band play.
Charlie (minus mustache) is a garishly dressed wife attending a
parade with her husband. As the film opens they have just arrived at
the bleachers and are quarreling. The wife sits down, leans backward,
and nearly falls off her seat. She shoves at Mack as if he's responsible.
He threatens her with clenched fist; she retaliates. Obviously hot,
Mack removes his hat and fans himself with it. She insists on being
fanned too. Then she blows her nose into her skirt. The woman to her

*Originally released with an educational short, *The Morning Paper*, directed by Joseph
Maddern.

left offers a handkerchief, but she pushes it away. At this point we catch the first glimpse of her umbrella.

The parade comes into view: a decorated car, two soldiers on horseback, a marching band, etc.

At the sight of the parade the wife grimaces, taps Mack's knee, and claps excitedly. Meanwhile, Mack is exchanging smiles with the young woman to his right. She gets up and walks away. He follows her, unnoticed by his wife. The wife gropes for her husband's knee and discovers that he has vanished. Frantic, she looks for him in all directions.

Rear view of a movie cameraman filming the parade. Hand-in-hand with the woman, Mack dashes across the path of the parade. The wife catches sight of her errant husband. Appalled, she topples back onto a man and a woman seated on the bleachers. She leaps into the air and runs across the path of the parade until she is out of sight. Then she returns and gesticulates at some soldiers in the parade.

Now the director comes forward and asks her to get out of the way. He takes hold of her fur collar and shows her the movie-camera. But instead of leaving, she steps back and poses for the camera. Once again the director takes her by the collar. She raises her boot to kick him but restrains herself. The director brings over a cop who orders her to clear off. In reply, she kicks the cop on the rump. When he falls, she kicks him again. Now the director makes a sudden leap at her and shoves her back onto a second cop at the bandstand. The cameraman resumes his filming of the parade. Meanwhile, the second cop boots the wife back toward the cameraman. She sprawls on the ground, does a half somersault and gets up. Then she raises her skirt and poses for the camera. The director tries to reason with her once more. Then he gives her a slight push. She brandishes her umbrella and raises her foot threateningly. He pushes her back onto the second cop at the bandstand. Holding onto the bandstand post, she boots the second cop onto the first one. Then she gets up, blows her nose, and weeps. Hands on hips, she looks into the camera with a grief-stricken expression on her face.

Suddenly she spies Mack and the woman joking together in front of a fence. Clenching her teeth, she pulls back her shoulders, hitches back her sleeves and lifts her skirt to make a violent kicking motion. She advances stealthily on the couple from the rear and pokes at the woman with her umbrella. The couple are thunderstruck. Then the woman flees. The wife aims a kick at her but slips and falls. She gets up and turns to Mack with a disarming smile. He smiles back. But her smile suddenly freezes, and she belts him on the jaw. He falls. She beats him down again with the umbrella and kicks him. He gets up again and strikes back, pushing her onto the second cop who slaps her face. She promptly knocks the cop flat. But he gets up and shoves her back at her husband. Undaunted, she boots Mack in the stomach several times until he seizes the opportunity to knock her down. Now the second cop dashes over and tries to grab the wife who by this time is throttling Mack. She shoves the cop aside; Mack collapses. The cop renews his attack but is booted away. Now Mack recovers and kicks his wife in the belly. Furious, he wipes the sweat from his brow.

At the bandstand the wife reengages the second cop. She shoves him in the face. He punches her jaw and orders her to clear off. In response, she boots him in the stomach. He leaps back onto her, but she fells him again, beats him over the head with her umbrella, and chases him away. Then she thumbs her nose at him.

Mack is visible among a crowd of bystanders. He looks upset. (Because of his wife or because he has lost sight of the other woman?) He watches speedboats racing in the harbor. The woman appears. They are delighted to see each other again.

Bandstand. The wife sashays in time to the music. She raises her skirt and climbs onto the grandstand platform. Rear view of her bow legs in ankle socks and men's shoes. Enraptured by the music, she swings on the grandstand post, loses her balance, and falls off the platform. Smiling, she does some high-kick dance steps—then touches her cheek coyly. After that she rumbas and does some back-kicks. The second cop reappears and orders her to leave. She promptly shoves him in the face and kicks dust back at him.

Mack and the woman are laughing together. He points out what is going on in the harbor.

The wife wanders over to the fence, leans against it, and weeps (with her back to the camera). Eventually, she turns, grimaces into the camera, and blows her nose into her skirt. Hands on hips, she glares ferociously in Mack's direction.

Bursting between her husband and the other woman, she strikes her rival and exchanges slaps with Mack. For a change, she belly-bumps him.

A low-angle shot of the crowded jetty. To the extreme right we see the husband and wife fighting. Mack suddenly shoves her off the jetty. She does a couple of somersaults before hitting the water with a big splash. Mack looks horrified.

Close-up of the wife splashing helplessly in the water. She disappears—then comes up for air. Exhausted at last, she sinks beneath the waves as the film comes to an end.

COMMENTS

1. *A Busy Day* is the first of three films in which Chaplin appeared as a woman. The other two are *The Masquerader* (Keystone no. 24) and the Essanay film, *A Woman* (1915). Detailed comparisons of these three films will be found in my comments on *A Woman*. It suffices to say here

that *A Busy Day* differs from the two later films in one major respect. In the first movie he is *supposed* to be a woman. In the later movies his female characterizations are merely masquerades.

2. *A Busy Day* is a companion piece to its immediate predecessor, *Caught in the Rain:* both films are about jealous spouses. However, *A Busy Day* is usually described as Chaplin's attempt to repeat the success of *Kid's Auto Race*, and it is similar to that film in two ways. (i) The sequence in which the wife obstructs the filming of the parade is, as Asplund (1976, 40) says, "a direct copy" of the earlier picture. However—unlike *Kid's Auto Race*—the film as a whole is not concerned with the Tramp character, with self-reflexivity, or with mirroring an off screen conflict of personalities. Moreover, the sequence in question is only an incidental *part* of a movie with a definable plot— which *Kid's Auto Race* doesn't have. (ii) A prefatory note to Blackhawk's prints of *A Busy Day* correctly states that both films "used a public event as the basis of improvized comedy scenes." The public event in the latter case was a town parade to celebrate the opening of San Pedro's new harbor. (A banner identifying the festivity is visible in at least one view of the parade.) Taking a leaf out of Lehrman's book, Chaplin rushed to San Pedro, dressed up in some of Alice Davenport's clothes, and made his film in two or three hours. For this demonstration of 'professionalism,' Sennett rewarded him with a bonus of twenty-five dollars.

3. The action of the film revolves around the two moments when the wife catches up with her philandering spouse. The first movement signals the wife's triumph: her remorseless battering of the husband. The second signals the wife's defeat: she is ditched into the ocean by her spouse. Note how the wife experiences one or more upbeat experiences prior to each of these moments: i.e., pleasure at watching the parade, frustration of the cops and the director, and a dance at the bandstand.

Despite its brevity this six-minute farce is action-packed. Seven sequences are discernible: (i) Prologue: Husband and wife quarrel, (ii) Forward movement: He chases after another woman, (iii) She tackles the director and the two cops, (iv) She tackles her husband, (v) Renewed assault on the second cop, (vi) Her dance, (vii) Finale: She's tossed off the jetty.

4. Female impersonation is probably as old as theater itself. Today it is usually associated with burlesque and farce, but in its earliest form we find it in tragedy. Euripides' *The Bacchae* (406 B.C.) has no less than four male characters who appear in women's garb. The play drew upon the myth of Dionysus and its attendant religious cult in which transvest-

ism was an established ritual. During the Christian era, female impersonation in the theater came about as a result of the exclusion of women from religious ceremonies. In the liturgical drama of the Middle Ages female characters were either played by boys or not represented at all. The secular mummers' plays seem to have introduced the earliest comic types in "drag," among them a boisterous, aggressive female character who was the remote precursor of the English pantomime "dames"—as well as the wife of *A Busy Day*. During the Elizabethan period it was widely held that the theater was an immoral place and therefore unsuitable for women. In consequence, boys and men were skillfully trained to perform all the female roles, among them some of the most sophisticated and demanding characters in Shakespeare. This practice came to an end with the Restoration of 1660 when actresses were at last introduced into the English theater. However, female impersonation in the theater was soon revived as a feature of pantomime. (John Rich played Mother Goose early in the eighteenth century.) By the end of the Victorian era it had become popular not only in the form of pantomime "dame" characters but also in vaudeville/ music hall "drag" acts. Years before Chaplin made his first film, the cinema adopted female impersonation from vaudeville as a popular subject for comedy. Typical examples of cross-dressing performances in film before 1914 are *The Old Maid in the Horsecar* (Edison 1901), *Dinah's Defeat* (Biograph 1904), and *Nearsighted Mary* (Lubin 1909).

On the subject of cross-dressing and "drag" performances, see further: Peter Ackroyd, *Dressing Up, Transvestism and Drag: The History of an Obsession* (New York: Simon and Schuster, 1979), Rebecca Bell-Metereau, *Hollywood Androgyny* (New York: Columbia University Press, 1985).

5. The obstreperous wife of *A Busy Day* was probably modeled on working-class viragos in the slums of Lambeth that Chaplin observed in his childhood. His parents also showed him all that he needed to know about marital discord. The female impersonations of Dan Leno, one of the great music hall stars of the Victorian era, may also have influenced this character. (Leno's costume as a pantomime dame in *Cinderella* looked strikingly similar to the wife's outfit in *A Busy Day*. See the illustration in Peter Leslie's study of the music hall, *A Hard Act to Follow* [New York and London: Paddington Press, 1978], p. 49.)

6. In any consideration of comedy based on female impersonation or cross-dressing the following questions will be useful. First, what *kind* of impersonation is it? Is the emphasis on a male *performer* who is supposed to be a female character (e.g., Chaplin in *A Busy Day*) or on a male *character* who is masquerading as a female character (e.g., the

aunt in *Charley's Aunt*, or the characters played by Jack Lemmon and Tony Curtis in *Some Like It Hot*). Second, on which of these factors does the comedy primarily depend: (i) cross-dressing, (ii) audience *awareness* that the performer is male, (iii) audience *discovery* that the performer is male, (iv) audience *awareness* of masquerade, (v) audience *discovery* of masquerade, (vi) the activities of the masquerader in a predominantly female environment, (vii) a supposedly female *character* displaying typically male traits, (viii) a male *performer* displaying typically female traits, or (ix) a male *performer* displaying highly exaggerated (or parodied) female traits?

Obviously, some of these questions do not apply to *A Busy Day*. But those that *do* apply indicate the nature of Chaplin's impersonation. What we see is not supposed to be a masquerade, and after the first minute or so, when we have had our laugh at the initial sight of Chaplin in women's clothes, the comedy does not depend on cross-dressing but on factors (viii) and (ix). It also depends on our willingness to accept or believe that the other characters unequivocally take Chaplin's character to be a woman.

The "typical" and exaggerated female traits in the portrayal reveal some of Chaplin's views of married women, if not of women in general. Husbands, as we have seen in *Caught in the Rain*, can be very jealous. The wife of *A Busy Day* is even more so. She has reason to be, of course. (By contrast to the first film in which the wife is quite innocent, in the second, the husband really *is* a philanderer.) The wife is also possessive, querulous, and aggressive. As in *Between Showers*, the umbrella she brandishes is unmistakably phallic and symbolizes her exclusive "rights" as a married woman. Being married (i.e., having "trapped" her man), she no longer sees any need for sex appeal and is hell-bent on preventing her spouse from responding to the sex appeal of other women. Paradoxically, she is also vain enough to expect the cinematographer to take her picture instead of the parade, and for this she even temporarily suspends her pursuit of the errant Mack. Chaplin's depiction of the wife particularly emphasizes her attitude to authority. In her marriage she's determined to "wear the pants"; at the same time she violently opposes any other authority. Three scenes somewhat mitigate this generally negative characterization. She exhibits a childlike pleasure in watching the parade. Later, she dances to express her delight in music. (Admittedly, it could also be interpreted as a premature dance of triumph.) This solo dance scene is, in its own way, rather charming as well as funny. It's also a first shot at the kind of clumsy-graceful terpsichorean performance that comes off even more charmingly in *Sunnyside* (1919). The third scene verges on pathos. After all her violent efforts to cure Mack of his philandering, she suddenly catches sight of him flirting with the other woman, and breaks into tears. Despite the usual behavior of this termagant, we are ready to be touched—but Chaplin immediately breaks the spell and gets on with the slapstick.

OTHER VIEWS

"In *A Busy Day* he actually combines aspects of the female roles. He is a battle-ax when he catches husband Mack Swain with another woman, and . . . he tries to wring laughter from his 'unfeminine' behavior, including repeatedly wiping his nose with his dress. Presumably at this stage Chaplin's fame was not such that he needed to make his identity as a 'woman' separate from his tramp character (he plays only the woman role in this film), but in the other films, he plays both male and female roles" (Kamin 1984, 66).

15.

The Fatal Mallet

(1914)

Original working title: *The Knockout*
Other titles: *Hit Him Again, The Pile Driver, The Rival Suitors;*
French: *Briseur de crânes, Le maillet de Charlot;* German: *Der Holz-hammer;* Spanish: *Charlot y su maleta, El mazo de Charlot;* Italian: *Charlot e il martello*

Length: 1 reel: 1063 feet (Asplund), 1120 feet (Lyons)*
Playing time: 18 minutes at 16 frames per second
Producer: Keystone
Director(s): Possibly a collaboration of Chaplin, Sennett, and Mabel Normand
Screenplay: Chaplin and/or Sennett
Photography: Frank D. Williams (?)
Cast:

The rival	Chaplin
The girl	Mabel Normand
Her admirer	Mack Sennett
Another rival	Mack Swain

Film completed or shipped: May 16, 1914
Released: June 1, 1914

SYNOPSIS

A Park. Charlie, a tramp, looking somewhat disconsolate, is standing beside a shed with his hands in his pockets. He points toward the girl (Mabel Normand) who is being escorted by her doltish admirer

---

*Note that the Glenn Photo prints—which appear to be in wide circulation—are only about half the length of the original film. Raoul Sobel and David Francis (1977, 186) publish a still that is unmistakably from the film (Mabel is wearing the right costume), showing Charlie delivering a swift kick to Mabel's behind. This scene does not occur in any American prints of the film that I examined. Gifford makes reference to the same scene, which presumably exists in British prints of *The Fatal Mallet.*

(Mack Sennett). Hand on cheek, he ponders the situation. Mabel evidently wants to sit on the swing, but Sennett has other ideas. He leads her past the swing and over to a tree where he puts his arm around her. She resists. Charlie follows them at a discreet distance. He stops, flips his cane upward, and accidentally hits himself on the head. Sennett removes his hat and then demonstrates how he can kick. Mabel is unimpressed.

From beside the swing, Charlie hurls a brick at Sennett. The latter dodges and the brick skims Mabel. Furious, she points at Charlie. Sennett imitates her. Then she picks up the brick and hurls it back, knocking Charlie off the swing. Mabel is obviously annoyed with Sennett for doing nothing. Unperturbed, he flexes his muscles and demonstrates how he intends to kick Charlie. Flinging out his arms he accidentally strikes her face. When he pats her consolingly, she slaps him. Now Charlie approaches with his arms open, appealingly. He confronts Sennett and glares at him. Mabel raises her hand to strike him, but he warns her not to—so she clenches her fist and signals to Sennett to deal with the intruder. Sennett moves toward Charlie hesitantly. He makes faces at him and then demonstrates how far he can spit. Charlie thumbs his nose in reply. Smiling, Sennett pulls up his sleeves and pretends he's about to attack—but it's a mere feint—he simply scratches the back of his neck. However, Charlie is taken unaware. He steps back and loses his hat. Sennett guffaws. Mabel remains unimpressed. Charlie strikes Sennett on the head while his back is turned. Mabel now watches, aghast, as Sennett flops, semi-consciously, against a tree. Charlie now demonstrates how far *he* can spit.

Another rival (Mack Swain) appears at the swing. He is stylishly dressed: swinging a cane and wearing a straw boater, a black tie, white shirt and pants, and a black jacket with a flower in the buttonhole. Mabel notices him and dashes over eagerly. He lifts her up and gives her a kiss. Meanwhile, Charlie examines the inside of Sennett's jacket and taps him on the chest. Sennett recovers consciousness. He points his finger at Charlie and spits into his hands as a gesture of defiance. Before he can do anything else, Charlie leaps toward him, his jacket half off. Sennett recoils. Once more Charlie shows how far he can spit. Then his attention is caught by the sight of Mack sitting on the swing with Mabel perched on his knee. Mack tickles her arm. They laugh.

Whistling and carrying a couple of bricks, Sennett and Charlie approach the happy couple from the rear. They disagree as to who should strike first, but Charlie wins. With all his might he brings his brick down on Mack's head. Mack shows no awareness of this. Sennett does the same—with the same result. The two attackers wipe their foreheads in consternation. Then, in unison, both slam their bricks down on Mack's head. Mack removes his hat and looks skyward to see if a bird has used him for target practice. Then he turns quite casually and notices Charlie and Sennett. Charlie hurls his brick at him and flees. Mack staggers but doesn't fall. Now Sennett hurls *his* brick and takes to his heels. Mack chases after them.

The shed. Charlie and Sennett dash inside and shut the door. Mack arrives outside, but he has lost sight of them. Unseen by him they peek out a window over his head. Vowing vengeance, Mack starts creeping round the shed. Sennett emerges, hits him with another brick, and retreats into the shed. Now Mabel reaches the shed. They peek out at her. She leans against the door. Sennett pushes it open, shoving her in the rump. He retreats once more. Charlie joins him in observing Mack's fruitless search. Exhausted, Mack leans against the door. Now Charlie pushes it open, shoving Mack in the rump. Suspicious, Mack peers into the shed—but it looks dark, and he assumes that no one is inside.

Back at the tree, Mabel calls Mack over to her. Charlie and Sennett creep out of the shed. The latter loses no time in hurling another brick at Mack who comes tearing back posthaste. Sennett beats a hasty retreat, carrying several bricks in his arms. Close behind him, Charlie seizes one of the bricks and flings it at their pursuer. He stops Mack in his tracks. He is about to hurl a second brick when Sennett turns and beats him on the rump. Charlie tries to retaliate with a kick but he slips. Recovered, Mack grabs an armful of bricks and continues his pursuit. He observes his adversaries about to sneak into another shed and promptly hurls a brick that knocks Charlie backward through the door.

Inside the shed. Charlie collapses alongside a packing case on which a large mallet is resting. Sennett scurries in and shuts the door. Charlie sits up dazedly.

A shot of Mabel counting her admirers on her fingers and shrugging her shoulders.

Inside the shed. Sennett peeks out the door and gets a brick full in the face. Charlie gets up and stretches his limbs. Sennett warns him that Mack is still outside, but Charlie wants to see for himself. As he peeks out, a brick hits him squarely on the nose. Sennett looks thoughtful. To arouse him, Charlie gives him a kick on the rump. Sennett returns the kick. Charlie is about to launch a full attack when Sennett points to the mallet. Charlie seizes it and waves it threateningly. Then he leaps forward. Sennett retreats. He flourishes the mallet in Sennett's face.

Outside. Mack heads back to Mabel. Sitting down on a heap of hay, she sighs and rests her chin in her hands.

Inside the shed. His cane hooked in his breast pocket, Charlie practices swinging the mallet. He flexes his muscles, looks thoughtfully at Sennett and then at the mallet. Gently removing Sennett's hat, he taps him on the head. Sennett staggers and clutches his forehead. Charlie considerately hands the hat back. He contemplates the mallet once more. Sennett retreats. Charlie looks toward the door (in Mack's direction) and then back at Sennett. The latter stares at the mallet and strokes his chin: he has grasped Charlie's purpose at last. Holding the mallet, Charlie heads toward the door. Then he hesitates, grins, and invites Sennett to go first. Sennett obligingly peeks out—whereupon Charlie prods him in the rear with the mallet handle. When Sennett turns around angrily, Charlie nonchalantly orders him to make haste. They creep out of the shed.

Sennett peers cautiously around the shed door and Charlie taps him on the rump. They argue briefly. Then Charlie notices that the shed door is unlocked. He hands the mallet to Sennett and turns around to fix it. A fatal error. Sennett immediately raps Charlie across the rump. Charlie strikes back with his cane, denting Sennett's hat. When the latter raises the mallet in a threatening gesture, Charlie merely thumbs his nose and marches off whistling. Sennett, carrying the mallet, follows rather sheepishly.

At the hay bale. Mack is on his knees to Mabel. He moves forward to embrace her, but she no longer appears interested in him.

Charlie has taken charge of the mallet. When Sennett protests he threatens him once more.

Charlie suddenly notices Mack joking with Mabel. He raises the mallet, accidentally striking Sennett on the nose. Sennett yelps and Charlie laughs uproariously.

Charlie advances stealthily toward Mack. Sennett follows and gets in another kick. They creep up behind Mack, and Charlie spends a few moments determining the best position from which to strike. At last he raises the mallet high above his head and delivers his mightiest blow. Mack sinks backward—unconscious. As Mabel turns to see what happened, Charlie conceals the mallet and politely raises his hat. Horrified, she gets to her feet and clasps her hands together while Charlie and Sennett pick up the body and cart it away.

They carry Mack to the second shed. Mabel stands outside, hands on hips.

Inside the shed. Charlie stumbles as they enter. They stretch Mack out in front of the packing case. Charlie puts his hat, cane, and the mallet on the packing case. He bends down to examine Mack's head, sniffing at it. Then he gets to his feet and shakes hands with Sennett.

Outside the shed. A small boy approaches Mabel and puts his arms around her waist. She pretends to be shocked—then strokes his hair.

Inside the shed. Sennett bends down and examines Mack. Charlie stands behind him, looking thoughtful. Then he raises the mallet and clobbers him. Sennett flops down beside Mack. Charlie walks over to collect his hat and exits from the shed, whistling.

Outside the shed. He carefully bolts the door, listens to hear if there is any movement within, and then thumbs his nose at his unconscious rivals.

Inside the shed. Sennett sits up, rubs his head, and dazedly looks around. He gets up and finds the door locked. He tries to force it. No luck. He points at Mack's body and then at himself. He's aghast at being trapped with his enemy.

Outside the shed. The boy escorts Mabel back to the hay bale. She is smiling as they sit down. She puts her arm around him.

A shot of Charlie, obviously pleased with himself, smoking, swinging his cane, and swaggering up and down.

Inside the shed. Mack gets to his feet. Near the door Sennett is visible trying to hide behind an old sheet. Mack clasps his head, vowing revenge. Turning, he notices Sennett's feet peeping out from under the sheet. He creeps over and pulls the sheet aside. Sennett begs for mercy.

At the hay bale. Charlie approaches. At the sight of him Mabel stops embracing the boy. The boy stands up and confronts Charlie. He raises his fist, but Charlie gently pushes him away, then boots him in the stomach, sending him sprawling. The boy gets to his feet and yells abuse.

Mabel stands up. Charlie shows her his flexed muscles and takes her arm. She sits down again and he sits beside her. He puts his arm around her. She looks bored.

Inside the shed. Sennett and Mack try to force the door. After several efforts it bursts open and they come hurtling out.

Mack immediately heads toward the hay bale. Sennett hesitates— then decides to follow.

At the hay bale. Charlie becomes ardent but Mabel doesn't respond. She puts his hat back on his head and shoves him away. Charlie gets the message but refuses to leave. He clasps his knees and starts whistling.

Sennett signals to Mack to be as quiet as possible.

At the hay bale. Charlie leans back onto Mabel. She pushes him away. Mack advances toward them. Sennett follows close behind. He intends to kick Mack, but when he looks back Sennett changes his mind. Mack points angrily at Charlie. Rejecting the idea of a surprise attack, he marches boldly up to him. By this time Charlie is stretched out on the hay alongside Mabel, but he hurriedly gets to his feet. Mack clenches his fists and kicks Charlie in the solar plexus. Charlie staggers back to the edge of the lake. He almost falls in. At a distance,

Sennett fastens his lowest jacket button and tries to look fierce. Mack advances toward Charlie. Charlie tries to argue with him but Mack swings a punch. Charlie ducks and counterattacks with a hefty kick. Mack stands his ground.

Lakeside. Mabel is watching the scene as Sennett wanders over to her. She shows no particular interest in her former boyfriend.

Mack throws another punch but misses again. Charlie is more successful. This time he boots Mack backward into the lake.

Sennett walks past Mabel down to the lakeshore. He reaches Charlie, who is standing with his back to the lake, crowing over his defeat of Mack. They shake hands. Then, suddenly, Sennett boots Charlie into the water. Two figures are visible struggling in the lake. Sennett raises his hat to them. Now Mabel rushes down the lakeside to join Sennett. He puts his arm around her and they march off together.

COMMENTS

1. David Robinson describes this film as "a low farce knocked up by Sennett and Mabel" (1983, 52). But we have no reason to assume that Chaplin didn't have a major hand in the knocking up.

Whatever else it may be, *The Fatal Mallet* is unique in presenting Chaplin's only on screen confrontation with Sennett. It is also the only film appearance of the quartet of Chaplin, Mabel, Sennett, and Mack Swain.

2. Structure: a series of fast-paced one-upmanship episodes in which male sexual rivalry for Mabel is translated into violence. (i) First attack: Charlie vs. Sennett. (ii) Second attack: Charlie and Sennett vs. Mack. (iii) Pursuit and retreat to the first shed: Mack chases Charlie and Sennett. (iv) Pursuit and retreat to the second shed. (v) Discovery of the mallet. (vi) Charlie's first use of the mallet: he deals with Mack. (vii) Charlie's second use of the mallet: he deals with Sennett. (viii) Charlie deals with his third and last rival—the small boy. Now the field is clear for him—but Mabel rejects him anyway. (ix) "Hinge" or turning point of the action: Sennett and Mack unite to escape from the shed and deal with Charlie. (x) Mack vs. Charlie: Mack is "liquidated." (xi) Sennett vs. Charlie: Charlie is "liquidated." (xii) Sennett winds up with Mabel—as he was at the outset.

3. Those commentators who even bother to mention this film usually write it off as nothing more than crude and unoriginal slapstick. For example, Gifford remarks: "The basic joke, Charlie thumping Sennett and Swain with a monstrous mallet, was old hat when Weber and Fields brought it to vaudeville" (1974, 45). It is indeed one of the crudest and

most violent of the Chaplin Keystones, but a closer look reveals rather more to it than is generally assumed.

The Fatal Mallet underscores two themes: (i) what women want as opposed to what men think they want, and (ii) how men "learn" violence and what their attitudes are to it. The first of these themes looks very Chaplinesque—in a very rudimentary way it anticipates Chaplin's *A Woman of Paris* (1923).

(i) At the outset we see that Mabel really wants a mild flirtation with a courteous man in which *she* will make the overtures and set the limits. She briefly gets this from Mack when they are together on the swing. But Sennett and Charlie, each in turn, misjudge her wishes or prefer to ignore them. Sennett wants to neck with her, while Charlie wants a tumble in the hay. The boy's approach to her is also sexually aggressive, but when they sit down together in the hay *she* becomes the one who does the embracing.

Mabel also expects her escort to protect her, and she's contemptuous of Sennett for not standing up to Charlie. At the same time, mere displays of masculine strength aren't attractive to her. Sennett fails to realize this in the opening scene. Charlie does too, and later on, when he clobbers Mack, he quickly conceals the mallet to convey the impression that it was his brute strength that knocked out his rival. Thereafter, when he kicks the boy aside he shows Mabel his flexed muscles and expects admiration. But she's disgusted with him. She rejects his advances, hands him his hat, and tells him to clear off. In violence as in flirting, Mabel also expects her man (whoever he may be) to know when to draw the line: i.e., she demonstrates in her change of attitude toward Mack that he has neglected her in order to pursue his obsessive revenge.

When Sennett winds up with Mabel it's not only because he has tossed both his rivals into the lake. He shows no interest in crowing over them or in hanging around to commit more mayhem. Thereupon Mabel rushes down to join him—because although he's an uncouth dolt, he isn't vengefully obsessive like Mack or a lecherous show-off like Charlie.

(ii) Each of the four male characters shows a different approach to violence. Charlie believes in combining his violence with cunning. His speciality is sneak attacks from the rear. Mack eschews such an approach. He believes in man-to-man "fair" confrontation—as he demonstrates when he discovers Sennett in the shed and, at the end of the film, when he decides not to creep up on Charlie from behind. Where violence is concerned, Sennett is primarily imitative, but he's terrified of getting hurt and obviously prefers making gestures to making attacks—as when he copies Mabel in pointing angrily at Charlie and indicates what he'd *like* to do to him, but stops short at actually doing anything. As the film continues, we see Sennett imitating Charlie, in making sneak attacks, in using bricks as weapons, and later, in trying out the mallet. Even his final coup de grace after the handshake is modeled on Charlie's cunning methods: it's the sort of thing Charlie himself did to the boy. Finally, the boy's procedure is to try and play David to Charlie's Goliath. He loses because Charlie has no compunction about using both cunning and brute force on anyone smaller than himself.

As the film proceeds, Charlie's cunning use of violence eliminates Mack, the representative of gentlemanly fair play. But at the end of the movie, when Charlie in turn makes the mistake of trying to behave like a gentleman (he shakes hands with Sennett), the latter—who has been educated in Charlie's methods—cunningly eliminates *him.*

Sennett and Charlie separately demonstrate violence as a learning experience. With Sennett, as we have noticed, this simply means imitation of Charlie. But with Charlie himself we actually observe the birth of an idea (the use of the mallet in place of bricks), and its development: the testing of the idea (Charlie first tries out the mallet on Sennett), further experimentation (he tries out its handle as well as its head), and its final application (he uses it on Mack). In contrast to the bricks (which everyone else uses) the mallet becomes Charlie's unique weapon, the product of his intelligence—even though, despite the film's title, it doesn't turn out to be fatal.

4. Chaplin's fondness for mallets as weapons is exhibited in many films: e.g., *Caught in a Cabaret* (Keystone no. 12), *Laughing Gas* (Keystone no. 20), and his Essanay films *The Tramp* (1915) and *Police* (1916).

OTHER VIEWS

"*The Fatal Mallet* . . . is a real film buff's curiosity, since it pits Mack Sennett himself against Chaplin in a struggle for Mabel's favors" (Moss 1975, 29–30).

"Then . . . the *Moving Picture World*, reviewing *The Fatal Mallet*, stated: 'This one-reeler proves that hitting people over the head with bricks and mallets can sometimes be made amusing.' Whether the review was correct or not is beside the point. What is more interesting is the underlying uncertainty it reveals. The writer is not quite sure if hitting people over the head with bricks and mallets *should* be made amusing; or, to put it another way, whether he should laugh at it. Otherwise he would not have used such a strong word as 'proves' " (Sobel and Francis 1977, 139–40).

16.

Her Friend the Bandit

(1914)

Original working title: *The Italian*
Other titles: *A/The Thief Catcher, Mabel's Flirtation;* French: *Le flirt de Mabel;* German: *Ihr Freund, der Bandit;* Spanish: *Charlot ladrón elegante, Un flirt de Mabel;* Italian: *Charlot bandito gentiluomo, L'ospite furfante*

Length: 1 reel; 993 feet (Asplund), 1000 feet (Lyons)
Playing time: 16 minutes at 16 frames per second
Producer: Keystone
Directors: Possibly Chaplin and/or Mabel Normand
Screenplay: Possibly Chaplin and/or Mabel Normand
Photography: Frank D. Williams (?)
Cast:

A bandit	Chaplin
Mrs. De Rock, a society lady	Mabel Normand
Count De Beans	Charles Murray

Finished or shipped: May 22, 1914
Released: June 4, 1914

No print of this film is known to exist. Synopses in the trade journals of the period suggest that the plot in some respects anticipated Chaplin's Mutual comedy *The Count* (1916) and the fancy-dress ball sequence of his First National comedy *The Idle Class* (1921).

OTHER VIEWS

"Mr. De Beans is captured by the bandit in question while on his way to a reception given by Mrs. De Rock. The bandit assumes Mr. Bean's evening suit and invitation card and, being a Keystone reception, he is taken on credit and has a gay time until the Keystone police are called in, who, it is needless to say, liven things up considerably and put the climax to an arousing farce" (*The Bioscope*, quoted in McDonald, Conway, and Ricci 1974, 51).

"Charles Chaplin and Charles Murray play the chief funny characters of this farce which is a bit thin, but has the rough whirlings of happenings usually found in farces of this well-marked type. It will amuse and make laughter and can be considered a safe rather than noteworthy offering" (*Moving Picture World*, June 4, 1914, p. 65).

"Chaplin's next . . . served to introduce Sennett's latest capture and colleague from the Biograph comedies, Charles Murray. Where Ford Sterling specialized in funny Dutchmen, Murray's main line was the funny Frenchman. His characterisation of the Gallic dandy fascinated Chaplin. He not only impersonated Murray in *Her Friend the Bandit*, but carried the character over into many of his later comedies, casting Leo White as the Count again and again" (Gifford 1974, 45).

17.

The Knockout
(1914)

Original working title: *Fighting Demon*
Other titles: *The Pugilist, Counted Out;* French: *Charlot et Fatty dans le ring, Charlot arbitre;* German: *Der K.O.;* Spanish: *Charlot arbitro, Charlot y Fatty en el ring;* Italian: *Il K.O., Charlot e Fatty boxeurs*

Length: 2 reels; 1591 feet (Asplund), 1960 feet (Lyons)
Playing time: 27 minutes at 16 frames per second
Producer: Keystone
Director(s): Either Mack Sennett and/or Charles Avery, or Roscoe "Fatty" Arbuckle
Screenplay: Chaplin (?)
Photography: Frank D. Williams (?)
Cast:

Referee	Chaplin
Cyclone Flynn, the champion	Edgar Kennedy
The challenger	Fatty Arbuckle
His girlfriend	Minta Durfee
The pug	Hank Mann
A cowboy	Mack Swain
Other spectators	Alice Howell
	Al St. John
	Slim Summerville
	Charley Chase
	Mack Sennett
Cops	Joe Bordeaux
	Eddie Cline
Keystone Kops	as themselves

Finished or shipped: May 29, 1914
Released: June 11, 1914

SYNOPSIS

A freight train. Two hoboes are riding on the roof. A railroad guard orders them off and boots them away from the train.

Exterior of restaurant. Fatty (later to become the challenger) emerges, eating, and carrying a pooch whose mouth he stuffs with food.

Street nearby. His girlfriend calls him over to her. She fusses over his dog.

Exterior of restaurant. The two hoboes appear. They mime that they are penniless and hungry.

Street nearby. Fatty asks his girlfriend for a kiss. She kisses him on the cheek. He's upset; then he "unscrews" the kiss and transfers it to his lips. Happily, they stroll away arm-in-arm.

Boxing compound. Fatty arrives with his girlfriend. When a pug tries to make up to her, Fatty blows smoke in his face and knocks him down. The pug intends to retaliate with a brick, but when Fatty glares at him he changes his mind. Fatty exits to buy some cigarettes. Undeterred, the pug again tries his chances with Fatty's girlfriend. This time *she* wades into him.

Exterior of town hall. The hoboes notice some posters advertising a forthcoming boxing contest.

Title: *"We'll pose as pugilists and make some coin."*

They shake hands on the deal. The boxing promoter has appeared. They accost him, and after some persuasion he invites them to follow him into the town hall.

Boxing compound. Fatty returns in time to separate his girlfriend and the pug. To her delight he takes on the pug himself and the fight becomes increasingly violent. (At one point Fatty bites his adversary's leg.) Eventually they start hurling bricks; one of them misses its target and knocks her unconscious. A Keystone Kop appears (he's about half the size of most of the men in the compound). He is struck by a brick and staggers away. The fight continues unabated. Several of the pug's sparring partners come to his aid, but Fatty brings the struggle to a triumphal conclusion by tossing all of them into a water trough. By this time his girlfriend has recovered: she rushes over to Fatty and kisses him. They leave the compound arm-in-arm.

A notice outside the town hall advertises a boxing match: *Cyclone Flynn will meet all comers—Winner Take All.*

The two hoboes receive bets on the fight.

Exterior of restaurant. Flush with money, they eagerly enter the restaurant.

Exterior of town hall. The pug, pretending that he is now Fatty's friend, shows him the notice and tries to persuade him to accept the challenge.

Title: *Pug shows his nerve.*

Exterior of restaurant. The two hoboes emerge, wolfing down pies.

Exterior of town hall. The pug calls the promoter over and introduces Fatty as a challenger. The girlfriend persuades the reluctant Fatty to participate. He follows the pug to the gymnasium. Close-up of a handwritten note being read by the promoter:

"I'll take up your fight proposition, and believe me, there'll be some fight. Pug."

He shows this note to the two hoboes.

Gymnasium. The two hoboes peek through a fence while the pug and his sparring partners put Fatty through a training session. Fatty's girlfriend urges him on.

Changing room. Fatty directs the camera to tilt upward as he removes his pants and pulls on a pair of boxer shorts.

Gymnasium. Fatty gives a show of strength, swinging a 500 lb. weight over his head and breaking a heavy chain with his bare hands. Until now the hoboes have expected that Cyclone Flynn will be the winner, but after witnessing Fatty's performance one of them is ready to flee. The other is more confident.

Title: *"Wait, I'll fix it."*

He tosses Fatty a note purporting to come from Flynn.

Title: *"It's unpleasant knocking out fat men, so lay down and we'll go halves on the coin."*

Title: *The real Cyclone Flynn.*

Railroad station. Flynn alights from a train.

Gymnasium. To the consternation of the hoboes, Fatty tears up the note and proceeds to give another demonstration of his strength by knocking out all his sparring partners.

Exterior of town hall. Flynn introduces himself to the promoter. The two hoboes appear and try to bribe him, but he beats them up for their affrontery.

Title: *Ready for the fight.*

The girlfriend's bedroom. Only men will be allowed to see the boxing match, so she has disguised herself in a man's suit and cloth cap.

Title: *One of the boys.*

Gymnasium. She turns up in her disguise. Fatty looks her over in amazement.

Title: *Cyclone Flynn fills the imposter's engagement.*

Gymnasium. Flynn enters, takes a look at Fatty's girlfriend, and removes her cap to reveal her long hair. She whispers to him to keep her secret. They are instantly attracted to one another, but she kisses Fatty as he exits for the fight.

Exterior of town hall. She enters along with a crowd of male spectators.

Boxing auditorium. She takes a seat in the front row as a boisterous crowd assembles for the big fight.

Dressing room. Flynn enters to get ready for the fight.

Exterior of town hall. Mack Sennett appears—then Mack Swain. Swain is dressed in a cowboy outfit and is sporting a long walrus moustache. The two men glare at each other. Sennett hastens inside. Swain follows him.

Fatty's dressing room. Swain enters. Brandishing a gun, he confronts Fatty.

Title: *"I'm betting heavy on you, so win or I'll kill you."*

Fatty looks terrified.

Boxing auditorium. The audience cheers wildly as the challenger (Fatty) climbs into the ring. One fan throws a pillow at him. Fatty throws it back, but it hits his girlfriend instead. Swain marches past Fatty and takes up his seat in a box beside the ring. As Flynn appears Fatty is drinking a bottle of milk and being fanned by his seconds. Now the referee (Charlie) dances into the ring, loses his balance and falls backward between the ropes. Getting up, he orders the two boxers to their places.

The fight begins. Charlie gets in the way of a blow from Flynn which sends him sprawling onto the ropes. Both boxers help him up. Next Charlie gets in the way of a punch from Fatty. He responds by kicking Fatty in the rear end just as Fatty is taking a punch from Flynn. Fatty collapses but manages to stagger to his feet before he can be counted out. Annoyed, Charlie kicks him again. Fatty takes a swing at Charlie but misses and topples over. Charlie raises his arms in grateful prayer. Fatty's initial setback is only temporary. Getting back on his feet, he pitches in to Flynn. Flynn rallies, driving Fatty into the ropes. Charlie intercedes—only to receive a hail of blows from Flynn. The audience goes wild. In his private box, Swain expresses a gamut of emotions. Fatty tries to fortify himself with a swig of milk, but as he is drinking, Flynn strikes him in the back and he spurts the milk over his girlfriend and the other spectators in the front row. As the fight resumes, the boxers get into a clinch. Charlie tries to break it up, but Fatty hits him and he staggers round the ring in a stupor. Another clinch—and this time Charlie gets caught in the middle of it. Flynn extricates himself, leaving Fatty wrestling with Charlie. Then, when the latter breaks loose and tries to referee the match, Flynn knocks him down. The round comes to an end with Charlie struggling between the ropes and hanging half out of the ring.

Round two. Fatty chases Flynn while Charlie hop-chases Fatty; then the chase is reversed. At last the two boxers confront each other and start swinging. Charlie gets in the way and is knocked back against the ropes. He recovers and doles out blows and kicks to both boxers. Then he climbs out of the ring and declares the end of another round. No use: the fight carries on regardless of him. At last Flynn downs Fatty and Charlie climbs back into the ring and starts counting. Fatty attempts to get up, but Charlie, tired of the match, shoves him back on the canvas with a poke on the rump. Fatty gets up anyway. As the fight resumes, Charlie slips upon the canvas, and from a sitting position watches Flynn down Fatty once more. This time he declares Flynn the winner even though Fatty gets to his feet before the count is over. At this egregious injustice, Fatty suddenly grabs Swain's guns and goes berserk, shooting at everyone in sight. Chaos ensues.

Exterior of town hall. Flynn flees with Fatty in hot pursuit, firing all the way. The promoter calls the Keystone Kops.

Interior of police station. The police chief takes the call and alerts his men. Their rush to answer the call leaves the police station in a wreck.

Exterior of police station. The Kops hurtle out, knocking a mailman into the air.

Street. Flynn momentarily turns the tables on Fatty, kicking him on the rump. Fatty continues shooting.

Exterior of town hall. The spectators exit in a mad rush.

A wild chase ensues. The Kops pursue Fatty as—firing all the way—he pursues Flynn over the rooftops, down a chimney, and through a sedate soiree. En route Fatty shoots himself in the foot and hits Flynn in the rear end. The Kops eventually get a rope around Fatty and try to restrain him. Flynn in the company of Fatty's (former) girlfriend watch the tug-of-war from a distance. The Kops lose. Fatty drags them through the streets to the seafront and leaps off the jetty, dragging them into the ocean after him.

COMMENTS

1. Since *The Knockout* is primarily a Fatty film, it does not require an extended commentary here. Chaplin's cameo role in the film may have been repayment for Fatty's walk-on in *A Film Johnnie*. Another such repayment would be made at Essanay the following year when Chaplin made a guest appearance in G. M. "Bronco Billy" Anderson's *His Regeneration* in return for Bronco Billy's bit performance as a ringside fan in Chaplin's *The Champion*. In the twenties, Chaplin made a number of other walk-ons and cameo appearances in such films as *The Nut* (1921), *Hollywood* (1923), and *Show People* (1928).

2. Although I have no way of proving it, I am convinced that Chaplin choreographed the boxing sequences of *The Knockout*, and that these

sequences were developed out of boxing-match mimes he had seen or appeared in when he was a member of Fred Karno's company, in particular *The Yap-Yaps*. (See further Adeler and West 1939, ch. 15.) The sequences in *The Knockout* have the same feel as Chaplin's better-known boxing parodies in *The Champion* (Essanay 1915) and *City Lights* (1931)–in which, by the way, Charlie appears as a boxer not a referee. It is noteworthy that in all three of these films there are frustrated attempts to bribe one or more of the boxers.

18.

Mabel's Busy Day

(1914)

Original working title: *Weine Story*
Other titles: *Love and Lunch, Charlie and the Sausages, Hot Dogs, Hot Dog Charlie;* French: *Charlot et les saucisses, Le flirt de Mabel, Mabel marchande ambulante;* German: *Mabels unruhiger Tag;* Spanish: *Mabel y Charlot en las carreras, Charlot y las salchichas;* Italian: *Charlot e le salsicce*

Length: 1 reel; 948 feet (Asplund), 998 feet (Lyons)
Playing time: 16 minutes at 16 frames per second
Director: Mabel Normand and/or Chaplin
Screenplay: Mabel Normand or Chaplin
Photography: Frank D. Williams (?)
Cast:

Mabel, a hot dog vendor	Mabel Normand
A cad	Chaplin
A woman	Billie Bennett
Cops	Chester Conklin
	Slim Summerville
	Edgar Kennedy
Unbilled	Wallace MacDonald,
	Al St. John
	Charley Chase

Finished or shipped: May 30, 1914
Released: June 13, 1914

SYNOPSIS

A fence concealing a motor race. A cop is guarding the main entrance. He notices Mabel, a hot dog vendor, peering through a hole in the fence and offers to let her in for free in exchange for a hot dog.

Inside the racetrack a cad tries to get fresh with her, but she knocks him down and kicks him in the rump.

Charlie appears at the main entrance, elegantly dressed in frock coat and derby hat and sporting a boutonniere. He tries to slip in without paying, but a track official orders him out. He tries again, but this time a cop intervenes. Undaunted, Charlie beats him up and dashes through the entrance. Two more cops advance on him, but Charlie knocks them down and gives them some hefty kicks. Then they start chasing him around the racetrack.

The motor race is in progress. A cop orders Mabel out of the vicinity of a parked car. Charlie, having shaken off his pursuers, wanders over to the parked car and discovers one of Mabel's hot dogs lying on the ground. At first he thinks it's a cigar. Then, realizing his mistake, he gulps it down. In the meantime, Mabel isn't doing much business. A would-be customer walks away without buying anything because she can't give him change. Charlie now turns his attention to three women—possibly a mother and two daughters—who are watching the race. He deliberately stands in front of them, blocking their view. When they push him aside, he looks into the camera and smirks. Renewing his unwelcome attentions, he leans his elbow on one of the young women. She promptly slaps his face. He raises his foot with the intention of kicking her but changes his mind when all three women turn and confront him. As soon as they turn back to the race, he filches the older lady's handkerchief and uses it to wave at the passing cars. When she notices what he has done, she grabs her handkerchief. Charlie grins, doffs his hat, and defiantly kicks his foot at her.

Before this encounter can get any further, he notices that Mabel is being pestered by another cad. Rushing to her aid, he attacks the cad and drives him away with a sharp left hook to the jaw. Pretending to console Mabel, he gently kisses her cheek. Suddenly, he grabs one of her hot dogs and bolts away with it. The three ladies try to stop him, but he evades them.

Mabel, now frantic, wakes up a sleeping cop (Chester Conklin) and reports what has happened. Meanwhile, Charlie dashes back to her hot dog tray and makes off with it, pushing and shoving several bystanders. Then he begins handing out free hot dogs to all comers. But several fun lovers now start to harass *him*, pushing his hat off and mussing his hair. He charges at them and knocks them down. Mabel observes what has become of her hot dog tray. She is about to attack Charlie herself when the cop stops her. He has a better idea. While she distracts Charlie, he will club him from behind. The plan almost works. She confronts Charlie and accuses him of stealing her tray, but in the nick of time he turns and discovers the cop behind him. Deftly, he grabs the nightstick and knocks the cop down with it. Simultaneously, Mabel boots Charlie in the rear end. The cop gets up, and with Mabel's assistance, manages to overpower Charlie. Then he makes the mistake of swinging at him. He misses and hits Mabel. Charlie gets to his feet and starts to spar with the cop. At the first opportunity he kicks him backward into several of the bystanders. Now he turns to face Mabel. She swings at him, but he dodges. The bystanders have now joined the fray. Charlie advances on Mabel with his fists swinging. But she breaks into tears and he cannot bring himself to strike a weeping woman. Changing his tactics, he tries to console her—even though she is lashing out at him. Then, grabbing her arm, he picks up his hat, raises it to the bystanders, and marches off arm-in-arm with Mabel, his new girlfriend.

COMMENTS

1. This concoction looks as if it had been whipped up at short notice to make use of a local motor race as background (compare with *Kid's Auto Race* and *A Busy Day*). It was the first of two one-reelers, made back-to-back, for which Charlie may have resumed codirection with Mabel Normand.

2. The film's structure anticipates that of Chaplin's *The Circus:* a series of contrasting parallel actions and scenes. (i) A cop admits Mabel to the racetrack, while (ii) Charlie beats up several cops to get onto the racetrack. (iii) Charlie finds a "free" hot dog, while (iv) Mabel can't sell any of her hot dogs. (v) Charlie pesters three women, while (vi) a cad pesters Mabel. (vii) Charlie rescues Mabel, but (viii) he steals one of her hot dogs. This is the first of the film's two reversals of action. (ix) Mabel reports his theft to a cop, while (x) Charlie doles out free hot dogs. I.e., he temporarily "becomes" Mabel, but (xi) his "customers" harass him. I.e., they treat him like Mabel. (xii) Cop and Mabel intend to attack Charlie, but (xiii) Charlie attacks the cop instead. (xiv) Charlie intends to attack Mabel, but (xv) he consoles her instead—second reversal. (xvi) They exit arm-in-arm.

3. It looks as if this film is Chaplin's "revenge" for *Mabel at the Wheel*. Although Mabel is at the racetrack again, this time she never gets near a wheel. She has a hard enough time trying to hang on to her hot dogs.

I find the two main characters of this film somewhat perplexing. Uno Asplund aptly describes Charlie as "an elegant flâneur with a flower in his buttonhole." Why should an individual dressed like this have to fight his way onto a racetrack? Is it likely that such a person would scoop hot dogs off the ground and devour them? In *City Lights* Charlie, dressed in a tuxedo and driving a limousine, suddenly dives out of his car and snatches a cigar butt from under the nose of an astounded hobo. The hobo is astounded because *he* doesn't know what the *movie audience* does: despite appearances Charlie *really is* just a penniless tramp. Unfortunately, *Mabel's Busy Day* tells us nothing that we need to know about the "elegant flâneur." What are his circumstances? Is he penniless or a would-be con man? What's he at the race for? There's no sign that he's really interested in it. If he hasn't any money, why isn't he trying to get some instead of pestering women and doling out Mabel's hot dogs for free? And what's a pretty girl like Mabel doing selling hot dogs at a racetrack? Her wares are obviously "phallic"—but it would make more sense in sexual terms if *Charlie* were selling them to *women.*

Mabel's Busy Day is one of the nastier Chaplin Keystones. (The only funny thing in it is Chaplin's dance around the cops who pursue him onto the racetrack.) Where *The Fatal Mallet* indicated some of the ways in which men misunderstand women, this movie invites its audiences to share in the sadistic pleasure of male characters pestering or abusing female ones. Of the various men Mabel encounters, only the two cops do not mistreat her—although she has to bribe one with a hot dog and gets very little help from the other. The others behave outrageously. One customer throws a hot dog in her face because she can't give change. A second openly attacks her—and Charlie only comes to her aid as a mean subterfuge for stealing one hot dog and then walking off with the entire trayful. His behavior toward the three ladies is downright insulting: he deliberately blocks their view of the race, steals a handkerchief belonging to one of them, leans his elbow on another, and almost kicks her when she understandably slaps his face. The tables are, of course, turned on him when he starts distributing the hot dogs for free. All his "customers" are men, and they harass *him* as if he were Mabel, again underscoring the film's view of male delight in tormenting females. Note that none of the bystanders comes to Charlie's aid—or Mabel's.

Charlie's final change of heart (or is it "discovery" of heart) is not totally implausible. He'd sooner stand up to cops and cads than resolute women. At his first encounter with Mabel he ran away after filching a hot dog. In his encounter with the three ladies, he demonstrates that he hasn't the guts to stand up to them when they turn on him. And so, when a weeping Mabel finally makes a frontal assault on him, he suddenly becomes conciliatory and consoling. But then Mabel hasn't any hot dogs left for him to steal. And he's also noticed at last that she's a very attractive girl.

OTHER VIEWS

"Roguery and rascality are as much a part of the 'Little Fellow's' make-up as his violence and vulgarity. There is hardly an occasion when he is not scoring off someone, kicking them or knocking them about (hardly ever with his fists, mostly with a weapon), by making them look foolish or clumsy, by outwitting them, by taking advantage of them. He is not averse to stealing the contents of a woman's handbag, as he does in *Mabel's Busy Day*, or picking someone's pockets, as in *In the Park*" (Sobel and Francis 1977, 175).

19.

Mabel's Married Life

(1914)

Original working title: *His Wife's Birthday*
Other titles: *When You're Married, The Squarehead;* French: *Charlot et Mabel en ménage, Charlot et le mannequin;* German: *Mabels Ehleben;* Spanish: *Vida matrimonial de Mabel, Charlot en la vida conyugal, Charlot y Mabel se casan;* Italian: *La vita coniugale di Mabel, Charlot e il manichino*

Length: 1 reel; 1020 feet (Asplund), 1015 feet (Lyons)
Playing time: 17 minutes at 16 frames per second
Producer: Keystone
Directors: Mabel Normand and/or Chaplin
Screenplay: Chaplin and/or Mabel Normand
Photography: Frank D. Williams (?)
Cast:

Mabel	Mabel Normand
Her ineffectual husband	Chaplin
Mr. Wellington	Mack Swain
His wife	Alice Howell
A friend	Hank Mann
Bar flies	Charlie Murray
	Harry McCoy
Delivery man	Al St. John
Second delivery man	Wallace MacDonald
Inquisitive neighbor	Alice Davenport

Finished or shipped: June 6, 1914
Released: June 20, 1914

SYNOPSIS

A park. Burly Mr. Wellington (Mack Swain), wearing a cloth cap and sweater and sporting a tennis racket, kisses his wife and heads for the nearest tavern, leaving her seated on a bench. Nearby but out of their view, Charlie (wearing a top hat) and his wife, Mabel, are also seated on a park bench. She is in a bad mood, disgruntled with her inadequate spouse who is busy examining his broken soles. He protests when Mabel bites off a large piece of his banana. Getting up, he also heads for the tavern where Wellington, who has already slaked his thirst, eyes him scornfully.

Returning to the park, Wellington sits beside Mabel and invites her to play tennis with him. When she refuses, he laughs and begins to make passes at her.

The tavern. Charlie helps himself to extra liquor when the bartender's back is turned. He tries to leave without paying, but the bartender is more alert than he had expected and insists on full payment. He hands over the money, spits in the bartender's face, and toddles out, slightly tipsy.

Back in the park, he comes upon Wellington annoying Mabel. She appeals to him to rescue her, and Charlie politely asks Wellington to desist, but the latter pulls out Charlie's tie, disarranges his hat, and returns to molesting Mabel. Charlie leans on Wellington's rump. No effect. He thumps it. Still no effect. He takes a flying kick at it but hurts his foot. Wellington just doesn't seem to notice his protests, so Charlie tugs at his arm and says:

Title: *"That's my wife."*

At this, Wellington tosses Charlie's hat out of sight. Mabel rushes over to her husband and appeals for aid, but Charlie dashes away to find his hat.

While Wellington drags Mabel over to the lakeside, Charlie retrieves his hat which had landed beside Wellington's wife. Curious, she follows him as he returns to the other bench and finds Mabel has gone. Suddenly they both notice Wellington and Mabel at the lakeside. The irate wife tells Charlie:

Title: *"That's my husband."*

She drags him over to the lake, cows her husband, and nearly throttles Mabel—despite Mabel's attempts to explain the situation. Charlie tries to intervene but is struck in the face for his pains. At last, Wellington and his wife stroll away, embracing each other. Mabel also walks away, throwing out her arms in despair at her husband's weakness.

Charlie makes his way back to the tavern to drown his sorrows in drink. At the bar, a tough-looking character in a striped sweater eyes him contemptuously and flicks ash in his face.

Meanwhile, Mabel arrives at a sporting goods store where she comes upon a life-size boxer's dummy for sale. It is dressed just like Mr. Wellington. She gets an idea and buys it, telling the shopkeeper:

Title: *"Send it up right away."*

Mabel's apartment: She mocks her absent husband with a remarkable mimicry of his comical walk and his behavior in the park.

At the bar. The tough pulls at Charlie's sagging pants, flips out his tie, and shoves his hat over his eyes. Mr. Wellington arrives—the tough is one of his pals. Charlie listens helplessly as his two tormentors joke about his humiliation in the park. Wellington mockingly shakes Charlie's hand then smacks his hat down with the tennis racket.

Title: *Delivered.*

Two delivery men arrive outside Mabel's apartment with the dummy. She is in pajamas and admits them only after wrapping herself in a tiger-skin rug. But when they bring in the dummy she drops the rug through sheer excitement. Embarrassed, she shoves the men out of the apartment. The dummy is fixed on a rocker base, and she has some fun pushing it and watching it sway back and forth. Then she gives it a hefty punch and it swings back and knocks her flat.

At the bar. All the barflies are now laughing at Charlie's discomfiture. But Wellington has gone too far. His temper aroused at last, Charlie launches a mighty punch and flattens his tormentor and everyone standing behind him. Then he kicks the tough and slaps the bartender. Everyone clears out, leaving Charlie alone to drink his fill. By this time he is quite drunk. Before he exits he picks up a bunch of onions from the free lunch counter as a "bouquet" for Mabel.

The apartment. Mabel goes to bed and waits for Charlie to return and confront the dummy. He doesn't notice it immediately because he is distracted by a distinctly unpleasant odor. After examining his shoes to make sure he hasn't stepped into anything, he realizes that he is holding a smelly bunch of onions. He tosses them aside—they land on Mabel. Now he spies the dummy and thinks it's Wellington arrived to plague him again.

Title: *"So you followed my wife home?"*

Mabel listens disgustedly as he politely asks "Wellington" to leave. But the dummy doesn't budge. Then Charlie drags Mabel out of bed and confronts her with her "lover." She tries to make him see reason, but he refuses to listen. Losing his balance, he falls back onto the dummy which starts swaying to and fro, knocking Mabel down. Angered at last, Charlie punches it—whereupon the dummy knocks him down too. The commotion arouses several neighbors who congregate outside the apartment. At last, Mabel manages to show Charlie that his adversary is merely a dummy. He is first aghast, then amused. Still drunk, however, he clutches the dummy and falls to the floor with it. Then it swings back and knocks Mabel down onto her hapless husband. As the film comes to an end, only the swaying dummy remains upright.

COMMENTS

1. Although Chaplin did not realize it at the time, this film was a turning point in his career. Thereafter he alone would direct all his films—with the single exception of *Tillie's Punctured Romance* (Keystone no. 33), directed by Mack Sennett.

2. One doesn't associate the Tramp with marriage, but then Chaplin did not invariably play the bachelor Tramp. *Mabel's Married Life* is the first of several films in which he appeared in the role of a married man. Other Keystones in this category are: *The Rounders* (no. 26), *His Trysting Places* (no. 32)—in which he is also a papa, and *Getting Acquainted* (no. 34). In *Tillie's Punctured Romance* (no. 33), he marries the elephantine Tillie (Marie Dressler) for her money, but the marriage is extremely short-lived and far stormier than his married life with Mabel.

3. The structure again anticipates that of *The Circus:* a series of contrasting situations and scenes. (i) The park: contrast of two married couples. (ii) Charlie remains with his wife while (iii) Mr. Wellington heads for the tavern. (iv) Charlie heads for the tavern while (v) Mr. Wellington returns to the park. (vi) Wellington makes passes at Mabel while (vii) Charlie tries to cheat a bartender. (viii) *"That's my wife"*: Charlie makes a feeble attack on Mr. Wellington. (ix) *"That's my husband"*: Wellington's wife makes a vigorous attack on Mabel. (x) The store: Mabel buys the dummy. This is the first "hinge" or reversal of the action. (xi) The apartment: Mabel mocks Charlie. (xii) The tavern: a tough and Mr. Wellington mock Charlie. (xiii) The apartment: the dummy is delivered. It flattens Mabel. (xiv) The tavern: Charlie flattens his tormentors—second reversal. (xv) The apartment: Charlie tries to deal with the dummy—but it deals with him (and Mabel).

4. Denis Gifford (1974, 46) notes that the film's final sequence was an elaboration of *The Football Match* and *Mumming Birds*, two Fred Karno sketches in which Chaplin had appeared prior to joining Keystone. *The Yap-Yaps*, another Karno sketch, which depicted both a barroom brawl and a comic boxing match must also have left its mark on the film. (See further Adeler and West 1939, ch. 15.)

Mabel's Married Life was more immediately a spin-off from several previous Keystones. It could hardly have been coincidental that the sequence with the boxer's dummy was made within a month after Chaplin had appeared in the comic boxing match of *The Knockout*. The film also combines elements of *The Fatal Mallet* and *His Favorite Pastime*. From the former it takes the situation of Mabel being escorted by a man who is too cowardly to defend her. From the latter it takes two situations: (i) Charlie getting involved in a tavern brawl and (ii) the husband returning home from a tavern and encountering an intruder he suspects to be his wife's lover. It should also be noted that in the barroom scenes of both *His Favorite Pastime* and *Mabel's Married Life*, Charlie has to deal with a tough wearing a striped shirt.

5. *Mabel's Married Life* is yet another film that emphasizes negative images of men. Dan Kamin (1984, 65) maintains that Mabel's relationship to Charlie in their films is one of equals. But this just isn't true of the film in question. Mabel is obviously the smarter of the two. She displays mockery and contempt for Charlie's weaknesses (physical and alcoholic) and sets up the dummy as a "test" that he must pass if he wants to sleep with her. He fails it miserably and they wind up not in bed but unconscious on the floor.

Between them, Charlie and Mr. Wellington exhibit a wide spectrum of male shortcomings: cheating and lying, cowardice and bullying, drunkenness and lechery. Charlie drinks up most of his money and then tries to look like a gentleman. But what's a man whose shoes are falling apart doing with a top hat? The film's original working title indicated that it took place on Mabel's birthday. Charlie's idea of celebration is to sit on *her* knee in the park, to object selfishly when she takes a big bite of his banana, and to toss her onions instead of orchids. Mr. Wellington flashes a tennis racket in front of his wife as an alibi to conceal his real intentions. As soon as she's out of sight he heads for the nearest tavern and then returns to the park to molest the first available woman. He takes a sadistic delight in bullying a weaker man (Charlie) but is terrified of incurring the wrath of his wife (who is half his size).

The two couples make an interesting contrast. When we first see the Wellingtons together he is kissing her; when we last see them together they are embracing. Superficially they look like a tender, loving couple. But we have seen what he gets up to whenever she isn't around. Obviously, Mrs. Wellington has too much faith in her sweet-talking husband and she totally *misperceives* what he's up to with Mabel. Despite all indications to the contrary she prefers to believe that Mabel is trying to seduce her "innocent" spouse. On the other hand, Mabel has no faith at all in *her* ineffectual husband. From her contemptuous attitude toward him it's obvious that they don't have much of a marriage.

Chaplin returns to these unvarnished impressions of married life in several of his later films, in particular his First National comedy *Pay Day* (1922).

The two women have different expectations of their husbands. Mrs. Wellington wants to believe that her spouse is faithful to her. Mabel wants a husband who's aggressive. The aggressiveness she has in mind involves their sexual relationship as well as Charlie's reactions to the aggressiveness of other men. The sexual aspect is underscored by the film's sexual innuendoes. In the park Charlie gets upset when Mabel takes a large bite out of his *banana*. In the tavern the tough pulls at Charlie's sagging pants (there doesn't seem to be much inside!) and flips out his tie (an obvious metaphor for a limp penis). In the apartment Mabel gets into her pajamas (compare with *Mabel's Strange Predicament*) to wait for Charlie. The two delivery men arrive first. They are obviously taken with the sight of her *en déshabillé*, but she wraps herself in a tiger-skin rug (a symbol for *her* aggressiveness) and kicks them out. Meanwhile Charlie is in no hurry to return home and bed down with Mabel: he prefers to get drunk.

Charlie does eventually turn out to be aggressive: not in the ways that Mabel wanted—but through alcohol and misperception. When he gets drunk enough, Dutch courage makes him a superman, and he pays back the tough and Mr. Wellington for the abuse they'd heaped on him. *Misperceiving* the dummy as Wellington, Mabel's "lover" who has invaded his apartment to humiliate him once more, he first tries to reason with it as he had with Wellington in the park. Then he takes a leaf out of Mrs. Wellington's book and accuses *Mabel* of adultery. Finally, he goes for the dummy when he thinks he's being attacked in his own home. The dummy is, of course, dressed like Wellington, and Mabel had intended it to be a harmless surrogate for him, a "sparring partner" with whom her husband can learn to be more aggressive. But it's also part of her mockery of Charlie: she has given him a dummy to fight because she knows he can't stand up to a real man. (Simultaneously, by the way, she symbolically reduces Mr. Wellington to what he really is when someone has the guts to confront him—a mere straw man.) Charlie's misperception of the dummy is on a par with Mrs. Wellington's misperception of her husband: Charlie sees what he *believes*, not what is really there. When Mabel manages to reveal the truth about the dummy—it's also the truth about the sort of man she's married to—it finally knocks them both out.

6. Some of Chaplin's funniest comic business in this film would, in due course, be appropriated by other comedians: e.g., Charlie putting his leg over Mabel's knee (a gag adopted by Groucho) and his cunning method for getting extra liquor (a gag taken over by Harpo). Chaplin himself reprised the battle with the dummy for a scene between Charlie and a punchball in his Essanay comedy *The Champion* (1915). The same battle probably inspired the football practice-session with a dummy in Harold Lloyd's *The Freshman* (1925) and Oliver Hardy's struggle with the gum-ball machine in *Two Tars* (1928).

Mabel Normand's mimicry of Chaplin has provoked much favorable comment. Asplund, for example, describes the scene as "funny and unique . . . [she] mimics to perfection Charlie's way of walking" (1976, 47). In fact the scene is quite brief and the mimicry is merely adequate compared to Gloria Swanson's vivid recreations of Chaplin's walk in *Manhandled* (1924) and *Sunset Boulevard* (1950).

OTHER VIEWS

"Sincerity is a hallmark of his [Chaplin's] appearances (and they are many) as a drunk. . . . In his complete inebriation, Charlie confronts the dummy as an intruder and attempts to convince "him" of the folly of remaining in the house. In ordinary hands this scene would be mildly amusing: with Chaplin, it is hilarious because Charlie's certainty that the dummy is real is so profound that we almost share it. The authenticity of Chaplin's drunkenness is an acting lesson. Unlike other comics who cleverly simulate drunkenness, Chaplin—like a real drunk—summons up his thoughts in an attempt to be *sober*. He is trying desperately to be sober. Chaplin looks at the drunk he is portraying from the *drunk's* point of view, not from the view of a skilled comedian trying to be drunk. It is the difference between great acting and clever impersonation. Reality" (McCabe 1978, 59–60).

"The complement to treating bodies as objects is treating objects as though they are alive. The first example of this type of transformation is Charlie's fight with a dressmaker's dummy [sic] in an early Keystone, *Mabel's Married Life* . . . . Not having noticed the dummy before, he is startled into believing that it is a person. . . . Charlie continues to treat the dummy as a man, even to the point of sniffing and concluding that it has been drinking" (Kamin 1984, 45).

20.

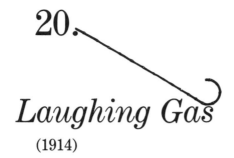

Laughing Gas

(1914)

Original working title: *Dentist Story*
Other titles: *Laffing Gas, The Dentist, Busy Little Dentist, Down and Out, Tuning His Ivories*; French: *Charlot dentiste, Charlot opère lui-même*; German: *Lachgas*; Spanish: *El gas de la risa, Charlot falso dentista, Charlot el buen doctor*; Italian: *Gas esilarante*

Length: 1 reel; 981 feet (Asplund), 1020 feet (Lyons)
Playing time: 16 minutes at 16 frames per second
Producer: Keystone
Director: Chaplin
Story and screenplay: Chaplin
Photography: Frank D. Williams?
Cast:

Dr. Pain, the dentist	Fritz Schade
His assistant	Chaplin
The dentist's wife	Alice Howell
Second assistant	Joseph Sutherland?
Man outside pharmacy	Mack Swain
Patients	Joseph Swickard
	Slim Summerville

Finished or shipped: June 26, 1914
Released: July 9, 1914

SYNOPSIS

Exterior of Dr. Pain's dental parlor. Charlie arrives dressed in a smartened-up version of his Tramp's outfit. (Actually he is one of the dentist's two assistants—but the audience doesn't know that yet.)

Waiting room. Charlie enters and contemplates two patients waiting for treatment: a lady with a bandaged face and an old man clutching his jaw in agony. In a dignified manner he removes his gloves and drops them into his derby. Then he places the hat and his cane on an armchair. The patients (and the audience) are under the impression that he's the dentist until he bends down and picks up a couple of spittoons—one of his usual jobs as dental assistant. He stumbles over the lady's feet on his way to an adjoining room.

Adjoining room. He puts the spittoons on a table to annoy the second assistant (a midget), who is eating his breakfast, and then takes off his jacket. Asked to remove the spittoons, Charlie first obliges— then grabs the midget's ear and tweaks his nose. The latter promptly retaliates with a punch that knocks Charlie sprawling. Temporarily accepting defeat—he offers the midget a handshake—he sets to work with the carpet sweeper, but at the first opportunity sneaks a blow to the midget's head and dashes back to the waiting room, carrying the carpet sweeper.

Waiting room. Two more patients have arrived by now: a pretty girl escorted by a bearded man. Charlie loses no time in making a nuisance of himself with the carpet sweeper, trying to provoke a fight with the old man, but the timely intrusion of the bearded patient changes his mind. He satisfies himself by returning to the adjoining room.

Adjoining room. He takes the midget by surprise, knocks him to the floor, and lands a few well-aimed kicks.

Waiting room. Meanwhile, the dentist, Dr. Pain, has arrived.

Surgery. Ushering the old man into the dentist chair, he administers laughing gas.

Exterior of dentist's house. Dr. Pain's wife exits, dressed in her most stylish outfit.

Surgery. As soon as the patient is unconscious, Dr. Pain extracts a tooth. Then, to his horror, he finds he can't wake up the old man. Panic-stricken, he calls to Charlie for assistance.

Waiting room. On his way to the surgery, Charlie stops to flirt with the pretty girl and to throw a magazine at the bearded man.

Surgery. Left alone with the patient, Charlie tries some gentle slaps on the wrist. He listens to the old man's heartbeats—then puts his ear to the sole of one of his feet.

Waiting room. Another patient arrives: a clean-shaven young man in a straw hat.

Surgery. As all other methods have failed Charlie resorts to drastic measures. He picks up a mallet and taps the old man on the forehead. Suddenly the patient starts to laugh uproariously. Flailing out his arms he hits Charlie who joins in the laughter, then suddenly silences the old man with a hefty blow of the mallet. Picking up a napkin, Charlie fans the unconscious patient as if he were a boxer. The dentist dashes in and hands Charlie a prescription to be filled. Charlie exits in haste.

Waiting room. Charlie smashes the surgery door into the face of the bearded man and steps onto his supine body on his way to the adjoining room.

Adjoining room. Charlie knocks down the midget, walks over him to retrieve his jacket, and then heads back to . . .

Waiting room. The bearded man stops Charlie to make a protest. He responds by smacking the man's face. The latter tries to retaliate, but Charlie ducks and the blow hits the lady with the bandaged face. Charlie dashes out, leaving a scene of chaos behind him in the waiting room.

Surgery. The dentist tries to cope with the patient who has recovered consciousness and is now laughing hysterically.

Exterior of pharmacy. A big man (Mack Swain) is blocking the entrance. Charlie raps him on the rump with his cane. As the bewildered Mack turns and stares at him, Charlie nonchalantly tosses his cane into the air and catches it. Then he rolls his derby down his arm, puts it back on his head, and raises it as if it were a lid. Disappearing into the pharmacy, he leaves Mack scratching his head in confusion.

Surgery. The frantic dentist glances at his watch. What's become of Charlie and the prescription?

Exterior of pharmacy. Charlie exits and gives the unsuspecting Mack a casual kick in the rear. This time Mack grabs him and protests. They slap each other. Just then the dentist's wife passes. Mack politely doffs his hat. Observing this, Charlie boots him in the belly and dashes after Mrs. Pain, leaving Mack writhing in agony.

Exterior of house with front steps. Charlie catches up with Mrs. Pain and tries to flirt with her. She gives him the brush-off—but he looks pleased with himself anyway. He swings his cane, knocking his derby off. She heads up the steps. He follows her but slips, grabs at her skirt, and pulls it off. Hearing her screams, Mack dashes over, catches sight of Mrs. Pain in her bloomers and faints away. Mrs. Pain flees in the direction of the pharmacy, colliding with a tall young man. Charlie flees in the opposite direction as Mack gets to his feet.

Exterior of dentist's house. Mrs. Pain knocks over a cop who is standing at the entrance. As he gets up to protest, she kicks him and runs into her house.

Street corner. Charlie hurls a brick at Mack. It catches him full in the mouth. Charlie sniggers. He hurls a second brick which misses Mack and strikes the tall young man in the jaw. Charlie flees as Mack comes after him.

Living room of dentist's house. Mrs. Pain flops into an armchair. Her maid calls up Dr. Pain.

Surgery. Dr. Pain hears the phone in the next room. He exits to answer it, leaving the old man writhing in the chair.

Next room. Dr. Pain receives the maid's call. He's aghast at the news.

Surgery. The old man gets out of the chair and finds that he's alone. Grabbing his hat, he gives a gesture of annoyance and exits.

Waiting room. Two bewildered female patients watch as the old man hastens past them, followed a moment later by the anxious-looking Dr. Pain.

Living room of dentist's house. The maid tries to calm her frantic mistress.

Exterior of dental parlor. Charlie comes into view, hopping on one foot. He looks back to see if Mack is still following him and then sneaks into the waiting room.

Waiting room. He eyes the two female patients, wipes the sweat off his brow, and enters the surgery.

Surgery. Charlie enters, looks around, and observes that the old man has gone. Pulling the prescription from his pocket, he dumps it into an ashtray.

Living room of dentist's house. The dentist arrives and listens to his wife's tale of woe.

Waiting room. Charlie tells the pretty girl to go into the surgery. The lady with the bandaged face objects (after all, she had arrived first), but a smiling Charlie gently back-kicks the girl into the surgery. The lady exits angrily.

Surgery. Charlie's big opportunity has arrived at last. He directs the girl to the dentist's chair. For a few moments he is uncertain what to do next. He peeks into the waiting room (to see if Dr. Pain and Mack are in sight?), then picks up a napkin and inadvertently starts polishing her shoes. They both realize his "error." When she starts laughing, he joins in—then puts one leg across her lap. Pushing him off, she shows him her bad tooth. They laugh again. However, Charlie is more interested in looking inside her dress than in practicing dentistry.

Waiting room. The tall young man arrives. In the background the bearded man is visible, stretched out on a sofa.

Surgery. Charlie flops backward onto the girl and looks into her mouth. Then he swivels the chair round until he falls dizzily to the floor. He tries climbing onto her lap once more but falls again. She laughs.

Living room of dentist's house. Dr. Pain is anxious to return to work. He tells his wife to put her skirt on.

Surgery. Charlie conceals his own and the girl's face with a napkin and kisses her. The midget enters. Charlie kicks him sprawling out of the room—onto the tall young man.

Waiting room. The tall young man hurls the midget onto the bearded man.

Surgery. Charlie seizes the girl's nose with a pair of tongs, turns her head toward him, and kisses her. She blushes. He tweaks his own nose with the tongs.

Waiting room. Mack arrives, nursing his injured mouth. He confers with the tall young man—presumably about Charlie.

Surgery. More tweaking and kissing. The girl doesn't seem to enjoy the treatment. Charlie is disgruntled. He lets the chair collapse backward, almost throwing the girl off it. She manages to extricate herself and exits hastily. Charlie now admits his next patient: the tall young man. Going to work on him with an enormous pair of forceps, he pulls out the wrong tooth, and boots the man in the face when he protests. Meanwhile, Mack has recognized the identity of the "dentist." He creeps into the surgery and confronts Charlie. They chase each other around the dentist's chair. Dr. Pain and his wife arrive. Charlie hurls a gladstone bag at Mack and knocks him backward onto Dr. Pain. Mack throws the bag back—it hits the tall young man in the face. Charlie charges at Dr. Pain, pushing him onto the tall young man who lands on top of Mack. At this point the midget rushes in swinging, but Charlie tosses him onto the others. He thinks he's victorious—but he has forgotten about Mrs. Pain, who knocks him out with a well-aimed blow to the jaw and then collapses onto the sofa.

COMMENTS

1. Satirical depictions of dentists were popular in the *commedia dell'arte* and this tradition resurfaced in Fred Karno's mime shows while Chaplin was working with the Karno company. Chaplin undoubtedly drew heavily upon his recollections of Karno's sketch *The Dentist* in creating *Laughing Gas*—which was probably the earliest film comedy on this subject.

Other comedy treatments of dentists and dentistry include: a sequence in Laurel and Hardy's *Leave 'Em Laughing* (1928) in which Stan and Olly react to laughing gas; W. C. Fields's famous short *The Dentist* (produced by Sennett, 1932), which was an adaptation of one of Fields's theatrical sketches; *The Paleface* (1948) in which Bob Hope plays a timorous dentist in the Old West; and two British comedies starring Bob Monkhouse, *Dentist in the Chair* (1960) and *Dentist on the Job* (1961). Black comedy treatments of the same subject occur in John Schlesinger's *Marathon Man* (1976), in which a fanatical Nazi dentist (Laurence Olivier) goes to work on Dustin Hoffman's teeth, and Erich von Stroheim's *Greed* (1923), in which Gibson Gowland plays a feeble-minded, unqualified dentist who is forced to stop practicing. (A scene in *Greed* when Gowland kisses one of his patients while she is in the dentist chair looks like a "serious" recreation of Charlie the dentist at work on the pretty girl.)

2. *Laughing Gas* is the first of a number of Chaplin films in which Charlie appears as an assistant to a workman, shopkeeper, or professional. Other examples: *His Musical Career* (Keystone no. 31), in which he is a piano mover assisting Mack Swain; *Work* (Essanay 1915), in which he is a wallpaper-hanger assisting Charles Insley; *The Pawnshop* (Mutual 1916), in which he is a salesman and general factotum assisting pawnbroker Henry Bergman; *Behind the Screen* (Mutual 1916), in which he is a sceneshifter in a movie studio assisting foreman Eric Campbell; *Sunnyside* (First National 1919), in which he is an odd job man at a hotel assisting manager Tom Wilson; and *Pay Day* (First National 1922), in which he is a construction worker at a building site assisting foreman Mack Swain. One special link between *Laughing Gas* and *The Pawnshop* is that in both films Charlie is engaged in a running duel with a rival assistant.

3. Structure. Three main plot movements: (I) the dental parlor—Charlie's accidental and deliberate mistreatment of patients (and his rival assistant); (II) interlude: the pharmacy—Charlie's accidental and deliberate mistreatment of passersby; (III) the dental parlor—Charlie's masquerade as a dentist, cross-cut with the real dentist's return home to his frantic wife.

(I) consists of seven scenes: (i) Prologue: Charlie momentarily creates the impression that *he's* the dentist. This is a mini-masquerade that foreshadows (III); (ii) Charlie fights his rival assistant; (iii) He tries to provoke a fight with a patient; (iv) Charlie's second fight with his rival; (v) The dentist overdoses his patient. His incompetence is "unmasked"; (vi) The mallet. Charlie tries to help the frantic dentist. This scene foreshadows the cross-cut scenes of (III) where the dentist tries to console his frantic wife; (vii) Charlie knocks down another patient and his rival.

(II) consists of four scenes: (i) Charlie's first assault on Mack; (ii) He rips off Mrs. Pain's skirt. She is "unmasked"; (iii) His second assault on Mack—kicks and bricks; (iv) Mrs. Pain's assault on the cop.

(III) consists of six scenes: (i) The dentist's return home cross-cut with (ii) Charlie "operating" on the girl; (iii) Charlie "operating" on the tall young man; (iv) Mack's recognition of Charlie. Charlie is "unmasked"; (v) Denouement.

4. In his book *Chaplin the Immortal Tramp*, R. J. Minney (1954, 42) claims: "The first notable development in the character of the tramp occurs in *Laughing Gas*." Minney follows up this comment with a description of Charlie's actions as he enters the dental parlor, but he does not enlarge on his statement. Frankly, I don't see anything in the film to support Minney's view. Charlie is klutzy, lecherous, mischievous, meddlesome, aggressive, malicious, bullying, vengeful, and sadistic:

i.e., he exhibits an accumulation of characteristics that are all evident in earlier Keystones. In many of those films he also anticipates his behavior in *Laughing Gas* by having fun at the expense of other, serious-minded characters. Even his penchant for masquerade was previously demonstrated in *Caught in a Cabaret* and *Her Friend the Bandit*.

What *is* developed in *Laughing Gas* is not Charlie's character but the range of his comic business and the functions of his violence.

The variety of the comic business is impressive. There's a clever sight gag early in the film when Charlie is trying to arouse the old man in the dentist chair. First he checks the patient's heart and then his sole—i.e., "soul." Then, having beaten him into insensibility with the mallet, he immediately mitigates his callous act by "transforming" the old man into a punch-drunk boxer who needs fanning with a towel. Outside the pharmacy he momentarily hypnotizes Mack (and probably the audience) with a slick display of legerdemain using hat and cane. Back at the dental parlor he applies a gentle version of his by now familiar back-kick to ease the pretty girl into his clutches. When he gets the girl and later the tall young man into the dentist chair, we are given a marvelous parody of a ruthless dentist on the job.

Charlie's behavior as a dentist makes a fascinating contrast with his treatment of Albert Austin's alarm clock in *The Pawnshop*. In the latter film the focus is on the object: Charlie's actions seem to transform the clock into a living form that he subjects to a medical examination and an operation. In *Laughing Gas* the focus is on the masquerade: Charlie's assumed role shows us a dentist exploiting his opportunities for lechery and sadism. What makes his behavior comical are his exaggerations (huge forceps), his lapses into inappropriate actions (polishing the girl's shoes), and, above all, the ludicrous assumption that motivates his masquerade: that he has *become* a dentist by *mimicking* the actions of one.

More vividly than in any of his previous Keystones Charlie also provokes laughter through his creative transformations of familiar objects, and (*pace* Henri Bergson) by treating *people* as if they were insignificant objects. Thus he nonchalantly turns two of the characters in the waiting room into his personal doormats, and later, in a twinkling, transforms his derby first into a bowling ball (using his arm as the bowling lane) and then into a flapping kettle lid. Patently, this is an individual who sees in others (particularly men) less than they see in themselves, but at the same time views the world of objects as one of endlessly creative possibilities. For Charlie objects *can be* and *are* easily adapted to suit his imaginative needs, but humans are less cooperative. They must be beaten, kicked, or bricked into conformity with his purposes. (E.g., a pair of tongs is ready to be used as a nose-tweaker, but the tall young man needs to be booted in the mouth if Charlie is to operate on him in peace.)

Laughing Gas is one of Chaplin's most anarchic early films: a wholesale mockery of order, dignity, and respectability. It is easy and misleading to see the film's violence as much of a muchness. Actually we are shown a variety of violent acts, and, more importantly, a *variety of motives* for them that reveal Charlie's attitudes to other characters. Charlie's attacks on his rival, the other assistant, begin as simple put-downs. He resents a mere assistant telling him to do something. As his rival is a midget, Charlie falsely assumes that he must be weaker and can be bullied without fear of retribution. After the midget demonstrates than he can take care of himself, Charlie changes his tactics and his motives: he makes vengeful surprise attacks.

In the waiting room he is mischievously provocative toward the old man whom he regards as another mere weakling. He stops short of a frontal assault when the bearded man intervenes. In the surgery a few moments later, he first tries out the mallet on the old man as a would-be "cure," but then uses it in vicious retaliation for the blows he has accidentally received from him.

En route to the pharmacy Charlie himself is responsible for accidental violence when he slams the door into the bearded man's face. Then, as previously noted, he casually uses his victim as a carpet. Accident or not, the blow from the slammed door provokes retaliation—a chain reaction of further violence. (This action, with similar consequences, is inflicted on one of Charlie's fellow waiters in the café sequence of *Modern Times* [1936].) Before Charlie enters the pharmacy he strikes Mack on the rump with his cane. Charlie is in a hurry, and Mack's rear, whether he knows it or not, is an obstruction. Booting Mack in the belly is another matter. What was its motivation? Jealousy? (Mrs. Pain smiles at Mack, not at Charlie.) A deflation of Mack's smugness? (He looks a bit too pleased with himself.) Contempt that Mack did not retaliate for the whack on his bottom? Whatever the reason, it is one of the most sadistic acts in all the Keystones. Before we have time to recover from it, Charlie has dashed after Mrs. Pain and ripped off her skirt. Another accident, of course, but something he'd doubtless like to do to her deliberately, in private. Notice that unlike Mack (who faints) and her husband (who goes into a tizzy over it), Charlie isn't shocked at the sight of a women in bloomers. A few moments later he's enjoying himself, hurling bricks at Mack, grinning at his agony—and inadvertently drumming up customers for the dental parlor. (This is surely the germ of that sequence in *The Kid* [1921] where little Jackie breaks windows to provide work for Charlie the glazier.)

It's not too clear why Mrs. Pain kicks the cop. Does she think that he is gawking at her? Is it a delayed display of bad temper at having her elegant outfit desecrated? Or is he simply in her way? Curiously, as soon as she gets indoors, she loses her aggressiveness and wilts helplessly into an armchair. Her husband has to rush to her aid. However, in the film's curious final twist of violence, this apparently helpless woman is allowed—if not the last word—at least the last blow.

OTHER VIEWS

"Charlie aids a dentist, Dr. Pain, with an amazing mixture of incompetence and self-interest. With most of the patients his tools are wrenches, hammers and overdoses of laughing gas, but with a pretty girl he uses a pair of forceps, gently and charmingly, to steal kisses" (Moss 1975, 27–28).

"The dentist's studio in *Laughing Gas* supplied him [Chaplin] with one of the most ancient of comic props—the enormous pliers with which he terrifies his patients. Il Dottore [of the *commedia dell'arte*] was brandishing them more than 200 years before Chaplin" (Sobel and Francis 1977, 199–200).

"Keystone comedy was filled with moments of violence and Mack [Swain] was often the object of spiteful Charlie's rage, as in *Laughing Gas*" (Lahue and Gill 1971b, 97).

"Charlie [was an] . . . intrusive lighthearted mischief-maker in such films as *Laughing Gas*" (Manvell 1974, 91).

21.

The Property Man

(1914)

Other titles: *The Roustabout, Props, Charlie on the Boards, Getting His Goat, Vamping Venus*; French: *Charlot accessoiriste, Charlot garçon de théâtre, Charlot dans les coulisses, Charlot monte sur les planches*; German: *Der Requisiteur*; Spanish: *Charlot tramoyista*; Italian: *Il trovarobe, Dietro le quinte*

Length: 2 reels; 1853 feet (Asplund), 2118 feet (Lyons)
Playing time: 31 minutes at 16 frames per second
Producer: Keystone
Director: Chaplin
Screenplay: Chaplin
Photography: Frank D. Williams(?)
Cast:

Props	Chaplin
Garlico	Fritz Schade
Hamlena Fat (angry vaudeville wife)	Phyllis Allen
Her husband, an old actor	Joe Bordeaux
Man (wearing pullover) in audience	Mack Sennett
The Goo Sisters	Norma Nichols
	Alice Davenport
Other roles	Lee Morris
	Harry McCoy
	Charles Bennett

Finished or shipped: July 18, 1914
Released: August 1, 1914

SYNOPSIS

A room next to the stage door in a vaudeville theater. Charlie, the property man, is in shirt-sleeves and wearing his derby. Behind him are several notices: "No Smoking," "Actors do not pose in front of your Posters," and "If your act is rotten, don't take it out on the Props." He drinks from a jug of beer, thirstily watched by his elderly assistant. The latter indicates that he wants his share. Charlie's reply is to wag his finger (You shouldn't drink!), give his ear a twist, and spew some beer in the assistant's face. Meanwhile, outside the stage door, a dignified old actor and his wife are examining a playbill on which the acts of Garlico the Strong Man and the Goo Sisters are prominently advertised. Charlie hands the empty jug to his forlorn assistant. He puts a corncob pipe in his mouth and gives the old man some money to get more beer. He exits up some steps at the rear of the room. Charlie dumps his pipe tobacco into his hand and shoves it into his mouth.

The old actor is smoking, nonchalantly. The wife looks disgusted. Title: *"Why, they haven't billed us!"*

The elderly assistant emerges from the stage door and overhears them. The wife insists that her husband follow her into the theater. They descend the steps behind Charlie who is now smoking his pipe. She starts to harangue Charlie. Unmoved, he casually takes some cotton wool from his pocket and stuffs it into his ears. They exit toward the dressing rooms. Charlie waves them goodbye.

Title: *"We'll take the Stars' dressing-room."*

The wife opens a door in the hallway. Behind her on the wall is a chalked caricature of Charlie below the word "PROPS." She enters the bare dressing room and shuts the door.

Title: *The "Strong Man" and his bride.*

The bride, a young woman wearing a large hat, descends the stage-door steps followed by the portly figure of her husband, Garlico the Strong Man, who is wearing a top hat and carrying a cane. Meanwhile, the wife is looking at herself in a mirror; she removes her hat and hangs it up. The bride opens the door and enters the dressing room. The two women angrily confront one another.

Charlie looks on as Garlico kicks aside a large trunk. He almost knocks Charlie's hat off with his cane. Then he grabs some letters that were attached to the wall and starts reading them. Charlie looks scared. He stares at Garlico who is puffing at a large cigar and is about to draw his attention to the "No Smoking" sign when—discretion being the better part of valor—he changes his mind. Reaching up to the sign, he turns it round to face the wall. Garlico scornfully flicks ash over Charlie and walks away. Charlie stands up and is about to kick him when Garlico turns round. Charlie quickly changes his mind again. Flexing his muscles, he stumbles up the steps and exits.

In the hallway a young man in a straw hat is sitting on a trunk. Garlico makes him stand up. Then the strong man lifts the trunk with ease, flips it over, examines it to see if it's his, and drops it on the young man's foot. He exits, leaving the young man hopping up and down in pain.

Outside the stage door Charlie wipes his hands, flexes his muscles, and hoists a large trunk onto his back. Garlico reenters the stage-door room. He looks angry and stumbles up the steps. Moving backward, Charlie inadvertently pushes the trunk into Garlico's face. Garlico's efforts to examine the trunk cause Charlie to lose hold of it. The trunk falls down the steps, and Charlie comes tumbling after it. Garlico marches down after him. He grabs Charlie, lifts him up, and shoves him aside.

Hallway. The bride slaps the wife's face. She howls. Nearby, her husband, the old actor, is talking to the young man. Hearing his wife's howling, he marches over to see what's wrong. She expects him to retaliate, but he raises his hat to the bride. Mrs. Garlico turns up her nose at his politeness.

Stage-door room. Garlico hoists the trunk onto Charlie's back. Charlie staggers around with it. Garlico steadies him—then gives him a shove that sends him hurtling across the hallway. He smashes into the old actor, knocking him sprawling into the stars' dressing room. Garlico dashes past the two women in pursuit of his trunk. Charlie apologizes but the old actor heaves him back onto Garlico. Then he slaps the strong man—intending the blow for Charlie. Garlico returns the slap in spades, knocking the old actor unconscious. This time Charlie apologizes to Garlico. The two women march in and carry on an angry altercation. Then the wife and Charlie pick up the old actor and carry him out of the room and across the hallway. Garlico now examines the trunk. It's the wrong one. He opens the door and calls for Charlie who comes running. Garlico orders him to remove the trunk.

Stage-door room. The elderly assistant hobbles down the stairs followed by the Goo Sisters, two young dancers. Meanwhile, Garlico hoists the trunk onto Charlie's back and hands him his hat. Charlie tries to put the hat on and almost loses his hold on the trunk. Garlico holds a casual conversation with him while he is staggering under its weight. The Goo Sisters are joking with the elderly assistant. Suddenly they turn, aghast, to watch what is happening to Charlie. Garlico has given him a hefty kick. He staggers but maintains his balance. He dances around the hallway with the trunk on his back, stumbles with it into the stage-door room, and collapses at the feet of the Goo Sisters. They laugh. But Charlie knows when to be polite. He gets up and doffs his hat. Then he takes the beer jug from his assistant and kicks him. The old man wearily exits up the steps. Chatting with the Goo Sisters, Charlie follows them into the hallway.

Trying to conceal his beer jug, he slips it into his capacious pants. When one of the Goo Sisters drops her reticule, Charlie makes the mistake of bending to pick it up. Hastily dropping it, he clutches at his wet trouser leg and walks away in an awkward bow-legged fashion. He turns and smiles at the two women. They stare at the wet floor and then at Charlie. Disgusted, they exit. Charlie shakes his leg and looks wanly after them.

Outside the stage door. Charlie is now "helping" his assistant move a huge trunk. He gets it onto the old man's back, checks that he's o.k., then kicks him in the face. He walks ahead of the old man, smoking his pipe and carrying a light hatbox. Maneuvering the trunk, the assistant follows Charlie down the steps. Charlie tries to tilt it off his back, but he collapses and the trunk lands on his stomach. Unable to shift it off his squirming body, Charlie pauses to relight his pipe. Now the bride appears in the hallway dressed in her bathrobe. Charlie climbs onto the trunk to take a rest. She stares at him. Telling the assistant to keep his cool, Charlie trots away to get help. He passes the bride. She calls him back. He stares at her *en déshabillé*, and she strokes his face affectionately.

An ordinary dressing room. The Goo Sisters enter. They peek over a screen behind which the old actor is fixing his wife's hair. The two groups confront each other, arguing about who has the right to the dressing room.

Charlie and the bride are now exchanging jokes while the assistant continues to squirm underneath the trunk. Garlico suddenly appears and notices his bride flirting with Charlie. Marching over, he kicks him and shoves him to the floor. Charlie gets up and delivers a feeble return kick, but a hefty belly-push from Garlico sends him sprawling back onto the trunk. Now Charlie tries to remove the trunk while he's sitting on it. He kicks the old man to silence his protests. In the hallway, Garlico turns to his bride and starts berating her. Rather belatedly, Charlie calls for help for his assistant. Garlico orders his wife back to her room: she isn't dressed. In the meantime, the Goo Sisters, the old actor and his wife have extended their quarrel into the hallway. They suddenly notice the assistant's predicament and rush to the rescue. They try—without success—to remove the trunk. Real strength is needed, and Garlico hears the call at last. He flexes his muscles and smirks at the camera. Swaggering into the stage-door room, he knocks Charlie off the trunk and lifts it aside with one hand. Then he flexes his muscles once more and exits. Miffed at being outclassed by the strong man, Charlie takes out his resentment on his assistant: he tweaks the old man's ear, slaps him on the back, and kicks him. Then he too flexes his muscles and exits.

Charlie is now shifting scenery in the wings. In the stars' dressing room the bride has changed into a ballerina-like costume. Garlico is wearing a tiger skin. They are quarreling. She exits in a bad temper, rushes up to Charlie (who's now mopping the floor), and hands him a pair of Garlico's tights. (For cleaning or repair?)

On stage a male singer is performing. Prominent in the front row of the audience is Mack Sennett. To his right is a lady holding a dog in her lap. To his left a drunkard is sleeping with his head on Mack's shoulder. The singer takes his bow. Backstage, Charlie throws a mop in his assistant's face and falls over a rope as he rushes to let down a new backdrop. It comes down on the singer's head—to enthusiastic applause from the audience. The assistant now adjusts the backdrop. Charlie walks on stage holding a broom. He sweeps up the garbage thrown by the audience. Then he faces them and holds his nose. The audience applauds good-humoredly. In the wings the singer takes his revenge on Charlie's assistant, causing him to drop the backdrop rope. The backdrop itself immediately falls onto Charlie. He gets up and scowls at the audience this time. The applause comes only from the lady with the dog. His assistant quickly resecures the backdrop, reaches out, and drags Charlie offstage. Charlie is furious. He chases after the old man, but falls over a bucket of water. The old man tries to pacify him, but Charlie won't be mollified: he gets up and kicks him in the belly. Momentarily, the commotion arouses the drunkard.

Now the Goo Sisters begin their act. From the wings Charlie eyes them as they dance on to the stage. Mack also eyes them eagerly. But when Charlie notices his elderly assistant peering at the two dancers, he blindfolds him and leads him behind the backdrop. Then he goes through the old man's pockets, removes the blindfold, and cautions him about looking at girls. Meanwhile, the Goos are dancing a variation on the cancan. Mack waves to them. Behind the backdrop Charlie is standing on a mat. He orders his assistant to pick it up. The old man obliges, tripping Charlie against the backdrop so that he bumps the Goos from behind. The audience applauds this as part of the show. Next the assistant drops a heavy prop on Charlie's foot. In a fit of rage, Charlie kicks him. At this the old man suddenly becomes combative. They exchange blows and it looks as if the old man is able to take care of himself. Then Charlie cunningly demonstrates some fancy sparring. Having confused the old man, Charlie tosses one of Garlico's weights at him and kicks him in the jaw.

Title: *"Hurry, get my tights."*

In the stars' dressing room the bride tells Garlico what she has done with them. Horrified, he orders her to get them back and shoves her out of the room. She shouts back at him from the hallway. Behind the backdrop, Charlie is arguing with his assistant. The bride anxiously asks Charlie for the tights. He can't recall where he put them.

Their first dance at an end, the Goos bow to the audience and dance into the wings. They shout that the scene is over. Charlie orders his assistant to change the backdrop, then rushes to grab the rope himself. They quarrel. Charlie suddenly notices Garlico's tights on the floor. He picks them up and hurls them at the assistant. They miss the old man and hit one of the Goos—who by now are performing their second dance. The stricken dancer throws the tights at the audience. They hit Mack and wake up the drunkard. Charlie creeps away, leaving his assistant to cope with the scenery. The Goo Sisters march offstage and confront the assistant. Behind the backdrop Charlie tries to calm the bride who is still demanding Garlico's tights. All he can do is mop his brow and blow his nose. The Goos, meanwhile, slap his assistant. Then they stalk past Charlie, who is now trying to flirt with the bride.

Sandwiched between the sleeping drunkard and the lady (who is now making a big show of eating candies), Mack tries to elbow himself into a comfortable position.

Garlico is late for his act. The assistant dashes off to get him. In the stars' dressing room Garlico looks upset. The assistant raps at his door and tells him he's wanted on stage. Frantic, Garlico heads towards the stage. Behind the backdrop he stops and stares glumly down at his legs. No tights—only underpants. Angrily, he confronts his bride, and then Charlie. At this moment the assistant pulls up the backdrop, inadvertently revealing a tableau at the back of the stage: Garlico in his underpants and his bride and Charlie pointing at him. The audience laughs uproariously. The bride dashes offstage followed by Charlie. In the wings she angrily confronts the assistant while Charlie mimes Garlico in his underpants.

On stage. Making the best of a bad situation, Garlico begins his act. He stands on a 500 lb. weight and flexes his muscles. Meanwhile, Charlie and his assistant trade slaps. The latter misses his target and hits the bride, knocking her out. Unaware of what has just happened, Garlico calls for her. But the show must go on: Charlie decides to take her place.

Garlico's act now follows. Charlie dances toward the strong man. The audience cheers. Garlico orders Charlie to move his barbells. With maximum effort Charlie drags them across the stage. Applause. Garlico tosses a handkerchief in Charlie's face. Charlie blows his nose in it. With a mighty effort the strong man lifts the barbells. The drunkard falls onto Mack. Mack slaps him back. Garlico lifts a weight with his right hand. An excited audience. Now Garlico lifts a weight with his left hand. Charlie stares at the strong man's underpants and laughs. Garlico raises the barbells above his head and drops them—right onto Charlie's foot. He hops painfully out of sight.

The wife turns up in the wings. She confronts Charlie: When is it her turn to go on? Garlico meanwhile has picked up an iron bar and is resting it on the back of his neck. With a mighty effort he bends the bar—and splits his underpants. Mack jeers. Charlie temporarily silences the wife by blowing smoke in her face. Then he picks up the still-unconscious bride and drags her away. Garlico is now lifting two weights (150 lb. and 500 lb.) while balancing the barbells on his neck. Charlie tries to keep the bride upright while he opens her dressing room door. At last he hits on the idea of holding her up by ramming his knee under her rump. Once inside the room he maneuvers her into a chair with great difficulty.

In a fury, the wife chases the assistant. When she catches up with him, he shoves his fist in her mouth; her husband merely stands by and watches. Meanwhile, Charlie fans the unconscious bride with a handkerchief. The assistant rushes back to deal with the backdrop: he lets it fall onto Garlico while he is in the middle of his biggest weight-lifting performance. More applause. Garlico drops his weights and disappears from view as the backdrop hits the stage. He shoves the couple in the face and stamps off in a rage. With downcast look, he pushes open his dressing room door and finds his bride with the property man.

Title: *The dramatic Act.*

On stage we see a scene from an old melodrama. The wife, holding a baby, is kneeling beside a bed. Her husband, the old actor, towers over her, holding a stockwhip. Disgusted at this part of the show, Mack gets out of his seat and points angrily into the camera. The drunkard also gets up—and burps in Mack's face. In a fury, Mack slaps him back into his seat, and holding his nose stamps out of the theater. The drunkard promptly flops across the empty seat into the lady's lap.

Garlico and Charlie trade blows, knocking down the old actor on the other side of the backdrop. Charlie swings the barbells, felling the singer. The bride, now recovered, hurls a weight which strikes the old actor. Charlie kicks Garlico then takes to his heels, knocking down his assistant. The strong man pursues Charlie onto the stage. The audience, of course, thinks it's all part of the show. Booting Garlico onto the bed, Charlie rushes offstage. The strong man continues the chase—only to ram his head against a wall. Taking advantage of his enemy's helplessness, Charlie smashes him on the head with the barbells.

To climax the mayhem, he picks up a hosepipe and deluges everyone on stage and behind the scenery. The audience rocks with laughter, but Charlie dampens their hilarity by training the jet onto them too, and he gives the drunkard an extra-special dose of cold water. The film ends with the whole company, its spirits well and truly dampened, grabbing the hosepipe from their aggressive property man.

COMMENTS

1. This was Chaplin's first film about the world of music hall/vaudeville that he had left behind just a few months earlier. It would be by no means his last.

The Property Man should, ideally, be viewed in conjunction with *A Night in the Show* (Essanay 1915), and *Limelight* (1954). In its own way, it is a more intriguing film than *A Night in the Show*, for where the Essanay film focuses on the show (a recreation of Karno's *Mumming Birds*), the Keystone film moves back and forth between the show (backstage and onstage) and its audience. *The Property Man's* farcical and satiric treatment of vaudeville also contrasts with the nostalgia of *Limelight*. In 1914, Chaplin was too close to the day-to-day realities of putting on shows in run-down flea-pit theaters to be nostalgic about them. Forty years later, after a lifetime of moviemaking, he could view that bygone world with affection as part of "the good old days." Yet even *Limelight* gives us one final glimpse of that harsher, tacky vaudeville world of *The Property Man* in the painful sequence in which the audience walks out on Calvero during his anonymous try-out at the Middlesex Theater.

Six other Chaplin films that bear significant comparison with *The Property Man* are *A Film Johnnie* (Keystone no. 5), *The Masquerader* (Keystone no. 24), *His New Job* (Essanay 1915), *Behind the Screen* (Mutual 1916), *His Musical Career* (Keystone no. 31), and *Work* (Essanay 1915). In the first four, set in film studios, we see a world behind the camera that resembles Chaplin's farcical vision of life backstage. (Charlie's job in *Behind the Screen* is also that of a sceneshifter.) In *The Property Man* Charlie treats his elderly assistant as a workhorse; in *Work*, as apprentice to house decorator Charles Insley, he himself becomes the workhorse: he literally has to drag his boss's cart. In *His Musical Career* Charlie the piano mover staggers under the weight of an upright just as he staggers under the weight of the trunk in *The Property Man*. *A Woman of Paris* (1923) contains an "in joke" on these scenes: Chaplin gives himself a mere walk-on part as a railroad porter who totters across the screen carrying a huge trunk.

2. Structure. The first reel consists of a series of comic misfortunes. (i) No beer for the elderly assistant. (ii) No billing for the old actor and his wife. (iii) Garlico can't locate his trunk. (iv) He drops a trunk on a young man's foot. (v) The wife is turned out of the stars' dressing room. (vi) Charlie has to move a heavy trunk. (vii) His problems with the beer jug. (viii) His elderly assistant is squashed under another trunk. (ix) Charlie is kicked for flirting with the bride. (x) The wife and the Goo

Sisters quarrel over another dressing room. (xi) Charlie feels outclassed by Garlico. The second reel revolves around three comic catastrophes: (i) Garlico's lost tights, (ii) his antagonism to Charlie, and (iii) the mistimed backdrop. The climax (Charlie and the hosepipe) is a development of (ii).

3. *The Property Man* is one of the earliest films in a long tradition of movies about putting on a show. It differs from most of the others in its slapstick treatment of the subject and the fact that it looks intermittently at three "shows": the one on stage, the one backstage, and the one in the audience.

As in *The Circus* these three shows relate to one another either ironically or superficially, and only we, the offscreen audience, are able to perceive the whole picture. The audience in the film never realizes that the melodrama on stage more or less inverts the real characters of the old actor and his wife. They know nothing of all those backstage antagonisms that we see in reel one. They are totally oblivious of the sufferings of the elderly assistant, while we, of course, have been made vividly aware of them. (The film here seems a hairbreadth away from that disturbing contrast in *The Circus* between our awareness of Charlie as a terrified fugitive and that of the audience under the big top who see him only as "The Funny Man.") They laugh (humiliatingly) at Garlico in his underpants without realizing that he's the top dog backstage. And they never know why he chases Charlie or that his conflict with him is really serious. Above all, until Charlie turns his hose on them, they are under the illusion that everything that goes wrong on stage was meant to be part of the show.

It's equally true that no one on or behind the stage relates in any significant way to the audience. The elderly assistant is too busy lifting trunks and moving the backdrop to pay any attention to them. Charlie sees them as garbage-throwers whose litter he has to sweep up. For the performers they mean only undifferentiated mass laughter, applause or mockery. But, for us, the film repeatedly cuts back to the front row where the audience is individualized. Instead of a crowd we see a lady who applauds in the wrong places or laughs when no one else does, a drunkard who sleeps through most of the show, and Mack who divides his attention between the antics on stage and the antics of his neighbors.

Although the backstage world is ostensibly dedicated to making the show run smoothly, its conflicts disrupt the program. At the end of the film all three "shows"—backstage, the melodrama, and the audience—are "washed up" by Charlie. Could this also have been Chaplin's verdict on vaudeville only seven months into his movie career?

4. Many critics have objected to the film's cruelty, referring specifically to Charlie's treatment of his elderly assistant. Some of the descriptions of what he actually does to the old man are more impressionistic than accurate. One such account, remarkably vivid despite its imprecision, is John MacCabe's:

> Charlie loads the trunk onto the back of the human wreck. The man staggers forward leaning on his cane. Charlie beats him like a mule, and the other collapses altogether, to lie, crushed under his burden, on the ground. To get him going again, Charlie leaps up on the trunk, thus adding to the burden of the old man, who now resembles nothing so much as a pathetic beetle pinned to the ground by some sick wit. (1978, 60)

McCabe goes on to concur with Raymond Durgnat that Chaplin was "easily the cruelest of Sennett's comedians." However, to this damning assessment he adds perceptively:

> One need not challenge this to point out also that the millions who loved these films in 1914 and later were not necessarily laughing at cruelty. One does not laugh at a cartoon—which is what *The Property Man* is—because it is real, but precisely because it is unreal, a caricature of life's troubles. We, all of us, soon or late get someone on our backs.

Kalton Lahue and Sam Gill make a similar comment more concisely: "In the Keystone world, everything was reversed. The strong looked on while the weak did all the work" (1971b, 39).

It is generally overlooked that the elderly assistant is not quite the "human wreck" that McCabe says he is. When Charlie provokes him sufficiently, he doesn't hesitate to take him on, and it takes cunning rather than brute force to beat him back into submission.

Without trying to mitigate the film's undoubted cruelty it seems worth noting that what we see in *The Property Man* could be viewed as a comic condemnation of wage slavery and ruthless hierarchy. (I haven't so far come across any criticism of Beckett's comparable comic depiction of "cruelty" in Pozzo's mistreatment of Lucky in *Waiting for Godot*.) Both the elderly assistant *and* Charlie obviously accept their sufferings as part of the exploitation that goes along with being a wage slave: i.e., if you need the job you have to put up with the kicks. It seems possible that in provoking his audiences to laugh at such cruelty, Chaplin may also have been making them sense the sort of injustice that lay behind it. (See further *His Musical Career* note 3.)

Most critics seem to focus on Charlie's mistreatment of the old man. But we should also notice Garlico's similar mistreatment of Charlie. The cruelty gets passed down the hierarchical ladder. Only in 1914?

OTHER VIEWS

"In *The Property Man*, one of Chaplin's memories of music-hall days, he plays a scrappy stagehand who boots, smashes, rips, and wrecks everything. The cruelest of his antics is to make a helpless, broken, feeble old man do all the heavy labor while Charlie sits around idly puffing on a pipe, occasionally booting and slapping the octogenarian for good measure. Charlie's only reason for torturing the old man is simply that comic torture was a staple of the Sennett product" (Mast 1979, 71–72).

"The *Property Man* provides amusing caricatures of vaudeville stereotypes—the sister song-and-dance act, the strong-man turn, the old-fashioned melodramatic 'sketch.' " (Huff 1952, 45).

22.

The Face on the Bar Room Floor
(1914)

Other titles: *The Ham Actor, The Ham Artist*; French: *Charlot fou, Charlot artiste peintre*; German: *Das Gesicht auf dem Boden der Bar*; Spanish: *Charlot pintor*; Italian: *Charlot pittore*

Length: 1 reel; 869 feet (Asplund), 1020 feet (Lyons)
Playing time: 15 minutes at 16 frames per second
Producer: Keystone
Director: Chaplin
Screenplay: Chaplin*
Photography: Frank D. Williams (?)
Cast:

The ham artist	Chaplin
Madeleine, his beloved	Cecile Arnold
The client who marries her	Fritz Schade
A model	Vivian Edwards
Drinkers	Chester Conklin
	Harry McCoy
	Wallace MacDonald
	Hank Mann

Finished or shipped: July 20, 1914
Released: August 10, 1914

SYNOPSIS

Barroom of a tavern. A drunken sailor is slumped over the bar (right foreground). Charlie enters, looking very disheveled and with a streak of paint on the side of his jacket. He walks up and down, eyeing the sailor's rump; then he pushes it and sniffs at it. Recovering, the

*Based on a poem of the same title by Hugh Antoine D'Arcy.

sailor offers him a drink. Charlie downs it while wiping away a tear. He coughs and puts his glass on the bar. The sailor resumes his nap. Surrounded by barflies, Charlie begins his tale. He peers earnestly ahead of him, one arm outstretched. Then, eyeing the sailor's rump once more, he draws a picture in the air.

An artist's studio. Dressed in a tuxedo, Charlie is holding a palette and brush. In the foreground to his left is his unfinished portrait of Madeleine, perched on an easel. Behind him several nude female statues are visible. A model in a harem costume is reclining on the floor. To Charlie's right, Madeleine is standing up and posing, with her rump aimed in his direction. Charlie turns to his canvas. He paints an outline of Madeleine's rump and adds what looks like a belt. Then he carefully shades in the rump and paints a distorted outline of one of her legs. After that he shades in the whole area below the waist, adding a handle above the rump so that she appears to be wearing a chamber pot. Fade out.

Fade in to the same setting. Holding Madeleine's arm, Charlie stares at her rapturously. He shows her the portrait, but she displays no interest in it. He raises his foot and inadvertently puts it down on the wet palette. She yawns and puffs on a cigarette. Taking her hand, he places it over his heart, then kisses it. Next he tries to kiss her on the lips, but she pulls away from him and dances out of the room, laughing. His back to the camera, Charlie gazes after her, his arms outstretched, longingly. He puts his hand to his brow. Then he turns to face the camera, walks forward, and stumbles over a polar bear skin stretched out on the floor. Picking up his paintbrush he contemplates the portrait. Absentmindedly, he touches his mouth with the wet paintbrush. He looks forlorn as the scene fades out.

Barroom. In a drunken daze, Charlie sways to and fro. One of the barflies steadies him. He flings out his arms, striking a man in the face. Then he falls backward. The barflies help him to his feet. Someone hands him another drink which he immediately knocks back, spitting the dregs into the sailor's face.

The studio. In the background, to Charlie's left, Fritz is posing for his portrait. In the foreground, to Charlie's right, is his caricature-like portrait of the sitter. Charlie prods Fritz's nose with a paintbrush to position his face. Then he turns to the canvas and twirls the brush into the portrait's ear-hole. While he is rearranging Fritz's posture, Madeleine enters, spies the portrait, clasps her hands together, and sighs. It's love at first sight. Charlie now introduces her to the sitter. Fritz is also smitten. They shake hands, and Fritz pulls her close to him. She kneels at his feet. Charlie looks shattered as he watches them engaged in intimate conversation. Distractedly, he daubs large blotches of paint on his white shirtfront. Now Fritz gets up, comes over to Charlie, and bows. He does a mime of Madeleine as a vase/chamberpot (i.e., her portrait). He shakes hands with Charlie and then with Madeleine. She clasps her hands together as he departs. At the exit he turns to gaze back at her. Fade out.

The studio. Madeleine is in street clothes and looks pensive. Fritz is holding his overcoat and a valise and has his arm around her. He invites her to elope with him. She sticks an envelope on the nose of Fritz's portrait. They exit hastily. A worried Charlie enters. He picks up a paintbrush, then turns to the canvas and notices the envelope. Ripping it open, he tosses the letter aside. Then he looks at the envelope, tosses that aside, and picks up the letter. Handwritten text of letter: "Goodby you great big hunk of man and remember not to fall over your feet. Yours that was Itsey Bitsey Madeline [sic]." Charlie reels—then looks around the studio and puts his hand to his brow. He sits down on the wet palette and rereads the letter. Howling, he wipes his head with the letter, then turns and notices the portrait of Fritz. He stands up with his back to the camera: the seat of his pants is covered with paint. Staring at the painting, he beats his breast. Then he rereads the letter. Suddenly, he attacks the portrait, ripping out its eyes and then the whole face. Then he tosses aside the broken canvas and flops onto the floor, weeping.

Park. Charlie, now a disheveled tramp, yawns and sits down on a deserted bench. He removes his hat to scratch his head, then bends forward to scratch the sole of his shoe. Behind him a miserable Fritz comes into view. Escorted by a very prim and proper Madeleine, he is pushing a baby carriage and has three other kids in tow. Agape, Charlie studies them. They stop for a moment near his bench. She berates Fritz. Charlie stands up and puts his hands in his pockets. Madeleine ignores or doesn't notice him, but Fritz stares at him enviously. Charlie stares back unenviously as the little procession passes out of sight. Now, facing the camera, he wipes the perspiration from his forehead. He sighs, sniffs, flings out his arms resignedly, shrugs his shoulders, and turns his back to the camera. A daub of paint is visible on his tattered jacket. Again he shrugs and flings out his arms before lurching away from the bench. Before exiting he stumbles over his shadow and stops to raise his hat to it. Then he continues on his way, marching briskly with one shoulder tilted higher than the other.

Barroom. One of the barflies hands Charlie a piece of chalk. He drunkenly sketches circles in the air and flops onto his back. Very unsteadily, he bends over and manages to chalk a circle (Madeleine's head) and two lines (her eyes) on the floor. Then he tumbles forward headfirst into the circle and somersaults across the barroom. Reversing the somersault, he resumes his drawing, adding lines to represent a nose and a mouth. After that he falls backward at the feet of his cronies. They help him to his feet. A man with a cigar orders him to clear out. He shoves him in the face. Charlie confronts the man and swings at him. But the man ducks and the blow knocks nearly everyone else to the floor. Now the sailor intervenes. He raises his fists— but Charlie boots him through the swinging doors, out of the tavern. Then he turns to the bar and helps himself to a drink. The man with the cigar suddenly punches Charlie in the belly, making him spew out his beer in a long jet. Otherwise unmoved, he puts down his glass and casually boots the man out of the tavern. Finally, observed by two terrified bartenders, he flops over, crawls to his sketch, completes it— then falls backward, spread-eagled on the barroom floor.

COMMENTS

1. The film is a parody of the following ballad by Hugh Antoine D'Arcy (1843–1925). The poem, originally written in 1887, appears in D'Arcy's *The Face upon the Floor and Other Ballads* (New York: The Author: Green Room Club, n.d.), 8–12. Note that Chaplin's film uses the more popular but inaccurate title of the poem. "The Face upon the Floor" has been parodied many times in verse, but aside from Chaplin's treatment of the ballad, the only visual parody I have seen appeared many years ago in an issue of *Mad Magazine* which also reprinted the text of D'Arcy's poem.

The Face upon the Floor

'Twas a balmy summer evening, and a goodly crowd was there,
Which well-nigh filled Joe's bar-room on the corner of the square;
And as songs and witty stories came through the open door
A vagabond crept slowly in and posed upon the floor.

"Where did it come from?" some one said. "The wind has blown it in."
"What does it want?" another cried. "Some whiskey, rum or gin."
"Here, Toby, sic him if your stomach's equal to the work—
I wouldn't touch him with a fork, he's as filthy as a Turk."

This badinage the poor wretch took with stoical good grace;
In fact he smiled, as though he thought he'd struck the proper place.
"Come, boys, I know there's burly hearts among so good a crowd,
To be in such good company would make a deacon proud.

"Give me a drink—that's what I want—I'm out of funds you know,
When I had cash to treat the gang this hand was never slow.
What? You laugh as though you thought this pocket never held a sou!
I once was fixed as well, my boys, as any one of you.

"There, thanks! that's braced me nicely. God bless you one and all!
Next time I pass this good saloon I'll make another call.
Give you a song? No, I can't do that; my singing days are past;

My voice is cracked, my throat's worn out, and my lungs are going
fast.

"Say! give me another whiskey, and I tell you what I'll do—
I'll tell you a funny story, and a fact, I promise, too.
That I was ever a decent man not one of you would think;
But I was, some four or five years back. Say, give me another drink.

"Fill her up, Joe; I want to put some life into my frame—
Such little drinks to a bum like me are miserably tame;
Five fingers—there, that's the scheme—and corking whiskey, too!
Well, here's luck, boys! and, landlord, my best regards to you!

"You've treated me pretty kindly, and I'd like to tell you how
I came to be the dirty sot you see before you now.
As I told you, once I was a man, with muscle, frame and health,
And but for a blunder ought to have made considerable wealth.

"I was a painter—not one that daubs on bricks and wood;
But an artist, and for my age was rated pretty good.
I worked hard at my canvas, and was bidding fair to rise,
For gradually I saw the star of fame before my eyes.

"I made a picture perhaps you've seen, 'tis called 'The Chase of Fame?'
It brought me fifteen hundred pounds and added to my name.
And then I met a woman—now comes the funny part—
With eyes that petrified my brain and sunk into my heart.

"Why don't you laugh? 'Tis funny that the vagabond you see
Could ever love a woman and expect her love for me;
But 'twas so, and for a month or two her smiles were freely given,
And when her lovely lips touched mine it carried me to heaven.

"Did you ever see a woman for whom your soul you'd give,
With a form like the Milo Venus, too beautiful to live;
With eyes that would beat the Koh-i-noor, and a wealth of chestnut hair?
If so, 'twas she, for there never was another half so fair.

"I was working on a portrait, one afternoon in May,
Of a fair-haired boy, a friend of mine, who lived across the way;
And Madeleine admired it, and, much to my suprise;
Said that she'd like to know the man that had such dreamy eyes.

"It didn't take long to know him, and before the month had flown
My friend had stolen my darling, and I was left alone;
And ere a year of misery had passed above my head
The jewel I had treasured so had tarnished, and was dead!

"That's why I took to drink, boys. Why, I never saw you smile!
I thought you'd be amused, and laughing all the while.
Why, what's the matter, friend? There's a tear-drop in your eye!
Come, laugh, like me; 'tis only babes and women that should cry.

"Say, boys! if you give me just another whiskey I'll be glad,
　　And I'll draw right here a picture of the face that drove me mad.
　　Give me that piece of chalk with which you mark the baseball score,
　　You shall see the lovely Madeleine upon the bar-room floor."

Another drink, and with chalk in hand the vagabond began
　　To sketch a face that well might buy the soul of any man;
　　Then as he placed another lock upon the shapely head,
　　With a fearful shriek he leaped and fell across the picture—dead.

2. In the absence of the film's scenario, it is impossible to be sure that any account of *The Face on the Bar Room Floor* describes the original *order* of scenes—let alone the entire film. The situation is complicated by the fact that the film exists in a number of different versions. (i) Uno Asplund says: "The entire poem is quoted in the script" (1976, 49–50). I presume he meant by this that the entire poem is quoted in *a print of the film* that he had seen. I, personally, have never come across a print that does quote the whole poem. The versions I *am* familiar with quote one or two verses at most, and it is evident from the design of the inserts that these were not provided by Keystone but by a later distributor. (ii) Apparently referring to the park scene, Asplund also states: "The farewell scene's proper position in the film is a matter of opinion. Several Chaplin experts place it in the middle. Chaplin's collapse in the bar, they think, should be the finale—like the hero of the poem he is giving up worldly things." Some versions end with the park scene, others with the collapse in the barroom. Asplund believes that the film originally ended with the scene in the park. "Personally," he says, "I am certain that Chaplin wanted his 'customary' blithe exit to come at the end." I must agree with his conclusion as to the order of these scenes (although I wouldn't describe Charlie's exit from the park as "blithe"). In the barroom it is obvious that Charlie hasn't yet got Madeleine out of his system, while in the park he demonstrates relief that he didn't marry her. The logic of the action surely indicates that the park scene should follow Charlie's collapse in the barroom. Nevertheless, the most complete print I have come across—and therefore the one I described—concludes with the barroom scene. (iii) Collectors in the United States have shown me prints of the film in which the scene of Fritz having his portrait painted *precedes* the scene in which Charlie is painting Madeleine's portrait. This must be an incorrect order of scenes. Unless audiences have already been shown Charlie's portrait of Madeleine, Fritz's miming of that portrait would have no meaning.

3. Parody is an imitation of a work—usually without any intention of devaluing it. If the imitation aims at trivializing the original, the result is a *travesty*. Chaplin's film deliberately mocked the original ballad, but

since D'Arcy's poem was trite to begin with, it could hardly be said to have trivialized it. If anything, the significance or "justification" for the corny original is that it inspired Chaplin's amusing parody.

The Face on the Bar Room Floor was probably the cinema's first parody of a literary work. Chaplin's most elaborate parody was to follow in 1916 when, for Essanay, he produced his *Burlesque on Carmen*, a take-off of two 1915 film versions of *Carmen* (De Mille's starring Geraldine Farrar and Raoul Walsh's starring Theda Bara).

Film parodies of Victorian melodrama were already popular when Chaplin entered movies, and, as David Robinson notes, *Mabel's Strange Predicament* was "a take-off of the Pearl White style" of movie serial. Throughout the teens and twenties one- and two-reel parodies of major feature films became frequent, among them: *Grief in Bagdad* (a parody of the Douglas Fairbanks *Thief of Bagdad*, with an all-star cast of chimpanzees), *Two Wagons, Both Covered* (a parody of James Cruze's *The Covered Wagon*), and *Mud and Sand* (a parody of the Valentino *Blood and Sand*). Movie parodies of other movies have appeared, less frequently, right up to the present: e.g., *De Duv* (parodying Ingmar Bergman's films), *High Anxiety* (parodying Hitchcock's films), and *Airplane* (parodying *Airport*).

4. The final barroom scene of *The Face on the Bar Room Floor* recalls the opening of *His Favorite Pastime*. But *Bar Room* is of special interest for its anticipations of later Chaplin films. (i) It is a burlesque treatment of one of Chaplin's major dramatic situations: Charlie losing the woman he loves to a more handsome rival, e.g., *The Tramp* (Essanay 1915), *The Vagabond* (Mutual 1916), *Sunnyside* (First National 1919), and *The Circus* (1928). (ii) In contrast to *Bar Room*, in *The Tramp* it is Charlie who leaves a farewell message for the woman he loves. Charlie's receipt of a misdirected note from the heroine is a crucial twist in the plot of *The Gold Rush* (1925). (iii) Charlie, who can't draw in *Bar Room*, demonstrates the same lack of talent in *The Vagabond* where, by contrast, his *rival* is an artist. (iv) His reaction of despair at losing Madeleine is repeated in *Sunnyside* where he believes he has lost his beloved Edna to the city gent. (v) Paintings also have important functions in the plots of *The Vagabond* and *A Woman of Paris* (1923). (vi) Madeleine's costume and pose for Charlie in the studio is paralleled in the dress and pose of the stripper at the party in *A Woman of Paris*. (vii) The park scene prefigures an important scene of *A Woman of Paris*: Pierre's mistress, Marie St. Clair, expresses her desire to marry and have children. Pierre thereupon directs her attention out of the window to the sight of a wretched married couple dragging their children through the street.

5. Flashbacks are very rare in Chaplin's films. Their first occurrence is in *Bar Room*. Thereafter he used this narrative device in only two films: very briefly in *Shoulder Arms* (1918) and extensively in *Limelight* (1952).

6. In his *Charlie Chaplin* (p. 72) John McCabe makes the curious assertion that this was the only film prior to *The Tramp* in which Chaplin played "an actual tramp." This claim overlooks *Recreation* (Keystone no. 23) in which Charlie is unquestionably a tramp, and it downplays various other Keystones in which Charlie wears the famous costumes although his status is unclear.

OTHER VIEWS

"One of the most direct anti-romantic statements from the Keystone period is in *The Face on the Bar-room Floor*. . . . A burlesque of a popular story [*sic*], it tells of an artists whose loved one has run off with another man. Having regaled a bar full of customers with his tale, Chaplin then comes face to face with his former love (Cecile Arnold), who is now gross and saddled with several children. His reaction is a mixture of distaste and relief at having escaped a dreadful fate" (Sobel and Francis 1977, 172).

23.

Recreation

(1914)

Original working title*: *In the Park*
Other titles: *Spring Fever*; French: *Charlot s'amuse, Fièvre printanière*;
German: *Erholung*; Spanish: *Fiebre de primavera*; Italian: *Divertimento*

Length: Split reel; 426 feet (Asplund), 462 feet (Lyons) **
Playing time: 7 minutes at 16 frames per second
Producer: Keystone
Director: Chaplin
Screenplay: Chaplin
Photography: Frank D. Williams (?)
Cast:

A tramp	Chaplin
A girl	Norma Nichols
A sailor	Charles Murray (?)

Finished or shipped: July 21, 1914
Released: August 13, 1914

SYNOPSIS

A park. A sailor and his girlfriend are seated on a bench. He has
fallen asleep. She is bored. Extracting her hand from his grasp, the
girl gets up and walks away from him.

A wooden bridge in the park. Charlie comes into view. He is wearing his Tramp's outfit. He feels in his pocket. No money. Contemplat-
ing suicide, he peers over the bridge and clasps his hands in prayer.
Then he puts one leg on the parapet and starts to pull the other one
up—only to fall backward onto the bridge, not into the water. Getting
up, he looks down at the water and changes his mind about that form
of death. He tries instead to run himself through with his cane. Just

---

*This film is frequently confused with *Tango Tangles* (Keystone no. 6) when the latter is
referred to by one of its reissue titles: *Charlie's Recreation*. Prints of *Recreation* are
extant despite claims to the contrary by some commentators.
**Originally spliced with a travelog, *The Yosemite*.

then the girl appears. They eye each other with interest, and Charlie forgets all about suicide. She looks him over and smiles. He smiles back, but she walks on past him. He thumbs his nose at the water and proceeds to follow the girl.

A second bench. The girl stops and looks around. Charlie walks up to her. Shyly, they pretend not to notice each other at first. He sits down and so does she—about three feet away from him. Each turns his back on the other. Then she turns and looks at Charlie, but when he turns to look at her she gazes in a different direction. Charlie now stares down on the bench at an armrest that forms a barrier between them. He gets up and moves past the armrest to sit beside her. Then he tries to make conversation, but she edges away. He exaggeratedly folds one bouncing leg over the other. Leaning toward her, still chatting, he swings his cane while one arm begins creeping round behind her.

First bench. The sailor wakes up. He discovers his girl has disappeared and starts looking around. Getting up, he heads in the direction of the other bench. He stalks across the bridge. He stops and looks around again. He is thunderstruck to see his girl apparently tête-à-tête with another man.

The second bench. Charlie flings his legs out wildly. He has edged very close to the girl.

Bridge. The sailor hitches up his pants and rushes toward the second bench.

The second bench. As yet unnoticed, the sailor moves onto the bench beside Charlie and watches his tactics. Charlie is gesticulating wildly; inadvertently he strikes the sailor in the face. The latter strikes back. Charlie and the girl are aghast at being discovered by him. But Charlie recovers quickly and delivers a swift punch to his attacker's jaw. The sailor tries to retaliate, but Charlie ducks and the girl gets the blow instead. Charlie flees—on one leg—to the safety of a nearby bush from which he observes the sailor haranguing the girl. Bending down, he pulls out a brick from the border of the footpath and hurls it. Bullseye! The sailor is struck in the eye. He collapses on the bench beside the girl who is too busy sulking to notice what has happened. Charlie is enjoying a laugh. Then the girl turns and is shocked to discover the effects of Charlie's target practice. The sailor is down but not out. Staggering to his feet, he picks up the brick. She tries to stay his hand, but he hurls it anyway. The missile lands on target, knocking Charlie off his feet. He gets up only to fall again. The girl is horror-stricken. The sailor clenches his fists and glares fiercely at Charlie.

Bridge. A cop twirling a nightstick comes into view.

Beside bushes. Charlie is nursing his bruised head, but undaunted, he hurls another brick. This one hits the girl. Charlie spits in his hands and is about to try again when a second cop appears behind him and stands watching with hands on hips. Aware that the law is taking an interest in his activities, Charlie pretends to examine the brick, dusts it, tosses it aside, and gives a nonchalant back-kick.

Bridge. The first cop rushes toward the second bench, grabs the sailor, who is on the point of taking aim at Charlie, and threatens him with the nightstick.

Beside bushes. Meanwhile, Charlie is trying to ingratiate himself with the second cop—but the officer looks at him suspiciously and questions him. Charlie assumes an innocent pose, doffs his hat, and strolls away.

Another part of the park. Charlie cups his hand over his mouth, wipes off perspiration, and looks apprehensively in the direction of the police officer.

The second bench. The sailor is arrested despite his protestations. The second cop comes over to find out what's going on. The first cop explains.

Another part of the park. Charlie observes the first cop dragging the sailor in his direction. He tries to slip past them unnoticed, but the sailor points him out to the cop. Before he can escape, Charlie is seized. The sailor accuses him of being the troublemaker.

The second bench. Finding the girl alone and unhappy, the second cop sits beside her. She explains the situation. He consoles her.

Another part of the park. Charlie makes counteraccusations. Then, noticing that the cop's attention is focused on the sailor, he crooks his stick around the cop's leg and pulls him over. Then he gives the sailor a parting blow and flees toward . . .

The second bench. Charlie sits down and suddenly observes the other cop beside the girl. He gets up and heads back the way he came, stopping beside the bushes to mop his brow.

Another part of the park. The first cop and the sailor get to their feet. The former slugs the latter with his nightstick; the sailor retaliates by felling the cop with a brick. Then he hurls another brick at Charlie—who ducks. The brick hits the second cop. The first cop recovers quickly and starts wrestling violently with the sailor.

The second bench. The cop gets up and joins in the struggle with the sailor, but the latter beats both officers to the ground.

Lakeside. The girl, looking frantic, leaves the bench and walks down to the water.

Bushes. Charlie sees her and assumes that she is going to throw herself into the lake. He looks around, hesitates, then dashes to the rescue.

Lakeside. The girl is bending down and peering into the water. Charlie eyes her posterior and is tempted to whack it with his cane when she stands up and stares at him. He tries to get friendly once again, leaning on his stick as he chats with her. She gives him a shove and he falls over. He gets up and gives her a playful kick. Meanwhile, the sailor, having escaped the cops, dashes up and boots Charlie in the rear end. Each swings at the other; both duck but the sailor loses his balance—whereupon Charlie kicks him into the lake. Charlie and the girl now watch as the two cops slug each other.

Another part of the park. The cops suddenly realize that their prisoner has escaped. They race after him toward the lake but make the fatal mistake of stopping to question Charlie. Without further ado, he kicks both of them into the drink. Turning back to the girl, he doffs his hat. She gives him a shove and he tumbles backward into the water, pulling her in after him.

COMMENTS

1. This is one of the rarest of Chaplin's Keystones. The only print I have seen is the one I obtained from Enrique J. Bouchard of Buenos Aires.

Like his earlier split-reel, *A Busy Day* (Keystone no. 14), Chaplin whipped up *Recreation* in a single day (in Westlake Park) and earned himself a twenty-five-dollar bonus from Sennett.

2. Structure. Prologue: The girl walks away from her sailor. (i) Charlie intends suicide but changes his mind when he sees the girl. (ii) Charlie flirts with the girl; the sailor interrupts him. (iii) Brick-throwing: Charlie vs. the sailor. (iv) Brick-throwing: the cops intervene. (v) The lakeside: Charlie gets rid of the sailor and the cops. Epilogue: The girl tries to get rid of Charlie but winds up in the lake with him.

3. *Recreation* recalls many earlier Keystones. The sleeping sailor of the opening scene was obviously taken over from Chaplin's previous film, *The Face on the Bar Room Floor*. The setting and story bear obvious resemblances to *Twenty Minutes of Love*, while the brick-throwing scenes look like a reprise of similar episodes in *Mabel at the Wheel* and *The Fatal Mallet*. But one moment of the movie also looks forward to a scene in *The Kid* (1921). In *Recreation* Charlie is about to hurl a brick when he becomes aware that a cop is watching him. Lowering his arm, he examines the brick, dusts it off, tosses it aside, and gives the cop an "innocent" smile. In *The Kid* little Jackie is about to throw a rock at a window when he realizes that a cop is right behind him. He reacts by more or less repeating Charlie's routine before making his escape.

4. The film is, for the most part, a little "ballet" of misdirected action—a cliché of Keystone's (and Chaplin's) slapstick. The sailor's

punch hits the girl instead of Charlie. The sailor's brick hits the cop instead of Charlie. The first cop arrests the sailor instead of Charlie. The cops wrestle with each other when they think they are tackling the sailor and Charlie, etc.

Yet there is just a little more to *Recreation* than routine slapstick. The film also gives us a couple of new perspectives on Charlie. First, he's not an intruder, a drunkard, or a lecher but a would-be suicide. Why? His gesture of turning out his empty pockets demonstrates that he's penniless. But it's hard to imagine the Tramp killing himself just for lack of money—not so difficult to believe that a woman like Madeleine (*The Face on the Bar Room Floor*) has driven him to despair and poverty. That frustrated suicide looks like a continuation of *Bar Room* or perhaps Chaplin's rejected idea of a finale for that film. At any rate, if one woman has forced Charlie to the brink of death, another's smile certainly saves him in the nick of time. (His most notable attempt at suicide occurs in *Sunnyside* [1919] and is also motivated by his [imagined] loss of the woman he loves.) See also *Those Love Pangs* note 3.

Second, although he's still a pretty violent fellow when attacked by a male rival, for a change Charlie's rather coy when it comes to flirting with a young lady. He follows the girl to a bench, but when she turns and looks at him he shyly pretends not to notice her. Then he sits down—not beside her but at the other end of the bench. Eventually he plucks up sufficient courage to move up to her and engage her in conversation. When she edges away, he tries to arouse her interest by bouncing his leg and swinging his cane in a devil-may-care manner. These are elaborate ruses to enable him to insinuate his arm around her. Compare this timorous behavior to Charlie's aggressive philandering in the park in *Twenty Minutes of Love* and *Caught in the Rain*. The girl in *Recreation* is, patently, more aggressive toward Charlie than vice versa. Toward the end of the film, when he finds her bending down at the lakeside he is mischievously tempted to whack her with his cane—but changes his mind. He can't bring himself to treat a pretty girl that way. On the other hand, the girl doesn't hesitate to knock *him* down or to shove *him* in the lake. At the outset, her smile arouses his amorous instincts and prevents him from jumping off the bridge, but, ironically, by the end of the movie his would-be flirtation arouses her aggressive instincts, and she winds up shoving him in the water anyway.

OTHER VIEWS

"In its composition the film is so extremely like the earlier *Twenty Minutes of Love* . . . that one may almost suspect it of using up a certain amount of leftover material from the earlier film, to which new takes have been added" (Asplund 1976, 51).

24.

The Masquerader
(1914)

Original working title: *Queen of the Movies*
Other titles*: *The Female Impersonator, Putting One Over, The Picnic, The Perfumed Lady;* French: *Charlot grande coquette, Charlot et l'étoile;* German: *Die Maskerade;* Spanish: *Charlot señorita bien, Charlot coquetea;* Italian: *Charlot attore, L'attore travestito*

Length: 1 reel; 968 feet (Asplund), 1030 feet (Lyons)
Playing time: 17 minutes at 16 frames per second
Producer: Keystone
Director: Chaplin
Screenplay: Chaplin
Photography: Frank D. Williams (?)
Cast:

Movie actor and beautiful stranger	Chaplin
Roscoe "Fatty" Arbuckle	as himself
Chester Conklin	as himself
Film director	Charlie Murray
The heavy (actor playing a murderer)	Fritz Schade
Heroine	Minta Durfee
Female extras/Charlie's admirers	Cecile Arnold
	Vivian Edwards
Male extras	Charley Chase
	Harry McCoy

Finished or shipped: August 12, 1914
Released: August 27, 1914

SYNOPSIS

Keystone studios. A dressing room. Fatty is getting dressed. Charlie (minus his mustache and wearing a straw boater) is smoking and brushing his coat. Fatty watches him.

*This film was sometimes confusingly rereleased as *His New Profession*—which is actually the title of Chaplin's next (i.e., twenty-fifth) Keystone film.

Studio set. The director instructs the heroine about her role in a movie melodrama. She has to gaze at her baby and clasp her hands above its cradle. The director gives instructions to his cameraman.

Dressing room. Charlie—without his mustache—sits at the table opposite Fatty who is drinking. Charlie is longing for a drink but Fatty isn't sharing. They stand up simultaneously and bump heads. Charlie applies his face powder too liberally and blows the surplus into Fatty's face.

Studio set. The director calls for Charlie but he doesn't appear. He sends the heavy to get him.

Dressing room. By this time Charlie is wearing his familiar costume and his mustache. The heavy appears and orders him onto the set. Charlie exits. Fatty and the heavy quarrel and throw objects at each other. Fatty is knocked down. The heavy flees.

Studio set. Charlie enters, poking the director's rump with his cane. The director checks Charlie's mustache and discovers that he has been drinking. Charlie pops a cough drop into his mouth to cover the smell. The director explains the action of the scene. Charlie will have to wrest a large knife from the heavy. But he is in too much of a hurry: he grabs the knife immediately, cutting the heavy's hand and zapping the heroine in the eye. Following instructions, he goes to the edge of the set to await his cue. He is standing against a door which turns out to be a piece of scenery. Two pretty girls open the fake door, notice Charlie, and start to flirt with him. One playfully shoves a teddy bear's leg into his mouth. Charlie takes a toy duck from the other girl, reaches into his pocket, and produces a golf ball which he turns into the duck's "egg." He lightly kisses each girl and playfully tastes the kisses. Meanwhile, the scene gets under way. The heavy attacks the heroine, tosses her aside, and raises his knife to stab her baby. This is Charlie's cue—but he misses it. He is preoccupied with the girls. But expecting his entrance, the heavy waits . . . and waits . . . and waits with knife upraised. The director calls out frantically. No response. At last, he picks up the dummy baby and flings it in Charlie's face. Now—better late than never—Charlie gets the message. He dashes over to the heavy, clobbers him with the dummy baby, grabs the knife, and sticks it in his rump. The director is furious. He orders Charlie to clear out. But he refuses to leave, so the director throws him off the set. Charlie falls backward, crashing onto some scenery and knocking down a couple of sceneshifters. They get up and slam the fake door in his face.

Meanwhile, the director has turned to Chester.

Title: *"He's rotten—you play the part."*

After being instructed in Charlie's role, Chester makes the mistake of standing next to him to wait for his cue. The melodramatic scene is now reenacted: the heavy raises his knife to strike the baby, and Chester is about to rush in and disarm him when Charlie grabs Chester's coattails and prevents him from moving. The director loses his temper once more. But Charlie is indifferent to his screams. He moves into action, kicking Chester backward onto the sceneshifters. Then he rushes onto the set and tickles the heavy under the arm before booting him onto Chester. Infuriated, the director chases Charlie off the set then peers out of the window to observe his flight. Undaunted, Charlie doubles back and kicks the director's rear end. Then he flees toward the dressing room.

Dressing room. Charlie is disconsolate. He flips his hat off his head and looks enviously at the other actors.

Title: *Fired*.

The director appears. As he is ordering Charlie out of the studio once and for all, Charlie cunningly shoves an open jar of cold cream under his elbow. Charlie pleads for another chance—to no avail. The director hands him his suitcase and tells him to clear out immediately. Charlie throws out his arms in a gesture of despair—then drops the case onto the director's foot. The latter picks up the case and is about to hurl it at him, but Charlie raises his foot in a threatening gesture, and the director politely hands it over. Charlie offers him a conciliatory handshake, but the director rejects it. Saddened, Charlie turns to leave. Then he suddenly flings the case into the director's face and rushes out of the dressing room. The director hurls the case after him but misses.

Studio set. Another scene is being filmed. Charlie dashes in and blocks the cameraman's view. The director appears in hot pursuit and throws the case at Charlie—who ducks. The case bowls over the cameraman and his camera. Charlie flees.

Exterior of studio. A cop (or studio guard) is standing next to a sign reading "Keystone Studio." The director (offscreen) throws the suitcase once more. This time it hits Charlie and bowls him over. Catching up with him, the director orders the cop never to readmit him. Then he gives him a parting kick.

Title: *A Beautiful Stranger*.

Exterior of studio. Accompanied by a chaperone, Charlie appears, disguised as a well-dressed young woman and sporting a large fur muff. The cop doffs his hat, and Charlie smiles flirtatiously at him. Both "ladies" are promptly admitted to the studio.

Studio. The heavy finds "Lady" Charlie alluring.

Title: *Everybody interested*.

All the men in the studio gather around Charlie, who acts coyly. The director approaches. He is also attracted by this beautiful new arrival and wants her for himself. After ordering a female extra to escort the chaperone around the studio, he asks Charlie to follow him.

Hallway. The director indicates by gesture that if Charlie wants a part in a film, "she" will have to be "nice" to him. Charlie appears agreeable, so he takes "her" along to his office.

Office. The director shows Charlie a contract and repeats his "deal." Then he starts getting ardent. Charlie screams for help. Responding to the call of a lady in distress, an assistant bursts into the office. The director hurls a book at him. Then he escorts Charlie out of the office.

Hallway. Charlie playfully strikes the director with his muff.

Dressing room. Several actors are present. The heavy waxes ecstatic about Charlie's charms.

Exterior of dressing room. The director leaves Charlie with the chaperone.

Dressing room. The director enters and orders everyone out so that the beautiful stranger can change. The actors obey reluctantly.

Exterior of dressing room. Charlie makes faces at the female extra. The actors exit from the dressing room, eyeing Charlie with renewed interest. The director appears, picks up Charlie's case, and carries it into the dressing room. Charlie follows him. They are alone again. When the director's back is turned, Charlie filches one of his cigarettes; then he playfully pushes a wig into his face. The director reacts by chasing "Lady" Charlie around the table. (At one point it is obvious—even though Charlie is wearing skirts—that he has made one of his typical street-corner turns, pivoting on one foot.) Charlie pretends to be coy once again—then tosses a brush at his pursuer. The director exits. Charlie shakes his fist after him. Then he hangs up his muff, removes his hat and wig and strips off his female clothes. He thumbs his nose in the direction of the door.

Office. The director reads over the contract.

Dressing room. Charlie sits at the table. He puts on his mustache.

Studio set. The actors are annoyed at having been ousted from their dressing room. With Chester as their spokesman they confront the director.

Dressing room. Charlie is now in his usual outfit.

Exterior of dressing room. The actors and the director arrive. The latter knocks on the door, then enters alone. He is astounded to discover Charlie and not the beautiful stranger. Charlie explains his masquerade. The director is not amused. He orders him to clear out, but Charlie merely laughs in his face. The director is furious. Before he can do anything, however, Charlie kicks him into a wardrobe and bolts for the door.

Exterior of dressing room. Charlie kicks over the waiting actors and flees toward the studio set. En route he knocks down a scene-shifter and walks over the man's prostrate body. Everyone gives chase. The sceneshifter catches up with Charlie. The two men slap at each other until Charlie tires of it and kicks his antagonist in the belly. He continues his flight.

A well. Charlie stops to hurl bricks at his pursuers. Then, finding no other avenue of escape, he drops down into the well and is submerged. The actors and the director arrive at the top of the well. They look down at Charlie, satisfied that the nuisance is removed. Turning to face the camera, the director smiles and removes his hat in a mock-reverential manner. The actors follow suit. The film ends with a close-up of Charlie's head as he bobs out of the water gasping for air.

COMMENTS

1. This is the second of the three films in which Chaplin appears in "drag": the others are *A Busy Day* (Keystone no. 14) and *A Woman* (Essanay 1915). It is also one of several Chaplin films located in film studios. See also *A Film Johnnie* (Keystone no. 5), *His New Job* (Essanay 1915), and *Behind the Screen* (Mutual 1916).

This film and *Tango Tangles* (Keystone no. 6) are the only Keystone movies in which Chaplin is seen without his mustache.

Half a century after showing Charlie putting on his make-up in *The Masquerader* Chaplin included a parallel scene in *Limelight:* Calvero removes his make-up in the dressing room of the Middlesex Theatre.

2. Structure. Prologue: Charlie's first transformation. He changes into his familiar costume. (i) He flirts with two pretty girls. (ii) He is ordered out of the studio after ruining his scene twice and preventing a replacement (Chester) from playing his role. (iii) Charlie's second transformation: He returns to the studio disguised as a woman. (iv) The director tries to flirt with Charlie. "Lady" Charlie teases the director. (v) Reversal: Charlie "unmasks." He's ordered out of the studio once more. (vi) The chase: Charlie disrupts the studio yet again. Epilogue: Charlie in the well.

3. An intriguing film, *The Masquerader* is thematically complex, drawing together several themes that occur individually in some of Chaplin's earlier Keystones: (i) images of women, (ii) on- and offscreen images of Chaplin himself, (iii) masquerade, (iv) misperception, (v) reflexivity, (vi) Chaplin's perception of cinema vs. Keystone's.

(i) It is enlightening to compare Chaplin's impersonations of women in *A Busy Day* and *The Masquerader*. In the earlier film Chaplin is *supposed* to be a woman, but he presents us with a caricature that seems more like a man *masquerading* as a woman. By contrast, in the later film Charlie's *masquerade* as a woman is astonishingly lifelike.

Isabel Quigly accurately describes the portrayal as "remarkably, undatedly attractive at this distance, in contrast to many of the actresses of the time, whose charm it is hard to see fifty years later" (1968, 29). Where *A Busy Day* underscores female jealousy and aggressiveness, *The Masquerader* depicts feminine seductiveness. In the smile, walk, and body language Chaplin captures the very essence of a recognizable female type. "Lady" Charlie is a coquette or sexual "tease," an extension of the sort of flirtatiousness that the two pretty girls had earlier displayed toward him. Interestingly, the film gives us two male reactions to this range of feminine seductiveness. When the girls flirt with him Charlie simply flirts back. Neither party is sexually "in control." But "Lady" Charlie's coy teasing excites the director's lechery. He loses control to the "lady" and winds up being humiliated when Charlie unmasks, exposing his blind impulses.

Passing mention should be made of the film's other female character. Minta Durfee plays an actress required to depict not a real woman but the cardboard figure of a victimized mother out of Victorian melodrama. The obvious triteness of this character contrasts with the vivid (and deceptive) femininity of Chaplin's "lady."

(ii) In *The Masquerader* Chaplin depicts himself in a continuous process of transformation. At the start of the film we see Chaplin himself, then Chaplin becoming Charlie (he is putting on make-up), then Charlie in his Tramp costume becoming, successively, Charlie the film actor, Charlie the flirt, slapstick Charlie, and "Lady" Charlie. (As Rebecca Bell-Metereau notes: "The audience becomes implicated in the cross-dressing situation because Chaplin allows us to witness every part of his metamorphosis from male to female . . ."[1985,26].) Thereafter, via a process of unmasking, "Lady" Charlie becomes Chaplin who once again transforms himself into slapstick Charlie for the film's finale. These changing images (plus our awareness that another, offscreen Chaplin is directing the film) provoke the same sort of questions raised by the filmmaker when the Tramp runs into the hall of mirrors in *The Circus* (1928). Which is the real Charlie? Who is the real Chaplin? What are their true relationships?

(iii) Charlie's impersonation is only one of many masquerades in this film. The film's title could refer to Chaplin as well as to his alter ego, Charlie. The film studio is, patently, a place where "fakery" is manufactured. Fritz and Minta pretend to be villain and heroine. Chester "becomes" Charlie. Doors and walls are not what they seem to be. When Chaplin masks and unmasks, when Charlie runs rampant destroying scenes and scenery, each destroys one set of illusions only to create others.

(iv) We (the audience) and characters in the film sometimes misperceive what is *not* disguised in addition to what *is*. The identity of Fatty's companion in the dressing room doesn't become apparent until he dresses up as the Tramp. (Fatty doesn't look too certain about him either.) Even before the director is taken in by Charlie's masquerade, we too will probably be fooled at our first sight of the beautiful stranger (the insert title is part of the trickery)—despite the fact that we were previously allowed glimpses of Chaplin without the mustache. Then, like Charlie, we will almost certainly misperceive some of the scenery around the studio. Charlie thinks (and so do we) that he is standing in front of a wall until it opens and reveals itself as a scenery door—a piece of fakery—yet it turns out to be solid enough when Charlie gets thrown against it. At the end of the film he seeks sanctuary inside a studio prop: the well. Well, it certainly looks like a prop when we (and Charlie) first perceive it. After all, what would a real well be doing inside a movie studio? However, the apparent fakery turns out to be the real thing— another aspect of that plastic, magic world of movies where things are not always what they seem to be.

(v) Like *Kid's Auto Race* (Keystone no. 2) and *A Film Johnnie* (Keystone no. 5) *The Masquerader* is a little essay in reflexivity. Chaplin has made a film about Chaplin (the film actor) playing Charlie (the film character) unmaking a movie melodrama (a film-within-the-film) that becomes, willy-nilly, part of Chaplin's film comedy. Two cameras (one visible and one offscreen) and two directors (Charlie Murray in the film and Chaplin offscreen) are involved in this filmic interaction.

(vi) The film's reflexivity is used to contrast two approaches to filmmaking: on the one hand melodrama and slapstick, on the other Chaplin's new view of comedy as an improvisational expression of character and character relationships. Chaplin deliberately uses Charlie's unintentional ruining of the film-within-the-film to impose his kind of comedy on the kind of crude melodrama that was popular at that period. The stereotypes of the movie melodrama are replaced by two genuinely comic characters: Charlie and the "lady." The melodrama's cliché actions, tightly controlled by director Charlie Murray are, similarly, replaced by Charlie's creative improvisations. I.e., having missed his cue, Charlie proceeds anyway. (What follows bears comparison with the audition sequence in *The Circus*.) Charlie improvises; he tackles the heavy in his own way—not the director's—clobbering him with the dummy baby and tickling him under the arm. The result is more original and far more entertaining than the film being shot, but the director fails to realize it. "He's rotten," he tells Chester, "You play the part." And he tries to substitute a comic *type* (Chester) for Charlie's richer comic *character*. Later on, director Murray also proves insensitive to the potentialities of Charlie's marvelous masquerade. Charlie offers him a brilliant *performance*, but like Henry Lehrman this director only wants crude *action*. (See *Kid's Auto Race*, comment 3.) He chases Charlie back to Keystone's routine slapstick with its brick throwing and its watery finale. In the end Charlie winds up in the drink, and Murray thinks he has the last laugh. But the picture that gets finished is not Murray's melodrama but Chaplin's *The Masquerader*, and its last shot is—a close-up of Charlie.

OTHER VIEWS

"*The Masquerader* had [a modern audience] . . . laughing, giggling and roaring throughout. Apparently something was operating beyond the plot and gags, which were rather primitive in this Chaplin film. I realized that the audience was responding much as an audience in 1914 must have—somehow the mere appearance of the Chaplin character was winning them over. Looking at the film more carefully, I noticed that even though he wasn't doing anything particularly ingenious, Chaplin seemed to be totally involved with what he was doing, and further, that his feelings at every moment were communicated to the audience with crystal clarity. A warmth came over the audience. We cared about how this fellow felt and what was happening in the film to affect him" (Kamin 1984, ix).

"Chaplin's imitations of women are extremely convincing because of his small stature and the delicacy and beauty of his features. More important, though, is the fact that he is willing to become a woman to the best of his considerable ability. He does not hesitate to adopt feminine mannerisms, to wear makeup, or to flirt with men as enthusiastically as a true coquette would do" (Bell-Metereau 1985, 25–26).

25.

His New Profession

(1914)

Original working title: *The Rolling Chair*
Other titles: *Helping Himself, The Good-for-Nothing;* French: *La nou-velle profession de Charlot, Charlot garde-malade, Charlot bon à rien;* German: *Seine neue Beschäftigung;* Spanish: *Charlot vago de profes-sion, Charlot faquin;* Italian: *Charlot infermiere*

Length: 1 reel; 971 feet (Asplund), 1030 feet (Lyons)
Playing time: 17 minutes at 16 frames per second
Producer: Keystone
Director: Chaplin
Screenplay: Chaplin
Photography: Frank D. Williams (?)
Cast:

Temporary wheelchair attendant	Chaplin
The invalid uncle	Fritz Schade
His nephew	Charley Chase
The nephew's girlfriend	Norma Nichols
Woman with a bag of eggs	Cecile Arnold
Cop	Harry McCoy

Finished or shipped: August 14, 1914
Released: August 31, 1914

SYNOPSIS

Close-up of a hand holding a copy of the *Police Gazette*. The magazine is lowered to reveal Charlie seated on a park bench. He looks incredu-lously at something on an inside page. Then he turns the pages, frowning, until his attention is caught by the picture of a bathing beauty on the front page. He looks up at the camera, smiles, and resumes his page turning. [Uno Asplund says: "He snips a bit out of the newspaper, per-haps because he sees he is 'wanted,' though this is not quite clear" (1976, 52). But this action does not occur in any print I looked at.]

Nearby in the park. A young man is explaining his problem to his girlfriend: he has to take care of his gouty and irascible old uncle, who is dozing in a wheelchair.

Title: *"I'll get someone to mind uncle."*

The girl stalks away, peeved because her young man cannot spend more time with her.

As she passes Charlie, she drops her reticule. In a flash, he pockets it, but the girl notices what has happened. She makes him hand over the pocketbook. He thumbs his nose at her as she disappears from view.

Nearby. By now the uncle has woken up and begun bossing his nephew. Annoyed, the young man starts wheeling him in Charlie's direction. Something obstructs the wheelchair, and Charlie obligingly renders assistance by hooking his cane around the invalid's neck and giving a tug. As the wheelchair works loose, the young man runs it over Charlie's foot; Charlie reacts by striking the old man on his gouty leg. While Charlie and the uncle are commiserating with each other, the young man has a bright idea. He whispers to Charlie.

Title: *"Push him around and I'll fix you up later."*

He informs uncle of the arrangement and dashes off to join his girlfriend.

Another part of the park. The young man creeps up behind the girl and plays peek-a-boo.

Beside the park bench. Uncle warns Charlie to avoid touching his gouty foot. But Charlie is a slow learner: he begins "his new profession" by walking into it. As soon as he starts pushing the wheelchair, he temporarily loses his grip on it and falls flat on his face.

A footpath in the park. A woman is talking to her husband. She carelessly drops a bagful of eggs. The couple walk hastily away to avoid the smell.

Beside the park bench. Charlie has difficulty in manipulating the wheelchair in a forward direction so he starts pulling it backward.

Footpath. He slips on the broken eggs and his pants-seat is soaked in egg yolks.

Nearby. The couple laugh at Charlie's mishap.

Footpath. Charlie tries to steady the wheelchair. He slips into the eggs a second time. He does a "dog act," trying to remove the mess on his pants by wiping his behind on the grass.

Nearby. The couple laugh at this too.

Footpath. Charlie has parked the wheelchair over the broken eggs. Uncle holds his nose. Charlie grabs the wheelchair handle but slips again and has to bend down to retrieve his hat. This time *he* holds his nose. Regaining his balance, he pushes the wheelchair toward the pier bar.

Exterior of pier bar. Charlie stops pushing the wheelchair. He coughs onto uncle's bald head and considerately wipes off the germs with his jacket. The old man orders him to continue toward the pier, but Charlie suddenly notices the pier bar.

Title: *"Slip me some change on account."*

The old man refuses. Feigning dire thirst, Charlie puffs out his cheeks, pokes out his tongue, and clutches his throat. All to no avail. Uncle insists on being pushed to the pier.

On the pier. Charlie positions the old man alongside a sleeping beggar—also in a wheelchair—who is holding a tin cup and a sign reading: "Help a Cripple." By now his charge has fallen asleep, and Charlie shifts the cup and sign onto uncle. Then he turns his back on his charge, pretending he has nothing to do with him. Immediately, a nurse passes by and obligingly drops a coin into the cup. Charlie helps himself to the money. Licking his lips, he heads back toward the pier bar.

Beside the park bench. The young man is joking with his girlfriend.

Exterior of pier bar. Charlie appears. He enters the bar with some difficulty—opening the swinging doors outward.

Beside the park bench. The young man and his girlfriend head toward the pier.

Interior of pier bar. Charlie pivots around on one leg, eyeing the free lunch. He orders a drink. When the bartender's back is turned, he quickly drinks up the dregs from all the other glasses.

Exterior of pier bar. The young man invites his girlfriend to go swimming with him.

Pier. The young man and his girlfriend arrive on the scene. He is horrified to find how Charlie has left his sleeping uncle. His girlfriend walks away, laughing scornfully. He follows her to the pier bar.

Exterior of pier bar.

Title: *"So that's the kind of uncle."*

Waving him away, she exits. He puts out his arms, appealingly.

Pier. A passerby drops a coin into the cup, arousing the beggar. In a fury, he seizes his cup and sign and whacks uncle across his gouty leg with a stick. The old man wakes up, howling. He strikes back, but the beggar retaliates more forcefully.

Exterior of pier bar. Charlie toddles out drunk. He heads toward the pier.

Pier. Uncle and the beggar are still exchanging blows when Charlie arrives. He contemplates the situation and then walks between the two wheelchairs, knocking the cup out of the beggar's hand. He bends down, helps himself to the money, and returns the empty cup to the beggar. Then he wheels uncle a short distance along the pier. Uncle wants to continue the ride, but Charlie feels tired. He takes a rest by sitting on the old man's gouty leg.

Park. The young man has caught up with his girlfriend. He pleads with her, but she spurns him.

Pier. Charlie pushes the wheelchair up to a bench. He wipes the old man's head with his dirty handkerchief; then he falls backward across the bench (which has no back). In retrieving his hat, he nearly falls off the pier into the sea. Sitting up, he straightens out the wheelchair by hooking his cane around the old man's leg.

Exterior of pier bar. The girl heads toward the pier.

Pier. To silence uncle's complaints, Charlie hands him his copy of the *Police Gazette*. The old man is delighted. He jokes with Charlie, who reacts by whacking him playfully across the leg.

The girl wanders back along the pier and sits down beside Charlie. She doesn't notice him but inadvertently puts her hand on his knee. He draws her attention to what she has done by scratching his leg. Then he gives her a playful poke. She laughs. They strike up a conversation. Getting excited, Charlie carelessly gives uncle's leg yet another whack. The old man protests. Charlie tells him to be quiet. He refuses, so Charlie kicks the wheelchair away. It rolls to the far end of the pier and stops.

Charlie resumes his flirting. He pulls the girl nearer to him with the crook of his cane. He tries to embrace her but she resists. The young man appears on the pier. He looks disconsolate. Then he notices Charlie flirting with his girlfriend. He is entertaining her by flapping his broken hat up and down as if it were a lid. Then he hooks her by the arm once more and renews his advances. The young man stalks over and sits on the bench. He does a slow burn, unseen by Charlie. Meanwhile, the beggar looks around to see if anyone is watching him. Removing his sign, he wheels himself in the direction of the bench. At last Charlie becomes aware of the young man's presence. The young man demands to know why Charlie isn't pushing the wheelchair. He grabs him by the tie and shoves him aside. Then he starts upbraiding the girl. Charlie gets up and swings a punch at him, but the young man ducks and pushes Charlie backward onto the beggar. They crash onto the floor. A cop rushes over and helps them up. The beggar promptly punches Charlie in the face. At this point uncle joins the fray. Wheeling himself back along the pier, he runs into the girl. The young man pushes him back to the end of the pier and resumes his quarrel with the girl. She slaps his face. A second cop intervenes. Assuming that the girl has been insulted, he shoves the young man backward onto a bench and takes a flying leap at him. He misses his target and hits the floor. The girl laughs. Charlie and the beggar are squaring off. The latter kicks Charlie sprawling. The first cop tries to intervene, but Charlie doesn't need help from the police. He flattens the cop and boots the beggar backward onto the second cop, pushing him into the ocean. (Long shot of the cop hitting the water.) Charlie staggers back and falls onto the first cop.

Now uncle comes rolling back along the pier; he has lost control of the wheelchair. Charlie kicks the first cop onto the passing vehicle which carries uncle and his "passenger" to the other end of the pier. The cop extricates himself and confronts uncle.

Title: *"You're pinched."*

He arrests the old man and wheels him away.

Observing this, Charlie laughs, then yawns and stretches himself. He wanders over to the girl, who is aghast at what has happened. He doffs his hat to her and casually kicks the beggar aside. Calmly taking the girl by the arm, he leads her off the pier.

COMMENTS

1. The film's close-up of Charlie sitting on a park bench reading the *Police Gazette* has remained enduringly famous. He is, of course, dipping into the most notorious, yellow-press publication of the period. (A comparable famous close-up from the same period depicts Fatty Arbuckle reading Elinor Glyn's scandalous novel *Three Weeks*.) Aside from its suggestion of Charlie's naughtiness at reading such a scandal sheet and the loneliness implicit in his sigh at the magazine's unattainable bathing beauty, the precise significance of the scene in *His New Profession* eludes me. Was there something special—say, a current joke long since forgotten—about that particular issue of the *Police Gazette?* What is there in the inside pages that holds Charlie's incredulous attention? What private jokes about the magazine does he share with uncle?

The film has a couple of noteworthy links with one of Chaplin's best-known Mutual films, *The Cure* (1917). Gouty feet are the target of Charlie's assaults in both films. Chaplin also elaborated on the wheelchair gags for the later movie but then decided to eliminate most of them, including a brilliant sequence—not unlike the climax of Ionesco's *The Chairs*—involving a "traffic jam" of numerous wheelchairs. The sequence was included by Kevin Brownlow and David Gill in their compilation, *The Unknown Chaplin*.

Other comic business. *His New Profession* contains some of Charlie's most dexterous (and sadistic) feats with his cane. The film also embodies his most explicit "dog act" (when he tries to clean off his pants). A variation on this sort of animal behavior occurs in *The Gold Rush* when he tries to conceal Big Jim's rifle in the snow. Charlie's rapid drinking of purloined liquor in the pier bar of *His New Profession* is outstripped by the extraordinary sequence in which he gulps down stolen cakes in *A Dog's Life*.

2. Structure. A series of episodes paralleling the problems of Charlie and the young man. Prologue: Charlie reads his paper. His problem: (i) no girlfriend. (I) The young man's problems: (i) What to do with uncle? (ii) How not to lose his girlfriend? (II) Charlie tries to filch the girl's pocketbook. (III) The young man's problems are temporarily solved: he hires Charlie. (IV) Charlie's new problems: (ii) the wheelchair and the eggs. (V) Charlie's additional problems: (iii) no money, (iv) no drink. (VI) The pier: Charlie resolves problems (iii) and (iv) by using uncle to beg for him. (VII) Charlie in the pier bar: he gets drunk. (VIII) The girl rejects the young man. (IX) The beggar attacks uncle—Charlie "rescues" him. (X) Charlie flirts with the girl and disposes of uncle—resolution of the young man's problem (ii). (XI) The young man attacks Charlie: melee. (XII) Uncle gets arrested. Epilogue: Charlie gets the girl—resolution of *his* problem (i).

3. *His New Profession* is a little potboiler about characters who all want something for nothing. The young man endures his uncle's demands because he is (presumably) after the old man's money. He hires Charlie to push the wheelchair and promises—rather dubiously—to fix him up later. Uncle wants Charlie to wheel him around but refuses to give him anything "on account." The girlfriend is a gold digger who only remains with the young man as long as she believes he has a rich uncle. Charlie attempts to get the money he needs by stealing her pocketbook. The beggar lives on charity, but Charlie appropriates his method and gets uncle, inadvertently, to beg for him. Charlie, the only character who demonstrates either ingenuity or any inclination to work, is also the only one who succeeds. He wants money, drink, and a girl and manages to obtain all of them.

Over the years the film has been frequently condemned for what Asplund calls its "disagreeably sadistic humour." The reference is to Charlie's persistent abuse of the uncle's gouty foot. In slight mitigation it should be noted that uncle behaves like a petty tyrant toward both his nephew and Charlie. One may feel sorry for his foot but not for the whole man.

OTHER VIEWS

"Charlie was back in Westlake Park for *His New Profession* with a plot that had worn out its welcome by 1907" (Gifford 1974, 49).

"It is a curious fact that, with the exception of *His New Profession*, all his park films contain episodes of Chaplin failing to make contact with another woman, a symbolic representation of his relationship with his mother" (Sobel and Francis 1977, 206).

26.

The Rounders*

(1914)

Original working title: *The Two Drunks*
Other titles: *Oh, What a Night!*, *Tip, Tap, Toe, Revelry, Two of a Kind, Going Down, The Love Thief*; French: *Charlot et Fatty font la bombe; Charlot et Fatty au café*; German: *Die Herumheiber*; Spanish: *Charlot y Fatty incoregibles, Charlot y Fatty en el café*; Italian: *Charlot e Fatty al caffè, I girovaghi*

Length: 1 reel; 971 feet (Asplund), 1010 feet (Lyons)
Playing time: 17 minutes at 16 frames per second
Producer: Keystone
Director: Chaplin
Screenplay: Chaplin
Photography: Frank D. Williams (?)
Cast:

Mr. Full	Chaplin
Mr. Fuller	Roscoe "Fatty" Arbuckle
Mrs. Full	Phyllis Allen
Mrs. Fuller	Minta Durfee
An elderly diner	Fritz Schade
Other diners	Wallace MacDonald
	Charley Chase
A bellhop	Al St. John

Finished or shipped: August 21, 1914
Released: September 7, 1914

SYNOPSIS

Exterior of hotel. Mr. Full (Chaplin), smoking a pipe and wearing his drunken dude's costume complete with cape, lurches drunkenly up the front steps. He loses his balance and falls on his face.

---

*"Rounder" was an old term meaning drunkard or good-for-nothing. It derives either from "rounds" of drinks or from "round the corner," a British slang expression common when Chaplin was a child, signifying "being drunk."

Hotel foyer. Eyeing a young woman, Mr. Full backs into Mr. Fuller (Fatty), who is leaning over the reception desk talking to the clerk. He doffs his hat to Fuller's rear end and retreats even further—still eyeing the young woman—until he falls back onto a staircase. He doffs his hat to the young woman and heads up the stairs.

Corridor. A bellhop sitting and reading a magazine watches Mr. Full as he tries, unsuccessfully, to walk along a straight line on the carpet. Realizing that he is about to fall over, the bellhop leaps up and steadies him.

Mr. Full's hotel room. He is late. His angry wife (dressed in white) looks at her alarm clock.

Corridor. The bellhop brushes Mr. Full down. The latter reaches into his pocket and produces a bill (a dollar?). He gives it to the bell-hop who dances away joyfully.

Mr. Full's hotel room. Hands on hips, Mrs. Full glares at her husband as he enters. He smiles at her, but she is not amused. He closes the door behind him and flops back against it. She offers him a chair, but pulls it away as he about to sit on it. He hits the floor, and she sits on the chair and looks scornfully down at him. Staggering to his feet, he gets caught up in his cape and falls over once more. Now he finds that he cannot stand upright because he has his foot on his cape. Instead of shifting the foot, he removes the cape.

Hotel foyer. Mr. Fuller, also drunk, staggers up the staircase.

Mr. Fuller's hotel room. He's also late. His despairing wife (dressed in black) is waiting for him.

Corridor. The bellhop, seated again, observes Mr. Fuller, with cigar, lurching toward him. He laughs uproariously. Mr. Fuller stops and looks at the bellhop. Then he pulls the chair from under him and toddles on until he reaches his hotel room.

Mr. Fuller's hotel room. Mrs. Fuller is weeping. Her husband staggers in, ignoring her.

Mr. Full's hotel room. Mrs. Full crooks her husband's walking stick around his neck. She pulls him toward her and starts hectoring him. He tries to retreat, but she pulls him back. When she removes the stick, he staggers back onto the bed, legs in the air. She rushes over and whacks him on the rump. He tries to evade her but manages only to flop onto the floor at her feet. She tosses him back onto the bed and hits him with a pillow. Then she shoves another pillow into his face.

Mr. Fuller's hotel room. Mrs. Fuller protests at her husband's condition, but he slaps her face. To his surprise, she replies with a straight right to the jaw. He collapses. She stands over him, looking disgusted. As he gets up, she pulls his jacket half off so that he cannot move his arms; then she belts into him, driving him against the door.

Under the weight of her attack, he slithers to the floor. She throws up her arms in a gesture of victory.

Mr. Full's hotel room. He is stretched out, unconscious, on the bed. Mrs. Full hears the noise from the room opposite. She goes to the door and listens.

Mr. Fuller's hotel room. He gets to his feet, leaps onto his wife, and starts to throttle her.

Mr. Full's hotel room. Disturbed by what she has heard from across the corridor, Mrs. Full arouses her husband, drags him onto the floor, and tells him he must go to Mrs. Fuller's aid. Just to make sure, she shoves him violently out of the room.

Corridor. Full hurtles against the door of Mr. Fuller's room.

Mr. Fuller's hotel room. The impact of Mr. Full's body sends Mr. Fuller sprawling. His wife gets to her feet and observes Mr. Full kicking her husband. Half-throttled but unfailingly loyal to her spouse, she orders her unwanted protector to clear out. When he hesitates, she reinforces her message by cracking him over the head with a basin. He staggers backward through the door.

Corridor. Mrs. Full rushes to her husband's assistance—then changes her mind: after helping him up she knocks him down again.

Mr. Fuller's hotel room. Mrs. Fuller peeks out to see what's going on.

Corridor. The two wives confront each other. In the background, Mr. Full is stretched out on the floor. As the women begin to quarrel, he gets up and tries to intercede. His wife tells him to keep out of it.

Mr. Fuller's hotel room. He gets up.

Corridor. Mr. Full tries to intercede again. His wife bumps him backward into Mr. Fuller's room.

Mr. Fuller's hotel room. He falls against Mr. Fuller, collapsing at his feet. The latter helps the intruder up, then uses his huge belly to shove him out.

Corridor. Mr. Full staggers against his wife, who pushes Mrs. Fuller into the Fulls' hotel room. Mrs. Fuller promptly retaliates, and Mr. Full gets shoved backward into Mr. Fullers' room.

Mr. Fuller's hotel room. This time the two men strike up an acquaintance: they obviously have much in common. The two wives move in—out of the corridor—to continue their quarrel. Unnoticed by them, Mr. Fuller uses his stick to hook up his wife's pocketbook. The two men—now the "rounders"—creep out of the room.

Corridor. Mr. Full puts his fingers in his ears to drown out the quarrel. Mr. Fuller closes the door of his room. His wife's pocketbook is dangling from his hand. He opens it, removes a few dollars, and tosses the pocketbook aside. Mr. Full invites his new-found friend into his room. He goes ahead of him and slams the door in Mr. Fuller's face.

Mr. Full's hotel room. Mr. Full staggers over to the bedknob to retrieve his hat. His friend enters. Mr. Full grabs a few dollars from *his* wife's pocketbook and shows it to Mr. Fuller. The latter grabs the money—Mr. Full grabs it back.

Mr. Fuller's hotel room. The women have almost come to blows.

Mr. Full's hotel room. Mr. Full drops his hat and bends down to pick it up. Mr. Fuller boots him out of the room and lurches after him.

Corridor. The rounders show each other their money and shake hands. Linking arms, they stagger drunkenly along the corridor away from their hotel rooms.

Hotel foyer. The rounders appear. They lurch past the seated bellboy.

Mr. Full's hotel room. Mrs. Full enters followed by Mrs. Fuller. She looks for her husband under the mattress. Both women now realize that their husbands have given them the slip. Their anger is immediately redirected to their wayward spouses.

Street. The rounders lurch along the sidewalk. Mr. Full collapses, but his fat friend drags him along anyway.

Mr. Full's hotel room. Mrs. Full now discovers that her husband has taken her money. Aghast, she shows her empty pocketbook to Mrs. Fuller. The two women fall into each other's arms. Mrs. Full weeps and vows vengeance.

Mr. Fuller's hotel room. Mrs. Fuller enters and puts on her hat and coat. Discovering that she too has been "robbed," she also vows vengeance.

Exterior of Smith's Café. Mr. Fuller drags his buddy into the Café, past a black porter.

Interior of Smith's Café. Mr. Fuller drags his buddy past seated diners and drops him beside a vacant seat. For a moment he contemplates Mr. Full's supine body. Then he crooks his stick around the latter's neck and tries to raise him from the floor. But he falls backward, and Fuller also loses his balance and tumbles head over heels in the opposite direction. Mr. Full gets to his feet, strikes a match on the bald head of a diner, and lights a cigarette. Mr. Fuller sits down on the vacant chair. His buddy uses the bald diner's head as a leaning post; then he grabs the man's napkin, blows his nose in it, and throws it into the man's face. Meanwhile, Mr. Fuller is using the waiter's champagne stand as a footrest and has pulled the tablecloth over himself as if it were a sheet. He starts to doze. Mr. Full peels off his jacket and tosses it aside. The he tears the tablecloth off the bald diner's table, flops to the floor below his buddy, and covers himself with the tablecloth. Mr. Fuller falls off his chair and lands beside Mr. Full. The diners watch, aghast at this behavior.

Exterior of hotel. The two wives, wearing overcoats, exit in search of their husbands. They discuss the most likely place to find them and set off in the right direction.

Exterior of Smith's Café. The wives arrive. They consider whether they should enter.

Interior of Smith's Café. The rounders get to their feet and attack some diners who try to eject them.

Exterior of Smith's Café. The wives ask the black porter if he has seen their husbands. He recognizes the descriptions and directs them inside.

Interior of Smith's Café. Getting too aggressive, Mr. Fuller falls over. The wives enter and approach their husbands. Mrs. Fuller belts into her spouse; Mrs. Full swings at hers, but he ducks and the blow catches the bald diner instead. The rounders shove their wives aside and rush out of the café.

Exterior of Smith's Café. The rounders dash away.

Interior of Smith's Café. The wives rush out after their husbands.

A park. A glimpse of the rounders still fleeing.

Exterior of Smith's Café. Mrs. Full brandishes her umbrella, knocking down the black porter. The wives head toward the park.

Lakeside in the park. A man is seated in a boat; his girl is about to climb in.

Park. The wives appear. They look around and head in the direction of their spouses.

Lakeside. Still fleeing, the rounders rush toward the water's edge. Mr. Full trips, knocking the girl into the water. Mr. Fuller jumps into the boat, sending the man hurtling after her. Mr. Full leaps into the boat which rocks violently.

Exterior of Smith's Café. Diners and waiters exit and dash toward the park.

Lakeside. The wives observe their husbands trying to row away from the shore. The man and his girl are struggling in the water.

Park. The diners and waiters appear, hot on the trail of the rounders.

Close-up of boat. The rounders look sick. They toss away their oars and gesture rejection of their wives. Fuller sticks out his tongue at his wife; Full thumbs his nose at his.

Lakeside. Angry diners and waiters reach the water's edge. The bald diner shows his battered hat—ruined by Mr. Full in the café.

Close-up of boat. The rounders are stretched out at the bottom as the boat fills with water.

Lakeside. Angry diners and waiters shake their fists at the two drowning men. The wives try to console each other.

Close-up of boat. The rounders and their boat sink out of sight.

COMMENTS

1. In its time, *The Rounders* was regarded as one of Chaplin's more unpleasant films. Uno Asplund (1976, 53) tells us that the Swedish censors banned the film (in 1915), referring to the two husbands as "perfect beasts," while in the U.S. *Moving Picture World* considered it "a rough picture for rough people" (McDonald, Conway, and Ricci 1974, 64). From the standpoint of violence the film seems relatively tame beside such Keystones as *The Fatal Mallet* and *The Property Man*, and despite complaints about its depictions of drunkenness, it contains nothing in that line that Chaplin (or Fatty, for that matter) hadn't done before without arousing comparable protest. The original criticisms may have been motivated by the unusual sight of wives manhandling their husbands.

Notwithstanding such objections, the film was one of Chaplin's most successful Keystones, due in part to his scene with Fatty in the Café. He went on to repeat that scene in two later films, teaming up with Ben Turpin in *A Night Out* (Essanay 1915) and with Harry Myers in *City Lights* (1931). In addition, the drunken dude character of *The Rounders*—a replay of one of Chaplin's most popular music hall acts—looks like a first-run performance for *One A.M.* (Mutual 1916), his best-known gentleman-drunk depiction. Compare also with his drunk roles in *A Night in the Show* (Essanay 1915) and *The Idle Class* (First National 1921).

In *The Rounders* Charlie is, of course, a married man yet again. See *Mabel's Married Life* (Keystone no. 19), comment 2. But this time his wife isn't Mabel but the formidable Phyllis Allen, who is also married to him in *Getting Acquainted* (Keystone no. 34) and *Pay Day* (First National 1922). In *The Kid* (First National 1922) she is not Charlie's wife but nevertheless beats him up when he tries to abandon baby Jackie in her perambulator.

The hotel foyer scene of *The Rounders* recalls scenes in two earlier Keystones, *Mabel's Strange Predicament* and *Caught in the Rain*.

Fatty dragging Charlie behind him to the Café anticipates a scene in *Pay Day* (First National 1922) where Henry Bergman pulls an equally inebriated Charlie through the streets by his overcoat.

Exceptionally, in *The Rounders* it is not Chaplin who makes the most dexterous uses of walking sticks. Phyllis Allen (in the hotel room) and Fatty (in the café) turn one of Charlie's favorite walking-stick gags against him. Charlie's best comic business in this film is his struggle with the cape; he does a comparable "turn" with a cloak in *The Great Dictator*.

2. Structure: three "acts" located respectively in the hotel, the café, and the park. Each act consists of two or more symmetrically contrasting scenes. Act One: (i) Charlie staggers up to his flat; Fatty staggers

up to *his* flat (ii) Charlie gets beaten up by his wife; Fatty gets beaten up by *his* wife. (iii) The two husbands become friends; the two wives become enemies. (iv) The husbands steal their wives' money; the wives discover the thefts. Act Two: (i) The husbands link arms and head off for the café; the wives console each other and set off in pursuit. (ii) Charlie and Fatty disrupt the café; the wives disrupt their husbands' fun. Act Three: (i) Charlie and Fatty flee to the park; the wives and the café clientele pursue them. (ii) Charlie and Fatty push a couple of people into the lake; they row away in a leaky boat and drown.

3. The film offers yet another of Chaplin's jaundiced views of marriage. Comparison with *Mabel's Married Life* indicates that Charlie's status as a spouse has actually deteriorated. Mabel was contemptuous of his physical weakness, but she tried to do something "positive" about it (the training dummy). She wants him to be a "he-man," and as a potential reward she puts on pajamas and waits for him in bed, seductively. Phyllis Allen is also contemptuous of Charlie's weakness, but she has, quite obviously, married a man smaller than herself in order to be the dominant partner. Her bed is not for sex (can one possibly imagine Charlie and Phyllis Allen making love?), it's the place where she demonstrates her power: she beats up her husband for returning home late and intoxicated. This is a marriage in which the traditional roles of husband and wife are, implicitly, reversed—as symbolized by the fact that Phyllis uses Charlie's cane against him. Similarly, in the Fuller flat, Minta turns the tables on Fatty by beating him up when he tries to silence her protests.

In *Mabel's Married Life* Mabel cares enough for Charlie to want to "improve" him, while Mack's wife persuades herself that her lecherous spouse is a loving, faithful husband. But the two marriages of *The Rounders* display neither expectations nor illusions. The relationship of the Fulls is that of oppressor and victim (a comic inversion of the brutal husband and battered wife). The relationship of the Fullers is that of a struggle between equals—i.e., each gives as good as he or she gets. There is not a trace of love, friendship, or understanding in these marriages. The men presumably took to drink in order to forget what was waiting for them when they returned home. But alcohol wears off. Ultimately, they prefer to drown themselves rather than go on facing their wives.

4. The café sequence provides memorable examples of comically creative treatments of people and objects. Charlie treats the elderly diner as if he were an object, striking a match on his bald head and using it as a leaning post. By contrast Fatty turns a tablecloth into a blanket and employs a champagne stand as a footrest. They transform the café into the sort of "home" their wives prevent them from having.

OTHER VIEWS

"Chaplin . . . never used Negroes as comic relief in his films, though in the 1914 Keystone comedy, *The Rounders*, there is a white man, in black-face, playing a bit part as a doorman" (Huff 1952, 261). [Huff overlooks the scenes with blacks in *His Favorite Pastime*, *A Day's Pleasure* and *His Trysting Places*.]

"Playing a drunk allowed Chaplin to indulge himself in his most characteristic behavior: that of dealing arbitrarily with the inanimate world. In *The Rounders* . . . he balances himself precariously along the straight border of the carpet" (Sobel and Francis 1977, 214).

27.

The New Janitor

(1914)

Original working title: *Caught*
Other titles: *The Porter, The New Porter, The Blundering Boob;*
French: *Charlot portier, Charlot concierge;* German: *Der neue Pförtner;*
Spanish: *Charlot portero, Charlot conserje;* Italian: *Il nuovo portiere*

Length: 1 reel; 984 feet (Asplund), 1020 feet (Lyons)
Playing time: 17 minutes at 16 frames per second
Producer: Keystone
Director: Chaplin
Screenplay: Chaplin
Photography: Frank D. Williams (?)
Cast:

Janitor	Chaplin
Elevator operator	Al St. John
Manager	Jack Dillon
President	Fritz Schade
Stenographer	Minta Durfee

Finished or shipped: September 3, 1914
Released: September 24, 1914

SYNOPSIS

[This is one of the few Keystones for which there is a detailed description elsewhere. David Robinson (1985, 693–97) supplies a shot summary. My description incorporates a few details from Robinson's account.]

The foyer of an office building. Charlie, the new janitor, is chatting with the elevator operator. He bends down to get his broom, dustpan, and brush, but before he can make it into the elevator, the operator deliberately closes the door on him. Disconsolate, he heads upstairs.
Title: *The top floor.*

Before Charlie gets to the top of the last flight of steps, the elevator arrives and the operator hops out. Amused, he watches Charlie wearily climbing the stairs, then dashes back to the elevator and closes the door behind him. Charlie wipes away his perspiration and removes his hat. He enters the top floor corridor equipped with dustpan and brush.

Manager's office (to the left of the corridor). The manager, seated at his desk, opens a letter.

Handwritten text of letter: *"Will call today to collect that gambling debt. Have the money ready for me or I'll expose you. Luke Connor."*

The manager looks around, scared.

Corridor. Charlie hangs up his hat on a hall stand. It falls off. He kicks it aside. [Robinson notes: "This looks like an accident: retakes were not encouraged at Keystone"]

Manager's office. Charlie the janitor enters with more letters. He knocks *after* entering. The manager buries his head in his hands, but Charlie doesn't notice this. He hands him the letters. Then he demonstrates his "dexterity": picking up the wastepaper basket, he rolls it up his leg. As a result, all the wastepaper drops out. He is about to exit when the manager orders him to pick it all up. Charlie obliges too eagerly: the manager has dropped a book on the floor, and Charlie shoves it into the basket along with the wastepaper. But the manager notices this and orders the janitor to return the book. Charlie exits.

The corridor. Charlie does some more juggling with the wastepaper basket. He collects his broom, dustpan, etc. and tries to enter the company president's office (to the right of the corridor) but blocks his own path by holding the broom horizontally. He solves the difficulty by climbing over it.

President's office. The president's desk and telephone are situated in the foreground (left) and another desk (the stenographer's) is located less conspicuously in the background near the door. In the foreground (right) a large safe is visible. Charlie wanders around the room with the broom on his shoulder. He yawns and proceeds to dust the telephone.

Corridor. The stenographer hangs up her coat and hat. She removes the manager's straw boater from its peg, looks at it fondly, presses it to her heart, and then replaces it.

President's office. The stenographer enters and glances at Charlie without much interest. She goes to the telephone. In the background Charlie eyes her with evident longing. She discovers a note (a love letter from Charlie?) by the telephone, glances back at him, and smiles. He dusts the safe, still eyeing her. She bends down to remove something from a drawer, and Charlie absentmindedly turns and dusts her behind.

Title: *Luke Connor.*

The manager's office. Connor enters. He is a tall man wearing a straw boater and sporting a mustache. He confronts the manager, demanding his money.

President's office. The stenographer reads her mail. Charlie continues to gaze at her until, absentmindedly, he puts his foot in his pail of water. She exits, dropping her handkerchief.

Manager's office. Connor gets more insistent. The manager pleads with him.

Corridor. The stenographer eavesdrops at the door to the manager's office.

Manager's office. The manager is still pleading.

Title: *"I'll get it by five o'clock."*

Corridor. The stenographer has heard enough. She passes on her way out of sight.

Manager's office. Connor, uttering threats, exits without the money.

President's office. Charlie stretches himself. He sits on the sill of the open window and almost falls out.

A high angle exterior shot shows him half out of the window. Traffic can be seen moving in the street far below.

Exterior ground floor entrance to office building. The company president, wearing a top hat, is chatting with two ladies.

President's office. Charlie removes his cleaning rags from the pail and squeezes them out of the window—onto the president and the two ladies. Then he loses hold of the pail handle. The pail falls out of the window.

Ground floor entrance. The president is drenched with dirty water. He looks up and shakes his fist at Charlie.

President's office. Charlie almost falls out of the window again.

Ground floor entrance. Enraged, the president enters the office building.

President's office. The window slips down, trapping Charlie.

Foyer. The president enters the elevator and orders the operator to take him to the top floor.

Top floor. The president stamps out of the elevator.

Corridor. The president shakes his hat and wipes his soaking head.

President's office. The president storms in and discovers Charlie stuck in the window. He boots him in the rump. Charlie wriggles free. He tries to make excuses, but the president refuses to listen.

Title: *Bounced.*

Charlie is ordered to clear out. He looks sadly at the president and bows politely. But the latter advances toward him ominously. Charlie retreats toward the door, falling as he goes. The president shoves him out of the office and slams the door in his face. Charlie falls backward into the corridor.

Title: *Going down.*

Exterior of top floor elevator. Charlie just misses the elevator again. He heads down the stairs.

President's office. The president is seated at his desk. The manager enters, holding a document. He eyes the safe. He hands over the document as the president talks about his mishap.

Foyer. Charlie reaches the bottom of the stairs. His bucket was left there, and he slips over it.

Janitor's room. Charlie puts down his broom, etc.

President's office. The manager exits. The president opens the safe.

Manager's office. The manager enters. He stands and ponders his next move.

President's office. The safe is now closed. The stenographer is typing at the desk in the background. The president shakes more water off his hat. He says a few words to the stenographer and exits.

Manager's office. The manager is slumped at his desk, pensive.

President's office. The stenographer covers up her typewriter and exits.

Corridor. She puts on her hat and departs.

Manager's office. The manager listens to her retreating footsteps, opens the door, and watches her heading for the elevator.

Corridor. The manager creeps across to the president's office.

President's office. The manager enters. He pulls down the window shades and goes to work on the safe's combination.

Exterior of elevator. The stenographer realizes that she has forgotten something. She turns and heads back to the president's office.

President's office. The manager now has the safe open. The stenographer enters and discovers him at the safe. Noticing her, he closes the safe door. She watches him suspiciously as he exits.

Manager's office. The manager grabs a gladstone bag and listens at the door.

President's office. The stenographer listens at the door. Then she exits.

Corridor. She listens at the keyhole of the manager's office.

Manager's office. He turns the door handle.

Corridor. The stenographer dashes back into the president's office.

Manager's office. He looks out, finds the corridor empty, and exits carrying the gladstone bag. He puts on his straw boater.

President's office. The stenographer hides behind the desk in the foreground. She watches as the manager enters, opens the safe, and tosses out the contents. He finds a wad of notes and begins counting them. Suddenly, he becomes aware of the terrified girl's presence. She rises and points an accusing finger at him. He drops the notes and starts to threaten her. She reaches for the telephone, but he hurls her to the floor.

Janitor's room. Charlie throws out his arms in despair.

President's office. The manager is throttling the stenographer.

Title: *The porter's button.*

As the manager pushes her backward onto the desk, she reaches out presses a button.

Janitor's room. Charlie hears the bell and ponders whether he should bother to answer it.

Close-up of bell ringing.

Janitor's room. Charlie gives a gesture of annoyance.

President's office. The manager pulls out a gun and waves it in the stenographer's face. She collapses in a faint.

Janitor's room. Charlie exits.

Foyer. He stands at the bottom of the stairs still undecided. At last, he makes up his mind and wearily heads upstairs.

President's office. The manager disconnects the telephone and turns his attention back to the safe.

Top floor. Charlie comes into view. He flops his head on the top step, exhausted. Then he stretches, rubs his feet, and heads into the corridor, puffing at a cigarette. He back-kicks the butt, swings his cane, and enters the president's office.

President's office. The manager is rifling the safe. The stenographer is prostrate, on the floor. Quickly sizing up the situation, Charlie whacks the manager on the rump and points at the girl. The manager reaches for his gun, but Charlie knocks it out of his hand with the cane. He swings at the janitor but misses. Charlie, a better shot, kicks him in the rear and sends him sprawling. Then he bends down and grabs the manager's gun. The latter advances upon the stooping janitor, expecting to take him by surprise, but Charlie is ready for him. From between his legs he points the gun at the manager, then steps over his own arm and stands upright, all the while keeping his crooked adversary in range. Now he orders him to pick up the girl and put her in a chair. Charlie tries to call for help but speaks into the telephone's base instead of the mouthpiece. The manager now advances toward him, threateningly. In desperation, Charlie fires a few shots out of the window.

The street below. A cop chatting with a girl is suddenly alerted by the gunshots.

President's office. Charlie fires another shot, but he has aimed in the wrong direction and grazes his own foot. The manager makes a rush at the janitor, but Charlie slams the safe door into him. By now the stenographer has recovered. She cowers helplessly in the background.

Foyer. The cop arrives at the elevator. The door is closed. He heads up the stairs.

Top floor. The president reappears. He is wearing casual clothes.
The cop arrives at the top of the stairs.

President's office. The president enters and finds Charlie covering
the manager with the gun. He kicks Charlie's behind and shoves him
backward. The stenographer intercedes.

Corridor. Charlie falls out of the president's office and lands at the
cop's feet. The cop grabs at him, but Charlie is quicker and kicks him
backward—into the manager's office. Then he slips and falls. The
manager gets up, seizes Charlie, and drags him into the president's
office.

President's office. By now the stenographer has explained everything, and the president has discovered the rifled safe. He confronts
the manager with it. The cop drags Charlie—the presumed culprit—
over to the president, but the latter points to the real criminal. The
manager is about to leave, in custody, when Charlie points the telephone at him. The manager cowers, thinking it's the gun. The cop
exits with his prisoner. The stenographer now praises Charlie's heroism. The president offers Charlie a reward. Charlie hesitates about
taking the money—then counts it and decides to keep it. The president
extends his hand, and Charlie gives him the telephone to shake.

COMMENTS

1. One of Chaplin's most carefully crafted films, *The New Janitor*
took no less than seventeen days to make—in contrast to *A Busy Day*
which was shot in a couple of hours.

One moment of *A Busy Day* borders on pathos (see comment 5 to
that film), but Chaplin himself singles out *The New Janitor* as the first
of his movies to be touched by a "desire to add another dimension . . .
beside that of comedy." He recalls:

> I was playing in a picture called *The New Janitor*, in a scene in which
> the manager [sic] of the office fires me. In pleading with him to take pity
> on me and let me retain my job, I started to pantomime appealingly that
> I had a large family of little children. While I was enacting mock senti-
> ment, Dorothy [sic] Davenport, an old actress, was on the sidelines
> watching the scene, and during rehearsal I looked up and to my surprise
> found her in tears. "I know it's supposed to be funny," she said, "but you
> just make me weep." She confirmed something I already felt: I had the
> ability to evoke tears as well as laughter. (Chaplin 1964, 153)

The New Janitor is Chaplin's first version of the story he would
remake as *The Bank* (Essanay 1915). See my commentary on *The Bank*
for a detailed comparison of the two films. A number of parallels with
other Chaplin films are worth noting here. (i) Plot analogues. Gerald

Mast observes: "In *The New Janitor*, an apparently respectable employee is an embezzler who robs the company safe. This Chaplin theme—that an apparently honest member of the Establishment uses that appearance as a disguise—recurs in *The Floorwalker*, *The Fireman*, *The Pawnshop*, and several other later films" (1979, 71). (ii) Thrill comedy. This is fairly infrequent in Chaplin's films. *The New Janitor* contains Chaplin's first (albeit very limited) use of thrill comedy. But Charlie's near fall from the high window gives us an early foretaste of his precarious escape from the hut in *The Gold Rush* and his foolhardy demonstration of skating blindfolded in *Modern Times*. (iii) Comic business. Several gags in *The New Janitor* recur in *The Tramp* (Essanay 1915). Among these: Charlie blocking his own entrance through a door with a broomhandle/pitchfork, and Charlie putting his foot into a bucket of water/milk as he is talking to a girl. The famous gag of Charlie poking a gun between his legs was repeated, most strikingly, in *The Immigrant* (Mutual 1917). (iv) Recasting. Al St. John, who had just played the helpful bellhop in *The Rounders*, reappears as the elevator operator, a mischievous variation on the same role.

2. Structure: a series of scenes contrasting the fates and fortunes of Charlie and the manager. Prologue: Charlie's misfortune—forced to walk up the stairs. (i) Connor threatens the manager (via letter). (ii) The manager is nasty to Charlie. (iii) The stenographer is secretly in love with the manager. (iv) Charlie is secretly in love with the stenographer. (v) Connor puts the screws on the manager. (vi) The president fires Charlie. (vii) The manager robs the safe and attacks the stenographer. (viii) Charlie intercepts the manager and rescues the stenographer. (ix) The president mistakes Charlie for the robber. (x) The cop does the same. (xi) The stenographer intercedes: Charlie is cleared; the manager is arrested. Epilogue: Charlie's good fortune—praised by the stenographer and rewarded by the president.

3. *The New Janitor* is a significant departure from Chaplin's previous Keystones. The film's slapstick is relatively inconsequential. The new emphasis is on a fusion of character comedy and melodrama.

Charlie's actions in the film serve not only to amuse us but also deepen our understanding of him, to enable us to perceive in him more than appears evident at the outset. While Charlie provides the comedy, the other characters and the plot resemble those of a typical D. W. Griffith Biograph melodrama, e.g., *A Burglar's Mistake* (1909). And, as David Robinson (1985, 693) notes, the film sometimes cross-cuts rapidly between parallel actions in the typical Griffith manner.

What marks *The New Janitor* as a film of special importance is that it is the Keystone movie in which Chaplin introduced Charlie into a serious story without either deliberate or accidental incongruity. His unheralded success in so doing was a development that would prove no less important than his discovery (in making the same film) that he had the power to evoke tears as well as laughter. For it implied that his character did not have to be limited to slapstick farces, that it would not be out of place—indeed, might even be more meaningful—in serious films.

4. The big theme of *The New Janitor* is "connections," a variation on the theme of perception/misperception. This is a film in which the characters communicate with one another at best only on a superficial level. They all misperceive Charlie, and most of them misjudge him too.

However, Chaplin enables the audience to make all the necessary connections. We see all that happens. At the outset, however, we will almost certainly misjudge Charlie. He looks and acts like a nebbish. That's all the elevator operator sees in him. Charlie tries to strike up an acquaintance with the elevator operator, but gets treated as a laughingstock. No connection there. We may modify our view of him as we see him forced to trudge all the way to the top of the stairs. Now he looks pathetic—like his mercilessly put-upon old assistant in *The Property Man*. But that seems to be all. We can pity him but cannot identify with him.

Charlie's encounter with the manager shows another nonconnection. The manager treats him like a menial, ignoring his politeness and reacting brusquely to his well-intentioned klutziness. The outcome of the story indicates the extent to which the manager failed to realize the potentialities of this klutz. Yet in his handling of the office wastebasket, Charlie shows that he can be nimble as well as klutzy, and when he demonstrates his nimbleness a second time, it is to disarm the manager at the scene of the crime. What provokes that crime is the manager's own "connection" problem with Luke Connor. Connor is obviously a bad connection—whether by mail or in person.

Both Charlie and the stenographer are too shy to make the connections they most desire. The stenographer secretly adores the manager and wants to know all about him. She fondles his hat and also spies on him. Charlie sighs for the stenographer behind her back as she reads a letter. She throws a smile back at him. Why? What is in this letter? We get to see the text of Connor's message, but we are not shown this one. Has Charlie written the stenographer a billet-doux because he is too timid to speak with her? He is, after all, only the new janitor, and he hasn't yet made good. Curiously, she appears to ignore Charlie while she's in the office but drops her handkerchief (for him?) as she exits.

Charlie's most direct connection is the one that gets him fired: he drops his bucket on the president's head. The latter refuses to listen to any of Charlie's explanations or pleas. Accident or not, president doesn't want him around. He considers the manager reliable and Charlie unreliable but doesn't know what either of them is really like.

The stenographer's first direct connection with Charlie is to press the *porter's button*. While she is summoning him, the manager *disconnects* the telephone. Charlie is now the only person who can rescue the girl. But he has doubts about responding to the call. After all, he has just been dismissed.

We don't expect much of this pathetic figure as he starts to shuffle wearily up the stairs. But something unexpected happens. Charlie has hidden possibilities. Entering the office, he springs into action in his unique way, disarming the manager and rescuing the girl. Now he needs help. He shouts into the wrong end of the disconnected telephone, then fires a few shots to alert the police. He had sized up the situation correctly as soon as he entered the office, but the cop and the president immediately make all the wrong connections. The stenographer puts them straight—but only after Charlie has been manhandled. (Charlie's deliverance by a girl he had previously rescued is a rare situation in Chaplin's films. The most memorable instance occurs in *Modern Times:* the gamine encourages Charlie, her former savior, to escape.) Charlie's heroism earns him praise from the stenographer. But he surely expects more—as he did with Mabel when he rescued her in *Caught in a Cabaret.* However, the social gulf between Charlie and the stenographer is, presumably, as unbridgeable as it was between Charlie and Mabel, the socialite. The president does, of course, offer him a reward. But Charlie's response sums up *their* relationship: in place of his hand he offers the president the disconnected telephone to shake.

In brief, the other characters in the film treat Charlie just as they view him: in a series of limited roles—as nebbish, drudge, klutz, savior, hero, etc. But the audience is able to make all the right connections. By the end of the film we can see Charlie as the sum of all these roles and also something more: as the would-be lover who doesn't get the reward he really wants.

OTHER VIEWS

"Charlie's method of saving the secretary from the thief is only a step away from Chaplin's mature style and theme. . . . Throughout the film, Charlie's strategies based on immediate, instinctive responses are consistently more effective than his more leisurely, planned methods of attack. . . . A further indication of the later Chaplin in the film is that, although the building has an elevator, Charlie, a mere laborer, must trudge up the stairs. . . . This allows him some funny business with climbing stairs, as well as social comment on who rides and who walks" (Mast 1979, 71).

"This is the first Chaplin film with a trace of sentimentality to it, when Charlie is fired and 'martyrised,' before making his comeback as victor" (Asplund 1976, 54).

"In the title role of *The New Janitor*, Charlie is unjustly dismissed and in consequence becomes something of a martyr. This is purely a side note and a good distance from the pathos yet to come in Chaplin films. He is still an integral part of the savage slapstick that is Keystone" (McCabe 1978, 60).

28.

Those Love Pangs

(1914)

Original working title: *In Wrong*
Other titles: *Busted Hearts, The Rival Mashers, Oh, You Girls!*; French:
Charlot rival d'amour, Joseph, rival de Charlot, Charlot et Joseph ri-
vaux d' amour, Charlot supplanté par Joseph; German: *Liebesqualen*;
Spanish: *Charlot rival de José*; Italian: *Quelle fitte d'amore*

Length: 1 reel; 974 feet (Asplund), 1010 feet (Lyons)
Playing time: 17 minutes at 16 frames per second
Producer: Keystone
Director: Chaplin
Screenplay: Chaplin
Photography: Frank D. Williams (?)
Cast:

A lovelorn young man	Chaplin
His rival (Joseph or Jose)	Chester Conklin
Their female interests	Vivian Edwards
	Cecile Arnold
Their friend	Edgar Kennedy
A landlady	Norma Nichols
A cop	Harry McCoy

Finished or shipped: September 19, 1914*
Released: October 10, 1914

SYNOPSIS

The dining room of a boarding house. Chester and Charlie are rivals for the affections of their attractive landlady. Charlie wants to
dash out into the hallway and flirt with her, but Chester pulls him
back by the seat of his pants and points to something interesting under

---

*This film was completed after *Dough and Dynamite* (Keystone no. 29) but released
earlier.

the table. When Charlie takes a peek, Chester dodges out into the hall and starts holding hands with the landlady. Realizing that he has been tricked, Charlie picks up a fork and jabs it through a door curtain into Chester's rump. Disturbed by his sudden contortions (is he drunk?), the landlady pulls herself away, leaving Chester nursing his buttocks. Chester knows who his assailant must be, but when he returns to the dining room Charlie is innocently pretending to play the fork like a Jew's harp. Chester slaps the fork out of his mouth—at which Charlie spits in his eye. Now it's his turn to dash into the hall and flirt with the landlady. This time Chester grabs the fork, and he is on the point of using it—but Charlie has taken the unchivalrous precaution of switching places with the landlady. Then he has second thoughts and moves her away from the curtain. But when he kisses her she's offended and pushes him away—onto the fork. His contortions also upset her (is he drunk too?), and she stamps away in a huff.

The conflict shifts into the hall. Charlie kicks Chester and bites his nose. Chester knocks Charlie onto the carpet. An apparent truce follows. But Charlie cunningly uses it to regain the advantage. Hooking his cane around Chester's neck, he drags him out of the house and down the front steps. Then he helps him to his feet, and they march off arm-in-arm.

Exterior of a tavern. Chester isn't interested in drink, and he walks away after Charlie has bummed some money from him. He heads for a park for a rendezvous with an attractive blonde (Cecile Arnold). Meanwhile, Charlie is about to slake his thirst when a pretty brunette (Vivian Edwards) passes. They eye each other with interest. Torn between liquor and sex, Charlie glances at his money and quickly makes up his mind. He follows the girl.

Street corner. Charlie catches up with the brunette, who is standing there waiting for someone. He attracts her attention with a couple of tricks: trying to swing his watch into his waistcoat pocket (he misses the pocket) and flipping his hat up and down like a lid. Before he can strike up a conversation, her boyfriend (a tall, well-built young man) arrives on the scene. He confronts Charlie menacingly. Charlie sizes him up and takes to his heels.

A park bench. Charlie nervously cleans his fingernails and picks his teeth with the end of his cane. His escape is only short lived, for the brunette and her boyfriend catch up with him. The young man towers over him, threateningly. But Charlie dodges under his rival's arm and escapes by crawling along the bench behind him. Then he strikes at the young man's straw boater with his cane and flees to safe distance.

Beside a tree. Charlie looks back at the young man and cups his hand over a smile. Chester and his blonde now come into view from behind the tree. Charlie doffs his hat, sighs, and faces the camera. He is listening to the couple, incredulously. The girl flings her arms around Chester and kisses him. He yawns. She grabs his hand and kisses it, then goes down on her knees to him. Charlie mops his brow. Chester yawns, stretches himself, and scratches his head. Charlie watches, hand on hip, as the blonde gazes rapturously up at Chester. Getting to her feet, she pulls him toward her. He strokes his mustache. She kisses him again and laughs, sneaking an amused glance at Charlie, who turns away in a daze, flinging out his arms in a gesture of despair. He falls back against the tree with a forlorn expression on his face. Then he pats his back, rubs his forehead, and turns to look at Chester, who is now being embraced by the girl. Chester stares back and doffs his cap. Disconsolate, Charlie observes the girl taking Chester's arm and walking away with him. Then he stares into the camera and throws out his arms once more. He tosses aside his hat and cane and pulls off his jacket. Looking skyward, he clasps his hands in prayer. He's about to leap into the lake when a cop grabs him by the seat of the pants and gives him a boot in the behind to bring him to his senses.

Seated on a park bench again, he jealously watches the blonde take some money from her shoe and stuff it into Chester's pocket.

Another bench. Chester and the blonde sit beside the brunette and her boyfriend.

Nearby. Charlie picks up a brick and polishes it.

He wanders over to the bench and provocatively drops the brick on the young man's foot. A chase follows.

In flight, Charlie pivots on one foot round a water fountain. He lures the young man to the lakeside. The latter threatens Charlie, but prevents him from toppling into the lake. Charlie is less concerned about his rival's safety. Hooking his cane around the young man's neck, he jerks him into the water. When his head bobs above the surface, he kicks it down.

Wandering away from the lakeshore, Charlie strikes a match on the back of his neck. He lights a cigarette and back-kicks the match.

Park bench. Both girls are now fussing over Chester. Charlie returns and confronts him, jabbing him in the stomach and hooking him around the neck with his cane. The girls exit. Chester's resistance is ineffective. A well-placed blow sends him sprawling face downward. Using him as a chair, Charlie fishes in his pocket and helps himself to his money.

Exterior of movie theater. The two girls buy tickets and enter. A poster outside the theater indicates that the show is *Helen's Stratagem*. [This looks like an ad for the 119-episode Kalem serial *The Hazards of Helen*, starring Helen Holmes; but the first episode of that serial, "Helen's Sacrifice," was not released until November 13, 1914, several weeks after the making of *Those Love Pangs*.]

Charlie follows the girls to the movie theater. At the ticket booth he removes a dollar from his pocket and blows it in to the cashier. He enters.

Park. The young man, having climbed out of the lake, revives Chester by wringing out his sopping jacket over him. Chester takes a swing at the young man—then realizes he's the wrong guy. Together, they go off in pursuit of Charlie.

Interior of movie theater. Charlie is now sprawled in a front row seat with an arm around each girl. He uses his feet to mime his embraces. His two rivals enter surreptitiously and change places with the girls while Charlie is napping. When he wakes and discovers the trick, he makes a vain attempt to escape, pushing himself backward and the whole row of seats along with him. Pandemonium breaks out: the audience rushes out of the theater while Chester and the young man fling Charlie through the movie screen and hurl bricks after him.

COMMENTS

Before starting this film and *Dough and Dynamite*, Chaplin planned to open the former film with a sequence showing Charlie and Chester as rival pastry cooks in a bakery. But the sequence was so funny and seemed to have so many possibilities that he decided to develop it in *Dough and Dynamite*. *Those Love Pangs* obviously combines elements of two earlier Chaplin films, *The Star Boarder* (Keystone no. 9) and *Twenty Minutes of Love* (Keystone no. 11). Isabel Quigly sums up this combination as follows: "Landladies and girls in the park, the only women a poor man might be expected to meet, were the main object of his [i.e., Charlie's] fancy. . . . In *Those Love Pangs* it was a case of both landlady *and* girls in the park, with Charlie and Chester Conklin pursuing both" (Quigly 1968, 36–38).

2. Structure. The film falls into two segments: a prologue (the boarding-house sequence and the main action (in the park). The prologue establishes the theme of male sexual rivalry; the action that follows rings a sequence of changes on that theme and introduces a second one: women are incomprehensible. Prologue: A stalemate—neither Charlie nor Chester wins the landlady. (i) Charlie has no girl but the young man and Chester have one each. (ii) First reversal: Charlie disposes of the young man; both girls are now with Chester. (iii) Second reversal: he disposes of Chester; both girls are now with Charlie. (iv) Third reversal: the girls clear off; the young man and Chester dispose of Charlie.

3. This is the second film in which we see Charlie attempting suicide. In *Recreation* (Keystone no. 23) his motive is uncertain but a flirtatious woman's entrance changes his mind. In *Those Love Pangs* the motive is

made perfectly clear (he's a failure with women), and he is saved by a cop's timely intervention.

The possession of women motivates the rivalry between Charlie and the other male characters. Where no women are available the antagonism ceases: i.e., Charlie and Chester bury the hatchet when the landlady rejects both of them. So far so good. But Charlie goes on to make three disturbing discoveries: he's the only man without a woman; women are incomprehensibly attracted to the "wrong" men; and women can be promiscuous.

Denis Gifford describes the two girls in the film as a "saucy a pair of flirts as ever winked and beckoned from a pre-permissive screen" (1974, 51). But it's Charlie who does the flirting—or at least attempts it. He tries to arouse the interest of the brunette on the street corner by doing a couple of tricks with his watch and hat. She doesn't really flirt with him. She seems to vacillate between curiosity about him and giving him the brush-off. But it is evident that she is waiting for her boyfriend, not for a pick-up.

The blonde doesn't flirt with Chester—she adores him. The scene in which they first appear looks like the opening of *The Fatal Mallet*, but it actually depicts the opposite situation. Both scenes occur beside a tree in the park. In the earlier film Charlie optimistically intrudes upon Mack trying to embrace a reluctant Mabel. In *Those Love Pangs*, by contrast, his expressions range pessimistically from envy, exasperation, disgust, and incredulity to downright despair as he observes the blonde going down on her knees to Chester while Chester nonchalantly yawns, stretches, and strokes his mustache. It's obvious why the brunette would prefer her tall handsome boyfriend to Charlie, but what is there about Chester that evokes such passion from the blonde? Charlie is confronted with the inexplicable taste of women. Why *don't* they care for him? Why *do* they dote on men with such contrary qualities?

In his perplexity and despair he attempts suicide. Rescued in the nick of time, he tries a new tack. Getting rid of the young man will, he presumes, make the brunette available. But the girls prove to be fickle and indiscriminate in their affections. Having dumped one of his rivals in the lake, Charlie discovers *both* girls necking with the other rival. This time, however, instead of despairing he sets about trading on their promiscuity by removing Chester and taking his place. In the absence of any other interested males, both girls are soon treating Charlie just as they had treated his rivals. But his triumph is short lived: the girls flee and his rivals launch a counterattack.

The film finally dissolves into violence, but not before it has farcically contrasted what sex appeal (supposedly) signifies for each sex. For the men: the more women the better. For the women: doting on whatever man is available.

4. Few of Chaplin's one-reel Keystones are as rich in comic business as *Those Love Pangs*. The film includes most of the already familiar gags and a few new ones. And even the familiar gags are sometimes given a new wrinkle. Sobel and Francis state: "Chaplin unerringly swings his fob watch into the pocket of his waistcoat with barely a glance" (1977, 187). In fact, Charlie flubs the trick (deliberately?): his watch swings *past* the pocket and swings below his waistcoat. The girl is unimpressed, so he demonstrates his old hat-lid trick to regain her attention. Later, in preparing for his assault on the young man, Charlie picks up a brick and starts to polish it. Previous Keystones have led us to expect a brick-throwing conflict, but he fools us by casually wandering over to the young man and dropping the brick on his foot. In earlier films we saw Charlie back-kick a cigarette butt, but for the first time we see him strike a match on the back of his neck.

The new gags are all very creative. He converts Chester into a "chair" and sits on him. He turns a dollar bill into a "feather" and puffs it into the cinema ticket booth. Finally and most memorably, with his arms around the two girls he suggestively mimes his "petting" by moving his feet as if they were his hands.

OTHER VIEWS

"Clothes, another good indication of class, are always given special attention by him [Chaplin]. *Those Love Pangs* shows Chester Conklin and himself as boarders at the same guest-house and as rivals for the same girls. There is nothing in the state of their dress to distinguish one from the other: baggy trousers, ill-fitting and creased jackets, large boots are common to both" (Sobel and Francis 1977, 162).

29.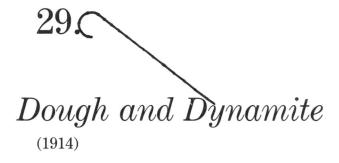

Dough and Dynamite

(1914)

Original working title: *In Trouble*
Other titles*: *The Cook, The New Cook, The Doughnut Designer;*
French: *Pâte et dynamite, Charlot pâtissier, Charlot mitron;* German:
Teig und Dynamit; Spanish: *Pastel y dinamita, Charlot panadero;* Italian: *Charlot panettiere*

Length: 2 reels; 2010 feet (Asplund), 2000 feet (Lyons)
Playing time: 34 minutes at 16 frames per second
Producer: Keystone
Director: Chaplin
Screenplay: Chaplin and Mack Sennett
Photography: Frank D. Williams (?)
Cast:

Pierre, a waiter and baker	Chaplin
Jacques, another waiter and baker	Chester Conklin
Monsieur La Vie, restaurant owner	Fritz Schade
Madame La Vie	Norma Nichols
Customer	Vivian Edwards
Waitress	Cecile Arnold
Bakers	Slim Summerville
	Edgar Kennedy
	Charley Chase
Diners	Phyllis Allen
	Jack Dillon

Finished or shipped: September 18, 1914**
Released: October 26, 1914

*In the 1920s, W.A. Films, Inc. rereleased this movie in a version reedited and inanely retitled by Chaplin's brother, Sydney.
**The film was completed before *Those Love Pangs* but released after it.

SYNOPSIS

Title: *Trouble*.

A combined bakery shop and restaurant. In the restaurant section Charlie, a waiter, is chatting with a waitress. He absentmindedly shovels leavings from one diner's plate onto a second diner's food and takes the latter's plate away. When the second diner protests, Charlie returns the plate. The diner protests again. Charlie removes the leavings with his finger, wipes his hands on his pants, and flicks a particle of food into the man's eye. More protests. Anxious to please, Charlie offers him some of the leavings. More protests. This time Charlie checks out the food by poking his finger into it, tasting some, and wiping his hand on the diner's jacket.

At the bakery shop counter a prominent sign is displayed, advertising "Assorted French Tarts." An attractive female customer enters (Vivian Edwards, wearing the outfit she wore in *Those Love Pangs*).

Restaurant. Charlie notices her, dumps the full plate of leavings in the second diner's lap and makes a beeline toward the counter. He smiles sweetly at her and inadvertently puts his hands in a plate full of tarts. The girl walks up and down alongside the counter, swinging her hips seductively. Enraptured, Charlie gazes after her, then stares knowingly at the sign. He offers her the tray of tarts, but they're broken. He carelessly flings them aside. One tart smacks into the second diner's eye. Charlie rushes to the rescue, scoops the tart off the man's face, and tosses it away. It lands on the first diner's ear; the man gets up and boots Charlie in the behind. Mistaking his assailant, Charlie smacks the second diner, who gets up, shoves Charlie into his chair, complains to the owner, and stalks angrily out of the restaurant. Upset, Charlie inadvertently puts his elbows into the food. Then he picks up some dirty plates and heads for the kitchen.

Kitchen. Stumbling, Charlie crashes into Chester, splattering his head with food. Chester hits him back with a dishcloth. Charlie retaliates, but hits a robust cook who is standing behind Chester. The fight that follows comes to an abrupt halt when Charlie smashes a plate over Chester's head and boots him in the face.

Bakery below the restaurant. Shot of bakers at work.

Restaurant. Chester tells Charlie to go below and get some bread. Charlie lifts up a trapdoor in the restaurant floor and starts descending a staircase to the bakery. Chester suddenly kicks him down the rest of the steps.

Bakery. Charlie lands on top of one of the bakers, who gets up and shoves him backward onto a kneading table. Large lumps of dough stick to his fingers and the seat of his pants. He uses the head baker's jacket as a convenient towel. Wandering over to the ovens, he burns his fingers trying to find out what's inside. Meanwhile, one of the bakers has, unwittingly, dropped a lump of dough on the floor. Charlie steps on it. He nonchalantly removes it by wiping his foot on a baker's rump and beats a quick retreat up the staircase.

Restaurant. Charlie closes the trapdoor on his foot. He wanders over to a couple of waitresses who are busily folding napkins and amuses himself by annoying the blonde one. He leans on the girl's shoulder and pulls out her hairpins. Then he takes one of the napkins and blows his nose on it.

Kitchen. Under the determined eye of the cook, he begins a short-lived truce with Chester. Volunteering to assist him with the dish-washing, he drops the crockery on the floor and accuses Chester of carelessness. There's another exchange of blows until Chester decides he's had enough.

Title: *The bakers want less work and more pay.*

Bakery shop counter. The owner vehemently rejects the head baker's demands.

Restaurant. The head baker descends the staircase, closing the trapdoor behind him.

Bakery. He joins a meeting of the other bakers, informs them of the owner's attitude and tells them to strike. They grab their jackets. The head baker finds that his jacket is covered with dough. He glowers into the camera. The bakers file up the staircase.

Bakery shop. An angry scene as the bakers confront the owner. They dump their aprons onto the counter.

Kitchen. Still arguing with Chester, Charlie exits into the restaurant.

Restaurant. He nearly falls through the open trapdoor. He closes the trapdoor.

Bakery shop. The owner calls to him. He wants Charlie to substitute as a baker.

Restaurant. Charlie eagerly rushes over to the bakery shop.

Bakery shop. The altercation is still going on. The head baker eyes Charlie suspiciously. Charlie grabs an apron. The head baker grabs the seat of Charlie's pants, pulls out a long knife, and points it at Charlie's chest. Charlie casually points the knife toward its owner and suddenly pounds on its handle. He dashes away leaving the head baker clutching his stomach. The bakers shake their fists, vowing vengeance at Charlie and the owner. They exit.

Exterior of shop. The bakers file out.

Kitchen. Charlie enters holding his apron. He back-kicks Chester, who is washing dishes. Leaning on the cook's fat belly, he tells Chester he must work in the bakery. Chester refuses. He exits.

Bakery shop. Chester tries to leave, but the owner hands him an apron and cap.

Restaurant. Chester flings out his arm in despair and descends to the bakery.

Bakery. He removes his jacket and puts on an apron and cap.

Kitchen. The cook hoists a huge sack of flour onto Charlie's back. His legs sag under him. She straightens them. He staggers out, knocking dishes helter-skelter.

Restaurant. He drops the sack onto a female diner.

Bakery. Chester slips on some wet dough and steadies himself by holding onto the staircase.

Restaurant. Charlie descends via the trapdoor. He drops the sack.

Bakery. Chester collapses under the sack. Charlie walks over it. Removing his jacket, he puts on his baker's outfit. He leans against the oven door and burns himself. He picks up a shovel, scrapes up the wet dough and dumps it into a vat. He tries levering some other dough off the kneading table, scrapes his boot with the shovel and sits down on the sack. He suddenly notices the prostrate Chester. Laughing, he lifts up the sack. Chester staggers to his feet and tells Charlie to get to work.

Title: *The strikers plot revenge.*

Shed. The head baker produces a box labeled "Dynamite." He points toward the bakery and mimes an explosion. The other strikers imitate his mime.

Bakery shop. Charlie enters, balancing a trayful of loaves on his head. One loaf falls. He bends down to pick it up, and the others topple off the tray. Picking them up, he tosses them at the owner, who flings one back in his face.

Restaurant. Eyeing two female diners, Charlie almost falls through the trapdoor.

Bakery. Chester calls up to Charlie.

Restaurant. Charlie drops his tray.

Bakery. The tray fells Chester.

Restaurant. Charlie descends staircase. He starts closing the trapdoor.

Bakery. Chester tugs at Charlie's legs.

Restaurant. The trapdoor closes on Charlie's neck.

Bakery. Chester tugs harder.

Restaurant. Close-up of Charlie's head caught in the trapdoor. He looks into the camera, grimaces, and fingers his neck. He wriggles free. The trapdoor cracks down on his head and closes over him.

Bakery. Charlie slaps Chester. Chester strikes back. They launch into a dough fight. Charlie uses wads of dough as if they were boxing gloves. He shoves Chester headfirst into the vat. They slash at each other with strips of dough. Chester trips and falls flat on his back.

Exterior of bakery shop. The head baker hesitates, then enters.

Bakery shop. He buys a loaf of bread and exits.

Bakery. At the ovens, Charlie burns himself again. He shoves a long paddle into the oven. He pulls it out, poking Chester in the face. He burns himself with a hot loaf and then with the paddle. Opening the furnace door, he warms his hands and rump. The two waitresses enter. They flirt with Chester. Charlie wanders over and orders Chester to tend the ovens. He flirts with the waitresses. Inadvertently, to Charlie's amusement, they sit down on a heap of wet dough. At the ovens, Chester stuffs ashes—and Charlie's jacket—into a sack.

Shed. The head baker shows his loaf to the other strikers. One striker (Slim Summerville) cuts a hole in the loaf.

Title: *A fiendish scheme.*

Shed. Close-up of the head baker stuffing dynamite into the loaf. The strikers clasp hands in a secret compact. The head baker exits carrying the loaf.

Bakery. Charlie kisses the blonde waitress. Behind his back, his hands become caught in a wad of dough. He extricates himself by stepping over his linked arms. Chester exits with the sack.

Restaurant. Chester trips over the trapdoor. He enters the kitchen.

Kitchen. He exits via the yard door.

Yard. He empties the sack into a garbage can.

Behind yard fence. Strikers peep through the slats.

Yard. They peep over the fence.

Behind yard fence. They pick up rocks and sticks.

Yard. They beat Chester over the head. He collapses. Recovering, he looks up. His attackers have disappeared. He dashes back to the kitchen.

Kitchen. He slides across the floor.

Restaurant. He descends the staircase.

Bakery. He tells Charlie he's needed in the kitchen. Charlie exits, leaving Chester with the waitresses.

Restaurant. Charlie stalks over to the kitchen.

Kitchen. The cook gives him a bucket to empty.

Yard. He tosses water over the fence.

Behind yard fence. The strikers are drenched.

Yard. The strikers peep over the fence at Charlie as he finds the sack and shakes out the ashes.

Behind yard fence. The strikers brandish sticks and rocks.

Yard. They beat Charlie over the head and disappear from view. Charlie gets up in a daze. He retrieves the bucket and looks over the fence.

Kitchen. The cook watches him stagger across the floor.

Restaurant. He stumbles over the outstretched legs of a diner and topples through the trapdoor.

Bakery. He takes careful aim and boots Chester. Then he fells him with a wad of dough. Horrified, the waitresses flee up the staircase. Charlie gets stuck to a wad of dough. Seizing his opportunity, Chester retaliates, kicking and pummeling his now defenseless adversary. Charlie extricates himself at last and beats Chester to the floor.

Bakery shop. The brunette waitress enters with flour on her face and rump. The owner looks at her suspiciously.

Bakery. Another dough fight. Chester gets his hands trapped in the dough.

Title: *The fatal loaf.*

Behind yard fence. The head baker hands the loaf to a little girl and tells her to take it to the bakery shop.

Exterior of bakery shop. The little girl looks around and enters.

Bakery shop. She hands the loaf to owner's wife and demands her money back.

Behind yard fence. The head baker is delighted.

Bakery shop. The little girl receives the money. She exits. The owner's wife examines the loaf. It feels too heavy. She shows it to the owner. He tells her to take it down to the bakery.

Bakery. Charlie flips strips of dough into baking pans as if they were flapjacks.

Bakery shop. The blonde waitress enters with flour on her face and rump. The owner is astounded.

Bakery. The owner's wife enters with the loaf. She watches Charlie at work. He rolls dough, making it into "bracelets," pushes the "bracelets" off his arm and lo!—bagels. He examines the loaf.

Title: *"Have it put in the oven and baked some more."*

She takes it over to Chester at the ovens. It's heavy—he almost drops it. Charlie hands his raw bagels to the owner's wife and pushes the loaf into an oven. He shows her a well-done loaf then escorts her over to the kneading table. She leans against the vat as he tries to flirt with her. Discouraging his advances, she exits.

Restaurant. The owner notices flour on her face and rump. He's furious.

Title: *"So my wife's been there too!"*

She protests her innocence. Growing wilder, he leaps into the air. Then he stamps over to the trapdoor and descends to the bakery.

Bakery. Approaching Charlie from behind, he kicks him, then slaps his face repeatedly. Charlie pleads with him. No use. At last, Charlie boots him back onto Chester. They collapse under a pile of loaves. The owner gets up and lambastes Chester. Charlie hurls flour into his face, then rushes up the staircase.

Restaurant. He flees into the kitchen.

Kitchen. The cook is holding a pie. Charlie grabs it.

Restaurant. The owner appears through the trapdoor.

Kitchen. Charlie hurls the pie.

Restaurant. The pie hits a diner in the face.

Kitchen. The owner rushes in. The cook swings a punch at Charlie—she hits the owner instead. Charlie kicks her and she flees. The diner enters. He swings at Charlie but hits the owner. Charlie exits with the owner in pursuit.

Restaurant. Charlie scampers down the staircase.

Bakery. Charlie kicks the owner as he descends the staircase. They chase one another around Chester. Charlie hurls a sack of flour—the owner flings it back. Charlie's next missile is a big pancake of dough, but just as he is about to throw it the ovens explode. The blast covers Charlie with his own pancake. Behind him, the staircase collapses.

Shed. The box of dynamite explodes, flinging the strikers into the air.

Bakery. Close-up of Chester and the owner buried in bricks up to their necks. They call for help then flop back, unconscious.

Close-up of a mound of dough, burying Charlie. His eyes gradually become visible through two holes.

COMMENTS

1. It appears that *Dough and Dynamite* was developed out of a bakery sequence originally intended for *Those Love Pangs*. Mack Sennett provides a confusing and somewhat misleading account of this development:

> Chester and Charlie worked out a situation in which they were both on the make for the landlady. This vague plot line faded after a few takes. Chester [Conklin] said, "Looky here Charlie, you're going to get credit as writer and director of this pastry, haven't you got a story?" Charlie said that chasing a landlady was the only idea he had. From there on he was stuck.(Sennett and Shipp 1954, 182–83)

Sennett conveys the impression that this situation was abandoned when in fact it became the opening episode of *Those Love Pangs*. He never mentions that film—but continues with a description of the origin of *Dough and Dynamite:*

> They [Charlie and Chester] left Edendale by streetcar that night, close to desperation. Then the trolley stopped at an intersection. . . . Across the street was a large bakery. Chester and Charlie peered at it and spotted a sign in the window: "Boy wanted." They turned to each other and said the same words at the same time: "This looks like our story." Next morning at Edendale they commandeered all the property men, painters, and carpenters they could lay hands on and built a bakery set.

When the flats were up, Conklin and Chaplin put their heads together and cast themselves not as pastry cooks but as strikebreakers. They gave a small girl the role of a customer, sent her in to buy a loaf of bread, and planned to have her return it with a complaint that the dough was not well baked. I . . . made a suggestion. "If you put a stick of dynamite in that bread and blow up the bakery, I think you'd have something, boys." We exploded the bakery with trick camera work and splattered dough for miles around. The picture was released as *Dough and Dynamite* and was Chaplin's best up to that time. (p. 183)

What Sennett meant was that it quickly proved to be one of the most *profitable* of Chaplin's Keystones—a fact that Chaplin confirms.

Sennett expected his directors to complete a two-reeler inside a week and at a total cost of less than a thousand dollars. But Chaplin (1964, 157–58) informs us that the film took him nine days and ran eight hundred dollars over the budget limit. As a result he forfeited his twenty-five dollar bonus. Sennett was, initially, disappointed at Chaplin's extravagance, but his attitude quickly changed when the film went on to gross over $130,000 in its first year of release!

2. Chaplin may have thought that his bakery idea was original. However, comedies about bakers and related subjects were popular almost from the inception of cinema, e.g., three 1898 British films: *The Miller and the Sweep, The Baker and the Sweep,* and *Whitewash and Miller;* also the American films *The Chimney Sweep and the Miller* (1902), *Fun in a Bakery Shop* (1902), and *Flour and Feed* (1904). Mention should also be made here of the Biograph comedy *A Catastrophe in Hester Street* (1904) which showed two drunken men blowing up a confectionery store.

3. Structure. The film interweaves several themes: (i) Charlie's multiple roles: klutz (as waiter), tease and flirt (with the waitresses), antagonist (with Chester and the owner), scab (as far as the strikers are concerned), and "creative" baker; (ii) Charlie's ongoing conflict with Chester; (iii) The strikers' revenge vs. Chester, Charlie, the bakery; (iv) the owner's jealousy.

4. Kalton C. Lahue comments: "For a Keystone, the film contained very few scenes, with majority of action occurring in five of them" (Lahue and Brewer 1968, 60–61). In fact, only six sets were used: (i) combined bakery shop and restaurant, (ii) bakery, (iii) kitchen, (iv) yard, (v) exterior of bakery shop, (vi) strikers' shed. For his comic business Chaplin made the maximum use of the film's props (plates, meals, tarts, loaves, dough, pie, paddle, knife, sack, bucket, etc.) and scenic structures (counter, trapdoor, staircase, tables, ovens, fence, etc.)

5. Those who see Chaplin as a political radical may find it difficult to square *Dough and Dynamite* with *Modern Times*. The film's hero is a scab, a servile tool of his ill-tempered boss, who is driven to reaction only after being unjustly beaten up. The striking bakers are treated negatively. Chaplin views them as shirkers, cynically representing their demands with the title: "The bakers want less work and more pay." Their leader is a vengeful fanatic whom they follow blindly. He turns them into a bunch of hoodlums and induces them to cooperate in his violent plot against the bakery. They are, in effect, crude caricatures of unionized workers, typifying reactionary attitudes to the American labor movement that prevailed prior to World War I in the wake of a series of violent strikes. Chaplin's radicalism is not evident in this film.

6. By contrast with the bakers, the conflict of Charlie and Chester is motivated by hierarchy, not by work or pay. Chester is a waiter like Charlie, but it's notable that we never actually see *him* waiting at the tables. Charlie seems to have (more or less) cornered the job for himself. The restaurant is, of course, a more interesting place than the kitchen. That's where he can eye the female diners and flirt with the waitresses. He leaves Chester in the kitchen to do most of the dishwashing and other menial tasks. Their disagreements begin with an accident: Charlie trips and spills a plate of leavings over Chester's head. But thereafter they are really battling over who gives the orders. As soon as the owner makes Charlie into a substitute baker, he goes into the kitchen and tells Chester to assist him in the bakery. But Chester prefers to quit rather than take orders from Charlie. Taking orders from the owner is another matter. He's about to walk off his job when the owner stops him and persuades him to go below and start work in the bakery. Nevertheless, Chester doesn't seem too taken with the idea of becoming a baker. Charlie, on the other hand, is obviously delighted with the job. Even before it is actually thrust upon him, we see him wandering around the bakery, exploring the ovens and having fun with the dough. When the two substitute bakers get to work, it's obviously Charlie who does all the "creative" bakery, making pancakes, bagels, etc. The only thing that will tear him away from his new job is the entrance of the two waitresses. Anxious to demonstrate to them who's running the place, he interrupts their tête-à-tête with Chester and orders him to see to the ovens. This time Chester obliges, but he makes Charlie pay for it: first by dumping his jacket into the disposal sack and later by sending him out to the yard to get beaten up too.

Charlie's relationships with women are somewhat better than he displayed in *Those Love Pangs*, but he still has to try much harder than Chester whose mysterious sex-appeal remains undiminished: i.e., the waitresses come down to the bakery to flirt with Chester, but they have to be trapped in dough before Charlie can sneak a kiss. Chester shows himself to be more or less indifferent to attractive women, but Charlie is tantalized by them (note his fascination with Vivian Edwards), and he also enjoys tantalizing them (note his mischievous behavior toward the blonde waitress). The visual-verbal pun—"Assorted French Tarts"—is emphasized by Charlie's glance from the sign to Vivian's seductive walk. But he's a voyeur rather than a seducer: other men get the "tarts," and, ironically, he is beaten up by his boss for the flirtation in which he is most signally rejected.

Charlie is even more of a failure as a waiter—his klutziness surpasses that of his first efforts as a waiter, in *Caught in a Cabaret* (Keystone no. 12). Of special interest here, however, is the fact that his klutzy behavior is strongly focused on *food:* the diners' meals, the tarts, the cook's pie, loaves of bread, masses of dough. Henceforth, in film after film, Chaplin will reveal a similar obsession with food, climaxing but not concluding with the feeding machine sequence of *Modern Times*. The obvious explanation for this—that it reflects his childhood privations—does not account for the fact that frequently, as in *Dough and Dynamite*, food is not treated possessively but used destructively, as a weapon. (Significantly, the film's title couples dough with dynamite.) It is, surely, relevant that Charlie is using (or abusing?) *food that does not belong to him.* To throw someone's food back in his or her face is an obvious rejection of dependence ("I don't need your food—you know where you can stuff it . . .!"). As a child, Chaplin may have known what it was like to go hungry, but his wild treatment of food in this and many later films does not reflect that hunger. It looks to me like a joyful affirmation of independence—whose antithesis is Charlie being force-fed by a machine in *Modern Times*. In *Dough and Dynamite* Charlie freely decides what to do with food: he doesn't eat it but uses it (missiles) on others or "creatively" (bracelets of dough) on himself. Chaplin himself revealed his pleasure in this:

> "Life's a funny thing," I said to myself. Then I made up as a baker, ordered a wagon-load of bread dough and flour and went out and romped through it hilarious, shouting with laughter whenever I was out of range of the camera. The result was *Dough and Dynamite*, and it clinched what I then thought was my success in the movies. (Chaplin 1916, 227; 1985, 135)

OTHER VIEWS

"Perhaps Chaplin's best Keystone with objects is *Dough and Dynamite*, one of his most famous. . . . Despite the purely Sennett premise of the film, it is dominated by the Chaplin style of paying close attention to what he can do with a bit of inanimate matter. Before the film has finished, Chaplin has used dough as boxing gloves, bracelets, quicksand, a mallet, a slingshot, a discus, a chair, and something to occupy his roaming hands while flirting with a girl" (Mast 1979, 70).

"Charlie arse-kicked in every conceivable variation known to human-kind, attacking his goal either from behind, to one side, or spinning past on the bias. . . . In *Dough and Dynamite* after some preliminary kicking early in the film Charlie is attacked by the usually genial Chester Conklin, who arse-kicks him five times in pile-driver fashion. And on and on. As a Chaplin gag, this is not a sometime thing" (McCabe, 1978, 61).

30.

Gentlemen of Nerve

(1914)

Original working title: *Attending the Races*
Other titles: *Charlie at the Races, Some Nerve;* French: *Charlot et Mabel aux courses, Charlot et Mabel à l'autodrome;* German: *Männer ohne Nerven;* Spanish: *Charlot y Mabel en las carreras**; Italian: *Gli sfaccendati, Charlot e Mabel alle corse*

Length: 1 reel; 961 feet (Asplund), 1030 feet (Lyons)
Playing time: 17 minutes at 16 frames per second
Producer: Keystone
Director: Chaplin
Story and screenplay: Chaplin
Photography: Frank D. Williams (?)
Cast:

Mr. Wow-Wow, an intruder at the motor races	Chaplin
Ambrose, his friend (another intruder)	Mack Swain
Walrus	Chester Conklin
Walrus's girlfriend	Mabel Normand
His old flame	Phyllis Allen
A cop	Edgar Kennedy
A waitress	Alice Davenport
Spectators	Slim Summerville
	Charley Chase

Finished or shipped: October 7, 1914
Released: October 29, 1914

SYNOPSIS

Outside the entrance to a motor-racing track. Mabel wants to see the race, but Chester Conklin (Walrus), her boyfriend, has no money for the admission. She strikes up an acquaintance with Mack Swain (Ambrose), hoping he'll take her in. In a jealous rage, Chester kicks

---

*This title suggests that in Spain the film was confused with *Mabel's Busy Day.*

Mack. The two men confront each other. Mabel attempts to play the peacemaker, but Chester tweaks his rival's nose and Mack kicks back. An innocent bystander gets caught up in the conflict. In the confusion, Mabel drags Chester through the entrance.

Interior of the racing enclosure. Mabel drags Chester along behind her. He stumbles and hurts his foot.

Starting post. The cars are ready to begin the race.

Interior of racing enclosure. Mabel points to the cars. Chester clasps his hand excitedly. They dash toward the bleachers.

Bleachers. They sit down. Chester removes his cap. Mabel sits on his right. To his left is seated Phyllis Allen, one of his old flames. She notices him and smiles.

Racetrack. The race begins.

Bleachers. Chester turns and notices Phyllis. She smiles at him. Disturbed by this unexpected encounter, he looks back at Mabel. While she is cheering the race, Chester turns his attention to Phyllis. He takes her hand. They start flirting. Mabel suddenly notices what her boyfriend is up to. She tweaks his nose and makes him stand up. Phyllis looks smug, so Mabel stamps on her foot. Grabbing Chester by the arm, she marches him away.

Outside entrace to racing enclosure. Mack is trying to enter without paying. Charlie (in his Tramp's outfit) wants to try his luck at the same game. He whacks Mack across the behind to make him stand aside. Mack turns upon him angrily, but Charlie pokes him in the belly, then politely doffs his hat. After that he tries to sneak through entrace by walking backward. But he is promptly ejected. Mack continues to protest, but Charlie silences him temporarily with a back-kick.

A wooden fence with a missing slat. Charlie tries to conceal himself among some barrels. No luck. Mack appears and whacks him on the head with a stick. A truce follows. They shake hands. They are perplexed about how to get into the enclosure until Charlie leans against the fence and falls halfway through the hole. They briefly contemplate the situation. Charlie starts to squeeze through first, but Mack insists on priority. He grabs Charlie by the jacket and pulls him back. Mack thrusts himself into the hole.

Interior side of fence. Mack is stuck in the hole.

Exterior of fence. Charlie tries pushing Mack's rump. Then he boots it. Mack doesn't budge.

Interior of fence. Bystanders observe Mack's gesticulations with amusement.

Exterior of fence. Charlie tries more shoving.

Interior of fence. Mack lurches forward onto a concession-stand waitress. But he's still trapped. She retrieves his straw hat and puts it on his head.

Exterior of fence. Charlie butts Mack's behind with his head. Then he steps back and tries his heftiest kicks. Still no movement. He picks up a pickaxe handle and tries to lever Mack out. Ineffective. He pokes Mack's buttocks. Then he jams him tight with the handle and resumes his kicking. Still no sign of movement. Exasperated, he pauses and leans on Mack's back.

Interior of fence. A helpful bystander tugs at Mack's arms. Losing his grip, the man falls backward. Mack is still trapped. The waitress chats with him.

Exterior of fence. Charlie starts to crawl between Mack's legs.

Interior of fence. Charlie's head and shoulders appear underneath Mack. He chats with him and doffs his hat.

Exterior of fence. Charlie kicks up his leg, booting Mack's rear. Mack kicks back.

Interior of fence. Charlie strikes Mack's face. He crawls through the hole into the enclosure. He smacks Mack again and mimes kicking him.

Exterior of fence. A cop appears. He notices Mack's rear protruding from the fence. Mack kicks out wildly and catches the cop on the behind. The cop retaliates, whacking him with his nightstick.

Interior of fence. Charlie seizes Mack's head and tugs.

Exterior of fence. The cop grabs Mack's jacket and tugs back.

Interior of fence. Charlie pats Mack's head. The waitress hands Charlie a soda siphon. She wants him to add soda to her drink, but he spurts it into his face.

Exterior of fence. The cop grabs Mack's body and tugs. Mack pulls away from him.

Interior of fence. Mack butts Charlie, spilling the drink. Charlie squirts soda in Mack's face.

Exterior of fence. The soda jet hits the cop in the face.

Interior of fence. Mack manages to struggle through the hole.

Exterior of fence. The cop staggers back as the jet still plays on him.

Interior of fence. Charlie squirts the cop while he's chatting with Mack.

Exterior of fence. The cop is driven offscreen by the soda jet.

Interior of fence. Charlie peeps through the hole. He sees that the cop has gone. He cheers. Then he stamps on Mack's foot and kicks him.

A mesh fence. Spectators are crowded behind it. Mabel and Chester are in front of the fence, cheering on the race. Charlie enters—also in front of the fence. A cigarette is dangling from his lips. He eyes Mabel with obvious interest. She drops her handkerchief. As Chester bends down to pick it up, Charlie strikes a match on his

rear end. He lights a cigarette and flings the match in Chester's eye.
Mabel is amused. They smile at each other. Chester is *not* amused. He
confronts Charlie, but Charlie shoves him back against the fence.
Another confrontation. This time Charlie leans forward and bites
Chester's nose. Mabel drags her boyfriend away. Charlie looks nonchalant. He picks at his teeth and spits. Looking into the camera, he
puffs at his cigarette. He twirls his cane in the faces of the spectators.
They protest. He raises his cane, threateningly. Then he punches one
spectator's face, doffs his hat, and thumbs his nose. He crooks his cane
around another spectator's neck, pulls him forward, and punches and
kicks the man in the head. Looking smugly at the camera, he turns
and blows smoke into the spectators' faces. Then he swings his cane
and accidentally knocks his hat off. The spectators laugh. Charlie responds with a slow burn. Then he puffs more smoke at them. Facing
the camera, he chuckles and clasps his hands.

The bleachers. Chester is nursing his nose. He sits down beside
Mabel and doffs his hat to Phyllis, who is seated on his left. They
shake hands and start chatting. Mabel notices this renewed flirtation.
Furious, she interrupts him, but he brushes her aside and turns back
to her rival.

Mesh fence. Mack appears. Charlie bends down to pick up his cigarette. Mack pokes him on the rump. Charlie gets up and presses his
lighted cigarette on Mack's nose. Then he kicks him in the belly,
punches his face, and whacks him across the head with his cane. He
strides away.

Bleachers. Mabel shoves Chester's head against Phyllis's.

Bleachers nearby. Charlie appears. He tosses his cane up and down
and catches it. He flexes his muscles and sits down. Beside him a
young lady, dressed in dark clothes, is sipping soda pop through a
straw. He swings his legs up and puts them across her lap. She pushes
him off and looks away from him. He sips at her soda. She turns,
suspiciously, but Charlie gazes skyward in seeming innocence. She
looks away once more, and he takes another sip. This time she catches
him with his mouth full. Unconcerned, he spurts out the drink and
wipes his mouth. She hands him the bottle and turns away. He offers
it to a woman in the row behind, but she ignores him. Facing the
camera, he points his nose in the air, miming her snobbery. He takes
another sip at the straw, then blows out a stream of soda. The young
lady edges away.

Bleachers. Chester spurns Mabel. He resumes his flirtation with
Phyllis. Enraged, Mabel seizes him by the ear. Then she stamps away.

Bleachers nearby. Mabel falls over Charlie's outstretched legs onto
a woman's lap. Looking unhappy, she sits down beside Charlie—right
on his hat. Contritely, she brushes it for him. He's upset; the crown of

the hat is broken. They stare at one another. He spits on the hat, wipes it with his sleeve, and puts it on.

Shot of the winning car.

Bleachers nearby. Mabel and Charlie point at the cars. She stands up. He makes her sit down. He loses his hat, then retrieves it. They both stand up. He pulls out his watch, tries to swing it into his pocket, but flubs the trick. Mabel is intrigued by him anyway. She takes his arm. They exit, smiling. Mack appears, dabbing his burned nose with a handkerchief. He catches sight of Charlie and heads toward him, but he trips over one woman's feet and knocks down another. He courteously raises his hat, but a spectator in the row behind boots him in the rear. He exits.

In front of wooden fence. Mack comes into view rubbing his buttocks.

Bleachers. Charlie and Mabel reappear. He's flirting with her. They sit down. He mimes his kicking of Mack. They laugh.

In front of wooden fence. The cop catches up with Mack.

Bleachers. Chester comes upon Charlie sitting there with his arm around Mabel. He tugs at her shoulder. She brushes him aside. He seizes her arm, pulls her upright, and tries to drag her away. She appeals for help from Charlie. Charlie's response is a study in casualness. He gets up with his back to Mabel, hands his cane to a bystander, and slowly removes his jacket. Meanwhile, Chester is shaking Mabel violently. Charlie flexes his muscles. Mabel shouts for help, but Charlie is doing calisthenics. At last, he is ready to help the lady in distress. With one hand he pushes Chester in the face; with the other he forces Mabel to sit down. Then he gives Chester a terrific swipe on the jaw, knocking him back among the spectators. Leaning forward, he drags Chester upright by his necktie and boots him in the direction of the wooden fence.

Wooden fence. Chester crashes into Mack, the cop, and a crowd of bystanders.

Bleachers. Charlie yawns and flexes his muscles.

Wooden fence. The cop has seized Mack in one hand and Chester in the other.

Bleachers. Charlie does a little knee-bend. Mabel gazes at him admiringly. He sits down. A spectator hands him his hat.

Wooden fence. Mack and Chester are arguing with the cop.

Bleachers. Mabel and Charlie are laughing at Mack and Chester.

Wooden fence. The cop drags Mack and Chester away.

Bleachers. The cop drags his protesting prisoners past Mabel and Charlie. Charlie whacks Chester with his cane. The spectators laugh at the sight of Chester howling with pain.

Close-up of Mabel and Charlie laughing. He turns to her. She offers him her cheek to kiss. He pretends to be shy—then tries to kiss her on the lips, but she pulls away. He takes her hand and kisses it; then he makes her hand into a clenched fist and kisses that. In response, she tweaks his nose, affectionately.

Bleachers. The cop hauls off Mack and Chester.

Close-up of smiling Mabel and Charlie.

COMMENTS

1. Another potboiler, cooked up in a single day. Despite the subject, it was probably made not on location but in the studio, using stock shots of the racetrack. At no point can any of the cast be seen in the same shot as the racetrack or the cars.

Uno Asplund dismisses the film as a "primitive burlesque farce, which is hardly worthy either of Chaplin or his art" (1976, 56). *Gentlemen of Nerve* is, admittedly, one of Chaplin's most violent Keystones (spewing, stomping, biting, and burning as well as the usual kicks and punches) and one of his least original: it continues Charlie's rivalries with Mack and Chester; the setting recalls *Mabel at the Wheel* and *Mabel's Busy Day*, Charlie's willful obstruction of the spectators is reminiscent of *Kid's Auto Race*, and most of the gags seem familiar from previous Keystones (e.g., the flubbed watch-trick is repeated from *Those Love Pangs*). However, the film does have one very funny slapstick sequence (Mack in the fence hole) using fluent cross-cutting, and several new gags that are memorable: i.e., Charlie trying to get into the racetrack by walking backward, his theft of soda pop, and his casual "preparation" to help Mabel in distress.

2. Structure. The film falls into two main segments. In the first part we see contrasting efforts to get into the racetrack without paying. The second part interweaves five groups of rivalries: (i) Charlie vs. Mack, (ii) Charlie vs. the spectators, (iii) Mabel vs. Phyllis for Chester, (iv) Charlie vs. Chester for Mabel, (v) the cop vs. Mack and Chester.

3. Chaplin's fondness for punning movie titles surfaces with this film. (Compare with such later title puns as *His Musical Career, Behind the Screen*, and *The Idle Class*.) Since the film's setting is a racetrack, the movie title would seem initially, to refer to the racecar drivers. But the movie title is actually a play on the word "nerve," a pun that underscores the film's main theme. *Gentlemen of Nerve* ignores the nerve of the drivers and focuses on the sort of nerve that signifies impudence, arrogance, or chutzpah.

The film is about three "gentlemen" with different kinds of "nerve." From Mabel's standpoint Chester has "the nerve" to flirt with another woman while he is dating her. From Chester's standpoint Charlie has "the nerve" to steal his girl. From Mack's standpoint Charlie has "the nerve" to try and push him around. From Charlie's standpoint Mack has "the nerve" to go in front of him (at the entrance and through the fence). Charlie triumphs because his "nerve" is stronger than his rivals. He gets the better of both of them and even has "the nerve" to taunt the spectators. On the other hand, Chester vacillates weakly between his two women, while Mack lacks Charlie's cunning and resourcefulness.

By contrast, the women are not "ladies of nerve." The generally formidable Phyllis Allen is more or less passive. And the usually spunky Mabel merely *reacts* to Chester's "nerve" in a fairly restrained manner: she tweaks his ear and stamps on Phyllis's foot. But Charlie proves shrewd enough not to take her restraint for granted. When she becomes his new girlfriend, he doesn't have "the nerve" to insist on a kiss immediately. After all, there's no telling what *she* might have "the nerve" to do to him if he gets too ardent. So, at the end of the film, just to be on the safe side, he folds her fingers down and makes the pacificatory gesture of kissing her fist.

Perhaps the most interesting aspect of the downplaying of the women's roles is that Mabel Normand was now very evidently playing in *Chaplin's* film and not vice versa. See my comment 1 to *Caught in a Cabaret* (Keystone no. 12).

OTHER VIEWS

"After Charlie gets several innocent people arrested, he winds up as a thief—stealing sips of refreshment through a straw from a bystander's pop bottle. It was one of his funniest pantomimes" (Sennett and Shipp 1954, 181).

"Somatic or body gags were as much a part of Chaplin's armour as they were of [the *comedia dell'arte*]. . . . Chester Conklin has his nose bitten in *Gentlemen of Nerve*. . . . The kicks Chaplin delivers to stomachs, shins and faces are legion, and would have been utterly familiar to any Commedia player. Even swinging a leg across a girl's lap . . . [was] part of Harlequin's repertoire long before Chaplin brought them to the screen" (Sobel and Francis 1977, 200–201).

31.

His Musical Career

(1914)

Original working title: *The Piano Movers*
Other titles: *The Piano Movers, Musical Tramps, Charlie as a Piano
Mover;* French: *Charlot déménaqeur, Charlot livreur de pianos, Les
déménageurs de pianos;* German: *Seine Karriere als Musiker;* Spanish:
Los cargadores de pianos, Charlot domina el piano; Italian: *La carriera
musicale di Charlot, Charlot facchino*

Length: 1 reel; 984 feet (Asplund), 1025 feet (Lyons)
Playing time: 17 minutes at 16 frames per second
Producer: Keystone
Director: Chaplin
Story and screenplay: Chaplin
Photography: Frank D. Williams (?)
Cast:

Assistant piano mover	Chaplin
Piano mover	Mack Swain
Mr. Rich, a wealthy client	Fritz Schade
Manager of a piano store	Charley Chase
Mrs. Rich	Alice Howell
Mr. Poor, an impoverished artist	Joe Bordeaux
Mrs. Poor	Norma Nichols

Finished or shipped: October 17, 1914. (Shipped later than *His Trysting Places* but released earlier.)
Released: November 7, 1914

SYNOPSIS

[The print described is Blackhawk's rerelease version derived from
an Australian negative which evidently lacks some footage at the end
of the final sequence. However, this is the most complete version I
have seen in the U.S.A.

His Musical Career is one of the few Keystones for which there is a published description elsewhere. David Robinson (1985, 697–98) supplies a summary. However, his description begins with the title *Mr. Rich buys a piano* and omits the original opening which appears in the Blackhawk version and is described below. See further my comment 1 on the film.]

The workshop of a piano store. The Piano mover (Mack Swain, in shirt-sleeves) gestures to his assistant Charlie (wearing his usual costume) that he needs building up. The latter demonstrates that he doesn't by lifting Mack's heavy pail of beer with one hand. This impresses Mack until Charlie decides to take a big sip. Mack reacts by slapping his assistant on the back, making him spew out what he has drunk. The manager calls Mack over for some instructions. Charlie seizes his opportunity to conceal the beer pail behind him, leaving another, seemingly identical pail in its place.

Title: *Varnish!*

Mack and Charlie joke together, but the former doesn't think it so funny when he picks up his pail and swallows a mouthful of varnish. This time, Mack does the spewing while Charlie does the laughing. Frantic, Mack stuffs a bandage in his mouth. Charlie tries to help by throwing some beer in his face. Then he pulls out the bandage, puts a towel around Mack's face, and starts cleaning him up.

Title: *Mr. Rich buys a piano.*

Piano showroom. Mr. Rich, an elderly gentleman wearing a top hat and frock coat, orders a new upright piano from the manager and gives him a card indicating the address for delivery. Mr. Rich leaves. The manager rubs his hands with satisfaction.

Workshop. Charlie removes his jacket, revealing that he is wearing a sleeveless shirt. He offers Mack one of the pails and laughs behind the latter's back when he rejects it. Charlie now hangs up his coat—on the floor. Then he shows off his biceps to the incredulous Mack. Standing in a weight lifter's exhibition pose, he proceeds to oil first his biceps and then his ear. After that he swaggers around and gives Mack a gentle slap. Mack is annoyed and starts to look threatening, so Charlie decides not to try his luck any further.

Showroom. Mr. Poor, an impoverished musician (typed by his long white hair and a scroll of music under his arm), enters and looks sadly at the pianos. He clasps his hands together in a futile appeal to heaven. The manager enters and the artist indicates that he's penniless. The manager shows him his account.

Title: *"If you can't keep up your payments, I'll take back your piano."*

Mr. Poor begs for more time, but the manager is hardhearted. Mr. Poor exits.

Workshop. Mack puts on his hat and work jacket and exits. Charlie spreads a towel over the keyboard of a piano, then stretches out on it for a nap. Unfortunately, it's too narrow a bed for him. He rolls off and hits the floor.

Title: *"Deliver this piano to 666 Prospect Street and bring one back from 999 Prospect Street."*

Showroom. The manager gives directions/invoice (?) to Mack.

Workshop. Charlie is smoking a corn cob pipe. He has a block and tackle over one shoulder. Absentmindedly he picks up one of the pails and is about to take a drink when he notices it's the varnish. He puts down the pail and sniggers. He exits.

Title: *No time to lose.*

Showroom. Mack and Charlie begin moving out the new piano ordered by Mr. Rich. Charlie slips and falls back onto another piano. Then, as Mack pulls Mr. Rich's piano out of the showroom, Charlie clings to it and gets a free ride.

Exterior of piano store. Mack hauls the piano while Charlie pretends to push it. No movement. Charlie starts fixing on the tackle with minimal effort and then indicates that he's "exhausted." He slips over once more. Mack is annoyed. Charlie gets tangled in the tackle. Mack extricates him and gives him instructions about handling the piano. This time Mack starts fixing on the tackle. Charlie assists by lifting up one end of the piano so that Mack can crawl under it. But as soon as he is well and truly underneath, Charlie lets the piano fall on him and leans on it. While Mack is squirming on the sidewalk, Charlie takes a well-earned rest. At last, he notices that Mack is calling him, so he bends down to see what's wrong. Mack's flailing arms catch him in the eye—at which Charlie gets up and boots his fallen partner. Before lifting up the piano to release him, he takes his time, removing his cuffs, etc.

Eventually, Mack staggers to his feet and roughs up Charlie. He boots him against the piano which rolls along the sidewalk. He retrieves it while Charlie tosses the block and tackle into a little donkey cart. The two men lift the piano upright onto the cart. Charlie takes the reins, and the donkey starts on his way with the piano balanced precariously behind them.

Mr. Poor's living room. A sign over the door reads: "God bless our home." Mr. Poor's wife tries to console him. *His* piano is visible in the background.

Close-up of the two removal men in the donkey cart. Mack is dozing while clutching another pail of beer. Charlie is thirsty and uses his pipe to ladle some out. Mack wakes up and discovers that most of his beer is gone. He looks suspiciously at Charlie who is somewhat tipsy.

The donkey stops. The piano suddenly slides backward shifting the balance of the cart. As a result, the donkey's legs are lifted completely off the ground. It struggles to regain its footing. This occurs several times until Charlie gets the animal to move on by booting its rump.

Title: *Taking Mr. Rich's piano to 999 Prospect, instead of 666.*

Exterior of apartment house. The cart comes to a halt. The two men remove the piano and wheel it over to a tall flight of steps. Charlie falls again. This time Mack seizes Charlie's cane and whacks him with it.

They proceed with the job of getting it up the steps. Mack goes first. Halfway up, Charlie drops his cane and bends down to pick it up, holding up the piano with one hand.

Mr. Poor's living room. The wife points out of the window at the removal men.

Staircase. Charlie can't hold up the piano. It slides back down to the sidewalk. Charlie, ahead of it, rolls head over heels. Mack, cursing, descends and orders him to get to work again. There is more pushing and shoving until they get the piano to the first level. Charlie now rushes back down to reclaim his hat and cane.

Mr. Poor's living room. Mack enters carrying his beer pail. Charlie follows, carrying the piano on his back. Enviously, he watches Mack finishing off the beer. There is no agreement about where the piano is to be placed. While Mr. Poor and his wife argue about it, Charlie staggers around the room with the piano on his back. At one point he is almost doing the "splits," but Mr. Poor and Mack push his legs together. At last, he is allowed to lower the piano to the floor, and he emerges from under it, walking in a crouch, like a bow-legged, humpbacked dwarf. He is unable to straighten up so Mack comes to the rescue. He grabs him by the neck and the seat of the pants and lowers him to the floor like an inverted "V". Then he presses his boot down on Charlie's rump. Charlie is flattened but also straightened out. Mack lifts him upright, puts his hat on his head, and hands him his pipe and cane. All's well again. Mack picks up his beer pail and the two men exit.

They descend the steps again. Charlie slips once more. They return to the donkey cart, which starts off before Charlie has fully climbed in. He falls into his seat.

Title: *Coming to get the Old Man's supposed piano at Mr. Rich's!*

The donkey cart pulls up outside Mr. Rich's house. The two men get out. Mack is still holding his beer pail. Charlie tries to pull the donkey closer to the curb, but the animal refuses to oblige. Charlie threatens it, but Mack rebukes him, so he changes his threat into a polite doffing of his hat.

Entrance to mansion. Mack checks the house number: it's 666.

Mack enters followed by Charlie, who falls up the steps.

Title: *They walked right in.*

Mr. Rich's living room. Charlie hands his hat and cane to Mack, flexes his muscles, and sets to work removing small ornaments from a piano located to the right side of the room. He tosses them to Mack, playing a game of mock baseball. Next the two men clear away a couch from the center of the room and begin wheeling out the piano. At this moment Mrs. Rich appears and demands to know what they are doing. Charlie's reply is to try flirting with her. At the sight of this, Mack wanders over, boots Charlie aside, and tries his own "appeal" on the lady. She isn't interested in either of them, so they return to shifting the piano. Mrs. Rich now calls in a liveried footman who tries to stop the piano movers, but Mack flings him aside, and the piano is shunted out of the house.

Exterior of Rich mansion. The piano is moved down the steps too quickly—Mack falls backward. He gets up and moves it again, leaving Charlie behind in an apparent state of collapse. But he staggers to his feet and follows Mack and the piano out to the sidewalk. Recovering somewhat, he leans on the piano. Mack promptly pulls it away, and Charlie collapses yet again. Mr. Rich comes into view. He contemplates Charlie spread over the sidewalk and eyes his "former" piano dubiously.

[This is where Blackhawk's rerelease print ends. But descriptions of European prints indicate that they have additional footage. Uno Asplund (Sweden) describes a print with this finale: "In the street they encounter the indignant Mr. Rich; the piano runs away down the hill, cannot be stopped, and finally, together with Charlie and Mack, ends up in a lake. Charlie manages to play a few final chords before it sinks" (Asplund 1976, 57). Denis Gifford (Britain) provides a similar account: "There is a hill for the piano and Charlie to run down, and a river for them to land in. Charlie adds his individual touch to this familiar finale: he plays a final requiem before the piano carries him under" (Gifford 1974, 52). Unfortunately, David Robinson's description of the same scene is unclear: "Sidewalk. Mr. Rich arrives. General Keystone mêlée" (Robinson, 1985, 698).]

COMMENTS

1. I have not come across a complete print of this film in the U.S.A., and it is possible that there are no complete prints in Europe. All the American copies I have seen omit the finale that (evidently) appears in European prints. David Robinson, in Britain, claims that his shot-by-shot summary was "recreated from the best available" copy of the film and is "believed to represent the complete and original form Chaplin

intended"—yet his summary makes no mention of the scene that opens the film in widely available American prints. A version that really is complete could, obviously, be created by conflating prints from both sides of the Atlantic.

2. Uno Asplund describes *His Musical Career* "in its last stages" as "an exact precursor" of Laurel and Hardy's Oscar-winning short, *The Music Box* (1932). "Both [films] contain precisely the same gags" (Asplund 1976, 57). The film is indeed a precursor of the Laurel and Hardy film—and also of Roman Polanski's 1958 short, *Two Men and a Wardrobe*—but it is certainly not an "exact" one. The basic situation is similar: two men with a horse and cart clumsily transport a piano. A few of the gags are identical: Stan and Ollie have to carry the piano box up a huge staircase; big fat Hardy gets trapped under the piano box; skinny little Laurel has to hold up the heavy end of their burden; but he sneaks a ride on it when Hardy is doing the pushing; they use a block and tackle; Laurel's limbs have to be straightened out after his exertions; they wreck someone else's house. But there are as many contrasts as similarities. The staircase sequence is a major episode of *The Music Box* but a fairly brief one in *His Musical Career*. Chaplin's plot is more elaborate and his characters and themes are quite different. (See further comment 6 below.)

3. *His Musical Career* relates, more appropriately, to several films in which Chaplin depicts an evolving imagery of work-slavery. As we noticed in an earlier commentary, *The Property Man* (Keystone no. 21), the first film in this group, shows a "hierarchy" of oppression in which the stronger imposes his will on the weaker: strong man, Garlico (Fritz Schade), turns Charlie into his beast of burden, and Charlie in turn savages his aged assistant when the old man lies squirming under Garlico's trunk. In *His Musical Career* Charlie switches roles and becomes the overburdened assistant, but the worst hauling is done by the poor donkey, who has to drag Mack and Charlie as well as the piano. In *Work* (Essanay 1915) Charlie literally becomes the workhorse. A vivid image links this film with *His Musical Career*: dragging a decorator's cart, Charlie finds himself dangling in the air just like the donkey in the earlier film. *Behind the Screen* (Mutual 1916) underscores the way in which rewards are apportioned for work-slavery. Charlie is Eric Campbell's assistant as sceneshifter in a movie studio. Big Eric does nothing and gets all the credit while Charlie—who does all the work—is accused of laziness. Chaplin's identification with the figure of the work-slave continues into his features. Significantly, his only appearance in *A Woman of Paris* (1923) is reserved for a walk-on as a railroad porter laboring under the weight of a huge trunk. In *City Lights* we see penni-

less Charlie (turned worker to earn money for the blind girl) reduced to shit-shoveler while his unpredictable friend, the millionaire, throws away his unearned income on wild binges and frivolous European vacations. Ultimately, of course, *Modern Times* and *Monsieur Verdoux* extend Chaplin's work-slave imagery to the entire modern industrial and economic system.

4. Structure. A series of inversions and contrasts. (i) Mack makes Charlie spew up beer; Charlie tricks Mack into drinking varnish. (ii) Mr. Rich orders a new piano; Mr. Poor is ordered to pay up or lose his piano. (iii) taking the new piano to Mr. Poor's home; removing an old piano from Mr. Rich's house. (iv) Mr. Rich is unable to stop Mack and Charlie; Mack and Charlie are unable to stop the piano.

5. David Robinson comments on this film: "At first sight it seems a regression in terms of narrative: in fact he [Chaplin] is boldly experimenting with quite a different style, much closer to that of his maturity. Having recognized that cutting is a convenience, not an obligation, he dispenses with the rapid editing which Keystone inherited from Griffith, and conceives the film in a series of much more extended shots which provide a stage for uninterrupted comedy routines" (1985, 697). But *His Musical Career* is not as abruptly innovative as Robinson maintains. Comparable use of extended shots in earlier Chaplin Keystones may be found in *The Face on the Bar Room Floor*, and to a lesser extent in *Mabel's Married Life*, *The Masquerader*, and *The New Janitor*. Chaplin's movement toward a more mature style was an evolutionary process, not a quantum leap.

6. Raymond Durgnat refers to *The Music Box* as "a perfect little epic of monotonous futility. . . . It's the myth of Sisyphus in comic terms, a little hymn to the uselessness of work . . ." (1970, 94). "Monotonous futility," "the uselessness of work"—in no way do these terms describe Chaplin's film. In the tradition of many nineteenth-century theatrical farces *His Musical Career* shows us error and confusion transforming an undesirable situation into a desirable one. The acquisitive Mr. Rich wants a second piano, while the worthy Mr. Poor, a musician, is threatened with losing the only one he has. This injustice is, coincidentally, rectified when Charlie and Mack confuse 666 and 999. Patently, their pains and problems in moving pianos are similar to those of Stan and Ollie, but in the final outcome there is nothing futile about their work. Their benign error suggests the mysterious workings of Providence, while (as Durgnat observes) Laurel and Hardy's labors point to the inexplicable absurdity of the human condition.

7. Note some new comic business that will be reused or developed in later films. Charlie oils his muscles to impress Mack; in *Pay Day* he oils his boots to stop their squeaking. The weight of the piano crushes him into a dwarf; in *Limelight* he incorporates a dwarf gag into the comic finale.

OTHER VIEWS

"Chaplin's manipulation of his body's size and weight is extended to his handling of objects. In *His Musical Career* . . . Chaplin's simulation of weight in the prop piano is effective, as is his ability to unbend after carrying the piano" (Kamin 1984, 17).

"He could elaborate on gags he had used before. In *Work* he staggers up the stairs of a house loaded with all the decorating equipment he has been dragging along for miles. In *His Musical Career* he is forced to carry an upright piano on his back. Both gags are incorporated in *Behind the Screen*, but with far greater artistry" (Sobel and Francis 1977, 198).

32.

His Trysting Places

(1914)

Original working title: *Ingratitude*
Other titles: *His Trysting Place*, The Henpecked Spouse, Very Much
Married, The Ladies' Man, Family Home, Family House;* French:
Charlot papa, Charlot en famille; German: *Sein Rendezvous;* Spanish:
Charlot papá; Italian: *Il luogo del convegno, Charlot gaga*

Length: 2 reels; 1912 feet (Asplund), 2000 feet (Lyons)
Playing time: 32 minutes at 16 frames per second
Director: Chaplin
Story and screenplay: Chaplin
Photography: Frank D. Williams (?)
Cast:

An inept paterfamilias	Chaplin
Mabel, his wife	Mabel Normand
Ambrose	Mack Swain
Mrs. Ambrose	Phyllis Allen
Clarice, writer of a love letter	Not named

Finished or shipped: October 1, 1914. (This preceded the shipping date
   of *Gentlemen of Nerve.*)
Released: November 9, 1914

SYNOPSIS

[The print described is the original Keystone version. A version
with humorous titles by Chaplin's half-brother Sydney is in wide circulation. It was released by W.A. Films in the 1920s.]

---

*Keystone's title card indicates that the last word in the title is plural— although many
writers on Chaplin (e.g., Theodore Huff, David Robinson, Denis Gifford, Kalton C. Lahue, John McCabe) render it as singular.

Title: *Family ties*

The kitchen of Charlie's home. His wife, Mabel, looking woebegone, is brandishing a horseshoe. She tosses it into the living room.

Living room. It hits Charlie in the eye. He picks it up.

Kitchen. Mabel points to her worn-out shoes.

Living room. He carries the horseshoe into the kitchen.

Kitchen. Mabel is seated, forlornly, at the table. Charlie closes the door behind him. He confronts her with the horseshoe and indicates that it had struck him in the face. He raises it above his head in a threatening gesture, but drops it on his foot. Tearfully, Mabel shows him her worn-out shoes. She puts her arms around Charlie and kisses him; then she points to their threadbare kitchen. But Charlie shouts at her and pushes her away. He is walking out in a huff when he catches his fingers in the door. Mabel renews her pleas—to no avail. He continues his exit, but she slams the door on his leg.

Living room. Charlie struggles in the door. In the background his little son, Peter, can be seen playing on the floor.

Kitchen. Mabel releases her pressure on the door.

Living room. Extracting his leg, Charlie brushes himself down and walks across the room without giving Peter a glance. The child stares after him.

Hallway. Charlie rubs his leg. Then he puts on his jacket and derby and brushes himself down. He uses the clothes brush to polish his shoes.

Living room. Mabel picks up Peter. She cuddles him and plays with him.

Hallway. Charlie polishes his fingernails with the clothes brush. He calls to Peter.

Living room. Mabel points at Charlie and tells Peter: "There's your father" (her words can be easily lip-read). She carries the child into the hallway.

Hallway. She shows Charlie his son. She kisses Charlie. He grabs her by the chin, scrutinizes her teeth, then kisses her. He flexes his muscles. Mabel smiles at him.

Title: *"I'll bring little Peter a present."*

Close-up of the trio. Peter is crying. Charlie tries to cheer him up by making funny faces.

He kisses the child. Then he orders Mabel to get his coat. She throws it at his head and drops his cane at his feet. He picks up his things and kisses her.

A shot from reverse position showing Charlie wiping his mustache after the kiss. Mabel hands him Peter to kiss. He holds the child by his legs and kisses his cheek. He exits.

Exterior of house. He trips over the front door mat. Then he picks up that mat and blows his nose into it. He looks in opposite directions, hesitating over which way to go. Then he marches off.

Hallway. Mabel is smiling and holding Peter. She closes the door behind her husband. She chats with Peter then carries him into the living room.

Living room. She shows him how to wave goodbye to Daddy and kisses him again.

Title: *A dark omen.*

Exterior of a drugstore. Charlie comes into view, carrying his overcoat over one arm. Outside the store is a local lounger—a black youth—who looks at him with interest. Charlie enters the store.

Close-up of Mabel cuddling Peter. She takes off the child's shoes and socks and kisses his feet.

Exterior of drugstore. Charlie exits from the store, carrying a small package. He opens it. Inquisitively, the black youth peers over his shoulder. Observing that the package contains a baby's feeding bottle, he points at Charlie, jeers at him, and walks away. Charlie stares after him, trying to look dignified. Then he stuffs the bottle into his overcoat pocket and exits.

Hotel foyer. In the foreground, Clarice, a hotel employee is seated at a desk, working. In the background the manager directs a female guest upstairs. When they exit, Clarice sneaks a look at a letter she has written.

Handwritten text of letter: *My darling: Meet me in the park this afternoon at our little trysting place. Don't fail me as I could not live without seeing you soon again. Clarice.*

Happily, she kisses the letter and stuffs it into an envelope.

Title: *Ambrose starts on one of his periodical strolls.*

A bedroom in the hotel. Phyllis Allen (Mrs. Ambrose) is fussing over Mack (Mr. Ambrose). She brushes his hair, kisses him, and puts a straw boater on his head. He picks up his walking stick and overcoat and exits, looking very pleased with himself.

Corridor. He trips over the carpet.

Hotel foyer. Clarice stops Mack and makes a request.

Title: *"Won't you post this letter for me?"*

He takes it and shoves it into his overcoat pocket. Raising his hat, he leaves, still smiling.

Exterior of hotel. Mack appears. He hesitates about which way to go, checks that he still has the letter, then exits.

Street. Mack stops outside a café advertising twenty-five cent dinners. He looks into the camera, rubs his stomach, points at the café, and enters.

Interior of café. Mack hangs up his coat and hat and sits on the only vacant seat at the lunch counter. In the foreground, beside him, is an old man with a beard. He watches with disgust as a filthy laborer walks past, wipes his dirty hands on a napkin, and tosses the napkin on the counter.

Exterior of café. A twenty-five-cent dinner also appeals to Charlie. He stumbles over his trailing overcoat and enters.

Interior of café. Charlie hangs up his coat and hat. There are no vacant seats at the lunch counter. Waiting for a place, he helps himself to a bite of the old man's donut, wipes his sticky fingers on the beard, and pretends to pick a flea from it. Insulted, the old man gets up, protests to the counterman, and stamps out of the café. Charlie moves into his seat, gesturing to the counterman that the old man must be crazy.

Exterior of café. The Old Man hesitates, then walks away in a bad temper.

Title: *Music.*

Interior of café. Two-shot of Charlie and Mack at the lunch counter. Charlie watches with disgust as Mack noisily drinks his soup. Putting his fingers in his ears, he mimes violin playing and points to Mack's bowl. Now Charlie receives a plate of soup. He picks up a pepper shaker and shakes it in the wrong direction—all over Mack. Mack reacts by sneezing over Charlie's soup, then burping. The counterman hands Charlie a plate containing a large steak. Charlie picks it up and chews it under his jacket to protect it from Mack's "spray." Mack reaches for the mustard and inadvertently drops some of it into Charlie's soup. Then he scratches his head with his soup spoon. Having finished with the steak bone, Charlie tosses it aside—onto Mack's plate. Mack is outraged; he strikes Charlie. Charlie retaliates by flicking soup into Mack's eye. They slap each other's faces several times. At last, tiring of this, Charlie throws the rest of his soup into Mack's face. [End of two-shot.]

Charlie is knocked to the floor, but he picks himself up and takes a flying kick at Mack, who sprawls backward, downing the other diners. Mack staggers to his feet and swings at Charlie, but he hits the counterman instead. Charlie, a better shot, boots his assailant and sends him sprawling once more. He also hurls a pie, but it hits another diner. By this time Mack has had enough. He grabs what he believes to be his overcoat and dashes out of the chaos.

Title: *He takes the wrong coat.*

Exterior of café. Mack's hasty exit astounds two passersby: an elegantly dressed gentleman and a lady. They watch as he dashes out of sight.

Interior of café. Charlie picks up another pie.

Exterior of café. The gentleman peers in at the entrance.

Interior of café. Charlie hurls the pie.

Exterior of café. The gentleman staggers back—the pie has hit him full in the face. The lady is convulsed with laughter.

Interior of café. Charlie picks up his stick, puts on his derby, and—unwittingly—takes Mack's overcoat. He exits.

Exterior of café. He slips on a fragment of the pie and knocks the gentleman down. The latter protests, but Charlie is in no mood to apologize. He shoves his fist in the gentleman's face, kicks him in the stomach, and raps him sharply over the head. Then he stalks away. The lady watches this scene with undisguised amusement.

Title: *Ambrose's wife feels restless.*

A bedroom in the hotel. Phyllis is wearing her hat. She sniffs, dabs her nose with a handkerchief, and exits, armed with an umbrella.

Corridor. She closes the bedroom door behind her. Puffing herself up, she turns her back to the camera and marches off down the corridor.

Pathway in the park. An agitated Mack wipes away his perspiration. A cop is visible in the background.

Park bench. Phyllis sits down.

Pathway. Mack spies his wife and heads toward her.

Park bench. Mack looks around nervously. Sitting down, he tells Phyllis (in mime) about his awful experience in the café. She embraces him consolingly.

Living room of Charlie's house. Mabel is sponging and pressing a skirt. Peter appears to need her attention. She picks him up. When she turns back to her ironing she finds the skirt has been scorched.

Exterior of Charlie's house. Charlie arrives. He looks back at the café and flexes his muscles. He ascends the front steps, stumbles, and enters.

Hallway. He hangs up his cane and Mack's overcoat.

Living room. Mabel hears him. With the iron in her hand, she rushes out to meet him.

Hallway. She greets him joyfully, but burns his hand as she embraces him. She places the iron on a seat and starts brushing his hat. Charlie sits down on the iron. Mabel tries to console him. He exits into the living room.

Living room. He picks Peter up by the scruff of the neck, kisses him, loses interest, and drops the child back in his cradle. He frowns at the scorched skirt on the ironing board. Inadvertently, he puts his hand in the jug of sponging water.

Hallway. Mabel is still brushing Charlie's hat. She stops and smiles as she remembers something.

Title: *"I wonder what he brought baby."*

She searches in the overcoat and discovers Clarice's love letter.

Text of letter is repeated.

Mabel's instant reaction is fury. She crumples up the letter and marches into the living room.

Living room. She confronts Charlie, momentarily disarming him with a sweet smile. He smiles back. Then she turns on him ferociously, dashing the sponge into his face. He staggers backward into the hallway.

Hallway. He looks aghast.

Living room. She flings a bowl at him.

Hallway. He falls. Then he gets up and clasps his hands in prayer.

Living room. She hurls the scorched skirt at him.

Hallway. It hits him in the face. He tosses it aside. Then he grabs his hat and coat and tries to exit.

Living room. She picks up the ironing board and rushes over to the hallway.

Hallway. She smashes the ironing board over his head. He shoves his hand into her face and exits.

Exterior of house. He stumbles down the steps, clutching his head.

Hallway. She jumps up and down, shaking her fist after him. Then she puts on her hat and coat.

Exterior of house. He rubs his head, looks back at the house, and exits.

Hallway. She wraps Peter in a shawl, then exits, carrying him.

Exterior of house. She looks to her right and left, shakes her fist, and exits.

Park bench. Phyllis is still embracing her "injured" spouse.

Title: "Wait. I'll be back soon."

She kisses the top of Mack's head and pats his cheeks. He strolls away (to slake his thirst at a nearby concession stand).

Park. A cop observes the agitated Charlie fleeing from Mabel. He gestures that he must be crazy. Charlie politely raises his hat and heads toward the park bench.

Park bench. Not noticing Phyllis, he flops down on her lap. She pushes him off. She's annoyed but calms down as he sits beside her and describes his domestic crisis.

Title: "My wife's gone foolish."

Concession stand. Mack buys himself a drink.

Park bench. Phyllis tries to console Charlie. He weeps into her handkerchief.

Pathway in the park. Mabel enters, carrying Peter in her arms. She looks upset. The cop offers assistance.

Park bench. Feeling tired, Charlie needs something to rest his elbows on. He pulls Phyllis's legs toward him with the crook of his cane. She shoves him aside.

Pathway. Mabel has spied Charlie. She asks the cop to take care of Peter.

Park bench. Unnoticed by Charlie, Mabel approaches. She thinks she has discovered her husband flirting with another woman. She swipes at him with her jacket but he ducks—Phyllis gets hit instead. Charlie flees.

A tree nearby. Charlie runs into an overhanging branch.

Park bench. Phyllis is appalled at Mabel's accusation. But Mabel follows it up by trying to throttle her.

Beneath tree. Charlie flings out his arms in despair. With his back to the camera he weeps into a handy garbage can.

Park bench. Mabel notices him. She turns away from Phyllis and rushes toward the tree.

Tree. She kicks Charlie into the garbage can. When he climbs out she swings punches at him, but he ducks them. He decides that it's safer to stay hidden in the can.

Pathway. The cop is still holding Peter. He looks bored.

Park bench. Phyllis needs a new handkerchief. Searching inside the overcoat (i.e., Charlie's coat—but she assumes it's Mack's) she finds the feeding bottle.

Title: *"Gracious! My husband has a child."*

She starts screaming.

Beneath tree. The garbage can brings no security to the hapless Charlie. Mabel pulls him out by his hair and punches him.

Concessions stand. Mack laughs at the sight of his enemy's sufferings.

Beneath tree. Charlie stands up in the garbage can and pleads with Mabel. Unmoved, she grabs his hair and punches him more violently than ever. He screams for help.

Concession stand. Mack laughs. He points and heads in Charlie's direction.

Beneath tree. Mack wanders over to Mabel and asks if she needs any assistance. Hearing this, Charlie slowly rises out of the can. A slow burn. Then he boots Mack in the rump. The two men circle each other belligerently. Mabel interrupts their gyrations by kicking Charlie. He falls and shoves Mack into the garbage can. Mabel gives her husband a violent shaking and throws him on top of Mack.

Park bench. The cop appears, holding Peter. He passes Phyllis.

Beneath tree. Mack is trapped in the garbage can. Charlie tries to punch him, but Mabel holds Charlie back by his jacket. The cop appears. He returns Peter to Mabel. At the sight of the law, Charlie courteously helps Mack out of the garbage can. The two foes smile and pretend they are the best of pals. The cop exits. Charlie immediately renews his attack. But Mabel hasn't finished with Charlie. She hands Peter to Mack and turns to deal with her spouse. Mack exits with Peter.

Park bench. The unsuspecting Mack shows the child to his wife.

She flops back in a faint. Bewildered, Mack fans her with his straw hat.

Beneath tree. Mabel is belting into Charlie. He tries to placate her. She stops to weep. He tries to console her. Then she shows him the love letter. Perplexed, he examines it.

Text of letter is repeated.

Charlie looks at the overcoat. Now he understands what happened. He explains the mixup to Mabel. She listens, contritely.

Park bench. Phyllis recovers consciousness and smacks her husband's face. She shows him the feeding bottle she had found in "his" overcoat. Mack examines the overcoat. Obviously it's not his, and he tells her so. He exits.

Beneath tree. Mack returns Peter to Mabel. He swaps overcoats with Charlie. The two men shake hands on the deal.

Park bench. Mack returns to his chastened wife. She kisses him. It seems like happiness for both couples. But not quite.

Beneath tree. Mabel asks Charlie to return "Mack's letter" to its rightful owner. He obliges.

Park bench. Charlie hands the love letter to Phyllis.

Title: *"Here is something that belongs to your husband."*

Charlie exits, falling over Mack's feet. Phyllis reads the letter.

Text of letter is repeated.

Phyllis turns on Mack and beats him with her umbrella.

Close-up of Charlie, Mabel, and Peter. They are seated on a park bench. Charlie is enjoying the sight of Mack's suffering. But Mabel draws his attention to his neglected son. Better late than never, Charlie produces the feeding bottle and hands it to the child. As the film comes to an end Charlie and Mabel are kissing Peter on the cheek.

COMMENTS

1. I have been unable to find separate verification for two of Denis Gifford's informational tidbits about this film. Gifford refers to the following scene which does not occur in any print I have come across in the U.S.A.: "Wifey [Mabel] tries to make bread and tend baby at the same time and on the same table, while hubby [Charlie] tries to relax with his feet up—and tips over a boiling kettle" (1974, 52). Gifford is generally a very reliable commentator. But he describes Mack Swain's hotel room in *His Trysting Places* as "an opulent apartment"—which it very evidently is not. So his recollection of that scene in which Mabel makes bread and Charlie scalds himself seems questionable.

Gifford also states that the film is based "on an old comic song his [Chaplin's] father had sung in vaudeville." He does not enlarge on this interesting "fact," but I presume he is referring to the song *Eh! Boys?*

by John P. Harrington and George Le Brunn. The sheet-music cover for this song is reproduced on page 44 of Chaplin's *My Life in Pictures* (1975). It depicts Charles Chaplin, Sr. (the comedian's father) in his typical lion comique/hail-fellow-well-met pose. Below the picture are three caricatures illustrating the history of a marriage: the one on the left shows a man contentedly seated in an armchair reading the *Sporting Times* while his housekeeper (presumably) stands behind him muttering: "Oh! I only wish I had you." The caricature to the right reveals that she has got her wish. She is married and has a drunken husband and two babies. The babies are squalling on the floor. The wife has seized a hot poker and is about to attack her terrified spouse. He recoils from her with the words, "Steady Darling steady. Don't be angry." Sandwiched between these two pictures is a third caricature depicting the final stage of the relationship. As she closes the front door on her hapless husband, the wife tells him: "You'll find your box in the front garden."

The notion that *His Trysting Places* is based on this particular song (or even on the song-sheet illustrations) is conjecture, not fact. Marital discord had become a popular subject for movie comedy several years before Chaplin arrived in Hollywood (e.g., the comedies of John Bunny and Flora Finch), and Chaplin's father certainly didn't have a corner on it as a vaudeville topic. More specifically, the marital discord in *His Trysting Places* is mainly motivated by the husbands' apparent infidelity whereas the song sheet points to drink (and perhaps gambling) as the overriding provocation. The song sheet also underscores the notion of marriage as a monstrous trap for both parties. The woman trapped the man into a loveless relationship in which she wears the pants; he trapped her into having children and turned her into his unpaid housekeeper. Their marriage culminates disastrously with the husband's eviction from the home. By contrast, the two marriages shown in the movie are based on affection (Mabel evidently loves Charlie, and Phyllis dotes on Mack) and the disruptions—at least in the case of Charlie and Mabel—look temporary.

2. Structure. The farce is developed out of a series of parallel contrasting situations: Prologue: Charlie's marital discord; Mack's marital harmony. (i) The two gimmicks: Charlie buys the feeding bottle; Mack acquires the love letter. (ii) Complications: the fight in the café; the overcoats are mixed up. (iii) Mack flees from Charlie; Charlie flees from Mabel. (iv) Mack meets his wife in the park; Mabel discovers her husband in the park. (v) More complications: Mabel finds Charlie "flirting" with Phyllis; Phyllis finds the feeding bottle in the overcoat. (vi) More fights: Mabel attacks Charlie; Charlie attacks Mack; Phyllis attacks Mack. (vii) Denouements: Charlie discovers the mix-up; Mack discovers the mix-up;

they exchange overcoats. (viii) Epilogue: Inversion of the contrast in prologue—Mack's marital discord; Charlie's marital harmony.

3. More than *His Musical Career, His Trysting Places* shows Chaplin moving between two cinematic styles: the use of frenetic cross-cutting (mainly for action scenes) that was typical of Keystone comedy and the use of longer, sustained shots (frequently to depict character and character contrasts) that would become increasingly basic to his mature technique. The editing of most of the film seems unexceptionally Keystone, but the eating scene, filmed in an extended two-shot, would not have looked out of place in one of Chaplin's Mutual comedies.

4. Chaplin's farcical visions of marriage continue with this film which seems in some respects like a sequel to *Mabel's Married Life* (Keystone no. 19). In the earlier film Mabel had serious doubts about her husband's virility. But since then they have produced a child, and her reservations about Charlie are now centered on his inadequacies as a breadwinner and as a father. As the film opens we can see that their marriage is seriously strained. They are out of luck (Mabel tosses away a horseshoe) and out of food (Peter doesn't even have a feeding bottle), and Mabel is wearing worn-out shoes. But Charlie is indifferent to all this. He is preoccupied with his aches and pains: he brushes aside her pleas and overlooks her little son. But Mabel is persistent. An affectionate wife and loving mother, she will not let him leave the house without a kiss and without his showing some sign of warmth toward the child.

Charlie's displays of affection are in marked contrast to Mabel's. Where she is spontaneously tender and playful toward little Peter, he has to be reminded of what is expected of him. When the child cries (is he hungry?) he makes funny faces at him instead of offering consolation. The "little present" he promises to bring Peter turns out to be not a toy but the feeding bottle the child should have had as a matter of course. Charlie treats his own son more as an animal or an object than as a child, picking him up by his legs on one occasion and by the scruff of his neck on another. (An anticipation here of a scene in *Easy Street* where Charlie feeds a family of little children as if they were chickens.) His treatment of his wife is in the same vein. Before responding to her kiss, he grabs her by the chin and scrutinizes her teeth as if she were a horse. Mabel seems to view that performance as a joke, but she certainly doesn't take kindly to being treated like a lackey. When Charlie orders her to fetch his overcoat she throws it in his face: a foreshadowing of her later reaction to what she will find in "his" overcoat.

Outside the drug store Charlie encounters his "dark omen," an equivalent of the horseshoe in the opening scene. His response to the black youth's mockery reveals that he is ashamed of being a father: he hastily conceals the feeding bottle in his overcoat. Before returning home he stops in at a café for a hearty meal. Whoever goes hungry in his family, it won't be Charlie.

When he does arrive home all seems sweetness and light. Mabel is overjoyed to see him and her gesture of brushing his hat looks like atonement for throwing the overcoat in his face. Then she discovers the love letter, and the violence of her reaction to it dramatizes her view of the marriage. She is prepared to put up with just about anything from Charlie—but not infidelity. Significantly, this time, instead of an overcoat she flings a skirt in his face. Shattering the ironing board over his head symbolizes what she believes he has done to their domesticity.

The other couple, Mack and Phyllis, have no domesticity to disrupt. They live in a hotel room, not a home of their own. They are middle-aged and childless—but Phyllis treats Mack like an infant, fussing over him, kissing the top of his head, brushing his hair, etc. It's the wife who wears the pants in this marriage, and the (phallic) umbrella—which she eventually wields against her luckless spouse—is her symbol of authority.

Mack has evidently been a "good boy," so Phyllis permits him to take a walk without her. For Mack—as for Charlie—self-gratification comes first. He doesn't take his wife to a restaurant but drops in at the nearest café to satisfy his stomach. Later on, he leaves Phyllis standing by herself in the park while he heads to the concession stand for a drink.

Self-indulgence is shown to be the male shortcoming; distrust and jealousy are the female equivalent. The men fight each other over (and with) food; the women become violent when they believe their marriages are threatened.

Their conflicts climax in the park, that "free zone" which is Clarice's "trysting place," the spot Mack and Phyllis had picked for a romantic interlude, and Charlie's refuge from Mabel's onslaughts. It is also the place where misperceptions (or most of them) are ultimately rectified.

In due course, each wife realizes that her husband has mistakenly been wearing another man's coat. Overlooking Charlie's very real shortcomings, Mabel concludes, contritely, that she had wronged him: the love letter wasn't intended for her husband, and his meeting in the park with Phyllis wasn't a tryst. Her marriage hadn't, in fact, been threatened by infidelity, and Charlie looks like a good father: he had, after all, remembered to bring a present for baby. Significantly, in the film's final shot the child appears at the center of their newfound marital bliss.

By contrast, Phyllis is relieved to discover that Mack is *not* a daddy. But her relief is short lived. She realizes (through Charlie) that the fact that her husband hasn't fathered another woman's child does not, after all, mean that he has remained faithful to her. Charlie suddenly turns manipulator and creates one final misperception (it's the only deliberate one in the film) by naughtily handing her that disastrous love letter ("Here is something that belongs to your husband").

In the finale, Phyllis's violent reaction and Mabel's reconciliation with Charlie reverse the original contrast of the two marriages. But since neither woman really knows what her husband is like (Phyllis believes surface appearances; Mabel believes what she wants to believe), the outcome seems purely arbitrary.

Aside from this toss-up view of marriage Chaplin's depiction of both sexes is distinctly unsympathetic. The two wives are jealous viragos; the men are unmitigated slobs. At home Charlie polishes his shoes with a clothes brush and blows his nose in a doormat. In the café sequence he competes with Mack in an orchestrated display of disgusting table manners. In addition, all the characters take pleasure in violence. The lady outside the café enjoys the sufferings of her male companion, the two wives lay into their husbands with gusto, and Charlie and Mack observe each other's beatings with undisguised relish.

In terms of comic characterization *His Trysting Places* is one of Chaplin's more effective and mature Keystones, standing in marked contrast to the crude stereotyping of *Tillie's Punctured Romance* (Keystone no. 33).

OTHER VIEWS

"When he wrote and directed *His Trysting Place*, he preceded W. C. Fields by many years with scenes in which he got laughs by being mean to a baby. The film ends with Mabel Normand batting him unconscious with an ironing board [*sic*]" (Sennett and Shipp 1954, 181).

"Chaplin's masculine disdain for the moral constraints of married life shows in the way he reacts to wife and baby in *His Trysting Places*" [sic] (Mast 1979, 70).

33.

Tillie's Punctured Romance

(1914)

Original working titles: *Dressler No. 1, She Was More Sinned against Than Necessary*
Other titles: *Tillie's Nightmare, Tillie's Big Romance, For the Love of Tillie, Marie's Millions;* French: *Un roman d'amour dégonflé, Le roman comique de Charlot et Lolotte;* German: *Tillies Romanze auf Raten;* Spanish: *Aventuras de Tillie, Charlot y Mabel, Novela de Amor Descha;* Italian: *Romanzo di Tillie*

Length: Originally six reels; 4796 feet (Asplund), 6000 feet (Lyons)*
Playing time: approximately 80 minutes at 16 frames per second; sound versions have considerably shorter running times
Producer: Keystone
Director: Mack Sennett
Screenplay: Hampton Del Ruth**
Photography: ?
Cast:

Tillie Banks	Marie Dressler
A city slicker	Chaplin
Mabel	Mabel Normand
Farmer John Banks	Mack Swain
Mr. Banks	Charles Bennett
Mr. Whoozis	Chester Conklin
Sheriff	Charles Parrott (Charley Chase)
Detective	Charlie Murray

*Prints of many different lengths exist. Donald W. McCaffrey notes: "Any analysis of *Tillie's Punctured Romance* runs into the problem of print validity. Many reruns and reedited versions of this highly popular feature have taken a toll. The film has been shortened to five reels and the titles have been altered" (1968, 17n). The most complete available American version (in 1985) appears to be that restored by Karl Malkames and marketed by Blackhawk Films of Davenport, Iowa.
**Based on *Tillie's Nightmare*, a musical comedy with book and lyrics by Edgar Smith and music by A. Baldwin Sloane. The show, starring Marie Dressler and the Gorman brothers, opened on Broadway on May 5, 1910, and ran for seventy-seven performances. Its songs included the famous "Heaven will protect the working girl."

Restaurant proprietor	Edgar Kennedy
Matron at jail	Phyllis Allen
Pianist in the cinema	Harry McCoy
Maidservant	Minta Durfee
Keystone Kops	Slim Summerville
	Hank Mann
	Al St. John
	Eddie Sutherland
	Joe Bordeaux
	Wallace McDonald
Party guest	Alice Davenport
Newsboy	Gordon Griffith
Preacher	Rev. D. Simpson

Shot: c. late April through July 25, 1914
Released: November 14, 1914

SYNOPSIS

[To avoid an inordinately long summary, I have limited the following description to individual scenes rather than detailing the very numerous shots.]

Hillside. His back to the camera, a city slicker contemplates a farmhouse in the valley below. As he turns to face us we recognize Charlie wearing a boater and cravat and smirking cunningly as he flourishes his cane and puffs on a cigarette.

Farmyard. Elephantine Tillie, the pride of Yokeltown and apple of her father's eye, is tossing bricks for her dog to chase. When one of them knocks Charlie down she rushes to his assistance but treads on him instead.

Interior of farmhouse. Helped in by Tillie, Charlie meets her father, Farmer John Banks, who pours him a drink. He enjoys flirting with Tillie, who has obviously fallen for him. But when he discovers that her father has a large bankroll he starts to woo her in earnest.

Farmyard. Charlie playfully tosses a brick in Tillie's direction. She hurls it back. It hits her father. Enraged, the farmer turns on both of them. They flee. Charlie suggests to Tillie that she should elope with him. He also urges her to bring along her father's bankroll.

Interior of farmhouse. Tillie picks up the bankroll but cannily insists on taking care of it until Charlie marries her.

A busy street in the wicked city. Charlie and Tillie experience some difficulty in dodging the heavy traffic. They are suddenly observed by Mabel, Charlie's confederate. Unaware that his interest in

Tillie is purely larcenous, she jealously seizes one of his arms while Tillie tugs possessively at the other. A passing cop prevents him from being pulled apart. Mabel skulks away, and Tillie marches off triumphantly, arm-in-arm with her fiancé.

Interior of restaurant. Mabel has followed the couple, and now she confronts Tillie. To prevent a fight, Charlie pulls Mabel aside and whispers his scheme to her. Meanwhile, Tillie, who has never tasted liquor, starts to get tipsy and insists on dancing with every man in sight. Charlie induces her to let him hold her pocketbook, and while she is cavorting wildly around the restaurant, he clears off with the bankroll and Mabel. Unable to pay the check, Tillie is kicked out of the restaurant.

Street. From a discreet distance Charlie and Mabel watch Tillie being arrested for being drunk and disorderly. Under police escort she dances her way to the police station.

Interior of police station. Tillie's drunken frolics create pandemonium. She refuses to reveal her identity and is dragged off to jail.

Jail. A prison matron discovers that Tillie is actually the niece of old Mr. Banks, the multimillionaire. Banks is telephoned.

Banks's mansion. Old Mr. Banks asks the police to release Tillie but not to turn her over to him.

Shopping district. Charlie and Mabel go on a spending spree with their ill-gotten gains.

Clothing store. They deck themselves out in expensive new clothes.

Interior of cinema. They arrive to see a Keystone movie entitled *A Thief's Fate*.

Onscreen. *A Thief's Fate* turns out—coincidentally—to be the story of a crook who steals a poor girl's money and hands it to a female accomplice.

Interior of cinema. As they watch the movie thieves being handcuffed and led off to jail, Charlie and Mabel become increasingly fearful and conscience-stricken. When they realize that they are sitting next to a sheriff who has begun eyeing them suspiciously, they make a hasty exit.

Mountain. To avoid any possible encounter with his niece, old Mr. Banks goes mountaineering.

Restaurant. Too proud to return to her father, Tillie has decided to remain in the wicked city and earn her own living. Despite her clumsiness, she manages to land a job as a waitress. By coincidence, Charlie and Mabel wander into the restaurant. More pandemonium ensues when Tillie spies her errant fiancé: she faints and drops a tray of food on him. Charlie and Mabel clear off. Tillie tries to pursue them, but the other waitresses restrain her.

Mountain guide's hut. A guide calls old Mr. Banks's mansion with the news that the multimillionaire has lost his life in a climbing accident.

Gathering of attorneys. Tillie is declared sole heir. The attorneys lose no time in organizing a search for her.

Park. Charlie reads a newspaper report of Tillie's legacy. He gives Mabel the slip and heads for the restaurant.

Restaurant. Arriving before the attorneys, he dashes in and embraces the bewildered Tillie, insisting that his former treatment of her had been a misunderstanding. Then he drags her—not unwillingly—away.

Church. Charlie and Tillie are married.

Restaurant. Tillie drags Charlie back to show off her husband to the other waitresses. The attorneys arrive and inform her that she has just inherited three million dollars. The news momentarily arouses her suspicion of Charlie's motives, but when he expresses outrage that she could possibly doubt his love, she gives him a bearlike hug and all is forgiven and forgotten.

Park. Mabel is furious at being deserted by Charlie and determined to get her share of Tillie's legacy.

Mountain slope. Old Banks is discovered—still very much alive and unaware that his estate has been handed over to his niece.

Interior of Banks's mansion. Charlie and Tillie move in. Losing no time in displaying their total lack of refinement and good manners, they lean on footmen and use valuable urns as ashtrays. They quickly whip up a lavish party complete with exhibition ballroom dancers in the style of Vernon and Irene Castle. Mabel arrives in the guise of a maidservant. Accosting Charlie, she demands a share of his new wealth. He is also confronted by Mr. Whoozis, a friend of old Mr. Banks, who accuses him of fortune hunting. Charlie turns his attention to the latter, and after a violent quarrel, succeeds in throwing him out of the house. Oblivious of the clouds that are gathering on her horizon, Tillie decides to join in the dancing. Charlie gallantly escorts her onto the floor. Mabel interrupts them while they are in the midst of a crazy tango. At first Tillie doesn't recognize the "maid." Later, however, she discovers Charlie kissing her. In a jealous fury she throws everything she can lay her hands on at them and at the assembled guests. Then, arming herself with a gun, she fires wildly at Charlie and chases him all over the house. He tries to hide in a huge vase, while Mabel crawls under a rug. But Tillie tracks them down and begins throttling her wayward spouse. His life is saved by the unexpected arrival of Tillie's uncle. Infuriated at the damage done to his home, old Mr. Banks orders everyone to clear out at once.

Exterior of Banks's mansion. Having second thoughts about the advantages of being married to Tillie, Charlie kicks her aside and takes to his heels in the company of Mabel.

Banks's mansion. Thirsting for revenge, old Mr. Banks calls the police and tells them to rearrest his niece.

Police station. Happy to oblige, the Keystone Kops leap into their squad car. A wild chase follows.

Seafront. Tillie—gun in hand—races after Charlie and Mabel. The Kops pursue Tillie. Charlie and Mabel stop in midflight and begin to quarrel. Catching up with Tillie, the squad car overshoots the mark and shoves her into the ocean. Charlie and Mabel resume their flight along the boardwalk as a rope is thrown out to the drowning Tillie.

Ocean. A police launch speeds to the rescue. It collides with a rowboat and capsizes it.

Pier. Kops manage to haul Tillie ashore. Charlie and Mabel are rounded up and brought face to face with their victim. But this time, instead of renewing her attack, Tillie hands Charlie his ring and gives him the cold shoulder. Her reaction melts Mabel's heart: she voices sympathy for all that Tillie has suffered and joins her in spurning Charlie for *never* having given *her* (Mabel) a ring. As the Kops drag Charlie away, Tillie embraces Mabel, her newfound friend.

COMMENT

1. Curious as it may seem, *Tillie's Punctured Romance* was evidently inspired by *The Birth of a Nation*. When Mack Sennett heard that D. W. Griffith was at work on a multireel epic picture, he decided that the time had come to make America's first multireel comedy. However, Sennett's inspiration was not shared by Kessel and Bauman, his controlling business partners at Keystone. They were grossing a fortune from Keystone's one- and two-reelers and could see no reason to risk any of it on such a dubious and undoubtedly very costly enterprise. Sennett managed to talk them round by offering to invest his own interest in Keystone in the financing of the picture and by guaranteeing that he could secure the service of Broadway showstopper Marie Dressler as star of the movie.

Sennett's acquaintance with Marie Dressler went back to the days of his callow youth (as Michael Sinnott) when, in an effort to break into theater, he had called on her with a letter of introduction from the family lawyer, Calvin Coolidge. Dressler in turn had written a letter of introduction to playwright-impresario David Belasco, who advised the young man to try his dubious talents in burlesque. Sennett took the advice. Thus began a career that culminated in his creation of Keystone, Hollywood's greatest fun factory during the era of silent cinema.

Dressler remembered Sennett when he approached her with an offer to star in a Keystone movie, and she was perfectly willing to accept his offer—as long as he agreed to her terms. But they were very steep for 1914. She demanded $2500 a week for a minimum of twelve weeks (the film actually took fourteen weeks to shoot) and exacted a *verbal promise* that her husband, James Dalton, was to have exclusive control of the movie's distribution. Sam Goldwyn is said to have remarked that a verbal agreement isn't worth the paper it's printed on. But this particular one wound up making a small fortune for several attorneys. For the parties most directly concerned it only created a big headache.

At the outset, when Sennett clinched the deal with Miss Dressler, there was neither script nor story. Then scenario editor Craig Hutchinson made the obvious suggestion: why not do a movie version of Dressler's Broadway triumph, *Tillie's Nightmare?* Sennett liked the idea. It wouldn't be as expensive and time consuming as cooking up a new script, and the success of the stage show would provide a valuable advertisement for the picture. In the final event, however, "Hampton Del Ruth and the idea department took a slim idea from Miss Dressler's stage play" as the basis of the film's scenario (Sennett and Shipp 1954, ch. 16). Meanwhile, Sennett brooded about what to call his masterpiece. He vacillated between *Dressler No. 1* and *She Was More Sinned against Than Necessary.* But Hutchinson and Del Ruth eventually came up with *Tillie's Punctured Romance,* a title that neatly combined an allusion to the original show with a hint of Keystone farce.

Work on the film turned out to be a highly erratic business. Dressler was the only performer who could devote uninterrupted attention to the movie. Chaplin and Mabel Normand worked on several other shorter films during the fourteen weeks that *Tillie's Punctured Romance* was in production.

In *King of Comedy*, Sennett recalls that Marie Dressler got on well with Chaplin, but that he (Sennett) had serious problems directing her, which may explain why the film took two extra weeks to shoot:

> No matter that this was her first motion picture, she was a great star, this was her own story, and she was still inclined to remember me as an awkward boilermaker from Northampton. In the midst of a comic scene I had planned carefully beforehand, Miss Dressler would say, "No, Mack, that's wrong. Now this is the way we're going to do it." I was the head of the studio and I was supervising this particular picture, but neither of these things influenced Marie Dressler. My arguments didn't influence her either. "Okay, Marie, you do it your way," I'd say. And I would leave the set. Usually a sweating messenger would arrive within an hour. Miss Dressler, who didn't know a camera angle from a hypotenuse, always threw the company into a swivet when she took over. "Mack, there's just a little technicality here you can help me straighten out," she'd say. "Sure, sure, Marie, call on me any time." (Sennett and Shipp 1954, ch. 16)

Despite Sennett's verbal agreement with Dressler, Kessel and Bauman went ahead separately and sold the film's distribution rights to the Alco Film Corporation for $100,000, netting an immediate $50,000 on the deal. Marie Dressler promptly brought legal action against Keystone, hoping to impede the deal with Alco and obtain legal rights to distribute the film. But the court overruled her claim, and she lost twice more on appeal. Incensed, she filed another suit against Keystone, charging that the company had misappropriated some of her salary. When a court-ordered audit found no evidence of fraud, she decided, reluctantly, to cut her losses and brought no further suit against Keystone.

Commercially, *Tillie's Punctured Romance* proved a huge success, grossing several million dollars during the years when it was in copyright. Marie Dressler went on to make two unsuccessful sequels: *Tillie's Tomato Surprise* (1915) and *Tillie Wakes Up* (1917)—for two other companies and without Chaplin and Mabel Normand.

Tillie's Punctured Romance gave Chaplin his first experience of acting in a feature film, but he did not regard it as a landmark in his career. In *My Autobiography* he polishes it off in three sentences: "During this time Mabel and I starred in a feature picture with Marie Dressler. It was pleasant working with Marie, but I did not think the picture had much merit. I was more than happy to get back to directing myself again" (1964, 158).

For additional factual information about the film see Lahue and Brewer (1967, ch. 7).

2. *Tillie's Punctured Romance* was the apogee of Sennett's brand of Keystone comedy. Chaplin's movement away from its slapstick clichés, stereotype characterization, and frenetic pacing toward a richer comic style is unmistakably evident in his own later Keystones. But Sennett seems to have been oblivious to Chaplin's development. The role in which he cast him was for the most part a recapitulation of the "sharper" character he had played in *Making a Living*.

3. The reader is recommended to consult the detailed critique and structural analysis of the film that appears in Donald W. McCaffrey's *4 Great Comedians*, pp. 16–22. McCaffrey's commentary concludes:

> In all, *Tillie's Punctured Romance* has many crudities, not only in primitive humour, but also in the acting and the technical use of the medium. Marie Dressler's acting is broad to the point of over-acting; Chaplin, although he has some effective moments ["moments" in a six-reel film!], is caught up in a whirlwind pace that makes him appear only slightly more talented than the run-of-the-mill Keystone comedian. . . . Camera shots and editing are often as primitive as the comedy. Poor framing of the subjects is often present, and few close-ups are used to

convey necessary information, let alone point up a gag. A goodly share of mismatched shots during a character's movements from place to place also occur in the film; and the establishment of locale is often fuzzy.

I have nothing to add to this summation.

OTHER VIEWS

"It is more than mere slapstick. It is a smart take-off of the old city slicker-country maiden cliché adding some pointed thrusts at the 'high society' of the period. The beginning of the picture betrays its stage origin, but it becomes more cinematic towards the end. At times the lips move in simulated 'soliloquies' and 'asides' that are actually pantomimed to the audience. About the middle of 1914, this device—a hangover from the stage and until then common in Sennett's and some other films— disappeared as the actors developed techniques more appropriate to the silent medium. Later it may be noticed that Chaplin seldom moves his mouth, relying on pantomime and action alone" (Huff 1952, 48).

"As in most of the Keystones, the plot simply supplies the pretext for a series of gags, mounting in rhythm and intensity, culminating in a rally. . . . Tillie's drunken dances—both alone and with tiny Charlie— are far more important to the film than the plotty attempts to swindle her out of some cash. The 'serious' motifs of the film are examples of the typical Keystone method of reducing all potentially serious material to predictable literary clichés" (Mast 1979, 55).

"There is a delightful burlesque tango danced by Tillie and Charlie, but the film, though deriving some strength from a good story, gave Charlie comparatively little opportunity to show his real worth, considering it is of feature length. The excessive resort to mere kicking is tedious and tasteless" (Manvell 1974, 84).

Tillie's Punctured Romance is still vital comedy, perhaps too vital. It is funny although much of its basic appeal may be to people who enjoy cockfights and mud-wrestling. It is arse-kicking brought to apotheosis, and Marie Dressler's stock in trade seems to be falling down, which she does unceasingly and with little provocation throughout" (McCabe 1978, 64–65).

34.

Getting Acquainted
(1914)

Original working title: *The Flirts*
Other titles: *Hello Everybody, A Fair Exchange, Exchange Is No Robbery;* French: *Charlot et Mabel en promenade, Charlot marié;* German: *Man Lernt Sich Kennen;* Spanish: *Charlot tiene una mujer celosa, Charlot y sa mujer celosa, Charlot y Mabel de paseo;* Italian: *Charlot e la moglie gelosa, Far amicizia*

Length: 1 reel; 951 feet (Asplund), 1025 feet (Lyons)
Playing time: 16 minutes at 16 frames per second
Producer: Keystone
Director: Chaplin
Screenplay: Chaplin
Photography: Frank D. Williams (?)
Cast:

Mr. Sniffles	Chaplin
Mrs. Sniffles	Phyllis Allen
Mr. Ambrose	Mack Swain
Mrs. Ambrose	Mabel Normand
A cop	Edgar Kennedy
A Turk	Harry McCoy
A girl	Cecile Arnold

Finished or shipped: November 22, 1914
Released: December 5, 1914

SYNOPSIS

The entire action of *Getting Acquainted* takes place in a park.

First park bench. Charlie is seated beside his sleeping wife (Phyllis Allen). A girl (the Turk's girlfriend) is passing by. She smiles at the couple. Interested in her, Charlie edges away from his wife to convey the impression that they are not connected. The girl stops and peers around—she is waiting for her date. Charlie imitates her actions.

Then he tries to flirt with her, but she spurns him. Leaving his sleeping wife, he starts to follow the girl.

He pursues her along a pathway, his cane hooked into his breast pocket. Catching up with her, he doffs his hat but decides not to push his luck when her boyfriend (a bearded Turk) suddenly arrives on the scene. Charlie turns his back on the couple and tries to look innocent, but the girl apprises the Turk of his behavior toward her. Pulling out a dagger, the Turk jabs him in the buttocks. Charlie flees.

Nearby, Mabel (Mack Swain's wife) is impatiently awaiting her husband. Charlie hops into view. He approaches her jauntily, sizing her up from behind. Accidentally on purpose he pokes her behind with his cane, then he doffs his hat and introduces himself. She gives him the cold shoulder.

A road close by. Mack is having a problem getting his racing car started. His driver watches him, mops his brow, and laughs.

Throwing discretion to the wind, Charlie puts his arm around Mabel. She slaps him.

Road. The driver watches as Mack tries to crank the engine.

Charlie "accidentally" crooks his cane in the hem of Mabel's skirt and raises it, doffing his hat at the same time. Mabel is outraged. Charlie reacts by spanking the cane for being "naughty." Then he resumes his flirtation.

A cop approaches them from behind.

Charlie flees with the cop in pursuit. Mabel watches the chase. She turns toward the camera and flings out her arms helplessly. She calls to her husband for help.

Road. Mack is still trying to crank the car.

Charlie returns and makes more advances toward Mabel. She slaps him again.

Road. Mack gets out of the car and heads toward his wife.

Mabel tries to tell her husband that Charlie has been pestering her, but Mack suddenly recognizes Charlie as an old pal.

Title: *Meet my wife.*

Charlie and Mabel are embarrassed. Charlie tries to creep away, but Mack stops him. He refuses to listen to his wife's protestations.

Road. The driver calls out to Mack.

As Mack turns to see who's calling, Charlie claps his hand over Mabel's mouth. Mack heads toward his car, cheerfully leaving his wife in Charlie's hands.

Road. Mack and the driver get the car started. They climb in.

Charlie renews his overtures; Mabel rebuffs him. He takes her arm. She calls out for Mack. No avail.

Road. The car drives off.

Charlie leans on Mabel's shoulder. She brushes him off and calls for help.

Road. Mack is tired of tinkering with the car. He gets out and walks away.

First park bench. Mack sits down beside Phyllis (Charlie's wife). She has woken up and eyes him suspiciously.

Mabel notices the cop creeping up behind Charlie. Changing tactics, she pretends to show an interest in him. They joke together. The cop stands behind Charlie and does a slow burn. Oblivious of danger, Charlie leans back against the cop (assuming he's a tree). At last he notices a nightstick waving ominously just a few inches from his nose. He takes to his heels.

The cop chases him around a bush and then makes the mistake of stopping to pick up his nightstick. Charlie jabs him in the rump with a pin.

The chase continues—around Mabel.

Second park bench. Charlie backs on to the Turk and gets another jab from the dagger.

The cop looks around for Charlie.

Second park bench. Charlie shoves the Turk into some bushes and dashes off.

Charlie in flight from the cop.

Second park bench. The cop asks the Turk if he has seen Charlie.

Charlie heads into the bushes.

Second park bench. The Turk's girlfriend points the cop toward Charlie.

The cop approaches Charlie but can't locate him.

First park bench. Mack tries to flirt with Phyllis. He chucks her under the chin. Insulted, she slaps his face and shouts for help.

The cop dashes toward Phyllis.

First bench. Phyllis boots Mack. He makes a hasty exit.

The cop stops beside Mack. Mack tries to look innocent. The cop is puzzled—he'd expected to find Charlie.

Charlie emerges from the shrubbery. He mops his brow.

First park bench. Phyllis calls out to the cop.

Mack is horror-stricken. The cop heads toward Phyllis.

First park bench. Phyllis informs the cop that it was Mack who had molested her.

Mack flees.

Charlie darts back into the bushes.

First bench. The cop heads away from Phyllis.

Mack passes the bushes where Charlie is concealed. Charlie emerges, sees the cop, then darts back into hiding.

Second park bench. Still in flight, Mack stumbles over the Turk who is kneeling (proposing marriage?) at the girl's feet.

The cop breaks through some bushes. He runs on in pursuit of Mack.

Second park bench. The cop catches up with Mack. He swings his nightstick but hits the Turk instead. Then, assuming the Turk is another molester, he deliberately clubs him and carries on his pursuit of Mack. The girl rushes to the aid of her battered escort.

Charlie emerges from the bushes and marches off.

First park bench. Looking confused and upset, Mabel sits down beside Phyllis.

Two-shot of the two women. Phyllis informs Mabel that there's a molester at loose in the park.

Charlie dashes into view. He removes his hat.

Mabel escorts Phyllis to a third park bench.

Charlie heads toward them.

Third park bench. Charlie flops down beside his wife. Phyllis expresses annoyance that he had left her alone. Then she introduces him to her new acquaintance, Mrs. Ambrose. Surprise! Charlie almost faints. Mabel starts to denounce him. But thinking quickly, he pushes Phyllis away and shoves his hand in Mabel's face. Then he back-kicks Mabel and exits after his wife. Mabel stares in his direction, a disgusted look on her face.

Second park bench. Mack is still fleeing from the cop. He passes the Turk again and evades his upraised dagger.

Mack flees into the bushes.

Second park bench. The cop appears, clubs the Turk, and continues his pursuit.

The cop rushes past the bushes where Mack is hiding.

A suspicious Phyllis interrogates Charlie about his association with Mabel. Charlie tries to pacify her.

Mack peers at the cop from behind foliage.

From beside the bushes the cop catches sight of Charlie.

Unconvinced by Charlie's explanations, Phyllis turns her back on him.

The cop creeps away from the bushes.

The cop creeps up behind Charlie.

Mack emerges from the bushes. He notices the cop and heads in the opposite direction.

Standing behind Charlie, the cop does a slow burn. Charlie notices him and flees. The cop heads after him.

The cop chases Charlie past the bushes.

Second park bench. Charlie runs toward the Turk. He sees the upraised dagger and flees in a different direction.

Charlie heads into the bushes.

The cop runs past the bushes—away from the camera.

The cop runs past the bushes—toward the camera.

Third park bench. Mack—nervously looking out for his pursuer—rejoins his wife. Mabel is angry with him for leaving her alone.

Phyllis is furious. She has turned round and discovered that harlie has left her alone once more.

Hands on hips, Phyllis marches toward the third park bench. She sits down beside the Ambroses. Mabel reciprocates Phyllis's courtesy:

Title: *"Meet my husband."*

Another Surprise! Phyllis denounces Mark and falls back in a faint.

Infuriated, Mabel drags Mack away. She starts to harangue him. He pleads with her.

The cop spies Mack.

Mabel is yelling at Mack.

The cop creeps toward Mack.

The cop does a slow burn behind Mack.

Charlie is strolling alone near the bushes.

Mack spies the cop and flees.

Charlie spies the cop and flees into the bushes.

The cop heads after Mack.

Mack darts into the bushes.

Mack finds Charlie hiding in the same bush.

The two outraged wives sit on the same bench and vent their anger at their philandering spouses.

The two husbands emerge from the bushes, mopping their brows. The cop creeps up and clubs them. They try to creep away but he grabs them by their coattails. He starts hauling them off to the police station.

A lengthy panning shot as he drags them past the two wives. As the three men recede into the distance, Charlie is facing backward and doffing his hat.

Two-shot of the two wives looking shocked.

The cop and Mack have stopped to argue. Charlie tries to slip away, but the cop catches him.

Two-shot of the wives. They are appalled at the sight of their husbands being manhandled.

The two wives approach the trio of men. Phyllis shows the cop her wedding ring and points to Charlie. She embraces her wayward spouse. Mack puts his arm around Mabel. Disgusted, the cop pushes a path through the two couples and stalks away.

Nearby, the cop comes upon yet another man molesting a woman. He beats the man up and chases him away.

The two couples are appalled at this spectacle. Then, in a concilia-

tory mood, each wife shakes hands with the other's husband. The two
men stare at each other and put their fingers to their lips. The two
women look shocked—then they smile. But Mack carelessly whispers a
flirtatious remark to Phyllis and she slaps him. Mabel is offended at
this, and Charlie tries to console her—but his consolation looks a little
too affectionate to Phyllis. Without further ado, she seizes him by the
tail of his jacket and frog-marches him out of the park. The Ambroses
watch this scene with smiles on their faces.

COMMENTS

1. Shot in a single day in Westlake Park, this was Chaplin's final
one-reeler for Keystone.

2. Symmetrical structure. An interweaving of parallel situations: (i)
Charlie deserts his own wife (Phyllis) and tries to pick up Mack's wife
(Mabel); Mack neglects his own wife and tries to pick up Charlie's. (ii)
The cop pursues Charlie the molester; the cop pursues Mack the molester. (iii) The two wives commiserate with each other on a park bench;
the two husbands take refuge together in the same bush. (iv) Mack
unsuspectingly introduces Charlie to Mabel; Phyllis does likewise; Mabel
unsuspectingly introduces Mack to Phyllis. (v) The cop arrests the two
husbands; the wives "liberate" them. (vi) Charlie makes peace with
Mabel; Mack makes peace with Phyllis. (vii) Phyllis is offended with her
husband's attentions to Mabel; Mabel is offended with Mack's attentions
to Phyllis.

3. A "park" film without either brick throwing or a watery finale,
and with one significant difference: unlike *Twenty Minutes of Love*,
Recreation, and *Those Love Pangs*, *Getting Acquainted* involves the
interaction of *married couples*. In the earlier park films Chaplin rings
the changes on rivalries and flirtations among single males and females.
But in *Getting Acquainted* the park's uninhibited free zone is not a place
for "innocent" flirtations or sexual rivalry between unmarried male
characters. Instead of mere flirtations, we see molestations and male
impulses to commit adultery.

The symmetrical situations applied to contrasting couples suggests
that what is being represented is typical human behavior. Marriage has
evidently ended whatever sexual interest Charlie and Mack once had for
the women they married. As soon as possible, each husband jettisons
his wife and tries to pick up the first unescorted female in sight. Both
couples are, of course, astonishingly mismatched. Charlie is married to
the formidable Phyllis Allen, so his impulse to walk out on her and pick
up someone as attractive as Mabel is quite understandable. But Mack

ignores Mabel in order to make passes at a battle-ax who looks twice Mabel's age. "Let's face it," says Kalton C. Lahue, "who would really want to pick up Phyllis Allen in the park anyway?" (Lahue and Gill 1971b, 98). The question overlooks the fact that Mack is philandering for its own sake—regardless of what the woman looks like. Charlie's impulse is exactly the same as Mack's, but he happens, just by chance, to come upon an unescorted woman who's attractive. Thereafter he pesters Mabel with total indifference to the fact that she finds him offensive. Mack presumably intends to treat Phyllis in the same way, but she proves too tough for him, and the cop scares him off more easily than he had scared off the more persistent Charlie.

The cop's exclusive function appears to be to protect unescorted women: a full-time job since every man in the park regards every woman in the park (other than his wife) as fair game. (Were parks really like that in "the good old days"?) In *Twenty Minutes of Love, Recreation,* and *Those Love Pangs,* the women (all single) join in the flirtation game. But in *Getting Acquainted* none of the women (including the single one who is molested toward the end of the film) shows any interest in picking up men. The wives are faithful to their faithless and neglectful husbands who leave them to be abused by the first man who passes by. They appear to get nothing out of their marriages other than the right to beat up their spouses. In the face of their flagrant mistreatment by men, the wives establish a female camaraderie similar to the newfound friendship of Mabel and Tillie at the end of *Tillie's Punctured Romance.*

By the end of the movie the film's title can be seen to have several connotations—most of them cynical. Each woman gets acquainted with what men are like when their wives aren't around; the wives get acquainted as fellow sufferers; the husbands as fellow molesters; the cop gets acquainted with the inexplicable behavior of women. It appears that where men and women are concerned "getting acquainted" is always sexually motivated—except, ironically, in the marriage relationship.

OTHER VIEWS

"As a farce it is astonishingly primitive to have been made so late in the Keystone series" (Asplund 1976, 61).

"His best and last Keystone quickie" (Gifford 1974, 55).

"Charlie often uses his cane as an extension of his arm in the early films. Holding it upside down in *Getting Acquainted* (1914), he raises his hand to his head which causes the cane to lift Mabel's skirt (whereupon he sternly reprimands it)" (Kamin 1984, 45). [But does one usually spank oneself? Is Charlie really using the cane as an extension of himself in this scene?]

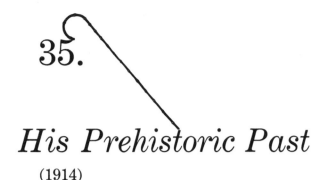

35.

His Prehistoric Past

(1914)

Original working title: *A Prehistoric Villain*
Other titles: *A/The Dream, The Caveman, King Charlie, The Hula-Hula Dance/Dancer;* French: *Charlot nudiste, Le passé préhistorique de Charlot, Le rêve de Charlot;* German: *Seine prähistorische Vergangenheit;* Spanish: *Charlot prehistorico, El sueño de Charlot;* Italian: *Charlot re per un giorno, Il suo passato preistorico*

Length: 2 reels; 1945 feet (Asplund), 2000 feet (Lyons)
Playing time: 33 minutes at 16 frames per second
Producer: Keystone
Director: Chaplin
Screenplay: Chaplin
Photography: Frank D. Williams (?)
Cast:

Mr. Weakchin	Chaplin
King Lowbrow	Mack Swain
Sum-Babee	Gene Marsh
Ku-Ku	Fritz Schade
Cavewoman	Cecile Arnold
Caveman	Al St. John

Finished or shipped: October 31, 1914
Released: December 7, 1914

SYNOPSIS

[The most complete prints of *His Prehistoric Past* that I have seen are copies of the W. A. Films rerelease version, edited by Sydney Chaplin and using *his* comic insert titles. The following description is a conflation of two varying copies of this version of the film.]

A park. Charlie, a tramp, heads for a rustic bench. He sits down, fans himself with his waistcoat flaps, and stretches out for a nap. Iris out.

Title: *Today when a man courting goes,*
He always has to carry
Flowers, candy, gifts galore,
If he expects to marry.

Title: *'Twas different in the long ago*
He'd never phone or knock
He'd waltz right in the lady's cave
And woo her with a rock.

Title: *South of 53—where the man with the biggest club has all the fun.*

A prehistoric encampment. The men are dressed in animal skins; the girls in grass skirts. Ku-Ku (Fritz Schade) is doing a ballet dance.

Title: *Ku-Ku the Court Jester entertains the King and his hand-picked harem.*

Ku-Ku takes a bow. He does a "pansy" walk and primps his hair. The king (Mack Swain) contemptuously scares him away with a flourish of his club.

Title: *A castaway.*

Near the seashore. Weakchin (Chaplin) appears. He is dressed in a bearskin but is also wearing his familiar derby and holding his cane.

Encampment. The king orders a girl (Gene Marsh) to fill a jug with water.

Title: *Sum-Babee, the King's Favorite Wife.*

To hurry her along, the king gives her a playful tap with his club.

Near seashore. Weakchin looks around. He plucks some hairs from his bearskin and stuffs them into his pipe. Picking up a piece of rock, he strikes it against his leg like a match and lights his pipe. He tosses away the rock, puffs at the pipe, and swings his cane.

Sum-Babee comes face to face with Weakchin. They start a flirtation. He notices her grass skirt.

Title: *"Shredded wheat is very becoming to you."*

They chat. He waggles his bearskin as if it were a tail.

They sit down on a rock.

Two-shot: He takes her hand.

Encampment. Ku-Ku minces back to the king but gets driven away.

Near seashore. Sum-Babee gets up to go.

A tree close by. Ku-Ku spies them together. He's aghast.

Weakchin kisses Sum-Babee's hand.

Ku-Ku fires an arrow.

Title: *Not so good a shot as Cupid.*

The arrow has hit Weakchin in the buttocks. Sum-Babee obligingly removes it, but Weakchin finds that it's painful to sit down.

Ku-Ku points at Weakchin.

Weakchin spies his attacker. He picks up a rock, spits on it, and hurls it at Ku-Ku.

Ku-Ku ducks.

Encampment. The rock lands in the king's lap. Consternation in the harem.

Sum-Babee creeps behind a huge boulder. Weakchin picks up a club.

Ku-Ku advances.

Thumbing his nose at Ku-Ku, Weakchin evades him by skipping behind the boulder. Sum-Babee follows Ku-Ku as he pursues Weakchin around the boulder.

Title: *Something tells his majesty that all is not well.*

The king picks up his club and stalks toward the boulder.

Sum-Babee exits. Ku-Ku jabs an arrow into Weakchin. Weakchin back-kicks his attacker. The chase around the boulder continues.

Club in hand, the king is advancing.

Encampment. Sum-Babee arrives. She joins the other girls.

Weakchin hurls another rock at Ku-Ku.

The rock hits the king.

The king joins in the pursuit around the boulder. Ku-Ku jabs him. Realizing his grievous error, he goes down on his knees and begs for mercy. Weakchin cracks his rival on the head, knocking him cold. Then, confronting the king, he offers him some "tobacco" and gets a hefty but good-natured slap in return. Weakchin explains how he happened to become a castaway.

Title: *"I started to swim out to the three-mile limit to get a drink and I lost my way."*

The king shows Weakchin a photo of his harem. Weakchin laughs and gives his newfound pal a friendly boot in the belly. The king takes the kick in good part. They shake hands and rub noses.

Title: *"You are now in the Solomon Islands where every man has a thousand wives."*

The king picks up Weakchin's cane and hands it to him.

Title: *"A thousand wives for every man? I wish I had brought a bigger club."*

The king generously exchanges his club for Weakchin's cane. They head toward the encampment.

Title: *"Don't worry. We catch 'em young, treat 'em rough and tell 'em nothing."*

They stop to laugh.

Title: *"You look healthy for a guy with a thousand mothers-in-law."*

Weakchin picks a flea from the king's chest, places it on the ground and crushes it with a blow of his club. The king is mightily impressed. Weakchin takes his arm.

Encampment. The girls of the harem point excitedly toward the king and Weakchin.

Encampment. Weakchin clubs a sleeping sentry. He marches toward the camera arm-in-arm with the king. They stop to joke. Weakchin jestingly swipes the king on the rear.

The girls of the harem bow formally.

The king retaliates for the swipe by pushing Weakchin backward over a groveling sentry. Weakchin gets up, doffs his hat, and cracks the sentry over the head. He swings the club for a second blow but strikes the king instead. The king accepts his apology. Then he orders the girls to rise.

The king invites Weakchin into his cave for a drink. He dances toward the cave. Weakchin follows, reluctantly. He is eyeing Sum-Babee.

Interior of cave. Weakchin enters. The king is seated at a table.

Title: *"Nothing is prohibited here except work."*

Weakchin sits at the table. He uses a sentry as a footstool. He shakes a cocktail and tosses the drink into the sentry's face.

Beside the boulder. Ku-Ku recovers consciousness. He clenches his fists and heads toward the encampment.

Interior of cave. Weakchin and the king are doing some heavy drinking. The latter is intoxicated. Weakchin tickles him under the arm with his club and exits.

Exterior of cave. Weakchin greets the girls.

The girls surround Weakchin and fuss over him. But they lose interest in him as a bearded caveman appears.

Title: *An irresistible masher.*

The girls exit, milling around the caveman. Several moments pass before Weakchin realizes that he has been abandoned.

Encampment. The girls are fussing over the caveman.

Exterior of cave. Weakchin examines his club, holds it behind his back, and wanders over to his latest rival.

Title: *Weakchin is some masher himself.*

He flattens the caveman. Impressed, the girls flock round him once more. Sum-Babee chucks him under the chin. They stroll away together.

Gully nearby. They are flirting.

Encampment. The girls laugh.

Gully. A torrent of water suddenly cascades onto Weakchin and Sum-Babee.

Sea shore. They are swept into the sea.

Encampment. The girls laugh.

Seashore. Weakchin and Sum-Babee are bombarded by the incoming waves.

Encampment. The king emerges from the cave. The girls point toward the seashore.

Seashore. Weakchin and Sum-Babee are struggling in the surf, but they appear to be carousing together.

Encampment. The king folds his arms. He is furious.

Seashore. Weakchin and Sum-Babee struggle onto dry land.

Encampment. The king confronts them.

Title: *"Keep away from my wives. You act more like a boarder than a guest."*

He grabs Sum-Babee and forces her back among the other girls. Weakchin tries to explain.

Title: *"She was drowning. If it wasn't for me you'd only have nine hundred and ninety-nine wives."*

The king accepts this explanation. He invites Weakchin to have another drink. He exits. Weakchin looks back at Sum-Babee and sadly follows the king.

Cave. The two men shake hands and bow to each other, conking heads in the process. Weakchin puts his feet on the table. The king pours wine.

Encampment. The girls are dancing. The caveman reappears, nursing his head and swearing vengeance against his attacker. Lovesick Sum-Babee is mooning about Weakchin.

Cave. The king is drunk. Weakchin sneaks out once more.

Encampment. Weakchin rejoins Sum-Babee. He is unnoticed by the caveman, who is speaking to the girls:

Title: *"That strange eater of cake with the feet like the flounder must die."*

Weakchin eyes the caveman and fingers his club. The caveman sees him and flees.

Nearby. The caveman stops and holds his aching head.

Encampment. Weakchin puts his hand over his heart and addresses Sum-Babee:

Title: *"Mrs. Solomon, you're one in a thousand."*

He invites her to dance with him.

Title: *"On with the dance. Let joy be unrefined."*

They dance. She catches him by the neck and swings him around. He staggers and falls. Rising, he doffs his hat.

Cave. The king realizes he has been left by himself. He looks out of the cave.

Encampment. Weakchin is enjoying a tête-à-tête with Sum-Babee.

Cave. The king grabs his club and marches out.

Encampment. He boots Weakchin in the rump. Then he hands him a bow and arrow and points.

Title: *Off to hunt big game.*

The king marches off, followed by Sum-Babee and Weakchin. The girls watch their departure.

Woodland. The king looks around for game. Weakchin eyes Sum-Babee. The king watches their flirtation with mounting annoyance. He orders Sun-Babee to clear off and berates Weakchin.

Clearing. Sum-Babee looks back and gestures to Weakchin to follow her.

Woodland. The king is angry with Weakchin. The latter stares at the king's belly, then shoots an arrow at it. The king is about to strike back when Weakchin points upward.

Title: *"Look! a Jersey eagle!"*

Close-up of bird in nest.

The king demands the bow and arrow, but Weakchin insists on using them. He fires upward.

Close-up of nest. The arrow punctures it.

Two-shot of Weakchin and the king. An egg hits the king on the head. Weakchin laughs. He looks up.

Close-up of nest. Another egg drops.

The king is hit again. Weakchin removes his derby and looks up.

Close-up of nest. Another egg drops.

Weakchin is hit in the face. The egg stinks; he holds his nose. He dodges yet another egg and shakes his fist at the bird.

A gully nearby. Ku-Ku and the caveman head toward the encampment.

Clearing. Weakchin has caught up with Sum-Babee. He kisses her.

Woodland. The king observes them together. Infuriated, he advances toward them.

Clearing. He creeps toward them. He raises his fist—intending to strike Sum-Babee. But Weakchin stays his hand. Then he shows the king his flexed muscle. The king isn't intimidated. He swings a blow at Weakchin—but Weakchin ducks. He waves his hat in the king's face. The king threatens Sum-Babee, but Weakchin orders her to clear off. She does so.

Nearby. She stops and looks back. She's scared.

Clearing. Weakchin is conciliatory.

Title: *"I like you, King, because I had a dog named Prince once."*

Cliff top. Weakchin glances at the slope behind the king. He's thoughtful. Then he cunningly maneuvers the king so that the latter's back is facing the slope.

Encampment. The girls look in the direction of the cliff top.

Cliff top. Weakchin kicks the king backward down the slope.

Slope. The king comes to rest on a ledge.

Cliff top. Weakchin looks down at the king.

Encampment. The girls scatter. They have caught sight of Ku-Ku and the caveman.

Cliff top. Weakchin mock-bows at the king. He nearly falls.

Nearby. Sum-Babee calls to Weakchin.

Encampment. Ku-Ku and the caveman return the girls' bows.

Nearby. Weakchin addresses Sum-Babee:

Title: *"Now I'm King and you're going to be Mrs. King."*

He orders her back to the encampment.

Encampment. The girls inform Ku-Ku that Weakchin has disposed of the king.

Clearing. Ku-Ku calls out to the king.

Encampment. The girls bow low as Weakchin appears. He stretches himself, walks over the girls' backs, and sits on his throne. Sum-Babee joins him. He kicks the caveman aside.

Cliff top. Ku-Ku still calling.

Encampment. Weakchin shoots an arrow into a sentry's rear end. He yawns.

Cliff top. Ku-Ku hears the king.

Ledge. The king shouts up for help.

Close-shot of Weakchin and Sum-Babee surrounded by the harem. He grabs Sum-Babee by the hair and pulls her toward him for a kiss.

Slope. The king is hauled up.

Encampment. Weakchin stands up and rubs his belly. He signals to Sum-Babee that he wants food.

Cliff top. Ku-Ku tells the king what Weakchin has been up to.

Encampment. Weakchin heads for the cave.

Gully. The king heads toward the encampment. Ku-Ku stops to primp his hair.

Encampment. The king waves his arms in a fury. The girls cower.

Cave. Sum-Babee sits at Weakchin's feet. He fondles her hair, then leans his elbow on her head.

Encampment. The king flexes his muscles. He picks up a big rock and heads toward the cave.

Cave. Weakchin is kissing Sum-Babee's hand as the king enters. Slow burn. He raises the rock above Weakchin's head.

Title: *Overpowered with the thought that he would never have to worry, work or go thirsty again.*

The king slams the rock down onto Weakchin's head. He slumps onto the table. Iris out.

Park. Charlie wakes up to find a cop clubbing him with a nightstick and ordering him to clear off. But he is too dazed to move. The cop grabs him by the necktie and yanks him onto his feet. Then he drops

Charlie's derby onto the ground. When Charlie bends over to pick it up, he gets clubbed again. Fully awake by now, he grabs his derby and takes to his heels.

COMMENTS

1. Chaplin had burlesqued a well-known ballad in *The Face on the Bar Room Floor;* his last Keystone film is another burlesque—of prehistory and primitive man, subjects of intense popular interest in the early years of the twentieth century. *His Prehistoric Past* was made in the same year as the publication of *Tarzan of the Apes*, two years after the publication of Conan Doyle's *The Lost World,* and three years after the sensational discovery of Piltdown man.

However, the immediate inspirations for the film were probably cartoon and comic strip treatments of prehistoric man and certainly D. W. Griffith's two films on prehistoric themes: *Man's Genesis* (1912) and its sequel, *Brute Force* (1913). In England Chaplin may have been familiar with E. T. Reed's comic prehistory panels originally published in *Punch* and appearing in book form as *Prehistoric Peeps* (1896) and *Mr. Punch's Prehistoric Peeps* (1902). Reed began a vogue that continued in England with Stafford Baker's *Stone Age Peeps in Puck* and in the United States with Frederick Opper's strip cartoon, *Our Antediluvian Ancestors.*

Several commentators maintain that turning the main story into dream-fantasy was an idea that Chaplin derived from *Jimmy the Fearless,* a show in which he had appeared during his theater years. Possibly. But he could also have picked up the idea from Winsor McCay's *Little Nemo* strip where it is a repeated device, or from *Man's Genesis* where a variation on the dream is used: an adult tells two modern children about prehistoric times, the film fades into the story he is telling (the main narrative), and ultimately returns to the story teller. The influence of Griffith's film is unmistakably evident in the naming of Chaplin's hero. In *Man's Genesis* the hero is called Weak Hands; in *His Prehistoric Past* the hero is named Weakchin. Griffith's film concerns a caveman weakling who (like the ape-man in *2001: A Space Odyssey*) invents a club to defeat his stronger rival. His superior intelligence wins him a beautiful cavewoman. Similarly, Chaplin's hero uses his cunning to triumph over the king and Ku-Ku, who are more powerful. But his victory is short lived. In a new twist to the story, Weakchin's adversaries bury their differences and contrive to overcome him.

2. In *My Autobiography* Chaplin describes how the film was developed out of an initial idea:

> In *His Prehistoric Past* I started with one gag, which was my first entrance. I appeared dressed as a prehistoric man wearing a bearskin,

and, as I scanned the landscape, I began pulling hair from the bearskin to fill my pipe. This was enough of an idea to stimulate a prehistoric story, introducing love, rivalry, combat and chase. (Chaplin 1964, 153)

Eight pages later he refers to his difficulties in completing the film. He was considering contract offers from Universal and Essanay:

Finishing my last picture, *His Prehistoric Past,* was a strain, because it was hard to concentrate with so many business propositions dangling before me. Nevertheless, the picture was eventually completed.

3. Structure. Prologue: Charlie falls asleep in the park. (i) The king vs. Ku-Ku. (ii) Ku-Ku vs. Weakchin. (iii) The king befriends Weakchin. (iv) Drinking session. (v) Weakchin goes hunting for Sum-Babee. (vi) The king vs. Sum-Babee. (vii) The king goes big game hunting. (viii) Weakchin pushes the king over the cliff. (ix) First reversal: Weakchin becomes the new monarch. (x) Second reversal: Ku-Ku rescues the king. (xi) Third reversal: the king eliminates Weakchin. Epilogue: Charlie has a rude awakening.

4. Dan Kamin refers to the final scenes of *His Prehistoric Past* as a "transition from romantic or heroic dream into gritty reality" (1984, 6). Not exactly. The awakening reality is certainly "gritty," but Charlie's dream is not unalleviated romance or heroism. To his disillusion, the ladies desert him for another man; his rule is extremely brief (the Tramp doesn't even become king for a day), and the real king uses his head for target practice. Charlie's dream reveals his desires, but it is a troubled fantasy.

Dreams show up in many later Chaplin films: *The Bank* (1915), *Shoulder Arms* (1918), *Sunnyside* (1919), *The Kid* (1921), *The Idle Class* (1921), *The Gold Rush* (1925), *Modern Times* (1936), and *Limelight* (1952). In *Sunnyside, The Kid,* and *Limelight* the heroes have dreams that are actually more troubling than reality.

5. Weakchin's initial entrance is the high point of the burlesque. Thereafter Chaplin seems to have lost interest in developing comic anachronisms. The few additional ones (Stone Age cocktail-shaking, for example) are virtually restricted to the first reel.

But prehistory is only the ostensible theme of the picture. Chaplin is really showing us a fantasy of masculine dominance. The location of the dream is an island—another free zone where all the women belong to the man in power, who can do with them as he pleases. (Weakchin symbolizes this by walking over them.) Of the three main male characters, Ku-Ku is gay and servile, Charlie is physically weak but cunning, and the king is strong but credulous. An effeminate man, by inference Ku-Ku doesn't need a woman; anyway, he wants to please the king, not challenge him. Weakchin *does* have his eye on the girls, but he's too weak to seize them. He feigns friendship for the king and moves in on the harem while the king is drunk. The girls are entranced by him—but only momentarily. They desert him for a handsome caveman. Weakchin can't compete with good looks, so he contrives to win back the girls with a display of power and cunning. He demolishes the handsome caveman with his club and cunningly shoves the king over the cliff. Then he takes over the harem and the throne. Weakchin's craftiness appears to have triumphed over the king's brute force. But the king isn't dead, and Weakchin has underrated Ku-Ku, who servilely rescues his monarch. The king's retaliation involves a mixture of his own methods (brute force) and Weakchin's (cunning); he creeps up behind the disarmed, unsuspecting Weakchin and smashes his head. The winner, as the dream ends, is the biggest guy with the biggest rock.

Strong-arm authority that reasserts itself in the dream also carries over into reality. Charlie is roughed up by a cop and driven out of the park. In both dream and reality the burlesque inverts the message of *Man's Genesis:* Weakchins never win fair ladies.

6. Later treatments of prehistory during the silent period. *His Prehistoric Past* should be compared with *The Three Ages* (1923) in which Buster Keaton paces the back of a dinosaur like a nervous sea captain, while Wallace Beery appears as a troglodyte riding a tame mammoth. Howard Hawks's *Fig Leaves* (1926) presents the full "Flintstones" treatment. The film's hero, Adam Smith, reads his stone-slab newspaper, then dashes off to catch the local commuter train—a cart filled with straphangers and pulled by a docile dinosaur. Eve, his wife, wanders off to the stores where there's a sale on fashionable fig leaves. When she is suitably adorned, along comes the serpent to lead her into temptation with a local gigolo.

OTHER VIEWS

"Chaplin's last film for Keystone was *His Prehistoric Past*, prototype of the other film dreams in which Charlie the tramp was transferred to some imaginative existence far from the squalid present. On the familiar park bench ('symbol of sadness') he lay and slept himself into prehistory. . . . Charlie woke to find a policeman looming over him. 'All I need to make a comedy is a park, a policeman and a pretty girl,' he told Sennett, and his last Keystone film, like so many of the others, proved him right" (Quigly 1968, 55).

"When he flirts with the grass-skirted maidens of the cave community he does so with his back to the camera, flapping his tail in lieu of coat-tails in a reprise of the back-view courtship he introduced to movies in *Between Showers*" (Gifford 1974, 55).

POSTSCRIPT

Chaplin's awareness of his star appeal is indicated in the titles he chose for several of his later Keystones: *His New Profession, His Musical Career, His Trysting Places,* and *His Prehistoric Past.* His name had yet to become a household word, but he had no doubts that the movie-going public would know which screen personality those pronouns referred to.

By August 1914, when Sennett was ready to discuss the renewal of his contract, Chaplin was convinced that he had become Keystone's most valuable talent. He asked for a thousand dollars a week. Sennett made a counteroffer: five hundred dollars a week starting immediately and progressive salary increases netting a thousand a week average over a three-year period. Chaplin turned it down. Sennett claims that he offered him a one-sixth interest in Keystone, but Chaplin rejected that too. For a while he dickered with an offer from Universal: Carl Laemmle was interested in financing Chaplin's films, but a thousand a week salary was out of the question. Then Jesse Robbins, a representative of the Essanay Company, came up with the handsome offer of $1250 a week plus a ten thousand dollar bonus before signing the contract. Chaplin accepted. His suspicions were aroused when Robbins came up with only six hundred dollars prior to the contract, but he decided to move over to Essanay anyway. It was a move toward greater artistic freedom, and anyway, Keystone had nothing more to teach him.

WHO'S IN WHAT?

ABBREVIATIONS:

ABD	*A Busy Day* (no. 14)
AFJ	*A Film Johnnie* (no. 5)
BS	*Between Showers* (no. 4)
CCL	*Cruel, Cruel Love* (no. 8)
CIC	*Caught in a Cabaret* (no. 12)
CIR	*Caught in the Rain* (no. 13)
DD	*Dough and Dynamite* (no. 29)
FOB	*The Face on the Bar Room Floor* (no. 22)
GA	*Getting Acquainted* (no. 34)
GN	*Gentlemen of Nerve* (no. 30)
HFB	*Her Friend the Bandit* (no. 16)
HFP	*His Favorite Pastime* (no. 7)
HMC	*His Musical Career* (no. 31)
HNP	*His New Profession* (no. 25)
HPP	*His Prehistoric Past* (no. 35)
HTP	*His Trysting Places* (no. 32)
KAR	*Kid's Auto Race* (no. 2)
LG	*Laughing Gas* (no. 20)
MAL	*Making a Living* (no. 1)
MAW	*Mabel at the Wheel* (no. 10)
MBD	*Mabel's Busy Day* (no. 18)
MML	*Mabel's Married Life* (no. 19)
MSP	*Mabel's Strange Predicament* (no. 3)
R	*Recreation* (no. 23)
TFM	*The Fatal Mallet* (no. 15)
TK	*The Knockout* (no. 17)
TLP	*Those Love Pangs* (no. 28)
TM	*The Masquerader* (no. 24)
TML	*Twenty Minutes of Love* (no. 11)
TNJ	*The New Janitor* (no. 27)
TPM	*The Property Man* (no. 21)
TPR	*Tillie's Punctured Romance* (no. 33)
TR	*The Rounders* (no. 26)
TSB	*The Star Boarder* (no. 9)
TT	*Tango Tangles* (no. 6)

THE PLAYERS:

Allen, Phyllis: CIC, ABD, TPM, TR, DD, GN, HTP, TPR, GA
Arbuckle, Roscoe "Fatty": AFJ, TT, HFP, TK, TM, TR
Arnold, Cecile: FOB, TM, HNP, TLP, DD, GA, HPP
Bennett, Billie: MBD, TPR
Bennett, Charles: TPM, TPR
Bordeaux, Joe: TK, TPM, HMC, TPR
Chase, Charley: TK, MBD, TM, HNP, TR, DD, GN, HMC, TPR
Clifton, Emma: BS

Cline, Eddie: TK
Conklin, Chester: MAL, MSP, BS, TT, CCL, MAW, TML, CIC, MBD, FOB, TM, TLP, DD, GN
Davenport, Alice: MAL, MSP, CCL, TSB, CIC, CIR, TPM, TNJ, GN, TPR
Dillon, Jack: TNJ, DD
Dressler, Marie: TPR
Durfee, Minta: MAL, AFJ, TT, CCL, TSB, TML, CIC, TK, TM, HNP, TR, TPR
Edwards, Vivian: FOB, TM, TLP, DD
Fitzpatrick, Charlotte: KAR
Griffith, Gordon: KAR, TSB, TML, CIC, TPR
Howell, Alice: CIC, CIR, TK, MML, LG, HMC
Jacobs, Billy: KAR
Kennedy, Edgar: CCL, TML, CIC, TK, MBD, TLP, DD, GN, TPR, GA
Kirtley, Virginia: MAL, AFJ
Lampe, Sadie: BS
Lehrman, Henry "Pathe": MAL, KAR, MSP
MacDonald, Wallace: CIC, MBD, MML, FOB, TR, DD, TPR
Mace, Fred: MAW
Mann, Hank: MSP, TML, TK, MML, FOB
Marsh, Gene: HPP
McCoy, Harry: MSP, MAW, CIC, MBD, MML, TPM, FOB, TM, HNP, TLP, TPR, GA
Morris, Lee: TPM
Murray, Charlie: HFB, MML, R, TM, TPR
Nichols, Norma: TPM, R, TLP, DD, HMC
Normand, Mabel: AFJ, MAW, CIC, TFM, HFB, MBD, MML, GN, HTP, TPR, GA
Pearce, Peggy: HFP
St. John, Al: MSP, MAW, TK, MBD, MML, TR, TNJ, TPR, HPP
Salter, Thelma: KAR
Schade, Fritz: LG, TPM, FOB, TM, HNP, TR, TNJ, DD, HMC, HPP
Sennett, Mack: AFJ, MAW, TFM, TK, MBD, TPM
Simpson, Rev. D.: TPR
Sterling, Ford: BS, AFJ, TT
Summerville, Slim: MBD, LG, DD, TPR
Sutherland, Joseph: LG
Swain, Mack: CIR, ABD, TFM, TK, MML, LG, GN, HMC, HTP, TPR, GA, HPP
Swickard, Joseph: TML, CIC, LG
Williams, Frank D.: KAR

BIBLIOGRAPHY

Adeler, Edwin, and Con West. *Remember Fred Karno?* London: Long Publishers, 1939.

Asplund, Uno. *Chaplin's Films.* South Brunswick and New York: A. S. Barnes, 1976.

Aubert, Charles. *The Art of Pantomime.* New York: Benjamin Blom, 1970.

Baldelli, Pio. *Charlie Chaplin.* Firenze: La Nuova Italia, 1977.

Balshofer, Fred J., and Arthur C. Miller. *One Reel a Week.* Berkeley and Los Angeles: University of California Press, 1967.

Bazin, André, and Eric Rohmer. *Charlie Chaplin.* Paris: Les Éditions du Cerf, 1972.

Bell-Metereau, Rebecca. *Hollywood Androgyny.* New York: Columbia University Press, 1985.

Benyoun, Robert. "L'assassin de Charlot." *Positif* 152–53 (July–August 1973): 6–18.

Bermel, Albert. *Farce: A History from Aristophanes to Woody Allen.* New York: Simon and Schuster, 1982.

Bessy, Maurice. *Charlie Chaplin.* London: Thames and Hudson, 1985.

Bessy, Maurice, and Robin Livio. *Charlie Chaplin, L'emigrant de l'illusion.* Paris: Denoël, 1972.

Biby, Edward Allan. "How Pictures Discovered Charlie Chaplin." *Photoplay* 15 (April 1919): 70–71, 105.

Blaisdell, George F. "Tillie's Punctured Romance." *Moving Picture World* 22 (December 19, 1914): 1680.

Bogle, Donald. *Toms, Coons, Mulattoes, Mammies, & Bucks.* New York: Viking Press, 1973.

Bowman, William Dodgson. *Charlie Chaplin: His Life and Art.* New York: Haskell House Publishers, 1974.

Brownlow, Kevin. *The Parade's Gone By.* New York: Alfred A. Knopf, 1968.

"Caught in a Cabaret." *Moving Picture World* 20 (May 9, 1914): 821.

Chaplin, Charles. *My Autobiography.* New York: Simon and Schuster, 1964.

———. *My Life in Pictures.* Introduction by Francis Wyndham. New York: Grosset & Dunlap, 1975.

———. *Charlie Chaplin's Own Story.* Indianapolis: Bobbs Merrill, 1916.

———. *Charlie Chaplin's Own Story.* Edited by Harry M. Geduld. Bloomington, Indiana: Indiana University Press, 1985.

Chaplin, Charles, Jr. *My Father, Charlie Chaplin.* New York: Popular Library, 1961.

Chevallier, Jacques. *Le cinéma burlesque americain 1912–1930.* Paris [?]: Service d'Édition et de Vente des Publications de l'Éducation Nationale, n.d.

Codd, Elsie. "Charlie's Early Days." *Picture Show* (London) 2 (April 17, 1920): 17; 4 (November 13, 1920): 4.

Condon, Charles R. "A Six-Reel Keystone Comedy." *Motography* November 14, 1914, 657–58.

Cotes, Peter, and Thelma Niklaus. *The Little Fellow.* New York: Citadel Press, 1965.

Cott, J. "The Limits of Silent Film." *Literature Film Quarterly* 3 (Spring 1975): 99–107.

Cremonini, Giorgio. *Charlie Chaplin*. Firenze: La Nuova Italia, 1974.

"Cruel, Cruel Love." *Moving Picture World* 20 (April 4, 1914): 58.

Delluc, Louis. *Charlie Chaplin*. London: Bodley Head, 1922.

Disher, M. Willson. *Clowns and Pantomimes*. New York and London: Benjamin Blom, 1968.

"Dough and Dynamite." *Moving Picture World* 22 (October 31, 1914): 642.

Durgnat, Raymond. *The Crazy Mirror: Hollywood Comedy and the American Image*. New York: Horizon Press, 1970.

Ennis, Bert. "Fame Came to Chaplin with Borrowed Clothes." *Motion Picture Classic* 23 (July 1926): 36–37, 76.

Everson, William K. *American Silent Film*. New York: Oxford University Press, 1978.

"Face on the Barroom Floor." *Moving Picture World* 21 (August 29, 1914): 1241.

"Fatal Mallet." *Moving Picture World* 20 (June 13, 1914): 1531.

"Film Johnnie." *Moving Picture World* 19 (March 7, 1914): 1238.

Fiske, Minnie Maddern. "The Art of Charles Chaplin," *Harper's Weekly* 62 (May 6, 1916): 494.

Fowler, Gene. *Father Goose: The Story of Mack Sennett*. New York: Covici, Friede, 1934.

Fussell, Betty Harper. *Mabel: Hollywood's First I-Don't-Care Girl*. New Haven and New York: Ticknor & Fields, 1982.

Gallagher, J. P. *Fred Karno: Master of Mirth and Tears*. London: Robert Hale, 1971.

Gehring, Wes D. *Charlie Chaplin: A Bio-Bibliography*. Westport, Conn.: Greenwood Press, 1983.

"Gentlemen of Nerve." *Moving Picture World* 22 (November 14, 1914): 932.

Gifford, Denis. *Chaplin*. London: Macmillan, 1974.

Grace, Harry A. "Charlie Chaplin's Films and American Culture Patterns." *Journal of Aesthetics and Art Criticism* 10 (June 1952): 353–63.

Haining, Peter. *The Legend of Charlie Chaplin*. London: W. H. Allen, 1982.

Hannon, William Morgan. *The Photodrama—Its Place among the Fine Arts*. New Orleans: Ruskin Press, 1915.

"Her Friend the Bandit." *Moving Picture World* 21 (June 4, 1914): 65.

"His Favorite Pastime." *Moving Picture World* 19 (March 21 1914): 1256.

"His Musical Career." *Moving Picture World* 22 (November 14, 1914): 933.

"His New Profession." *Motion Picture News* 10 (August 29, 1914): 66.

"His Trysting Place." *Moving Picture World* 22 (November 14, 1914): 933.

Hoyt, Edwin P. *Sir Charlie*. London: Robert Hale, 1977.

Huff, Theodore. *Charlie Chaplin*. London: Cassell and Company, 1952.

Jacobs, Lewis. *The Rise of the American Film*. New York: Harcourt, Brace & Company, 1939.

Kamin, Dan. *Charlie Chaplin's One-Man Show*. Metuchen, NJ: Scarecrow Press, Inc., 1984.

Kerr, Walter. *The Silent Clowns*. New York: Alfred A. Knopf, 1975.

"Knockout." *Moving Picture World* 21 (June 4, 1914): 65.

Lahue, Kalton C. *World of Laughter: The Motion Picture Comedy Short, 1910–1930*. Norman: University of Oklahoma Press, 1966.

Lahue, Kalton C., and Terry Brewer. *Kops and Custards: The Legend of Keystone Films*. Norman: University of Oklahoma Press, 1967.

Lahue, Kalton C., and Sam Gill. *Clown Princes and Jesters*. New York: A. S. Barnes, 1971a.

———. *Mack Sennett's Keystone: The Man, the Myth and the Comedies*. South Brunswick and New York: A. S. Barnes, 1971b.

"Laughing Gas." *Motion Picture News* 10 (August 15, 1914): 56.

Leprohon, Pierre. *Charlot ou la naissance d'un mythe*. Paris: Corymbe, 1936.

———. *Charles Chaplin*. Paris: Melot, 1946.

Lyons, Timothy J. *Charles Chaplin: A Guide to References and Resources*. Boston: G. K. Hall, 1979.

"Mabel at the Wheel." *Moving Picture World* 20 (April 25, 1914): 518.

"Mabel's Busy Day." *Moving Picture World* 20 (June 27, 1914): 1829.

"Mabel's Married Life." *Moving Picture World* 21 (June 4, 1914): 65.

Macdonald, Dwight. *On Movies*. Englewood Cliffs: Prentice-Hall, 1971.

Madden, David. *Harlequin's Stick—Charlie's Cane*. Bowling Green, Ohio: Popular Press, 1975.

"Making a Living." *Moving Picture World* 19 (February 17, 1914): 678.

Manvell, Roger. *Chaplin*. Boston: Little, Brown & Company, 1974.

Mast, Gerald. *The Comic Mind: Comedy and the Movies*. Chicago: University of Chicago Press, 1979.

McCabe, John. *Charlie Chaplin*. Garden City: Doubleday & Company, 1978.

McCaffrey, Donald W. *4 Great Comedians: Chaplin, Lloyd, Keaton, Langdon*. London and New York: Zwemmer & Barnes, 1968.

———, ed. *Focus on Chaplin*. Englewood Cliffs: Prentice-Hall, 1971.

McDonald, Gerald D. *The Picture History of Charlie Chaplin*. New York: Nostalgia Press, 1965.

McDonald, Gerald D., Michael Conway, and Mark Ricci. *The Films of Charlie Chaplin*. Secaucus, New Jersey: Citadel Press, 1974.

Mellor, J. G. "The Making of Charlie Chaplin." *Cinema Studies* (London) 2, no. 2 (June 1966): 19–25.

Minney, R. J. *Chaplin the Immortal Tramp*. London: George Newnes, 1954.

Mitry, Jean. *Tout Chaplin*. Paris: Seghers, 1972.

Moss, Robert F. *Charlie Chaplin*. New York: Pyramid Publications, 1975.

Naremore, James. "Film and the Performance Frame." *Film Quarterly*, Winter 1984–85, 8–15.

"New Janitor." *Moving Picture World* 21 (September 26, 1914): 1777.

Niver, Kemp. *Motion Pictures from the Library of Congress Paper Print Collection 1894–1912*. Berkeley and Los Angeles: University of California Press, 1967.

Noble, Peter. *The Negro in Films*. London: Skelton Robinson, 1948.

Oldrini, Guido. *Chapliniana*. Bari: Editori Laterza, 1979.

Payne, Robert. *The Great God Pan*. New York: Hermitage House, 1952.

"Pie Pioneer." *Theatre* 28 (November 1918): 319, 325.

Poulaille, Henri. *Charlie Chaplin*. Paris: Grasset, 1927.

Pratt, George C. *Spellbound in Darkness*. 2 vols. Rochester: University of Rochester Press, 1966.

"Property Man." *Moving Picture World* 21 (August 15, 1914): 961.

Quigly, Isabel. *Charlie Chaplin: Early Comedies*. London: Studio Vista, 1968.

Ramsaye, Terry. *A Million and One Nights*. New York: Simon and Schuster, 1926.

"Recreation." *Moving Picture World* 21 (August 29, 1914): 1242.

Robinson, David. *The Great Funnies: A History of Film Comedy*. London: Studio Vista, 1969.

————. *Chaplin: The Mirror of Opinion*. London and Bloomington: Secker & Warburg and Indiana University Press, 1983.

————. *Chaplin: His Life and Art*. London: Collins, 1985.

"Rounders." *Moving Picture World* 21 (September 19, 1914): 1645.

Sadoul, Georges. *Charlie Chaplin, vie de Charlot: ses films et son temps*. Paris: Les Éditeurs Français Reunis, 1957.

Savio, Francesco, ed. *Il Tutto Chaplin*. Venice: Biennele de Venezia, 1972.

Seldes, Gilbert. *An Hour with the Movies and the Talkies*. Philadelphia: Lippincott, 1929.

Sennett, Mack, and Cameron Shipp. *King of Comedy*. New York: Pinnacle Books, 1954.

Smith, Edward H. "Charlie Chaplin's Million Dollar Walk." *McClure's* 47 (July 1916): 26.

Smith, Julian. *Chaplin*. Boston: Twayne Publishers, 1984.

Sobel, Raoul, and David Francis. *Chaplin: Genesis of a Clown*. London: Quartet Books, 1977.

Soupault, Philippe. *Charlot*. Paris: Plon, 1931.

"Star Boarder." *Motion Picture News* 9 (April 11, 1914): 52.

"Those Love Pangs." *Moving Picture World* 22 (October 17, 1914): 337.

Towsen, John H. *Clowns*. New York: Hawthorn Books, 1976.

Turconi, David. *Mack Sennett*. Rome: Edizioni del Anteneo, 1961.

Tyler, Parker. *Chaplin: Last of the Clowns*. New York: Horizon Press, 1972.

Ulm, Gerith von. *Charlie Chaplin: King of Tragedy*. Caldwell, Ohio: Caxton Printers, 1980.

Viazzi, Glauco. *Chaplin e la critica. Antologia di saggi, bibliografia ragionata, iconografia e filmografia*. Bari: Editori Laterza, 1955.

Wagenknecht, Edward. *The Movies in the Age of Innocence*. Norman: University of Oklahoma Press, 1962.

Warren, Low. *The Film Game*. London: Werner Laurie, 1937.

Weinberg, Herman G. "Slow, Fast and Stop Motion: A Discussion of their Origin and Use." *Movie Makers* 5 (January 1930): 40, 50.

Whitcomb, E. V. "Charlie Chaplin." *Photoplay* 7 (February 1915): 35–37.

Wiegand, Wilfried, ed. *Ueber Chaplin*. Zurich: Diogenes, 1978.

Yallop, David. *The Day the Laughter Stopped*. New York: St. Martin's Press, 1976.

Index of Titles

NOTE: A full index to *Chapliniana* will appear in volume III.

Editor:	Chris Holly
Book designer:	Matthew Williamson
Jacket designer:	Matthew Williamson
Production coordinator:	Harriet Curry
Typeface:	Linotron Century Expanded
Compositor:	Huron Valley Graphics, Inc.
Printer:	Thomson-Shore, Inc.

Harry M. Geduld, Professor of Comparative Literature/Film Studies at Indiana University, established Indiana University's Film Studies Program in 1963. He has published sixteen books on various aspects of literature, film and popular culture, including *Birth of the Talkies* and *Filmguide to Henry V*. Editor of four internationally-known series of film books, including *Filmguides, Film Focus,* and *The New York Times Film Encyclopedia,* he has also published several hundred reviews and articles on books, plays and films. He is currently editing a series of critical editions of science fiction classics ("Visions" series) for I.U. Press.

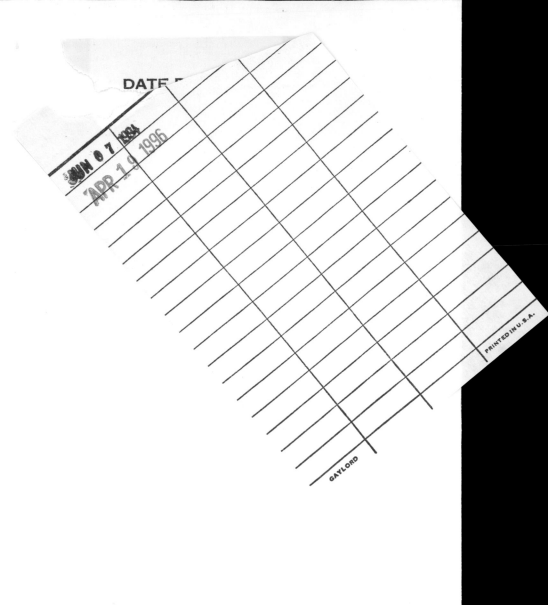